CANADIAN SOCIETY

MEETING THE CHALLENGES OF THE TWENTY–FIRST CENTURY

EDITED BY DAN GLENDAY AND ANN DUFFY

OXFORD

UNIVERSITY PRESS

OXFORD
UNIVERSITY PRESS

70 Wynford Drive, Don Mills, Ontario M3C 1J9
www.oupcan.com

Oxford University Press is a department of the University of Oxford.
It furthers the University's objective of excellence in research, scholarship,
and education by publishing worldwide in

Oxford New York

Athens Auckland Bangkok Bogotá Buenos Aires Calcutta
Cape Town Chennai Dar es Salaam Delhi Florence Hong Kong Istanbul
Karachi Kuala Lumpur Madrid Melbourne Mexico City Mumbai
Nairobi Paris São Paulo Shanghai Singapore Taipei Tokyo Toronto Warsaw

with associated companies in Berlin Ibadan

Published in Canada
by Oxford University Press

Canadian Cataloguing in Publication Data

Main entry under title:

Canadian society : meeting the challenges of the twenty-first century

Previously published under title: Canadian society : understanding and
surviving in the 1990s.
Includes bibliographical references and index.
ISBN 0-19-541437-3

1. Canada—Social conditions—1991–   . 2. Canada—Economic conditions—1991–   .
I. Glenday, Daniel, 1948–   . II. Duffy, Ann. III. Title: Canadian society : understanding
and surviving in the 1990s.

HN103.5.C35 2000   971.064'8   C00-932296-5

Cover Design: Joan Dempsey

1 2 3 4 – 04 03 02 01

This book is printed on permanent (acid-free) paper ∞ .
Printed in Canada

For Rich Boutin and Dusky Lee Smith

CONTENTS

introduction

The Challenges Facing Canadian Society

A s we move past the events of the 1990s and turn our attention to the present and possible future(s) for our country, most Canadians are confident that we are prepared to meet the challenges. Indeed, the last two decades brought profound changes, and most Canadians who experienced this period in our history marked it as a crucial turning point in the evolution of Canadian society. Each day, newspapers provided evidence of the growing tension around such pivotal issues as the need for trade unions in a post-industrial information society; the violence of racism in urban centres; gender inequalities; poverty; the economic, political, and environmental fallout from US governmental policies; and the relationship, if any, of Quebec in the Canadian confederation. Even the messengers, the print and visual media, were not immune, especially when two individuals, (the would-be lord) Conrad Black and Lord Beaverbrook, own and control the overwhelming majority of newspapers in this country. With little if any real competition, it is not surprising that the print medium is not without its detractors, who insist that the presentation of the news contains bias or prejudice.

Today, Canadians from coast to coast to coast recognize that they are faced with a rapidly changing and more complex world. We have been told by politicians and businessmen that this is due to the restructuring of national economies, otherwise known as 'globalization'. Every day, men and women workers in the manufacturing and service industries and in the public sector are told to become more flexible in their workplace or face permanent layoff. While education and training are pitched as necessary ingredients for future job security, tragically, Canadians read about the excessively high levels of youth unemployment while significant numbers of the adult population in Canada remain illiterate.

This book is a modest attempt to address some of these issues. The contributors to this second edition of *Canadian Society* not only provide accessible, original, and critical analyses of their topics, but include personal considerations of the policy and practical implications of their analyses. However, the time is ripe to consider the link between what we in sociology and other social sciences say about our society and its institutions and what this knowledge tells us about the prognosis for a humane and prosperous future.

As we see it, Canadians require understanding to 'face the next round of hard truths'. We tell our pollsters we are prepared to meet the challenges of the New Information Age, and yet, in the flood of information, there is little understanding of what lies buried in the headlines. Canadians will be asked to make sacrifices, and have been asked in the past to do so, when only one side of the story is offered as evidence for change. The contributors to this text offer other points of view, other sides of particular stories, in order to challenge conventional wisdom.

The basic theme that connects all of the contributions is inequality. In Part One, 'Canada in Conflict: Burdens of Past Inequality', the authors explore how exclusionary practices have exacerbated demands for fair and equitable treatment from organized labour, the poor, Aboriginal peoples, and Canada's visible minorities. Chapter 1 explores the growth of trade unions in Canada, their progressive role in fashioning that which we cherish in Canadian society, and their hopeful future. Setbacks brought on by recent Supreme Court challenges, the restructuring of the economy, and the state's clawbacks from public-sector institutions should have left Canadian unions 'on the ropes'. Instead, unions in Canada have weathered the storm better than their counterparts in the US, and in this chapter Dan Glenday provides important insights into why this is so. Chapter 2, by J. Rick Ponting, makes visible the all too often invisible mechanisms that have resulted in the long-standing exclusion of non-whites, including Native peoples, from full participation in Canadian society. Recent incidents in Manitoba, British Columbia, and Ontario suggest the possibility of a growing racist undertone in Canadian social relations. In Chapter 3, Ann Duffy and Nancy Mandell explore the extent to which in Canada, recently, 'the rich get richer and the poor get poorer.' Increasing income inequalities and ineffectual government efforts in providing adequate housing and social assistance have set the stage for collective and creative adaptation to housing in Canadian cities and the struggles of poor people in Canada for a better life. These themes overlap with what has been called 'the feminization of poverty' in Canada. Over the past several decades, women comprised a disproportionate percentage of adults and children living in poverty and well over half of single-parent female families lived below the government-set poverty lines.

Part Two, 'Institutions in Crisis', examines what governments have done and have failed to do as the Canadian society and economy have changed. In Chapter 4, Norene Pupo emphasizes the dramatic growth of the Canadian state (which includes the federal, provincial, and municipal governments). One indication of this expansion is that one in five Canadians today is employed either directly or indirectly by the state. Moreover, state policy impacts on virtually all aspects of our lives—for example, the ramifications for women workers of the different state policies on day care. Pupo considers the various competing explanations for understanding the state's role in Canadians' lives. Drawing on a number of recent studies, David Livingstone, in Chapter 5, examines the growing gap between the skills acquired by Canadians and the jobs they hold. Even though many Canadians seek out new learning experiences both formally and informally, there is increasingly less likelihood that these skills will be used on the job. Livingstone concludes with concrete suggestions for the future. Kelly Hannah-Moffat, in Chapter 6, examines the public perception of increasing crime in Canadian cities, towns, and rural communities in the light of current research into crime and criminality in this country.

Part Three, 'Movements Towards Social Change', considers how recent public policy helped to shape the contours of the feminist, gay and lesbian, and youth movements in Canada. In Chapter 7, Peta Tancred and Huguette Dagenais discuss the similarities and differences in the institutionalization of the feminist movement in Canadian and Quebec universities. The larger Canadian cities have been the centres for social action in the struggle for equality of gays and lesbians, while the federal court system has been the place where issues of equality have had to be played out. While significant legal gains have been made, as Gary Kinsman reveals in chapter 8, gays and lesbians remain outcasts in this society. As we move into the next millennium, the struggles for social equality will face opposition from the religious and political right. Chapter 9 concentrates on the present-day proletarianization of youth in this country. James Côté and Anton Allahar offer an explanation for its development and the ramifications for young people.

Finally, Part Four, 'Sociological Frontiers into the Twenty-First Century', looks at our current and future physical and political health in terms of the deterioration of the physical environment and the role played by Quebec in defining our national identity. Chapter 10 is an exposition of the accepted wisdoms in English Canada about Quebec. Hubert Guindon has spent close to four decades as a sociologist engaged in the debates and public policy alternatives about the future of Canada. His contribution is a welcome ballast to the hegemonic platitudes/invectives about Quebec that frequently emanate from English Canada. Environmental issues remain at the top of both political and public agendas, as Kathleen Reil explains in Chapter 11. Addressing the environment involves grappling with a history of subordination to other, more 'important' issues. Grassroots environmental groups confront a complex and often ponderous bureaucratic government structure and 'unclear' federal, provincial, and international political boundaries, especially in an era notorious for its neo-liberal rhetoric of individualism and personal responsibility.

Taken as a whole, these essays provide the basis for serious consideration of what form Canadians want their country to take as we face the hard truths and meet the challenges confronting us. Over the past quarter-century, Canadian society has undergone substantial modifications and continues to change shape and substance while the issues of sexual orientation and gender and racial/ethnic inequalities, and the social movements they engender, are reshaping our existing legal and social arrangements. Moreover, the erosion of the physical environment continues unabated. However, shifting the arena from politics (the politicians) to the courts (the legal battles) has opened possibilities for progressive change in this area. Finally, the role of Quebec in Canada is a fact to be reckoned with and one that requires our public attention and recognition. These are among the changing and complex realities Canadians are facing today and will struggle with in the coming years. Ultimately, Canadians who work at understanding the social transformations at hand will find themselves in a better position to make the important choices of the near future.

Acknowledgements

We acknowledge our generous contributors who have taken great time and care to provide accessible, thoughtful analysis of their respective issues. We also wish to express our thanks to all the Oxford University Press editorial staff, especially our editor Richard Tallman, and to our family members—Rick, Dusky, Mayra—who have supported, or at least tolerated, our involvement in this project. We want specially to thank Phyllis Wilson for her gentle prodding during the project's lengthy gestation. Her encouragement and her insistence on several reviewers' comments helped make this a better book.

Ann Duffy and Dan Glenday

Dan . . . I would like to thank you for keeping things going.

Ann

part one

Canada in Conflict: Burdens of Past Inequality

More and more Canadians find themselves shortchanged when it comes to opportunities for good jobs, for the good wages and protections found in most collective agreements, or for equal access to such public goods as university education, decent housing, and even fresh air and clean water. Indeed, much of Canadian history can be understood as an ongoing struggle against inequality between those who have been marginalized and kept back from full participation in Canadian society and those on the inside who have sought numerous ways to affirm their privileges and power. We have seen how, in the past decade, these conflicts, particularly as they pertain to the labour movement, visible minorities, and the poor, have intensified.

In the opening chapter, Dan Glenday describes organized labour's often bitter battles for legal recognition, if not social acceptance, against business and government in Canada. Most of the social programs Canadians now take for granted were advanced as social reforms by the labour movement—e.g., unemployment and disability insurance and parental leave. Today, new reforms such as universal child care and employment equity are being championed by organized labour. In recent memory, we have had a political climate marked by wide-ranging policies such as the Canada-US Free Trade Agreement (FTA) and the North American Free Trade Agreement (NAFTA), aggressive, anti-union assaults by employers, and several setbacks before the Supreme Court of Canada that appeared to put trade unions in this country in serious jeopardy. Many trade unions began to fight back. The trade union movement today is strengthened by the new inroads in the service sector and a renewal of social activism sparked, in part, by the increasing proportion of women in the trade union movement.

If Canadian trade unionists have often been made to feel dispensable by the unequal treatment they have received from those in power in Canadian society, this has been doubly true for our racial minorities. As J. Rick Ponting explains, the history of Canada, contrary to our non-racial mythology, is inter-woven with racial conflict and violence. In contemporary Canadian society, under a dark cloud of neo-conservative rhetoric, racist and exclusionary atti-tudes persist in our major institutions, including schools, the police, and the labour market. Moreover, explicitly racist organizations such as the Aryan Nation and the Western Guard have found fertile ground in the present polit-ical climate. Increasingly, racial minorities in our urban centres and Native Canadians are losing patience with the largely symbolic responses to these manifestations of racism. The challenge now is to overcome exclusionary atti-tudes and practices. The strength to continue is coming from and draws on those directly affected.

Visible minorities often have borne the brunt of economic marginaliza-tion. However, as discussed by Ann Duffy and Nancy Mandell, poverty impacts on a broad range of Canadians. The experience of inequality has been expressed in terms of harassment and discrimination at work or housing, denied opportunities for social advancement, and limited entry to formal and informal contacts with those who can 'open doors'. No matter at what point in our history, poverty, more than any other social condition, has signified the pernicious burden of inequality. In the postwar period, certain strides in Cana-dian public policy were made to address poverty. One important initiative was family allowances. Today, this and other advances made to assist the poor, espe-cially children, have been eroded or eliminated altogether. Few imaginative public policy alternatives are advanced other than 'tax breaks for families' and the conservative mantra of hard work and individual responsibility. Poverty and economic disenfranchisement have persisted as pivotal social issues facing increasing numbers of Canadians. As Duffy and Mandell explain, all indications suggest that poverty—as evidenced by increasing numbers of the homeless and of children living in poverty, as well as large numbers of 'unofficial' poor—has deepened throughout the past decade, even while the country as a whole boasted high levels of economic growth. However, the gap is growing and by all accounts will continue to expand in the foreseeable future. In recent years, social activists, trade unionists, some academics, and other Canadians have joined with anti-poverty groups in their struggle for social inclusion.

chapter one

Off the Ropes? New Challenges and Strengths Facing Trade Unions in Canada

Dan Glenday

Where Do Unions Come From?

Are Unions Socially Harmful or Socially Progressive?

Today, many Canadians view unions as unnecessary, even antiquated. To them, trade unions may have served a purpose long ago when employers and governments were virulently anti-union—when unarmed workers lost their lives at the hands of armed police, security guards such as Pinkertons, and even the Canadian army. But today, they point out, we live in a free and democratic society where employers and governments respect the law—where all workers are granted protections such as those embedded in the Charter of Rights and Freedoms, provincial human rights legislation, and the extensive federal and provincial employment and labour relations laws. For these Canadians, unions have outlived their purpose. Well, have they? Are there no longer tangible benefits for someone to belong to a union?

In a recent Statistics Canada study, a full-time unionized worker in the first half of 1997 received an average hourly wage of $18.87, in contrast to a non-unionized worker's rate of $15.32—a difference of $3.55 an hour, which amounts to $142 a week or $7,384 a year! If you were a unionized part-time worker, the average hourly rate was $16.68 compared to the non-union average of $9.97 an hour or an additional $268.40 a week or $13,956.80 more a year! Plus, unionized workers were twice as likely to receive non-wage benefits such as employer-sponsored pension programs, health and dental plans, better vacations, paid sick leaves, and improved working arrangements such as job-sharing.

Moreover, trade unions in Canada continue to improve the lives not only of their constituency in the workplace but for many less fortunate in the larger society as a whole. Trade unions have made a significant contribution to the building of Canada as a maturing capitalist nation. Many of the taken-for-granted rights enjoyed by Canadian unionized and non-unionized workers alike (old age pensions, workers' compensation, minimum wage legislation, unemployment insurance, and family benefits) were advanced by the trade union movement

(Palmer, 1992). Workers in non-union sites such as Dofasco Steel Corporation in Hamilton, Ontario, benefit when company management routinely 'negotiates' a contract of wages and fringe benefits for their employees at 'the going union rate'. Several major unions, such as the Canadian Union of Postal Workers (CUPW), have struggled to advance women's rights and opportunities. For example, in 1982, CUPW was the first Canadian trade union to negotiate paid maternity leave, now seen by many non-union employers as a basic employee right (White, 1987). In cases such as these and others, trade unions in Canada are progressive trend-setters. Therefore, the struggles for respect, dignity, and material benefits in the workplace are as relevant today as they were a century ago.

As we move into the next millennium, the present and future role of unions in our society is, in large part, conditioned by the past. How we got to where we are now is coloured by what we did yesterday and the many years before yesterday. Therefore, it is important to understand our past in order to help us explain the present and hopefully prosper in the future.

A Brief History of Trade Unionism in Canada

Since the beginning of the nineteenth century, if not earlier, workers' have waged struggles for better workplaces and a better life for their families, children, and future generations. The gains made over the years since then have not been easy ones. Four distinct phases of unionization—craft, industrial, public sector, and the emerging private service sector—are chronicled in Table 1.1. In the first wave, skilled artisans sought to organize what were then called 'secret societies' because trade unions were outlawed organizations. In the second, factory workers and miners mobilized into separate industrial unions. This was a period of intense sectoral fragmentation and ideological quarrels within the Canadian labour movement. In the third, blue- and white-collar workers in the public sector organized trade unions in their workplaces. Today, we have entered another phase in the progress of trade unionism in Canada, one noted by the unionization of the private service sector and the strategic role played by young Canadian workers in this new development.

1. THE FRENCH COLONIAL WORKING CLASS

The time of the French presence in North America (about 1534 until the Conquest in 1760) witnessed the rise and demise of the French empire in North America. The beginning of a colonial working class is documented in the shipbuilding industry during the latter part of the French regime (New France). Some Quebec historians have discovered evidence suggesting that by the end of the French colonial period there existed a small class of skilled workers concentrated in Quebec City. Still others point out that the close to 10,000 *coureurs des bois* could be included as a social class of 'workers' who were employed in the French colonial fur trade because they constituted 'a group of individuals united by a common economic interest' (Chirot, 1977; see also Wallerstein, 1979).

Table 1.1 A Short Chronology of the Canadian Labour Movement

Period of Conspiracy Doctrine

1825	Strike by carpenters in Lachine, Quebec, for higher wages
1827	Printers organize in Quebec City: first trade union in Canada
1867	Confederation (British North America Act)
1871	British unions won statutory relief from criminal conspiracy doctrine
1872	Toronto Typographical Society's strike that resulted in John A. Macdonald exempting trade unions from criminal and civil liabilities imposed by British law

Craft Unions

Struggle for Legal Recognition and Collective Bargaining Rights

1886	Trades and Labour Congress (TLC) formed by international craft unions
1889	Royal Commission on the Relations between Capital and Labour
1900	Federal Department of Labour created
1902	'Berlin Declaration': TLC renounces all but US-based international unions
1907	Canadian Industrial Disputes Investigation Act: first national labour legislation, emphasizing conciliation
1919	Winnipeg General Strike: most complete general strike in North American history
1921	Canadian and Catholic Confederation of Labour formed in Hull, Quebec
1925	British courts rule that most labour legislation falls within provincial jurisdiction
1935	US National Labour Relations (Wagner) Act
1937	United Auto Workers sit-down strike at General Motors, Oshawa, Ontario
1939	TLC expels Canadian affiliates of US CIO unions
1940	CIO affiliates form the Canadian Congress of Labour (CCL)
1943	Order-in-Council PC 1003 guarantees labour's right to organize (combining principles of the US Wagner Act with compulsory conciliation)
1945	99-day Ford strike and the Rand Formula: mandatory check-off of union dues

Industrial Unions

Nationalism and Public-Sector Unionism

1947	Taft-Hartley Act (US) set limits on closed union shops while granting individual state governments the right to override union-shop provisions
1948	Industrial Relations and Disputes Investigation Act (grievance arbitration mandated into all collective agreements)
1949	Asbestos strike: Catholic union struck in defiance of the law; workers lose the strike but some argue it set off 'La Revolution Tranquille' (the Quiet Revolution)

Public-Sector Unions

Table 1.1   cont'd

1956	Merger of the TLC and CCL to form the Canadian Labour Congress (CLC)	**Public-Sector Unions**
1965	Quebec Civil Service Act grants unionization rights to all public-sector employees except the police; limitations on the right to strike	
1967	Federal government grants the public service employees bargaining rights; other nine provinces follow suit	
1968	Federal Task Force on Labour Relations (Woods Report)	
1972	First Canadian breakaway union: Canadian Paperworkers' Union (CPU)	
1975–8	Federal government imposes first peacetime wage and price controls	
1982	Federal government enacts the Charter of Rights and Freedoms; construction unions withdraw from CLC to form the Canadian Federation of Labour	

The New Service Economy

1996	First Starbucks in North America to be organized, by the CAW in Vancouver	**Private Service Sector**
1998	First McDonald's Restaurant unionized by the CAW in Squamish, BC	

The staple trade in furs, however, constituted the economic basis upon which the French and later this British colony survived (Innis, 1999). Neither during the French regime nor in the early years of British rule over New France could the colonial trade in furs support the creation of a class of workers who shared a common economic interest outside of the fur trade. Since the Aboriginal tribes caught the animals and cured the furs, this enclave staple economy became dependent on strategic alliances with varying groups of indigenous peoples. The trade in furs probably paid for the upkeep of the colony because virtually all necessities had to be imported from France. The meagre agricultural production from the settlers along the St Lawrence was insufficient to support a large population based in Montreal and Quebec City. During the concluding decades of the French colonial period and the beginning of the nineteenth century, economic diversification into the lumber and small-scale shipbuilding industries created a nascent working class. However, not until the second decade of the nineteenth century were workers in a position to begin collectively to advance their common class interests. For example, skilled carpenters in Lachine, Quebec, sporadically struck for higher wages during the first quarter of the nineteenth century (Creighton, 1956; Ryerson, 1963).

2. THE GROWTH OF CRAFT UNIONS IN THE ERA OF THE CONSPIRACY DOCTRINE

The second period, which takes us from the British Conquest of New France and the American Revolution of 1776 to Confederation and the National Policy of

1879, has been called the age of 'proto-Industrialization'.[1] Essentially, these hundred years constituted Canada's takeoff period of industrialization and were characterized by the staple exports of furs and later lumber, the beginnings of commercial agriculture, especially in Ontario, the start of US ownership and control of Canada's manufacturing and natural resource industries, and the subdivision of labour into different forms of handicraft production (see Palmer, 1979, for handicraft production). The rise of cities in Upper Canada and the Atlantic provinces occurred amid the dominance of the Montreal merchant and commercial classes. Meanwhile, the majority of the French-speaking colonists of Lower Canada worked subsistence farms under the watchful eyes of the clergy and a small professional class of lawyers and doctors (Gérin, 1964; also ch. 10, this volume).

Collectively, the colonial working class of skilled craftsmen may have constituted a social class, defined as a social group who see themselves united by a common economic interest; nevertheless, they were divided and parochial. During this period, craftsmen were numerically small, territorially dispersed, heterogeneous (that is, made up of Toronto typographers, Montreal brewmasters, Hamilton shoemakers, and so on), and fractured along ethnic lines (for example, workers of Irish and Scottish descent). It was also the era of the 'Conspiracy Doctrine'. Under British common law, combinations of workers for purposes of collective bargaining were treated the same as conspiracies to commit murder, because their purpose was to restrain trade—a criminal offence. Therefore, early trade unions in Canada were often called benevolent societies or journeymen's clubs. Throughout this period of development 'the English trade union movement provided an important training ground for craftsmen who emigrated to Canada. Upon their arrival in North America, their presence gave added impetus to the early growth of the labor movement' (Willes, 1984: 27). As fraternities of working men, they helped unemployed members find work and supported comrades in disputes with their employers over wages, working conditions, and craft rights.

In the early stages of the Canadian trade union movement, sickness and accident benefits were the more important issues affecting members. As in Britain, early Canadian unions were largely local in outlook, since communities were relatively isolated and transportation links were primitive. The trade union movement gained strength in the latter part of the nineteenth century for a number of reasons. First, the development of the railway system opened up vast territories for commercial agriculture, lumbering, and mining ventures. Second, the immigrants who settled these tracts of land created markets for manufactured goods produced by large manufacturing firms. Last, but certainly not least, the laws prohibiting trade unions as organizations of workers were repealed. In 1871, British unions won statutory relief from the criminal conspiracy doctrine. The following year, in 1872, the Trade Union Act was passed in Canada by the Conservative government of John A. Macdonald. It stipulated that the mere combination of workers to increase wages or to lower hours was not a conspiracy and did not violate the common law.

3. THE DOMINANCE OF CRAFT UNIONS AND THE EMERGENCE OF INDUSTRIAL UNIONS

The roughly four decades from the National Policy (1879) to the outbreak of World War I was a time of unprecedented industrial development in Canada. In British North America, the building of the Canadian Pacific Railway (CPR) linking central Canada with the Pacific Ocean and of the Intercontinental Railway, which integrated the eastern provinces with central Canada, was not the only major economic achievement. The discovery of a new strain of wheat at the beginning of the century created the means for a new prosperity in the Prairies based on the export of an agricultural staple. Prospects for a new and better life and the concerted and selected efforts of the CPR agents in Eastern Europe led to a steady stream of immigrants to settle the newly created provinces of Alberta (1905) and Saskatchewan (1905). Immigrants from Eastern Europe also worked in the mining communities of northern Ontario. Clearly, this period was crucial in diversifying the ethnic mix of Canada's working class. An ethnic mosaic began to leave its stamp on Canada's growing working-class movement.

These years witnessed the founding of craft trade unions in central Canada, the creation of city labour councils, and the initial attempts at a national labour organization. Craft unions predominated because factories, as we know them, did not yet exist. The many large machines needed for large-scale, mass production were not yet commercially viable. The manufacture of goods such as clothing, furniture, and home utensils occurred in small shops that required most workers to own their own tools. These men acquired numerous necessary skills through years of experience working with master craftsmen. Entrance into these 'professions' was strictly controlled and women were seldom allowed entrance to skilled crafts. However, as John Porter (1965) correctly noted, the demand for skilled labour in Canada was supplied predominantly from abroad. The few instances of locally developed craft skills were never enough to meet the demands of employers. New immigrants were the method of choice.

Since the support provided by these early workers' fraternities was generally limited to the resources of their membership, local trade unions began to realize the potential benefits of city-wide and then national organizations as a response to the growth of capitalist industrial organizations. A city-based labour organization provided greater resources and could act to co-ordinate the activities of various local unions. The first steps towards such organizations were the city labour councils based in Hamilton, Toronto, Montreal, and Brantford. These organizations, in turn, led to the establishment of the Canadian Labour Union (CLU) in 1873.

Improved transportation and communication allowed unionized craftsmen in both Canada and the United States to have more frequent contact with one another. These contacts facilitated the growth of international unions based in the United States to move into Canada. International trade unionism began in Canada in the 1850s in response to the desire of Canadian local unions to be part of something bigger and stronger. Moreover, membership in US-based international trade unions would make it easier for members to move to the US when Canadian jobs became scarce.

In 1886, international craft unions formed the Trades and Labour Congress (TLC). Subsequent years witnessed the expulsion of British craft unions from the TLC and the consolidation of an apolitical, US-inspired ideology within the leadership of this craft-dominated national labour organization. The formal alliance between the TLC and its American counterpart, the American Federation of Labor (AFL), was cemented with the signing of the 'Berlin Declaration' of 1902 at the TLC convention in Berlin (later Kitchener), Ontario, which stipulated that it would not recognize a national Canadian union in a jurisdiction where an international union existed. John Flett, the newly elected president of the TLC, proudly postured that 'the Congress (TLC) is the legislative mouthpiece of the international unions' (Lipton, 1967: 137).

In contrast, the 1880s also gave rise to the remarkable Knights of Labor, the first workers' movement in North America 'to envision and to attempt the organization of the working class in its entirety, transcending divisions of skill, sex, race and ethnicity' (Kealey, 1981: 235). The early success of their organizing drives made many employers and government officials fearful of potential future gains in wages, working conditions, and hours of work. Moreover, their mandate to organize all workers contradicted the exclusionary practices of the US international craft unions and their recently created national organization, the Trades and Labour Congress. The combined efforts of employers, the state, and the international craft union leaders sealed their fate. By the turn of the century, the Knights had become a nonentity.

For much of the period leading up to World War I, Canadian industrialization had been kick-started by US investors. US-based branch plants employed increasing numbers of skilled and semi-skilled Canadian workers in factories manufacturing consumer and producer goods. A few notable Canadian manufacturers, such as Stelco, carved a niche for themselves in the Canadian internal market. As well, American investment found its way into the newly discovered mineral riches locked in the Canadian Shield. The mining communities of Sudbury, Kirkland Lake, and Timmins, to name a few, suddenly appeared in northern Ontario and were linked together and to the south by the Ontario Northland Railway. Most of the workers in these fledgling towns had come from Eastern Europe. They formed the backbone of a uniquely independent spirit that would come to characterize life in Canada's northern regions.

These years bore witness to the importance of the federal state in regulating the economic activities of the newly created nation, including the regulation of labour. First came the Royal Commission on the Relations of Capital and Labour (1889), which revealed, in sordid detail, the despicable working conditions in Canada's early factories and sweatshops. In 1900, the federal Department of Labour was created to gather statistics about the conditions of labour in Canada and new legislation was enacted, the most important being the Industrial Disputes Investigation Act (IDIA) of 1907.

In summary, the first phase in the history of the Canadian labour movement takes us from the founding of the French regime to World War I. At the start of this period, the transformation of the colonial economy resulted from a shift in staple exports from furs to timber and a colonial economy comprised of commercial agriculture and small-scale manufactories. The development of a small internal market gave rise to the demand for craft workers who possessed scarce skills and the appropriate tools for their trade. Only at the end of this period did craft-based trade unions mature to form the first national trade union federation in Canada— the Trades and Labour Congress. By the beginning of the twentieth century, the emergence of the factory system and the exploitation of Canada's natural resources gave rise to a new type of worker and, as a result, a new form of trade union. The need for semi-skilled and unskilled labour to work the factories and mines meant the rapid growth in demand for workers who possessed *no tools and few skills to protect*. Certainly, the interests of factory and mine workers in organizing into trade unions are different from those expressed by tradesmen in the craft-based trade union movement in Canada. The creation of an industrial working class at the beginning of this century led to the formation of industrial trade unions—labour organizations reflecting the interests of semi-skilled and unskilled factory and mine workers.

4. The Rise of Industrial Unionism and the Struggle for Legal Recognition

The next phase takes us through the Great Depression to the end of World War II. Industrialization entrenches and expands into hitherto untouched regions of Canada. However, the first few years of this period are known for the great defeats inflicted on the Canadian labour movement. Prominent examples are the Winnipeg General Strike of 1919 and the Cape Breton coalminers' and Sydney steel strikes of 1922 and 1923. In all three instances, federal troops and special police were dispatched to put down the 'insurrections'.

The continued growth of factories meant an ever larger proportion of the Canadian working class was made up of semi- and unskilled production workers. These men, and not a few women, came from diverse ethnic and religious backgrounds. Increasingly, more and more factory workers wanted to join trade unions and fought with employers to get legal recognition to bargain collectively for better wages and working conditions. The growth of industrial unions, with their cocksure Communist and social democratic organizers, was sure to lead to a confrontation with the apolitical leaders in the craft-based unions controlling the Trades and Labour Congress.

At the onset of World War I, skilled craftsmen ruled the workplace and the trade union movement in Canada. These artisans were known to be fiercely loyal to their craft and had strict rules for entry into their workplaces and 'professional' associations. They were noted for clinging to their status as skilled craftsmen and, for the most part, did not support any one political party. On the other hand, the newly created industrial unions were organized by Communists, socialists, and social democratic ideologues with committed political agendas, something the craft-based unions in the US and Canada had consciously avoided. Differences in ideologies proved to be formidable obstacles for admitting semi-skilled and unskilled workers as equal partners in the TLC. The intensity of the debates split organized labour in Canada into competing, national organizations when, in 1939, the TLC expelled the Canadian affiliates of the international industrial unions. The international industrial unions affiliated with the US Congress of Industrial Organizations (CIO) formed their own national federation, the Canadian Congress of Labour (CCL).

The 1930s saw the ascendancy of industrial trade unions in Canada. The heart of industrial unionism in Canada was southern Ontario and Montreal. If the traditional TLC unions were not responding to the needs of Canada's factory and mine workers, these men and women would turn for support to US-based industrial unions. The sit-down strike of Oshawa General Motors workers in 1937 was the most dramatic of these initiatives. The Canadian workers had decided to mimic their American comrades at the General Motors plant in Detroit. Their intention was to achieve the union recognition and collective agreement that followed the Detroit sit-down strike. Surprisingly, and in spite of the weight of the provincial government against the workers, they succeeded, and the United Auto Workers were ensconced in Canada. Other international industrial unions, such as the Steel Workers Organizing Committee (later to become the United Steelworkers of America) and the Communist-led International Mine, Mill and Smelter Workers, soon followed.

In addition to organizing workers, industrial trade unionists advanced different political and ideological agendas. Industrial unions became the hotbed of ideological struggle among communism, a pro-capitalist business unionism, and a social democratic, made-in-Canada political alternative known as the Co-operative Commonwealth Federation (the CCF, later the NDP). On a different front, the Canadian and Catholic Confederation of Labour (CCCL) was founded in Hull, Quebec, in 1922. Presented as a 'Catholic and Christian' alternative to the materialism of secular trade unionism, its adherents were prepared to wrest control of the minds of Quebec's workers from the clutches of communism and secular dogma.

By the end of World War II, the picture of trade unionism in Canada was complicated by sectoral differences (skilled vs industrial unionism), ethnic diversity (Eastern European, Scottish, Irish, French-speaking Québécois, and so on), the predominance of international unionism, ideological conflict (Communist vs social democratic ideas), and competing provincial and national organizations. As well, the provincial and federal governments had allied with employers and were quick to use the stick (that is, the RCMP, federal troops, or provincial police) when necessary. However, the use of force to sanction property relations in the workplace became ineffective when the numbers of militant combatants kept growing and growing. The larger the industrial working class in Canada grew, the more difficult it was for the state to settle industrial conflict by simply using armed force against striking workers.

The crescendo of workers' struggles by the middle of the war led the federal government to legislate the rules necessary to settle disputes over wages, benefits, and working arrangements in the workplace. Enacted under the auspices of the War Measures Act, PC 1003 remains, to this day, the hallmark of federal and provincial labour law in Canada. Combining the principles of the US Wagner Act of 1935 with compulsory conciliation, this truly Canadian law covered all of Canada's employees for the duration of the war. Nevertheless, by 1947 the federal government conceded most of the jurisdictional authority in labour matters to the provinces. However slow the provinces were to enact similar labour laws, PC 1003 stood as the standard for their own provincial labour legislation.

5. THE STRUGGLE FOR LEGITIMACY: CERTIFICATION AND CHECK-OFF

Immediately following the war, almost all private-sector employers tried to reverse the union movement's wartime gains, particularly in the areas of union recognition and security. Normally, union recognition means the employer is forced by the state, through legislation, to recognize representatives from the employer's workforce. These individuals will then be in a position to sit down with representatives from the employer to negotiate freely for better wages and working conditions for all employees. Customarily, it involves a process known as certification.

To become certified as the legally recognized bargaining agent for a group of employees, the organizers for the particular trade union (usually people from the workplace) must first sign up individual workers. Once a high enough percentage of workers have agreed to join (45–55 per cent is the accepted minimum range), the union petitions the appropriate labour relations board (provincial or federal) for certification as the independent bargaining agent of the employees. This quasi-governmental body is ordinarily comprised of three representatives—one from organized labour, one from the employer group, and a mutually acceptable third person. Once an organizing drive by a trade union has begun, employers are constrained from taking certain actions. If, for example, the employer fires an employee for assisting in the organizing drive or coerces employees to sign a counterpetition to the one presented by the union, then the labour relations board (LRB) has the authority not only to reinstate the dismissed employee(s) but may not accept the company's counterpetition.

On the other hand, the union organizers must follow a number of rules. For example, an employer has the right to be informed of who signed the union's petition to the labour relations board. Moreover, from the time the employer is informed of the organizing drive until the time the LRB makes a decision for legal recognition of the bargaining unit, the employer is free, within certain limits and depending on the jurisdiction (that is, the province or the federal government), to set in motion strategies to discourage workers from certifying. For example, the employer may improve sanitation and safety standards or provide a modest increase in wages and/or benefits in order to offset the perceived need, on the part of employees, of a union. On some occasions, these gestures from the employer have been sufficient to stall the legal recognition of the union.

However, a union is recognized by the state as an independent organization in that particular workplace once the labour relations board confirms the majority of workers want to be represented by a union and establishes it is not funded by the company. Unions depend on dues collected from each employee in order to finance all of their own operations. The union's financial security rests on what is commonly called the 'check-off' of union dues by the company—a procedure that companies early in the history of trade unionism in Canada flatly rejected until Justice Ivan Rand's ruling in 1945 in Ontario forced all employers to deduct union dues from their employees and pass them on to the union.

A historic 99-day strike at the Ford plant in Windsor, Ontario, in 1945 concluded with Justice Rand of the Supreme Court of Canada providing for a compulsory 'check-off' of union dues for all employees in the bargaining unit, whether union members or not. His ruling stipulated that the company was required to deduct union dues from a worker's paycheque and immediately turn over the money to the union executive. However, the financial security of the trade union was not all that Justice Rand had in mind when he made his ruling. He was equally concerned with making certain that the union officials would carry out the rules negotiated in the collective agreement. In Justice Rand's judgement, in return for 'policing' the workplace during the term of the collective agreement (i.e., enforcing the negotiated rules in the collective agreement), the trade union, as an organization, receives a fee from each employee in the bargaining unit (i.e., union dues). This provision has become known as the Rand Formula (see Russell, 1990).

6. The Rise of Nationalism and Public-Sector Unions

As the economies of the Western industrialized countries grew over the course of this century, so did the role played by the central government in labour-related matters—except for Canada. As a bilingual federal state, Canada is unique. Only in Canada do close to 90 per cent of workers come under the 10 provincial labour relations acts, while merely 10 per cent fall within the federal jurisdiction.[2] In the United States, by contrast, approximately 90 per cent of employees fall under Washington's authority and only 10 per cent of the workforce are covered by individual state laws. Federal jurisdiction over organized labour in the United States explains why it was possible for President Reagan in the early 1980s to fire all of America's striking air traffic controllers, while our Prime Minister cannot directly intervene with striking autoworkers, steelworkers, or hydro workers. All these employees come under the authority of provincial governments.

Between the end of the war and the beginning of the 1960s, foreign (mainly US) direct investment dominated the manufacturing and resource sectors of the Canadian economy. As well, the Quebec economy was shifting from a basically agricultural hinterland to a modern industrial economy. French-speaking Québécois from the countryside were finding jobs in the factories and mines of the newly expanding towns and cities of rural Quebec. Everett Hughes, in his classic analysis, *French Canada in Transition* (1948), pointed out the potentially explosive atmosphere generated by the 'ethnic division of labour' in Quebec's booming factories and mines. However, he was quick to suggest that it was not the newly created working class that would have difficulty adjusting to the changes in Quebec society. They had everything to gain and very little to lose. On the contrary, the traditional élites in Quebec—the clergy and the Francophone professional groups—and the 'stable and traditional' middle-class way of life were threatened by 'foreign-controlled' industrialization. The legitimacy of their pivotal and historical role as brokers between the French-speaking rural majority and the English-speaking political and economic élites was breaking down. In seeking a new role for themselves, some of the members of the traditional élites wanted to cling to the past. Others searched for new ways of accommodating the past with the emerging present by seeking political power, as Pierre Elliott Trudeau did, or, like Jean Marchand, by working within the Quebec labour movement. The trade union movement in Quebec, especially the Catholic trade union federation, became one of the important institutions that was modernized and initially put in the service of grounding a new relationship with English-speaking political and economic élites—a role the newly created CSN (Confédération des syndicats nationaux) or CNTU (Canadian National Trade Unions) would quickly eschew for a left-wing, pro-Quebec nationalist ideology.

The phenomenal growth of the public-sector institutions of health, education, and welfare started in the early 1960s, not only in Quebec, where it became known as 'the Quiet Revolution', but throughout Canada. Traditional institutions in Quebec such as the Catholic Church no longer possessed the legitimacy or expertise to accommodate the passage into a mature, welfare capitalist regime. High growth in the public-sector institutions of health, education, and welfare ushered in a new middle class of salaried bureaucrats and experts who were quick to assert their rights to organize and negotiate for collective agreements. In 1965, the Quebec Liberal government of Jean Lesage passed legislation allowing Quebec's public-sector workers to organize into trade unions. In 1967, the federal government followed suit after a short period of intense public-sector workplace conflict across Canada. In the following months the remaining nine provinces passed similar legislation. White- and blue-collar workers in the public sector of the provincial and federal governments and parapublic institutions such as universities rapidly organized. By the early 1970s, the majority of public-sector workers at the federal and provincial levels were organized into trade unions and enjoyed the legal protections afforded to them in their collective agreements. At this time, the labour movement in Canada was comprised of craft, industrial, and the newly created public-sector unions.

7. Trade Unions, English Common Law, and Collective Agreements

In Canada and the United States, the *collective agreement* is the cornerstone of collective bargaining. The agreement carries the force of law and is binding on both parties. It is the basis for and governs the relations between the trade union, which speaks for the employees, and the employer. Collective agreements are normally small, pocket-sized documents. They vary in length from about 20 to over 200 pages. In any collective agreement, a number of clauses will always appear—dealing with wages and fringe benefits, establishing union recognition and management's rights, dealing with job security and job opportunities more commonly known as seniority, and outlining the procedures for settling disputes or grievances. However, many clauses in collective agreements are written in general terms. In practice, several provisions written in the collective agreement are fleshed out by memos, bulletins, various plant rules, customs, and oral understandings.

Canadian agreements, unlike most in the United States, make provision for *compulsory and binding arbitration* as the last step in the grievance procedure. Arbitration must be distinguished from conciliation. Arbitration is the last step in a grievance made by a member of the union about the misconduct of a supervisor. An individual arbitrator or a board of three is agreed upon by both the trade union and the company. Arbitrators are usually judges, but sometimes university professors have been appointed. After hearing evidence from both sides in the dispute, the arbitrator arrives at a decision that is legally binding on the company and the union. This process, however, is a very expensive way of settling disputes that arise in the day-to-day operations of a normal working environment.

When union members and employer representatives negotiate a new or renewed collective agreement, *conciliation* is needed when an impasse occurs over some of the items to be settled. These problems are viewed as a normal part of the collective bargaining process between representatives from organized labour and the employer. Conciliation is normally compulsory in Canada. A conciliator is government-appointed. His/her job is to help the parties overcome the impasse and achieve a mutually agreed settlement. In Canada, recommendations made by a conciliator or a conciliation board are rarely binding on the two parties. However, if conciliation does not work, the union may be in a legal position to strike or the employer to lock out the employees.

It must be said that one of the important gains for workers made by trade unions and collective bargaining has been to 'qualify to a great degree the traditional power of an employer under the law of master and servant to dismiss without cause' (Bilson, 1985: 750). It must not be forgotten that the arbitrary power exercised by a master over his/her servants in early modern Europe constitutes the legal framework for current employer-employee relations. As mentioned earlier, trade unions were illegal. They were outlawed by the state. Not so long ago, an employer could dismiss any employee on a whim. Trade unions and collective agreements have helped to eliminate these arbitrary uses of power.

Employees represented by a trade union are accorded some share of respect and dignity in the workplace. This is an intangible that is often sorely lacking in a non-union environment. Weiler (1980: 31) correctly identifies collective bargaining with 'subjecting the employment relationship and the work environment to the "rule of law"'. He goes on to note this function of 'protecting the employee from the abuse of managerial power, thereby enhancing the dignity of the worker as a person, is the primary value of collective bargaining, one which entitles the institution to a positive encouragement from the law.'

On the other hand, trade unions, as organizations, have lost much of their edge as active agents for social change in Canada. With few exceptions, trade unions are not actively pursuing innovative solutions to the restructuring of employment in the Canadian economy. Unfortunately, space does not permit us to explore the innovations begun by some trade unions. One example, though, is the Solidarity Fund of the Quebec Federation of Labour (QFL).

Instead, for many unionized employees in Canada, trade unions are viewed as agents of relative job security in an era of increasing uncertainty. This role may not be sufficient for unions to prosper in the present environment, especially since most of the economic and political power remains with the employer and the state. For example, if they so desire or they do not want to work with trade unionists in this country, there are employers who will relocate to other countries where there are no unions or where there is cheaper labour.

Today, employers are much freer to move than are workers. Briefly, 'runaway shops' (factories and offices moving to areas of cheap labour) are more prevalent today for several reasons. First, new information and communications technologies have eliminated many of the jobs that were once necessary to the labour process while making co-ordination of activities easier to manage from one location. Second, so long as there are few, if any, government regulations to keep an employer in a community, province, or country, the employer is freer today than ever before to move operations wherever there is an economic advantage. Solutions to the new problems posed by changes to the political and economic realities of present-day Canada require trade unions to become innovators in labour-management relations.

8. THE NEW ECONOMY

The changes to the workplace and job creation brought about by information and communications technologies (ICTs) and globalization have yet to be fully documented, but some indicators are clearly present. The proliferation of 'non-standard work', defined as part-time, temporary, and self-employment, is evident in all advanced industrial societies, including Canada. Homework or telework is another work arrangement made possible by ICTs and globalization (Devine et al., 1997). Not surprisingly, homeworkers are overwhelmingly women who are frequently paid low wages, receive few if any benefits, and are often 'closed-off from one another as they increasingly work one-on-one with computers' (Menzies, 1996). The increase in part-time service jobs is attractive to many young people and some seniors who need the money. Many teenagers are coaxed by their parents into taking these short-term jobs because they offer added 'pocket money' and workplace discipline—training many parents feel their children could benefit from.

Times change quickly. These short-term jobs are now stable employment for many young people. Moreover, new ICTs provide employers with ways of minimizing costs but short-changing their young employees, who have acquired considerable experience while doing their jobs. At Starbucks, for example, the new 'Starbucks' Labour Scheduling' (SLS) system can minimize labour costs by selecting lower-paid new employees over more experienced and more costly workers. This system can track sales in 15-minute intervals and then project inventory and labour requirements for the next day, the next week, even the coming month! When SLS was implemented in 1996 at its outlets in Vancouver, experienced full-time servers paid at an hourly rate of $8 were displaced by new employees paid at $7 an hour. The SLS system sparked an organizing drive that ended with a collective agreement in August 1997 after employees won their fight for hours at work based on seniority and experience.

Today, the Canadian Auto Workers (CAW) is one of the more active trade unions organizing workers in the service sector. In British Columbia alone, as of late 1998, the CAW had organized 2,275 employees at 50 Kentucky Fried Chicken outlets, 11 Starbucks, and 18 White Spots. What are the major issues? 'Wages are not the issue. These people are coming to us based on three primary issues: job security, benefits and being treated with some level of respect and dignity' (John Schreiner, *Financial Post Daily*, 28 Aug. 1998, 17).

In Quebec the two major labour federations, the FTQ and CSN, have been embroiled in labour conflict over certification of young workers in the service sector. Young ushers, cashiers, and concession-stand employees at 10 Cineplex Odeon cinemas are now organized by an affiliate of the FTQ, while workers at five Montreal-area Famous Players theatres have been certified within two CSN locals. After two years of struggle the over 500 workers at Terre des Homme, the amusement park from Expo '67, were certified and won a union contract. Quebec was the scene for the first organizing drive at a McDonald's franchise in Canada. After a long and bitter struggle to unionize and just before the certification vote in March 1998, the owners of the St Hubert McDonald's franchise closed that outlet. Financial difficulties were cited as the explanation, yet none of their other five restaurants shut their doors. This 'McDo' (McDonald's is popularly known in Quebec as 'McDo') incident sparked widespread media attention and community support. According to one poll conducted in early March 1998, 86 per cent of Quebecers had heard of the 'McDo' union drive and 72 per cent among those aged 18-34 supported the workers.

A Profile of Trade Unionism in Canada

Today, over 500 trade unions represent and protect skilled craftsmen and blue-collar and white-collar occupations in the private and public sectors of the national economy. Of these, over 400 are national unions, some 50 are international unions with headquarters in the United States, while the remainder represent federal and provincial government employees.

As Table 1.2 shows, the vast majority of Canadian workers today belong to

Table 1.2   Membership of National and International Unions in Canada, 1960–1997

Year	International Affiliation	%*	National Affiliation	%*
1960	1,051,997	72	320,118	22
1965	1,124,741	71	389,746	25
1970	1,359,346	63	752,373	35
1975	1,478,583	51	1,324,076	46
1981	1,557,792	45	1,812,983	52
1988	1,265,797	33	2,425,411	63
1990	1,283,000	32	2,563,000	64
1997	1,217,000	30	2,663,000	65

*Percentages do not add up to 100 due to the exclusion of 'Other' affiliations, normally independent locals.

Source: *Directory of Labour Organizations in Canada*, Ottawa, selected years.

national (Canadian) trade unions. A shift in the affiliation from international or US-based organizations to national union membership has been facilitated by a number of factors, including the unionization of public-sector workers and the breakaway in 1985 of the CAW from the American UAW (United Auto Workers). In all, over 15,000 trade union locals are spread across Canada, representing more than 3,880,000 workers out of a total of over 11 million non-agricultural workers.

Table 1.3 provides a further breakdown of trade union membership by province and sex for 1997. The evidence reveals differences in provincial rates of unionization as well as variations in the gender breakdown of unionized workers in Canada. With 41.7 per cent of workers union members, Quebec is the most unionized province in Canada. Only a decade ago, Newfoundland and British Columbia held this distinction, with 74.9 and 50.5 per cent, respectively, but such relatively high rates of unionization have fallen with the decline of these provinces' traditional resource-based industries. With the second largest industrial economy in Canada, Quebec's rank at the top marks a significant shift in jurisdictional power for unions in Canada. On the other hand, Ontario's position has diminished significantly, with only 29.9 per cent in comparison to the 1988 figure of 38 per cent. In 1997, Ontario and Alberta stood closely together, with PEI, as the provinces with the smallest percentage of the paid workforce represented by trade unions, a situation that can be explained at least in part by the fact that Ontario and Alberta for the past several years have had Conservative governments that are strongly pro-business and antagonistic towards labour.

When comparing rates of unionization by sex, the most recent statistics reveal

Table 1.3   Unionization by Province and by Sex, 1997

	Total Employed (000s)	Total Unionized (000s)	% Unionized	Female (000s)	Male (000s)	% Female
Nfld	163.6	67.2	41.1	30.3	36.9	45.1
PEI	48.5	14.0	28.9	7.8	6.2	55.7
Nova Scotia	329.6	101.4	30.7	45.7	55.7	45.1
New Brunswick	268.2	81.7	30.5	36.5	45.2	44.7
Quebec	2,747.8	1,147.1	41.7	504.5	642.6	43.9
Ontario	4,498.6	1,346.9	29.9	581.5	765.4	43.1
Manitoba	438.3	164.2	37.5	80.0	84.2	48.7
Saskatchewan	351.5	128.6	36.6	68.0	60.6	52.9
Alberta	1,148.1	292.5	25.5	148.3	144.1	50.7
BC	1,458.5	536.7	36.8	243.4	293.3	45.4
Canada	11,452.6	3,880.3	33.9	1,746.1	2,134.2	45.0

Source: Statistics Canada, Ottawa, 1998. Catalogue no. 71F–0004–XCB.

the progress made by women. As was predicted a number of years ago, substantial growth potential existed for unionizing women since only 28 per cent of all female paid workers were union members in 1985 (Glenday, 1994). In 1997, women made up a majority of unionized workers in three provinces—PEI, Alberta, and Saskatchewan. Moreover, in no province does the proportion of unionized women workers fall below 40 per cent—unlike 1988, when a majority of provinces (7 out of 10) had percentages below 40 per cent.

Linda Briskin and Pat McDermott's *Women Challenging Unions* (1993) and Julie White's *Sisters and Solidarity* (1993) both address issues of concern to feminist trade unionists in Canada. Briskin and McDermott bring together a group of mostly feminist academics who cover topics ranging from 'women and strikes' and 'the politics of gender within the union movement' to specific concerns such as women's occupational health in Quebec and the particular problems faced by women in the garment industry. White contextualizes the women's and trade union movements in Canada by situating women in the larger historical context of changes to the trade union movement in Canada. She also examines the problems of access to the top of union bureaucracies and the remaining controversies women need to face inside unions.

Many Canadian unions are responding to the challenges posed by the new economy and antiquated labour relations legislation that creates unnecessary barriers to the certification of workers in the service sector. While some gains have been made, governments and business have not been friendly to unions or the desires of their employees for fair and respectful workplaces. However, the fight is far from over and Canadian unions are well poised to meet these challenges.

Setting the Stage for the New Economic and Political 'Realities'

The Retreat from the Postwar Industrial Relations System in Canada

The growth of good jobs in the post-World War II Canadian economy came from large, mainly US-owned or -controlled manufacturing companies and the expansion of government positions in health, welfare, and education. Today, large companies are restructuring and downsizing and the federal and provincial governments push for deregulation and deficit reduction while they shed many of the good jobs and shy away from directly creating numerous secure, high-paying, and challenging jobs (Glenday et al., 1997).

The impetus for change certainly began earlier than the 1980s recession. Starting with the OPEC oil crisis in 1973 and continuing over the next two decades, the Canadian and US economies witnessed high inflation, then tight monetary controls to fight inflation, the deregulation of communications and transportation industries, and the signing of the FTA and then NAFTA. All these events have added new fuel to the abandonment of the economic and political arrangements and progressive climate created in the first few decades of the postwar era (Teeple, 1988). The new information and communications technologies, changing economic circumstances, and the rise of neo-conservative political ideas and policies in Canada and the United States are the leading social forces transforming the primary labour markets and their accompanying postwar industrial relations system. These forces, by creating the present context for the increasing polarization of Canadian society (the rich are getting richer and the poor are getting more numerous) and the progressive balkanization of the country (increasing provincial autonomy while the national government, more and more, takes on the role of resource of last resort), are transforming what made Canada a maturing nation in the 1960s and 1970s.

In Canada and the US, but with varying degrees of success, the progressive erosion of the labour relations system built up over the first three decades following World War II marks public-sector and private-sector industrial relations policy over the past two decades. In Canada, this process probably began with the federal government's wage and price controls of the mid-1970s, otherwise known as the anti-inflation policy, and took off with the more recent policies of deregulation. The deregulation of transportation and telecommunications are good examples of the federal government's role in this transformation. The push towards concession bargaining from management (there is a strong presence of US managers and managerial ideologies in Canada), the federal and provincial governments' assault on public-sector unions in the 1980s (Glenday, 1994; Panitch and Swartz, 1988), and the more recent attempts to relax provincial labour laws are all part of the 'hollowing out' of the post-World War II institutional arrangements between management and labour that gave Canada (and the US) a solid middle class.

The only political jurisdiction in North America that has not been vigorous in its attacks on both public- and private-sector labour legislation in North America is Quebec.[3] For example, as a result of changes to the province's labour laws passed during the first Parti Québécois term of office (1976–80), Quebec was the first jurisdiction in Canada to prohibit the hiring of scab labour and remains the only province to have such legislation on the books. For a province that was notorious for its militant labour movement and violent strikes during the 1960s and early 1970s, the more than 20-year legacy of progressive labour legislation must be credited for the relative calm that today surrounds Quebec's labour relations. However, the political climate in Quebec has changed. Today, much like the other provinces, the PQ government in Quebec under Lucien Bouchard struggles with balancing budgets, deregulation of industries not under its control, and so on. And, like his counterparts in the other provinces, Bouchard (one should not forget he was a minister in Brian Mulroney's Progressive Conservative government) sees little difficulty in attacking the public-sector unions to achieve some of his political goals: witness the severity of the nurses' strike in the dying months of 1999.

Unlike the US, the assaults on trade union freedoms in Canada have been fiercest against *public*-sector unions. For example, a 1986 headline in the *Globe and Mail* read: 'UN body censures B.C. Government for flouting widely accepted international labour standards'.[4] British Columbia joined Alberta, Ontario, and Newfoundland, which were also censured by the same United Nations agency—the International Labour Organization (ILO)—for outlawing free collective bargaining. This judgement followed the visit by an ILO mission—the first to Canada—to investigate public-sector union harassment by these four provincial governments. Canadians are not accustomed to being singled out for violations of what the United Nations accepts as basic human rights—the right to join trade unions and to have these organizations pursue the collective interests of their members through vehicles such as free collective bargaining.

Was the ILO incident an aberration in an otherwise progressive labour regime? Some might say it was, while others have written that it was not. Leo Panitch and Donald Swartz (1988) labelled the 1980s the beginning of an era of 'permanent exceptionalism' when the federal and provincial governments set aside prior legislative precedent and opted for curtailing, even outlawing, hard-won pro-labour legislation. After the relative calm of the 1950s and 1960s, a period when trade unions were accepted as legitimate organizations within liberal democracy, Panitch and Swartz argue that beginning in the 1970s the federal and provincial governments started to resist and erode legitimate trade union practices.[5] Trade unions, which for over 100 years both protected and advanced the rights and interests of the average worker, must continue to counter the legal and political attacks on their role in society. The future of work, politics, and power in Canada hinges on current changes to the legitimacy of trade unions and collective bargaining and what their place will be in Canadian life.

Moving Off the Ropes: The Charter and the Legal Future of Organized Labour in Canada

The passage into law of the Charter of Rights and Freedoms in 1982 meant trade unions were to face different and formidable challenges to their role in Canadian society. It must not be forgotten that the Canadian Labour Congress (CLC) remained outside of the 1982 constitutional discussions.[6] As a result of its silence, the collective rights of trade unionists were never seriously discussed for possible inclusion in the Charter. The labour trilogy, as three Supreme Court cases decided simultaneously have since become known, challenged the legislative protections afforded to trade unions in Canada. The first case, *Reference re Public Service Employee Relations Act* (*Alberta Labour Reference*, 1987), dealt with whether the Alberta government's prohibition against strikes and lockouts for firemen, policemen, and hospital workers violated the Charter's guarantee of freedom of association. The second, *Public Service Alliance of Canada v. The Queen* (1987), asked the Court to rule on the federal government's 1982 wage restraint package on the civil service, popularly dubbed the '6 and 5' program. Finally, in *Retail, Wholesale and Department Store Union, Local 580 et al. v. Saskatchewan* (1987), the Saskatchewan government had enacted emergency legislation to prohibit a work stoppage in that province's dairy industry. The trilogy sought to overturn government attempts to curb the collective interests of trade unionists by recourse to individual rights under the Charter of Rights and Freedoms. That is, certain legal safeguards over whether trade unions in Canada could act collectively in the interests of their members were threatened. In two of the three cases, different public-sector unions were pitted against their employers—the federal and provincial governments.

Essentially, the Supreme Court of Canada was being asked to rule on whether the right to form associations as laid down in Section 2(d) of the Charter extends to workers the right to act collectively to protect their interests. In a 4–2 ruling, the Court upheld federal and provincial legislation. These were important cases because the Court's decision diminished the ability of trade unions to exercise rights earlier guaranteed by Canadian governments and by the United Nations. In light of these initial rulings, Leo Panitch and Donald Swartz (1988) identified the provincial and federal government encroachment into organized labour's legal protections as 'permanent exceptionalism'. In other words, the state could act unilaterally in the pursuit of what it saw as its own concerns without regard for trade union interests. But the story does not end here. It gets worse.

A fourth legal challenge to the Supreme Court, *Dolphin Delivery*,[7] involved 'secondary picketing'. The issue began with a strike between Purolator Courier and its employees in Vancouver. The company had subcontracted some of its business to Dolphin Delivery. The union claimed Purolator was sidestepping the strike and therefore collective bargaining by continuing, indirectly, to give business to Dolphin. The union attempted to picket Dolphin. Dolphin sought and received an injunction prohibiting secondary picketing. The Supreme Court's judgement rejected the union's position and refused to confer Charter protection under the section guaranteeing freedom of expression to secondary picketing.

Given these Court decisions, trade unionists expected the worst from the long-awaited *Lavigne* case (*Lavigne v. Ontario Public Service Employees Union* [1991]). Lavigne sought to avoid the compulsory payment of union dues at his unionized workplace. Contributions for his legal fees came from the National Citizens' Coalition, a right-wing, anti-union group started by a London, Ontario, businessman that receives the bulk of its support from Ontario and western Canada. The *Lavigne* case went to the heart of union security as an organization, as established in the Rand Formula nearly a half-century earlier. The compulsory payment of union dues by all members, known as the 'check-off', goes to maintaining the union as an organization. As an organization, the union has an obligation to meet the needs of its members through collective bargaining with the employer, in grievance arbitration, and possibly by promoting some of the political objectives of the NDP. To put an end to compulsory dues payment would cripple union finances since some workers would opt out of the payment while still enjoying the advantages (wage increases, better working conditions, and better benefits) of a unionized workplace.

The Supreme Court ruled that the compulsory payment of the equivalent of union dues by a person within the bargaining unit, but who may not want to be a member of the union, does not infringe on his freedom of expression, even if the union voices opinions contrary to her/his own. The Court argued that the union's expression of its views is not made on behalf of an individual member and the individual is not bound by it. In its ruling, the Court also recognized the union member's obligations during a lawful strike, which include not being paid salary or benefits.

Clearly, the check-off of union dues and strike pay from union coffers existed *before* the Supreme Court's decision. Trade unions in Canada already had these rights. In *Lavigne*, however, the Court not only reconfirmed these rights in Canadian law, but helped to consolidate the union's presence in the workplace. Had the Court ruled against the union, trade unions across Canada would have been weakened as effective organizations pursuing the collective interests of Canadian workers. Undoubtedly, many trade unionists would have viewed this as a return to pre-World War II Canada when trade unions did not enjoy legal protections that guaranteed their organizational stability. Presumably, such a decision could have led many trade unionists to adopt a more aggressively militant stance. Moreover, as a country, Canada likely would be more closely scrutinized for violations of basic human rights by the ILO.

Over the past two decades trade unionists found themselves on the defensive, as employers, both state and private companies, attempted to erode past gains won, not only in wages and benefits (i.e., the workplace) but in the social contract that helps bind our country's citizens, including workers and employers, to the political legitimacy of the Canadian state. While the circumstances surrounding the survival of the Canadian labour movement are not as grim as they were a few years ago, the struggles for a better workplace and society are far from over.

Trade Unions in the US and Canada

In both Canada and the US common forces are associated with the retreat from the post-World War II industrial relations system, yet enduring differences exist in the character of the US and Canadian trade union movements. How is it that two countries that are sharing more look so different when it comes to the role of trade unions in society?

The Uneven Sectoral Distribution of Organized Labour in Canada

Table 1.4 traces the trends in unionization for the 10 industrial sectors of the Canadian economy. Between 1971 and 1992 every sector of the economy except manufacturing and forestry reported an increase in unionization, from a high of 79 per cent for public administration to a low of less than 5 per cent for finance. From 1981 until 1992, the rate of unionization for manufacturing declined from 44.4 per cent to 35.2 per cent. The historically anti-union sectors, such as finance and wholesale and retail trades, continue to exhibit extremely low levels of unionization. However, six of the 10 industries—public administration, construction, transportation, communications and utilities, forestry, and mining—report levels above 50 per cent.

While uneven in distribution across the 10 industrial classifications of the Canadian economy, traditional union concentrations in mining, construction, forestry, and public administration continue, while manufacturing, which may

Table 1.4   Workers in Unions by Industry in Canada, 1971–1992

Industry	1971	1981	1992	1981–92 % Increase/ Decrease
Fishing and Trapping	20.5	37.5	53.5	+42.7
Public administration	64.0	69.1	79.2	+14.6
Construction	50.5	54.0	65.2	+20.7
Transportation, communications, utilities	52.2	53.2	53.4	+0.4
Manufacturing	41.7	44.4	35.2	-20.7
Forestry	30.9	56.2	53.0	-5.6
Mining (metal mines)	35.6	35.5	52.0	+46.5
Services (excluding education, health, & social services)	21.8	25.6	35.7	+39.8
Wholesale and retail trade	8.4	8.9	11.9	+33.7
Finance	0.8	2.8	4.7	+67.9

Source: *Corporations and Labour Unions Returns Act*, Part II, Labour Unions, Catalogue no. 71–202.

never have achieved a rate of unionization above 50 per cent, can still boast strongholds in autos and steel.

The complete picture today is difficult to ascertain, primarily because the Canadian government no longer provides data for all unions from the CALURA or Corporations and Labour Unions Returns Act. As a result, scholars must depend on the Labour Force Historical Review, a survey that uses a sample of one respondent to every 200 people in the workforce. Therefore, the two data sets cannot be compared over time. However, estimates for union density of the public and private sectors for 1997 stand as follows: 72.2 per cent for public administration; 84.7 per cent for the rest of the public sector, including education, health, and social services; and 24.3 per cent for the private sector as a whole.

Tables 1.5 and 1.6 summarize the trade union movement in the US over the past 15 years. In every sector except the public service there has been a precipitous drop in trade union membership. Roughly a third of unionized workers were lost in construction, transportation and utilities, manufacturing, mining, services, wholesale and retail trade, and finance, insurance, and real estate; the government sector gained a modest 2.7 per cent. Table 1.6 gives a further breakdown by sector, sex, and age. The toll has been felt by both sexes and all age groups. However, with losses in the 20 per cent range, 45–54-year-olds and females reported the least percentage drop.

Certainly, the persistence in the disparities in trade union density between the US and Canada is a remarkable trend given how much closer our ties, in economic terms, have become with the signing of the FTA and NAFTA. In Canada, union density has begun a slide downward in traditional provincial strongholds such as

Table 1.5   Workers in Unions by Industry in the US, 1983–1996 (percentage of workers in unions)

Industry	1983	1996	1983–96 % Increase/ Decrease
Government	36.7	37.7	+2.7
Construction	27.5	18.5	-32.7
Transportation and public utilities	42.4	26.5	-37.5
Manufacturing	27.8	17.2	-38.1
Mining	20.7	14.1	-31.9
Services	7.7	5.7	-26.0
Wholesale and retail trade	8.7	5.6	-35.6
Finance, insurance, real estate	2.9	2.4	-17.2

Source: *Statistical Abstracts of the United States, 1997*, US Department of Commerce (Economics and Statistics Administration), Washington, 1997.

Table 1.6   Workers in US Unions by Sector, Sex, Age, 1983–1996
(percentage of workers in unions)

Sector	1983	1996	1983–96 % Increase/ Decrease
All union members	20.1	14.5	-27.9
Public-sector workers	36.7	37.6	+2.4
Private-sector workers	16.5	10.0	-39.4
Sex			
Male	24.7	16.9	-31.6
Female	14.6	12.0	-17.8
Age			
16 to 24 years old	9.1	5.5	-39.6
25 to 34 years old	19.6	12.0	-38.8
35 to 44 years old	24.8	16.8	-32.2
45 to 54 years old	27.0	21.4	-20.1
55 to 64 years old	26.9	18.8	-30.1

Source: *Statistical Abstracts of the United States, 1997,* US Department of Commerce, Washington, 1997. Catalogue no. 89–503E, 77.

Ontario (except Quebec, which has strengthened its position). However, the breadth and depth of unionization in the public sector, the inroads being made in the new service sector, and the strength of women's participation in the union movement are undeniably strong indicators of a vibrant and adaptive trade union movement in Canada. This stands in sharp contrast to the US, where the negative impact has been felt in all sectors (except government), at all ages, and among both sexes. In an era marked by a common thread of similar new technological, economic, and political realities, what explains the disparities in the social character of unionism in the two countries?

'The Continental Divide'

THE STRUCTURAL EXPLANATION

Canada's publicly funded national health-care system and the wider, publicly financed support for all four levels of education (primary, secondary, community colleges, and universities) may be a partial explanation for the larger percentage of unionized workers in Canada than in the US because, proportionally, there are more public-sector workers to draw on in Canada than in the US (Kumar, 1993).

However, this fact alone cannot account for the push to 'Canadianize' the labour movement in Canada or for the marked differences in the American and Canadian labour relations systems.

Trade unions in Canada have been structurally compared to their counterparts in the United States. A sketch of these differences is presented in Figure 1.1. The complexities attendant to the two countries' trade union histories, their different organizational structures, and their dissimilar institutional mechanisms for conflict resolution are simplified here, yet this does capture the more salient features differentiating Canada's labour regime from the one in the US.

While sharing a common heritage as European white settler colonies, each nation has created its own trajectory into the modern and post-modern age. The historical or horizontal axis covers two dimensions: trade unions as social movements and as social organizations, a characteristic more or less shared by the labour movements in the US and Canada, and a second reflecting the increased differentiation of the trade union movement that today includes skilled tradesmen, industrial workers, and the private, public, and parapublic (e.g., universities) office workers. These divisions, of course, correspond to the increased social and economic complexity of each society. The political and economic dimension is shown along the vertical axis and specifies the complex relationships among trade unions, employers, and the state, with business unionism at the bottom and social unionism at the top.

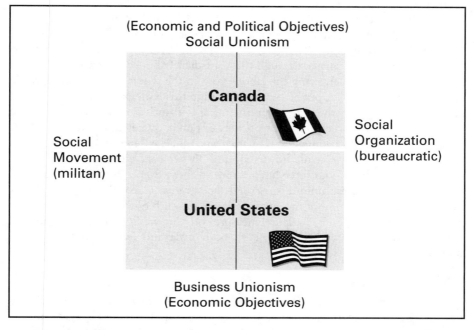

Figure 1.1 Labour Regimes in the US and Canada

In their important essay, Cella and Treu (1982) make a distinction between *business unionism* and *competitive or social unionism*. The former is characterized by 'its mainly economic objectives, pursued strictly through collective bargaining, outside stable political initiatives, and by relying mostly on direct organization in the workplace', while competitive or social unionism incorporates a much broader strategy, such as 'basic socio-economic reforms [that] are pursued by initiatives both on the economic and political fronts, often highly conflictual, with a close but not necessarily institutionalized relationship with the political system'.

As argued by McIntosh (1989: 16), the distinction belongs to a 'hierarchy of interests with business unionism defining the minimum set of interests (i.e., workplace specific) and competitive (or social) unionism having the maximum set of interests (i.e., workplace specific, plus general societal/political concerns)'. As trade unionists move away from the strict confines of the workplace (business unionism), they take up agendas requiring more direct political participation in addressing not only the expanding parameters of workplace problems (e.g., computer training) but public and social policy issues (e.g., family violence, child care). The US falls into the former category while Canada occupies the latter.

Huxley et al. (1986) and Cella and Treu (1982) detect three more influences that identify a country's shift from business to social unionism. The first is the degree of formal linkage between trade unions and political parties. The second is the degree of state intervention in the economy. Finally, a benchmark of 30 per cent unionized workers is set as constituting the upper limit for defining a labour regime dominated by business unionism.

On all the above, Canada differs from its southern neighbour. First, the Canadian political regime contains the only social democratic parties in North America—the New Democratic Party and the Bloc Québécois. It is also true, however, that trade unions in Canada, through the Canadian Labour Congress (CLC), have been unsuccessful in delivering the labour vote to the federal NDP. Second, while Canada's 'experiments' in public ownership of industries are presently under attack and all levels of government are experimenting with privatization of these public assets, there remain some important pockets of public ownership of industry, such as hydroelectricity (no longer in Ontario) and nuclear energy. Third, the trade union membership in Canada hovers around 35 per cent while the US share of the non-agricultural labour force has not moved above 20 per cent for the past two decades. Together, these unique structural factors give Canada's labour regime a healthy dose of social unionism. By extension, the health of the trade union movement in Canada depends, in large measure, on the vitality of social unionism expressed by its rank-and-file members, both male and female, in the private, public, and parapublic sectors.

THE 'VALUES' EXPLANATION

Seymour Martin Lipset (1991) places the bulk of the explanation for the 'Continental Divide' between Canada and the US, including differences in trade unionism,[8] on the dissimilar values that characterize the two nations' 'organizing principles'. In his words, 'US institutions reflect the effort to apply universalistic principles emphasizing competitive individualism and egalitarianism, while the other's [Canada's] are an outgrowth of a particularistic compact to preserve linguistic and provincial cultures and rights and elitism' (Lipset, 1991: 225). These differences in historically rooted values, according to Lipset, explain the relative lack of 'class consciousness, support for socialist or social democratic parties, or a strong union movement' in the US (ibid., 170). For Lipset, the emphasis placed on competitive individualism works against the need for collectivist solutions to individual and social problems, including those of the workplace. Simple, apolitical, 'bread and butter unionism' complements the US national values of 'competitive individualism and egalitarianism'.

Lipset argues for three, not two, labour regimes in North America. He sees Quebec, once the 'most conservative province in Canada', as occupying one end of a contemporary continuum of values with English Canada somewhere in the middle and the US at the opposite end. Lipset asserts that 'the attitudinal evidence indicates that, on most issues, Francophones are at one end of the spectrum, Anglophones in the middle and Americans at the other. Quebec has become the most liberal on social and welfare issues' (ibid., 216). Both value differences and a dissimilar judicial system make the Quebec labour regime distinct in North America.

In summary, a combination of factors, including structural dissimilarities and contrasting cultural values, continue to influence the trade union trajectories of the US, English Canada, and Quebec. Differences may persist; however, the wearing down of the social and political cohesion of Canada and the increasing strength of some provincial governments, such as Ontario, Alberta, and British Columbia, are factors contributing to widening the differences in labour regimes in the country as a whole.

The Vitality of Social Unionism: A Case Study

In regard to membership in trade unions, women in the US are losing ground while in Canada the percentage of women in trade unions is increasing. Interestingly, the public sector is the only sector that is growing in the US while in Canada, since at least the 1980s, the public sector has been under siege from both levels of government.

If increasingly greater numbers of women are embracing trade unionism in Canada, especially in the public sector and the new service economy, it would be instructive to know something about their perceptions on matters that concern them and how they see the role of their union in society. Do rank-and-file women, for example, see issues such as child care, family violence, and sexual harassment as being adequately addressed by their union or society at large? How satisfactorily are unions in Canada responding to the needs of Canadian women? For trade unions in Canada to exhibit characteristics of social unionism, these are among the issues they should be addressing. A partial answer to these questions can be offered in the following case study.

A Report from Rank-and-File Women in Ontario and Quebec

Table 1.7 shows the results from a 1995–6 survey of mostly female clerical, secretarial, and technical university (parapublic sector) workers in Ontario and Quebec. The strength of social unionism was measured by examining the responses to questions that covered non-workplace issues such as women's rights, AIDS, family violence, environmental issues, help centres for unemployed workers, and the trade union's role in society. It would not be accurate to conclude that these responses are statistically representative of unionized women workers in Canada. However, these results can be taken as a benchmark for evaluating the relative strength of social unionism among women trade unionists in Canada.

Employees were asked how active their union should be—more active, less active, undecided, about the same, or not active at all. On all five non-workplace issues Quebec respondents scored higher than their Ontario counterparts. These results not only support Lipset's contention that Quebecers express more liberal values than either their English-Canadian or US counterparts. They also are indicative of a socially active rank and file. This is not surprising since Quebec has the highest percentage of workers in trade unions in Canada, while Ontario hovers close to the 30 per cent figure considered a critical benchmark for social unionism by Huxley (1986) and Cella and Treu (1982).

In regard to satisfaction with their union's ability to represent their interests, a large majority (75 per cent of Quebec unionists and 65 per cent of those in Ontario) reported their union had done very well or well in representing the overall needs of members in contract negotiations. While not an unusual finding, it is interesting to note that the Quebec rank and file reported a higher percentage level of satisfaction than their Ontario counterparts.

Finally, Table 1.7 reports on four items dealing with the union's role in society. Here, the results are virtually identical. Over 80 per cent of the respondents in both Quebec and Ontario see unionization playing a major role in benefiting workers. Between two-thirds (Ontario) and three-quarters (Quebec) report that unions are necessary because current legislation is inadequate to protect workers' rights. Also, close to 90 per cent of workers from both provinces do not accept the point of view expressed at the beginning of this chapter, namely, that unions are no longer necessary because management is now willing to listen to workers. It is evident that women employees stand strongly and squarely behind their union. Finally, a clear majority do not agree that unions are too closely connected to the NDP (Ontario) or Parti Québécois (Quebec).

As we move into the next millennium, this last finding, in particular, may need to be revised. For Ontario workers in particular, the fiasco of the early 1990s with the Social Contract and the Rae NDP government has put NDP support from both public-sector and some private-sector unions in jeopardy. Quebec workers, especially in the public sector, are looking more cautiously at the social democratic, pro-labour past of the Parti Québécois by concentrating on the Bouchard government's recent handling of the nurses' strike.

Table 1.7   Vitality of Trade Unions

	Ontario	(N)	Quebec	(N)	Response Categories
Non-Workplace Issues					
Women's rights	64%	(173)	80%	(161)	More/About the same
	19%	(51)	7%	(15)	Should not be active
Health issues (AIDS)	55%	(150)	61%	(123)	More/About the same
	23%	(62)	24%	(49)	Should not be active
Environmental issues	69%	(191)	75%	(152)	More/About the same
	16%	(44)	13%	(26)	Should not be active
Help centres for	60%	(164)	64%	(128)	More/About the same
unemployed workers	16%	(43)	17%	(35)	Should not be active
Family violence	44%	(118)	65%	(132)	More/About the same
	26%	(71)	16%	(32)	Should not be active
Union Representation of Worker Interests					
How well does your union					
represent the overall needs	65%	(181)	74%	(156)	Very well or Well
of its members in contract	27%	(76)	20%	(42)	Somewhat
negotiations?	8%	(23)	6%	(12)	Not at all
Trade Unions' Role in Society					
Unionization plays a major	84%	(238)	83%	(184)	Strongly agree/Agree
role in benefiting workers	5%	(14)	3%	(6)	Don't know
	11%	(45)	15%	(33)	Disagree/Strongly disagree
We don't need unions	7%	(18)	6%	(14)	Strongly agree/Agree
because managements are	6%	(17)	4%	(10)	Don't know
now willing to listen to	88%	(250)	89%	(198)	Disagree/Strongly disagree
workers and unions are no					
longer necessary					
We need unions because	67%	(189)	75%	(168)	Strongly agree/Agree
existing government	13%	(37)	5%	(11)	Don't know
legislation is inadequate to	21%	(58)	20%	(44)	Disagree/Strongly disagree
protect workers' rights					
The unions are too closely	13%	(37)	21%	(47)	Strongly agree/Agree
connected to the NDP	36%	(102)	24%	(53)	Don't know
(or PQ)	52%	(145)	56%	(124)	Disagree/Strongly disagree

Conclusion

This chapter addressed four related questions. First, by examining the historical progress of trade unions in Canada, we spoke to the question of whether unions are agents of progressive social change. Second, in an era marked by the retreat from the post-World War II social contract between government, business, and trade unions, are their persistent national differences in the social character of trade unionism in the US and Canada? What explanations have been offered to account for the persistence in what Lipset calls the 'Continental Divide'? Last, what do women in one sector of the Canadian economy have to say about their union's organizational and strategic direction?

As a result of substantive changes to the organization and management of work in Canada and elsewhere in the world economy that started to take hold during the 1980s, trade union and management goals and priorities are changing. Where trade unions' interests were once directed at achieving gains in wages and benefits for their members, their focus today is often on gaining provision for job security in the collective agreement. On the other hand, management in both the private and public sectors (which includes Crown corporations) seeks concessions from trade unionists in order to achieve lower costs. Examples of concessions demanded by management include greater flexibility in work rules, the subcontracting of work, and lump sums of money in lieu of regular wage increases.

New information and communications technologies have been credited with levelling the hierarchy of virtually every organization. A flatter organization, especially at the bottom, means fewer job classifications, which in turn result in compressed promotion ladders and a smaller wage-based hierarchy. Workers find themselves doing more because several jobs have been combined into one new job category. Doing more also means spending more time in that job category (possibly decades if they are lucky enough to keep their jobs) because promotions now take more time because there are fewer jobs to move into. Moreover, because of new technological developments, fluid market conditions, changing government priorities, and/or increased global competition, most workers today are threatened with unemployment the longer they spend on the job.

For most Canadians who will have jobs, work in the new millennium promises flat or marginally increasing incomes, new work-related health problems, more stress and anxiety, less security, and few prospects for promotion. In addition, part-time and limited contract jobs are increasing in number. And, while many jobs disappear altogether, some jobs are resurrected into private 'contractor' jobs where the onus of paying for benefits, pensions, and so on is placed on the new employee, not the employer. These conditions, historically, have been fertile ground for the growth of trade unions. Consequently, organizing the new service workers in the years to come should remain at the top of the agenda of organized labour in Canada.

Why are Canadian trade unions well poised to take advantage of changes in the conditions of work and variations in the employment relationship? We saw that among the reasons put forward for the different trajectories of the trade union movements in the US and Canada were distinct historical and structural factors and, interestingly, dissimilar cultural values. Canadians are different from Americans and Québécois are different from both. Each group manifests distinct sets of values that would seem to have an effect on community support for trade unions— Quebec is the most liberal and the US the least, with English Canada somewhere in between. Today, Quebec boasts the highest percentage of unionized workers in Canada. Given the support for the 'McDo workers' among Quebec's youth and the successful organizing of young service workers in British Columbia by the CAW, there is fertile ground among young people in Canada for trade unionists to nurture.

Canadian employers will continue to seek trade union concessions to achieve lower costs, improved productivity, and greater profits. Among the more important areas to be targeted are (1) wage freezes or cuts; (2) the elimination or postponement of cost-of-living allowances; (3) compensation linked to individual performance; (4) greater use of part-time employment and subcontracting; and (5) changes in job classification, work rules, and seniority. Union gains in the future are likely to be in areas that will lead to only minimally higher labour costs. Job security will remain a crucial area, especially in view of rapid technological change, plant closures, and government and business downsizing. These provisions, however, are inherently difficult to negotiate. Very often, the employer will agree to limit layoffs or to confine the contracting out of work to special circumstances in exchange for wage rollbacks or wage freezes. The efforts of trade union officials to enhance job security will include negotiating for (1) reductions in working time and the sharing of available work; (2) restrictions on overtime as a means of distributing existing work; (3) voluntary early retirement with full pension rights; (4) improved training, retraining, and job transfer clauses; and (5) a halt to subcontracting.

Trade unions in Canada have the capacity to meet these challenges successfully because they remain permanent social movements. That is, their democratic structures, their numerous and various struggles over the years with employers and governments, and their ceaseless organizing in a variety of working environments make them especially able to adapt to and meet new challenges. Most trade unionists in Canada recognize the need to combine the gains made at the bargaining table with progressive change in the political arena. Only in this way can trade unions remain significant contributors to a safe and humane workplace and a more equitable and free country.

Questions for Critical Thought

1. Describe the ways trade unions in Canada are socially progressive?

2. How has the Charter of Rights and Freedoms affected the legal rights of trade unions in Canada?

3. Why do Canada and the US appear so different in regard to the role of trade unions in society?

Glossary

'**Conspiracy Doctrine**': Under British common law combinations of workers for purposes of collective bargaining were treated the same as conspiracies to commit murder because the purpose of collective bargaining was viewed as an act to restrain trade—a criminal offence.

PC 1003: The principles of federal and provincial labour law in Canada were set down in 1943–4 by this Order-in-Council. It incorporates the principles of collective bargaining as stipulated in the US Wagner Act of 1935 with compulsory conciliation, a uniquely Canadian twist.

Social unionism: This ideology pursues workers' interests not only through workplace organizing and collective bargaining, but also includes political demonstrations and actions for social change beyond the workplace.

Business unionism: This is an ideology that pursues workers' interests exclusively through workplace organizing, collective bargaining, and political lobbying.

'**Continental Divide**': Seymour Martin Lipset described the value differences between the US and Canada and Quebec with this term. Quebec stands as the most liberal, English Canada in the middle, and the US at the other end of the spectrum.

Suggested Readings

Glenday, Dan, and Ann Duffy, eds. 1994. *Canadian Society: Understanding and Surviving in the 1990s*. Toronto: McClelland & Stewart. This is the original collection of essays that the present volume has expanded upon.

Duffy, Ann, Dan Glenday, and Norene Pupo, eds. 1997. *Good Jobs, Bad Jobs, No Jobs: The Transformation of Work in the 21st century*. Toronto: Harcourt Brace. This is a collection of original essays about the changes to work largely brought about by information and communications technologies. Essays focus on telework, casino culture, underemployment, unemployment, the double day, and part-time work.

Heron, Craig. 1996 *The Canadian Labour Movement: A Short History*, 2nd edn. Toronto: James Lorimer. This is the only short and readable volume on the history of the labour movement in Canada.

Notes

I would like to acknowledge the technical assistance of Moira Russell, Documents Librarian, Brock University. Her always cheerful smile made asking difficult questions all the easier.

1. See Grint (1991: 57) for a more detailed description of proto-industrialization: 'Whatever else the pre-industrial world of work was like, it certainly does not appear to have been composed of a mass of skilled craft workers, nor was it a world where employers or their agents always rode roughshod over the interests of employees or labourers.'

2. A major turning point occured in 1925 when Lord Judge Haldane, speaking for the Judicial Committee of the British Privy Council, the highest court in the land, struck down the Canadian government's Industrial Disputes Investigation Act of 1913. Also, see Frank Scott's passionate plea for reversing the divided jurisdictions following Haldane's 1925 decision (1977: 337).

3. Within months of being elected, the Mike Harris government in Ontario bulldozed Bill 7, Ontario Labour Relations Act, 1995, through the provincial legislature. Billed as returning 'equality to labour relations' in the province of Ontario, the new Labour Relations Act replaced the NDP's Bill 40. Written for the government by one of Toronto's leading labour law firms, the new law permits employers to hire 'scabs' and makes it more difficult to organize workers into trade unions. Under the name of 'economic development and industrial democracy', the PC government of Ontario passed Bill 31 in July-August 1998, taking away many of the remaining 'irritants' for business that had been overlooked in Bill 7 and, incidentally, laid the groundwork for the subcontracting of non-union workers by school boards and municipalities. Taken together, many argue these measures provide fewer protections than the original legislation adopted in the 1940s.

4. *Globe and Mail*, 6 Mar. 1986, A10. The United Nations Universal Declaration of Human Rights of 1948 protects freedom of association under Article 20; the International Covenant on Economic, Cultural and Social Rights under Article 8 and signed in 1976 protects the right to form trade unions; and Articles 2 and 3 of the 1984 International Labour Organization's Freedom of Association and Protection of the Right to Organize Convention protects the right to form trade unions, the right of unions to write their own constitutions without interference, and the protection from public authorities of interference in union activities. Despite Canada's endorsement of all these United Nations documents, the ILO concluded that the legislative guarantees afforded to public-sector trade unions in this country had been violated.

5. For a more balanced view of the federal and provincial assault on public-sector unions in Canada, see Russell (1990: 245–75).

6. This position was due, in large part, to the insistence of senior officials from the Quebec Federation of Labour.

7. *Retail, Wholesale and Department Store Union v. Dolphin Delivery*, in Russell (1989: 460–70).

8. On several occasions throughout the book, Lipset sees the 'tory heritage' on the one hand and the 'Catholic heritage' on the other as two conservative value orientations (Lipset prefers Max Weber's 'weltanschauung' to convey the two different world views) that were historically anti-socialist but in their present-day secular versions favour the plight of the poor and an interest in social democracy. For example: 'Ironically, the conservative effort has stimulated an emphasis on group rights and benefits for the less privileged' and 'the American social structure and values foster an emphasis on competitive individualism, an orientation that is not congruent with class consciousness, support for social or social democratic parties or a strong union movement' (Lipset, 1991: 225, 170).

References

Bilson, R.E. 1985. 'A Workers' Charter: What Do We Mean by Rights?', *Canadian Public Policy* 11, 4: 749–55.

Briskin, Linda, and Patricia McDermott. 1993. *Women Challenging Unions: Feminism, Democracy and Militancy.* Toronto: University of Toronto Press.

Cella, G., and T. Treu. 1982. 'National Trade Union Movements', in R. Blainpain, ed., *Comparative Labour Law and Industrial Relations.* Deventer, Netherlands: Kluwer, ch. 10.

Chirot, Daniel. 1977. *Social Change in the Twentieth Century.* New York: Harcourt Brace Jovanovich.

Creighton, Donald. 1956. *Empire of the St. Lawrence.* Toronto: Macmillan.

Devine, Kay, et al. 1997. 'The Impact of Teleworking on Canadian Employment', in Duffy et al. (1997: 97–116).

Duffy, Ann, Daniel Glenday, and Norene Pupo, eds. 1997. *Good Jobs, Bad Jobs, No Jobs: The Transformation of Work in the 21st Century.* Toronto: Harcourt Brace.

Gérin, Leon. 1964. 'The French Canadian Family—Its Strengths and Weaknesses', in Marcel Rioux and Yves Dofny, eds, *French Canadian Society*, vol. 1. Toronto: McClelland & Stewart.

Glenday, Dan. 1994. 'On the Ropes: Can Unions in Canada Make a Comeback?', in Glenday and Ann Duffy, eds, *Canadian Society: Understanding and Surviving in the 1990s.* Toronto: McClelland & Stewart, 15–48.

———. 1997. 'Lost Horizons, Leisure Shock: Good Jobs, Bad Jobs, Uncertain Future', in Duffy, Glenday, and Pupo (1997: 8–34).

Grint, Keith. 1991. *The Sociology of Work.* Cambridge: Polity Press. 1991.

Hughes, Everett. 1948. *French Canada in Transition.* Chicago: University of Chicago Press.

Huxley, Christopher, et al. 1986. 'Is Canada's Experience Especially Instructive?', in S.M. Lipset, *Unions in Transition: Entering the Second Century.* San Francisco: Institute for Contemporary Studies, 113–32.

Innis, Harold. 1999. *The Fur Trade in Canada: An Introduction to Canadian Economic History*, with a new introductory essay by Arthur J. Ray. Toronto: University of Toronto Press.

Kealey, Gregory. 1981. 'Labour and Working Class History in Canada: Prospects in the 1980s', *Labour/Le Travailleur* 7: 67–94.

Kumar, Pradeep. 1993. *From Uniformity to Divergence: Industrial Relations in Canada and the United States.* Kingston: IRC Press.

Lipset, Seymour Martin. 1991. *Continental Divide: The Values and Institutions of the United States and Canada.* New York: Routledge.

Lipton, Charles. 1967. *The Trade Union Movement in Canada, 1827–1959*, 3rd edn. Toronto: NC Press.

McIntosh, Thomas A. 1989. *Labouring Under the Charter.* Kingston: Industrial Relations Centre, Queen's University.

Menzies, Heather. 1996. *Whose Brave New World?* Toronto: Between the Lines.

Palmer, Bryan D. 1979. *A Culture in Conflict: Skilled Workers and Industrial Capitalism in Hamilton, Ontario, 1860–1914.* Montreal and Kingston: McGill-Queen's University Press.

———. 1992. *Working-Class Experience: Rethinking the History of Canadian Labour, 1800–1991.* Toronto: McClelland & Stewart.

Panitch, Leo, and Donald Swartz. 1988. *The Assault on Trade Union Freedoms: From Consent to Coercion Revisited.* Toronto: Garamond.

Porter, John. 1965. *The Vertical Mosaic.* Toronto: University of Toronto Press.

Russell, Bob. 1990. *Back to Work? Labour, State and Industrial Relations in Canada.* Toronto: Nelson.

Russell, Peter H. 1989. *Federalism and the Charter: Leading Constitutional Decisions.* Ottawa: Carleton University Press.

Ryerson, Stanley. 1963. *The Founding of Canada: Beginnings to 1815.* Toronto: Progress.

Scott, F.R. 1977. 'Federal Jurisdiction over Labour Relations: A New Look', in Scott, *Essays on the Constitution.* Toronto: University of Toronto Press, 336–52.

Wallerstein, Immanuel. 1979. *The Capitalist World-Economy: Essays by Immanuel Wallerstein.* Cambridge: Cambridge University Press.

Weiler, Paul. 1980. *Reconcilable Differences: New Directions in Canadian Labour Law.* Toronto: Butterworths.

White, Bob. 1987. *Hard Bargains: My Life on the Line.* Toronto: McClelland & Stewart.

White, Julie. 1993. *Sisters and Solidarity: Women and Unions in Canada.* Toronto: Thompson.

chapter two

Racism and Resistance

J. Rick Ponting

Mention the word 'racism' or 'racist' today and various images come quickly to mind, such as white power groups and violent 'skinheads', the murder of Victoria-area teenager Reena Virk, the torture of Somali youth Shidane Arone by members of the Canadian Airborne Regiment, police abuse or even shootings of black and other 'visible minority' individuals in various Canadian cities, residential schools for Natives, the Indian Act of Canada, the backlash by east coast lobster fishers against the Supreme Court of Canada decision granting Native fishing rights in the Donald Marshall Jr case in 1999, racist music and Web sites, and certain right-wing politicians and media commentators. Contrary to what the myth-makers would have us believe, these are not isolated phenomena, for racism permeates Canadian society.

As Satzewich (1998: 12) notes, the term 'racist' is both a sociological concept and a powerful political epithet used in contemporary discourse to discredit and silence people so as to close public debate. In academia, in the mass media, and in conversation, the term is used with little precision or consistency. Indeed, the meaning of 'race' itself changes over time, as the categories of people subjected to the process of 'othering' that is inherent in racialization have at times been based on ethnic origin, on religion, on social class, and on skin colour. For instance, Kelly (1998: 35) illustrates that 'whiteness' is *socially constructed*, for she quotes a 1908 newspaper columnist who refers to Ukrainian immigrants to Canada as non-whites. What is clear, though, is that underlying the phenomenon of the emergence of racial categories are social psychological processes of *boundary maintenance* and *identity formation* (Satzewich, 1998: 32–4). What is also clear is that the expressions, forms, and targets of racism vary on the basis of historical, social, and economic conditions (Miles, 1989: 77–84).

We Canadians have prided ourselves on our 'tolerance' of diversity since at least the middle of the twentieth century, when American racial conflicts were boiling over in brutal violence perpetrated by the state, and perhaps as far back as the mid-nineteenth century when Canadians gave refuge to fugitive slaves. At times we have adopted a 'holier than thou' orientation towards the United States.

However, such smugness is quite ill-founded, for racism has been a long-standing feature of Canadian society. For instance, slavery was not abolished in Canada until the passing of the Emancipation Act by the British Parliament in 1833. Admittedly, racism in Canada has often been subtly expressed. It has often been covert and aversive, rather than overt and confrontational. That, however, is of little comfort to its victims.

Non-whites now comprise the majority of immigrants to Canada. By the time of the 1996 census, so-called 'visible minorities' (excluding Aboriginal people) constituted about one-third of the populations of Toronto and Vancouver[1] and over 11 per cent of the total Canadian population. However, only 70 per cent of the over three million visible minority individuals in Canada are immigrants. Furthermore, racism is not an outcome of the arrival of larger numbers of non-whites. Nor is racism merely a product of economic downturn or of First Nations' militancy. Rather, for many generations racial discrimination has been structured into key institutions of Canadian society, such as the Immigration Act and other laws, the schools, the ideology, the economy, the real estate market, and the criminal justice system.

Adapting the definition of sociologist Pierre van den Berghe (1967: 11), we can say that, strictly speaking, racism is a set of *beliefs* about the alleged inferiority of individuals who are socially defined as members of a certain group (a 'race') distinguished by its physical characteristics. This set of beliefs is usually accompanied by an ideology, often religious, which involves values, assumptions, historical interpretations, and other claims to 'justify' the treatment of individuals from that group as inferior. In particular, it is used to justify allocating those individuals to particular economic positions and excluding them from receiving certain economic rewards and political rights (Miles, 1989: 3). Thus, the racial ideology rationalizes, legitimizes, and sustains patterns of inequality (Barrett, 1987: 7). Box 2.1 expands on this from a Marxist perspective.

Physical attributes are used to define social groups ('races') only insofar as those attributes are socially recognized as important because they are believed to be associated with other intellectual, moral, or behavioural characteristics (Li, 1990: 5–6). Thus, 'races' are social constructs, not objectively identifiable physical realities, for there is much genetic variation within so-called races that are superficially similar in physical appearance. Sociologically, the *racialization* process, whereby a category of such superficially similar people comes to be socially defined as a 'race', is very important. The state often plays a pivotal role in this process, as it did with such peoples as the Chinese and First Nations through government enactment of policies and laws that restricted their power and resource base (Li, 1988: 23–40; Li, 1990: 13–15).

With the advent of the Black Power movement in the United States in the late 1960s, the term 'racism' took on a broader meaning than indicated above. Now, the term 'racism'—as 'institutional racism' or 'systemic racism'—is also used to describe outcomes of the operation of institutions when those outcomes differ systematically for people of different 'races', regardless of the intentions of the individuals

Box 2.1: Marxian Conceptions of Racism

Classical Marxian scholars saw racism as emerging out of class relations in society. In particular, they regarded racist ideologies as myths invented by the capitalist class to justify the exploitation of certain sectors of the population as a reserve army of cheap labour (Bolaria and Li, 1988). They regarded racism as a form of 'false consciousness' on the part of white workers, dividing the working class into 'fractions' that make them less likely to unite under a consciousness of their working-class status to challenge effectively the capitalist class.

More recent Marxian approaches, based on the writings of Antonio Gramsci, regard racism as one of the ways in which people attempt to make sense of their experiences (Satzewich, 1990). Gramsci sees the content of racist belief systems as varying from one class to another. Yet other contemporary theorists offer new conceptualizations of race and racism with much analytic promise, for instance, in rectifying the narrow-minded biases that have distorted our understanding of the situation of non-white women (see Stasiulis, 1990).

staffing those institutions. Often individuals making the decisions in those institutions have no discriminatory intent; they merely subscribe to the notion of equal rights for all individuals. It is important to note that that radical conceptualization of equality—equality as uniformity—and its associated rights discourse operate to perpetuate institutional racism. These linkages are discussed later in this chapter in the section on the Reform/Canadian Alliance Party, most of whose members, it should be noted, adamantly denied being racist.

Even though the term 'discrimination' would suffice, the term 'racism' has also been used to describe the behaviour of individuals who consciously engage in discrimination against members of other 'races'. Thus, there is no consensus on the proper use of the terms 'race' and 'racism'. Indeed, some social scientists, like Miles (1989: 72), feel strongly that these terms should be 'confined to the dustbin of analytically useless terms'. Given the prominence of the terms in popular parlance, that is unlikely to happen. Furthermore, it is important that readers understand the essentially social nature of 'races', the historical roots of racial discrimination in Canadian society, and the mechanisms by which discriminatory outcomes are perpetuated despite the intentions of the actors in the system. Only with such an understanding can realistic policy options be formulated.

Historical Background

Like the tap root of the common dandelion, racism's roots extend deep below the surface of Canadian society. They extend far back into our history, where they are intertwined with a pronounced ethnocentrism (belief in the superiority of the culture of one's own group). In fact, since the time of early British contact with the Aboriginal people, Canadian legal traditions have assumed that Indians were too primitive to have a legal system that could be considered 'civilized' and 'worthy' of recognition by the British-based courts. The non-Christian Aboriginals were considered to be 'pagans'. It was assumed that they had no law, and English law was imposed.

One law that was imposed on the Native people by the British was the Indian Act of 1876, which is still in effect today in amended form. The Indian Act approximates what sociologists call a 'total institution'. It not only establishes a system of dependency and control in which Indians are at the mercy of a paternalistic institution (the Department of Indian Affairs and Northern Development and its minister), but also operates to change the very identity of those who are subjected to it. Box 2.2 provides a few excerpts from the present-day Indian Act, which, like the race laws of the apartheid era in South Africa, applies to a category of people defined in terms of their 'race'.

Racial discrimination has been entrenched in various other Canadian laws. Examples include the labour laws of certain provinces, especially in their failure to offer the protection of the labour code to female domestics, who are often non-white. However, the federal Immigration Act offers even more glaring examples of racism.

Although Asians were allowed to enter Canada to help in the dangerous and demanding work of building the Canadian Pacific Railway, soon after the task was accomplished the immigration regulations were turned against others of similar origin. For instance, in 1900 a 'head tax' of $100 was imposed on Chinese immigrants as a deterrent to their entry. It was increased to $500 in 1903[2] and in 1923 an outright ban on Chinese immigration was imposed. After the race riots in Vancouver in September of 1907 the Canadian and Japanese governments entered

Box 2.2: Excerpts from the Indian Act

Sec. 61(1) Indian moneys shall be expended only for the benefit of the Indians or bands for whose use and benefit in common the moneys are received or held, and subject to this Act and to the terms of any treaty or surrender, the Governor in Council [federal cabinet] may determine whether any purpose for which Indian moneys are used or are to be used is for the use and benefit of the band.

Sec. 76(1) The Governor in Council may make orders and regulations with respect to band elections . . . .

Sec. 80 The Governor in Council may make regulations with respect to band meetings and council meetings . . . .

Sec. 82(2) A by-law . . . comes into force forty days after a copy thereof is forwarded to the Minister . . . unless it is disallowed by the Minister . . . .

into a so-called 'gentlemen's agreement' whereby Japan agreed to limit emigration of labourers to Canada unless specifically requested otherwise by the Canadian government (Palmer, 1973: 9–10). The following year Canada enacted the 'continuous passage' rule, which precluded immigration from India unless the ship did not stop at any ports along the way; at that time no ships met that criterion.

Later, Canada refused entry to thousands of Jews fleeing the pogroms and Hitler's holocaust, including 907 aboard the passenger ship *St Louis* in 1939. After Cuba refused to honour the entry visas it had already granted the passengers, the *St Louis* was refused landing rights in the US and all Latin American countries. Canada was the last hope of these desperate refugees, but anti-Semitic senior officials in Ottawa, fully sympathetic to the mood of latent anti-Semitism prevalent in Canada at that time, refused them admission at Halifax. The passengers were returned to Europe, where, subsequently, many were probably rounded up and killed by the Nazis (Abella and Troper, 1982: 50–1, 63–6). The *St Louis* incident was similar in some respects to an infamous incident in 1914 when 400 would-be immigrants from India, citizens of the British Empire, were denied permission to disembark from the freighter *Komagata Maru* at Vancouver.

When the immigration flow to the United States was diverted to Canada as a result of the introduction of American restrictions, Canada developed a list of 'preferred' and 'non-preferred' countries from which to select immigrants. Racial discrimination in the Immigration Act was later formally abolished with the introduction of the 'points system' whereby immigrants would gain eligibility to enter Canada by amassing a certain number of points for job skills, official-language fluency, education, etc. However, even for several years after the introduction of that system in 1967, administrative practices involving the placement and staffing of immigration offices continued to work to the systematic disadvantage of people from primarily non-white countries.

The same assimilationist (Anglo-conformity) goals and ethnocentrism that informed Indian policy were also inherent in immigration policy. Canadian immigration law and policy were built on the assumption that the closer a prospective immigrant's resemblance to the white, Anglo-Saxon, Protestant in appearance and culture, the better. This orientation was an integral part of the dominant ideology espoused by the opinion leaders of the day. For instance, in 1928 R.B. Bennett, who two years later would be Prime Minister, said in the House of Commons:

> It is because we desire to profit by the very lessons we learned there [the United States] that we are endeavouring to maintain our civilization at that high standard which has made the British civilization the test by which all other civilized nations in modern times are measured. . . . We must still maintain that measure of British civilization which will enable us to assimilate these people [immigrants] to British institutions, rather than assimilate our civilization to theirs.[3]

Two decades later, as Canada was about to embark on a major nation-building project, another Prime Minister, Mackenzie King, exhibited another facet of the same ethnocentric, racist bias when he told Parliament:

With regard to the Japanese, I stated, on August 4, 1944, at which time we were at war with Japan, that the government felt that in the years after the war the immigration of Japanese should not be permitted. This is the present view and policy of the government. . . . There will, I am sure, be general agreement with the view that the people of Canada do not wish, as a result of mass immigration, to make a fundamental alteration in the character of our population. Large-scale immigration from the Orient would change the fundamental composition of the Canadian population.[4]

King's remarks are important, for they not only bring to mind the national shame of the forced relocation of Japanese Canadians from the west coast, but they also point to a strain of racist thinking that persists in Canada today—the notion of preserving the 'fundamental character' of the Canadian population. Notwithstanding the changes in the ethnic composition of the Canadian population that have resulted in the proportion of non-whites (including Aboriginal persons) rising to about one in seven residents of Canada, it is presumed by many that the 'fundamental character' of Canadian society is white and should remain white. Public opinion polls in the 1980s found a large minority (e.g., 30 per cent in one poll) of Canadians favoured restrictions on non-white immigration.

The treatment of Japanese Canadians during and after World War II was a national disgrace of major proportions (Adachi, 1976; Sunahara, 1981). Under an order issued in 1942 pursuant to the War Measures Act, approximately 22,000 Japanese residents of British Columbia, many of whom were Canadian citizens, were required to turn themselves over to Canadian authorities. Many were held in conditions unfit for humans at the barns of the Pacific National Exhibition before being sent inland, some to detention camps, some to do forced farm labour, others to resettle far away. Their homes, fishing boats, possessions, and businesses were confiscated and sold at prices far below market value. Even after the war, efforts were made to deport them and their freedom of movement was curtailed, as some municipalities in Alberta passed by-laws prohibiting persons of Japanese ancestry from living within the municipality (Palmer, 1982: 167). Secret government documents released many years later revealed that police and military authorities did not regard the Japanese Canadians as a security threat. That is, their forced removal and subsequent exploitation and victimization were politicians' responses to an intensification of the long-standing racist political pressures emanating from the British Columbia population. After years of delay, the government of Canada finally issued an official apology and token compensation payments in 1989.

Persons of Japanese ancestry are not the only ones in Canadian society to have been scapegoated and persecuted because of their ethnicity. Joining their ranks are Native people, blacks, Chinese, Jews, Ukrainians, Italians, Germans, Hutterites, and others. We conclude this introduction with a cursory overview of the tribulations faced by blacks as a result of their race.

Slavery was legal and practised in Canada from almost the time of the first European settlement in New France. By 1750 there were over 4,000 black slaves in New France, according to Anderson and Frideres (1981: 233). More blacks came as Loyalists around the time of the American Revolution against Britain. In the nineteenth century the main concentrations of blacks were in the Halifax area of Nova Scotia and in southwestern Ontario (e.g., Chatham)—a terminus for the 'underground railway' used by fugitive slaves from the United States. In the early twentieth century, concerted lobbying, such as by the Edmonton Board of Trade and the Imperial Order of the Daughters of the Empire, was conducted in an effort to prevent black immigration to Canada (Kelly, 1998: 38). With the liberalization of Canadian immigration policy in 1967 and 1978, and the determination of the Quebec government to attract French-speaking immigrants (e.g., Haitians and North Africans) to Quebec, Toronto and Montreal also became centres of large black populations, while smaller but still substantial black communities developed in numerous other urban centres, such as Calgary.

Stereotyping is a salient part of the life experience of blacks and other people of colour. It is rampant in the larger society, as is discrimination based on it. That discrimination occurs in numerous spheres of life, but is especially widespread in public facilities, employment, and housing. For instance, Henry and Tator (1985) report that Windsor, Ontario, was the last municipality to desegregate its public facilities—in 1975! In Calgary, even during the economic boom of the early 1980s, 25 per cent of Ponting and Wanner's non-random sample of 140 blacks reported having personally experienced discrimination in housing, and 32 per cent reported having personally experienced discrimination in employment. One-third of the respondents reported having personally experienced discrimination in more than one of 15 different institutional spheres (e.g., education, housing, stores, city police, recreation, etc.). Particularly troubling was the finding that almost 20 per cent of these black respondents reported having forgone one or more job opportunities because they expected to encounter discrimination in hiring. This illustrates how, once racism is ingrained in a social system, discriminatory outcomes can occur even though members of the dominant group are relieved of 'having' to make discriminatory choices.

Racism in employment and housing, while prevalent, receives much less attention in the mass media than certain other manifestations of racism, such as police behaviour towards blacks and other racial minorities. Perceived and actual racism on the part of police has escalated to crisis proportions in Toronto, Montreal, Winnipeg, Saskatoon, and elsewhere. The case of Marcelus François, described in Box 2.3, illustrates not only the increasingly frequent use of lethal force by police against non-white minorities, but also the racism underlying the police behaviour. This account of an encounter with police resonates with the experience of law-abiding blacks and other people of colour throughout much of Canada (e.g., Kelly, 1998: 18–19). Later in this chapter we shall consider some other sociological dynamics involved in police interactions with non-whites.

Kelly provides a contemporary account of black students' encounters with racism in the schools and elsewhere. Black students interviewed by Kelly (ibid., 19) report that when whites in positions of authority view them 'it is often with a specific gaze that sees "the troublemaker", "the school skipper", or "the criminal".'

Box 2.3: The Case of Marcelus François

On the evening of 3 July 1991, Marcelus François, a 24-year-old black male, was in a car with three friends driving through the financial district of downtown Montreal after having made a purchase of illicit drugs. At the same time, equipped with a poor-quality photocopy of a 'mug shot', Montreal Urban Community (MUC) police were looking for a suspect in an attempted murder that had occurred two days earlier. They placed the car under surveillance and an entourage of four 'ghost cars' and a SWAT team truck followed it from late afternoon until they stopped it around 7:25 p.m.

In their physical appearance François and the suspect were similar only in their colour and their gender. François was short and had short hair. The suspect was tall with long hair and a scar over his eye. Indeed, the police tape recording of the conversation between the dispatcher and the officers tailing François reveals that the officers believed there was only about a 75 per cent resemblance between François and the wanted man. Those same tapes record the police officers' references to 'two niggers with their noses pressed against the windows' of the car.

The officers stopped the car near the intersection of McGill and Saint Antoine Streets. When the SWAT team members aimed their weapons at the occupants of the car, three of the occupants got out of the car. Sitting in the front passenger seat, François did not immediately get out. Instead, he reached under the seat, where police later found a bag of drugs. An eyewitness reports that at that point the unarmed François was shot in the forehead by a member of the police SWAT team, 34-year-old Sergeant Michel Tremblay, a veteran of more than 10 years of police experience. It was left to friends to notify next of kin of the tragic case of mistaken identity.

Marcelus François died two weeks later. He left behind a common-law wife and two children under the age of four. Premier Robert Bourassa refused at the time to establish an inquiry into the treatment that blacks receive from the police and the province's criminal justice system. He insisted that it was premature to conclude that the shooting was racially motivated. Months later, the MUC police chief concluded that the incident was not racially motivated and therefore that Sergeant Tremblay would not be disciplined. However, the chief also concluded that the tactical team had 'bungled the operation from start to finish', which led to a protest 'March for Respect' by over 2,500 MUC officers calling for the chief's resignation. A coroner's inquiry into the Marcelus François case was held. Pursuant to other incidents, complaints of physical abuse and disrespect continued to be lodged against the MUC police by visible minorities and homosexuals.

Sources: *La Presse*, 5, 9 July 1991; CBC News, *The National*, 27 Sept. 1991; *Calgary Herald*, 10 Feb. 1992; *Globe and Mail*, 14 Feb. 1992.

That gaze, of course, is rooted in stereotypes. As Kelly emphasizes, it is a control-ling gaze, for it has the effect of subduing many of those who receive it and making them wish to be invisible. Police, shopping mall security staff, and store clerks are particularly prone to this gaze of surveillance, which Kelly describes as 'social subjugation . . . achieved by social illumination'. Ironically, rather than submitting to the gaze, 'some Black students accentuate their visibility, thus providing a "glare" of light to interrupt the gaze' (ibid., 20). That is achieved through a combination of dress, walk, posture, attitude, and moving in a group.

Racist and Other Attitudes

The study of racist attitudes has long fascinated social psychologists, sociologists, and others. Social scientists have offered a variety of explanations for attitudes towards members of other 'races' and for opinions on policies intended to assist disadvantaged members of those out-groups. Those explanations run the gamut from psychological factors to sociological to cultural.

For instance, Adorno and his colleagues (Adorno et al., 1950) sought to explain prejudice in terms of personality type—the so-called 'authoritarian personality' who is fundamentally insecure. Blumer (1961) sought to explain prej-udice as a response to a perceived threat to one's historically acquired sense of group position. Marxists have viewed race prejudice as a weapon of imperialism and class conflict (see Box 2.1). In Canada, Dunk (1991: 101–31) found northern Ontario working-class males' prejudices towards First Nation people to be a polit-ical-cultural phenomenon—a product of those men's ideology of regional alien-ation and anti-intellectualism and their stereotypes of 'Indians'. Through hostile attitudes towards Natives, Dunk's interviewees were able to establish their own moral worth and their difference from the perceived dominant power bloc of southern Ontario, city-dwelling, liberal, gullible intellectuals whom they saw as naïvely developing pro-Aboriginal policies that accorded special privileges to Natives. For Dunk's interviewees, 'the Indian' stood as a symbol of local white powerlessness in the face of the domination of that external power bloc.

Other scholars have offered yet other explanations of hostile opinions towards government policies designed to assist disadvantaged out-groups. For instance, for Bobo (1983) and many others before him, the key explanatory factor is competi-tion for scarce resources, while for Kluegel (1990) and some others the key is a 'blaming the victim' mentality. Yet another explanation (Kluegel and Smith, 1986) for hostility to affirmative action policies is that of value conflict—because such policies for disadvantaged out-groups are perceived to promote equality of economic outcomes, they are opposed by those who do not favour such a concep-tion of equality. Near the end of this section, as an introduction to our considera-tion of right-wing extremist groups, we shall encounter yet another explanation that can be invoked to explain extremely hostile racial attitudes—namely, Lipset and Raab's status preservationist backlash theory. First, though, let us consider some empirical evidence of racist and other hostile attitudes among Canadians.

With the explosion of public opinion polling in the late twentieth century, it is now easy to obtain indicators of the prevalence of attitudes that, if translated into behaviours by their holders or by the policy-makers who read the poll results, would produce racially discriminatory outcomes. A few examples will suffice.

Now that the majority of immigrants to Canada are non-white, Canadians' receptivity to immigration can be used as a proxy indicator of racist sentiment in Canadian society. Veteran pollster Allan Gregg (Gregg and Posner, 1990: 171) reports his firm's finding that in 1987 and 1989 virtually half of Canadians expressed the view that too many people from different races and cultures had been allowed to live in Canada. On the basis of this and other data, they note:

> One could fairly conclude that a significant portion of the Canadian population is uncomfortable with not just the idea of freer immigration but with the very notion of multiculturalism—one of the bedrock building blocks of the modern Canadian mosaic. We salute the abstraction; we seem to resent the reality. And the persistence of these attitudes through the 1980s, in times of economic wellbeing as well as of hardship, strongly suggests they aren't going to change for some time—if ever. (Ibid., 172)

Findings from other studies tend to be in the same direction. For instance, an Angus Reid survey done in early 1990 for Southam News found that one-third of Canadians agree with the notion that Canadian society is being threatened by immigrants (59 per cent disagreed), while one-quarter agreed (and 65 per cent disagreed) with the idea that 'there should be more white immigrants taken into Canada and fewer non-white immigrants.' In a 1994 national study (cited in Reitz and Breton, 1994) a majority (53 per cent) expressed the view that too many immigrants are coming to Canada, but a 1998 national survey conducted for the Citizenship and Immigration Department found Canadians evenly divided on that question (Cobb, 1998). In her study on racial attitudes in metro Toronto in the late 1970s, Henry found that about 16–19 per cent of respondents could be described as hard-core bigots, while 'thirty-five per cent have racist tendencies' (Henry and Tator, 1985: 323). In a 1998 national survey, the Angus Reid Group (1998: 111–13) identified 11 per cent of Canadian adults as 'Confident Hard-Liners' on Aboriginal issues. They are strong opponents of the stances taken by the national Aboriginal leadership. For instance, the 'Confident Hard-Liners' believe that Aboriginal people are largely responsible for their own problems, see no particularly inherent value in cultural diversity, and adopt an assimilationist orientation towards Natives, reject the idea of Aboriginal self-government as having any merit, and have a profound dislike for Aboriginal rights or special status for any group in society.

Moving beyond racist attitudes *per se*, in my own national survey in 1986 I found widespread insensitivity to the negative impact that the behaviours of people from the dominant white society can have on visible minorities. Some of these questions offered the advantage of getting the respondents' reactions to a 'real-life' situation rather than to an abstract idea or policy. For instance, in one question respondents were told 'A person from Pakistan reads in the newspaper that some teenagers have painted "Pakis Go Home" on the side of a building' and were asked what his reaction would likely be. Only 50 per cent chose the response, 'He would take it seriously and wouldn't like it at all' from among three others: 'He would probably regard it as a harmless teenage prank—something that they'll grow out of in time' (15 per cent); 'Unless it was a building that he owned or passed by often, he would probably not pay too much attention to the incident' (8 per cent); and 'One cannot judge fairly without knowing more about the particular Pakistani person who read the newspaper article' (28 per cent).

Other questions on the survey were combined to form scales to measure generalized sympathy for Natives and, more narrowly, for Indians (Ponting, 1987: 20 and Figures 1–2). Results suggested that fewer than 5 per cent of Canadians hold consistently and strongly negative views towards Indians and other Natives. This is in the same general range as the Angus Reid Group finding cited above. Note also that the consistently and strongly anti-Aboriginal element in the 1986 sample is more than offset numerically by people holding consistently and strongly positive views towards Aboriginals. However, on yet other questions I found strong evidence of the assimilationist pressures characteristic of Canadians' attitudes to immigrants and Aboriginals for generations.

The 1986 national survey offers some important insights into the causes of hostility towards government policies designed to help Aboriginal people. Using advanced statistical techniques, Langford and Ponting (1992) have determined that ethnocentrism is a minor to negligible determinant. Instead, the key determinants of respondents' policy preferences are prejudice, perceptions of conflicting group interests[5] as between Aboriginals and themselves, and economic liberalism[6] (the 'free enterprise' belief that government should minimize its role in economic relations and refrain from encumbering the property rights of business owners with such things as mandatory affirmative action programs). Furthermore, there is a noteworthy *interaction effect* between prejudice and perceived group conflict.

Importantly, prejudice has very little impact on the dependent variables (policy preferences on Aboriginal issues) when the level of perceived group conflict is low. However, when perceived group conflict is high, prejudice again becomes an important determinant of other Canadians' policy preferences towards Aboriginal people. Otherwise stated, whether prejudice has any appreciable effect on a person's support for Native self-government or on his/her support for special status for Natives depends on the extent to which that person perceives there to be an underlying conflict between his/her own group and Natives. The relationship can be examined from the other side, also: whether perception of group conflict has any appreciable effect on a person's support for those same two pro-Native government policies depends on how prejudiced that person is.

Our findings suggest the utility of distinguishing between two types of prejudice: dormant and activated. Prejudice against a group is dormant when it is unattached to any sense of conflict with that out-group. Dormant prejudice has minimal effects on policy preferences vis-à-vis that out-group. On the other hand, prejudice against a group is activated when it is linked to a perception of contemporary conflict with the out-group. Such activated prejudice has important effects on policy preferences.

The individual rights emphasis of economic liberalism is clearly at odds with the collectivist emphasis of Aboriginal rights advocates. It is perhaps no surprise, then, that regardless of whether prejudice is dormant, activated, or absent, economic liberalism produces antagonism towards Aboriginals and their preferred policies. Aboriginal people and their supporters might despair at that finding, in light of the facts that economic liberalism has been a dominant ideology in Canada and that substantial state economic intervention will be necessary to overcome the effects of past and present racism. However, with the advent of balanced government budgets and even multi-billion dollar surpluses, economic liberalism loosened its grip somewhat on the Canadian political agenda. It could well become less dominant in the twenty-first century. Until the fate of economic liberalism and social conservatism is known, though, the practical significance of our finding of the relationship between economic liberalism and antagonism towards Aboriginals is unclear.

The question remains as to what accounts for extremist, right-wing backlash movements against Aboriginal people and other non-whites (especially non-white immigrants). Examples of such backlashes include the media and public opinion reaction against the 1998 Nisga'a Treaty in British Columbia, against the alteration of RCMP dress regulations to permit the wearing of a turban, and against boatloads of immigrants arriving illegally on Canada's shores.[7] American sociologists S.M. Lipset and Earl Raab (1970) suggest that such reactions are rooted in three factors. These are: the participants' adherence to the ideology of economic liberalism, as in our above findings concerning policy preferences on Aboriginal issues; 'monism', or the intolerance of differences; and the so-called 'quondam complex' in which individuals attach their identity to symbols and values that were dominant in the past but are now being displaced by social change. Those chosen as the target of hostility are those perceived to be responsible for the social change that threatens the values and identity of people characterized by these three factors.

Lipset and Raab's conceptualization of extremist, right-wing backlash movements is as a *status preservationist backlash*. However, the causal impetus for a right-wing response could be any one of a number of other closely related factors. For instance, the vociferous non-Native reaction against 'special treatment' provisions in Aboriginal land claim settlements strongly suggests that some mixture of envy and fear of loss of privilege could be at play. A propos anti-immigrant backlash, some observers would suggest that fear of losing a taken-for-granted view of how one's society is constituted, or even the fear of losing the power to 'set the rules of the game',[8] is the operative explanatory factor. Canadian research on racist organizations, as we shall see, lends support to the preservationist emphasis of these various explanations and to the monism component of Lipset and Raab's theory.

Racist Organizations

Racist organizations and others promoting intergroup intolerance have a long history in Canada.[9] For instance, Li (1988) catalogues a long list of organized efforts in the nineteenth century and more recently to persecute the Chinese, especially in British Columbia. The Ku Klux Klan was active in Ontario and west of Manitoba in the 1920s and numerous fascist organizations were active, especially in Quebec, in the 1930s. In the late twentieth century there emerged numerous small extremist organizations, such as the Ku Klux Klan in British Columbia (see Sher, 1983), the Western Guard in Toronto, the Aryan Nation in Alberta, the Canadian Nazi Party, Campus Alternative, the Council of Public Affairs in British Columbia, and the White Canada Council. In his landmark study of the right in Canada, *Is God a Racist?*, Barrett lists 60 organizations of the 'radical right' and another 70 less extremist organizations of the 'fringe right', all of which have emerged since World War II (Barrett, 1987: 357–60). Our concern below is with the 'radical right', which Barrett defines as 'those individuals who define themselves as racists, Fascists, and anti-Semites, and who are prepared to use violence to realize their objectives' (ibid., 9).

In the 1970s and 1980s there was a resurgence of white supremacist organizations in Canada—Barrett (ibid., 28–9) identified 18 major radical right organizations, another 25 minor ones, and a further 17 that were 'front' organizations for one of the other 43. Although four were Canada-wide, over 70 per cent were exclusive to Ontario. However, the linkages among them and with other similar organizations abroad are quite extensive and often computerized. They are part of a broad international network of white supremacist organizations.

Barrett identified only 586 members of radical right organizations in Canada, but is confident that thousands more like-minded individuals live in Canada. In their beliefs, the members of radical right organizations tend to be anti-black, anti-Semitic, anti-communist, anti-immigration, anti-foreign aid, anti-egalitarian, anti-feminist, and anti-homosexual. They regard blacks and Jews as subhuman, mere animals. Not surprisingly, therefore, having dehumanized their victims, they tend to be firm believers in the appropriateness of violence in pursuing their goals (ibid., 30). Recruits, overwhelmingly male urban dwellers, tend initially to be focused on a single issue. However, they go through a socialization process known in the social movements literature as *frame alignment* (Snow et al., 1986) whereby their existing prejudices are expanded into a broader racial perspective of the world, specifically, one that sees an alleged Jewish conspiracy as a driving force in history. Within their very narrowly bounded system of rationality, all evil and misfortune can be traced back to the 'Jewish conspiracy'.

These organizations are characterized by constant internal squabbling, suspicion, and schism, and therefore much circulation of members occurs from one organization to another. To a significant degree they are also infiltrated with informers and undercover agents, according to Barrett (1987: 184). Some, like the Aryan Nation, are heavily armed and their members are known to police for their record of thefts, assaults, and worse. For instance, Carney Nerland, who participated in the Aryan Nation's cross-burning in Provost, Alberta, in September 1990 and is alleged to be the group's leader in Saskatchewan, was convicted of the January 1991 manslaughter slaying of Leo LaChance, a Native man whom Nerland shot in the doorway of Nerland's Prince Albert gun store (Wagg, 1991). Similarly, the five young men convicted in the January 1998 murder of Nirmal Singh Gill, a care-taker at a Sikh temple in Surrey, BC, were linked by police to a skinhead white supremacist group called White Power (Cernetig and Matas, 1998; *Vancouver Sun*, 1999).

Some recruitment to the movement occurs in prisons among persons we might assume to have fairly pronounced needs for such positive reinforcement of their personal identity as the racist ideology offers. Importantly, though, Barrett found that those 141 members of the radical right for whom he could obtain occupational data were definitely not concentrated on the bottom rung of the occupational ladder. Indeed, 18 per cent were professionals. In their ethnic back-grounds Barrett found a heavy overrepresentation of Eastern Europeans (anti-communists) and of people of British origin who, as Lipset and Raab would predict, 'see the rampant changes in society as a threat to their social position, and lament the dilution of the British flavour brought about by Third World immigra-tion' (Barrett, 1987: 38).

Barrett concludes that an overriding concern knits together all of the issues on which white supremacists focus—'the presumed decay of Western Christian civi-lization' (ibid., 327). James Keegstra, the Alberta schoolteacher convicted of spread-ing hatred for his anti-Semitic classroom teaching, is a living embodiment of this (Bercuson and Wertheimer, 1985). As Barrett (1987: 339) notes, theological racism in the Christian tradition can accommodate all the significant strands in the white supremacist's belief system (e.g., communism as anti-Christian, homosexuality as an abomination before God, etc.). However, this religious-based anti-Semitism of the radical right is merely an extension of a lingering anti-Semitism in the main-line Christian churches and Christian theology.

Systemic Racism

Systemic, or institutionalized, racism has been defined in various ways. Jones (1972: 130), for instance, defines it as the situation that exists when the norms of an insti-tution are predicated on assumptions of racial equality that are not met in the soci-ety. Often those norms involve irrelevant and inflexible standards and qualifications intended to be 'universalistic' (race neutral), but that actually militate against non-whites. The application of the institution's policies and procedures then produces discriminatory consequences, even though there might have been no discrimina-tory intention on the part of the actors involved. This notion of discriminatory consequences existing independently of the volition of the actors is a common thread running through most definitions. As Anderson and Frideres (1981) note, systemic racism emerges initially from individuals' racist beliefs, but once created it survives independently of individual racism by virtue of being entrenched in the laws, customs, and practices of the society or organization.

A classic example of racist outcomes occurring in the absence of racist intentions is to be found in Frideres and Reeves's (1989) research on the Canadian Human Rights Commission. They found a higher rate of dismissal of complaints based on any one of race, colour, ethnicity, or national origin than of complaints based on gender or disability. This bias, according to the researchers, resulted from unrecognized racist features of the Commission's 'fact-finding' procedures and use of documents.

Crucial to an understanding of the persistence of systemic racism (and of systemic discrimination against non-racial minorities) is the role of individual rights ideologies in perpetuating it. Such ideologies usually attach paramount value to the equality of individuals. They tend to have nothing but disdain for the notion that collectivities have rights and for the notion that, by virtue of their membership in a particular collectivity, some individuals should have opportunities (through affirmative action programs) that are not available to other individuals.

Also crucial to understanding systemic discrimination is the notion of the *web of institutional interdependencies*. For example, racial controls and differentiation in one institutional sector, such as the real estate market, fit together to feed into or reinforce distinctions in other institutional sectors, such as schools and the labour market (Baron, 1969). Thus, it is highly significant that, in a survey done by their own trade association, 92 per cent of all personnel officers surveyed admitted to racial discrimination in hiring or promotion.[10] When racism is so pronounced in such a pivotal institution as the labour market, its effects will be felt across a broad range of other spheres of daily life. For instance, a person of colour refused a job appropriate to his/her level of training and education could be excluded thereby from certain real estate markets. That, in turn, will probably determine the school his/her children attend and the probability that they will graduate from university, which, of course, affects their job prospects. Thus, Canadians will often be relieved of 'having' to make an explicitly racist choice (e.g., against those children) because it is made for them earlier in a chain of institutional linkages.

Calliou (1997: 229–30) recounts the fable of the giraffe and the elephant (Box 2.4). It is a powerful metaphor for the systemic barriers faced by many immigrants and Aboriginal people admitted to the institutions of the larger society, whether under affirmative action programs or not. Calliou asserts that post-secondary educational institutions are like the giraffe and its house. That is, they and other corporate structures that say 'welcome' to Aboriginal people, immigrants, women, visible minorities, and handicapped people have not changed the structure of their organizations. Nor have they changed their mindsets, their policies, their operating practices, their teaching styles, etc. truly to welcome those who are different. They operate more in an assimilative mode ('Leave your culture at the door') than an accommodative mode. That takes us to cultural racism.

Box 2.4: The Fable of the Giraffe and the Elephant

There once was a giraffe which expressed to the world that all elephants are welcome at its house, anytime, just as most universities, colleges and corporations tend to express a similar welcome to the aboriginal community, people with disabilities, women, and visible minorities. One day the elephant knocked on the door of the giraffe. The giraffe opened the door to his opulent house and said to the elephant: 'Welcome! Finally you've come to my house. Do come in.' The elephant began to enter but got stuck in the doorway because the doorway was made for giraffes, narrow and tall. So, the giraffe said, 'Oh, why don't you go around to the back of the house. My basement is on the ground level. I'll chip away my basement so you can fit in and come into my house.' The elephant walked around the huge house and by the time he got to the back he heard the chinking of the cement where the giraffe was making a hole so the elephant could come in through the basement. Finally, the elephant entered the basement and the giraffe said, 'Welcome! Make yourself at home.' Just as he finished saying those words, the doorbell rang upstairs. He told the elephant, 'I'll just go check who that is. Make yourself at home.' The giraffe then went up the stairs and did not come down. The elephant stood on his legs and shuffled from one side to the other and then said, 'I'm getting tired waiting for the giraffe.' The elephant saw a bedroom in the corner of the basement and thought, 'Well, he did say that I should make myself at home, so maybe I'll go lay down.' However, in trying to enter the bedroom he once again found that he could not fit through a doorway, as the door was narrow and tall for giraffes. The elephant noticed a grease pail in the corner of the basement and proceded to grease himself, in the hope that he'd be able to slide into the bedroom to take a rest. He got in a little bit further, but still could not get through, so backed away. Getting tired, the elephant leaned against the wall of the basement and the wall started caving in, because it was not made for the weight of an elephant. Finally, after standing around for a long time, the elephant said 'I'd better go check to see what's keeping the giraffe. I'll go upstairs.' So, the elephant started climbing the stairs and the stairs started giving away because they were not made for the weight of the elephant. The elephant and the giraffe never did get together again.

Source: From an account by Roosevelt Thomas, founder of the American Institute for Diversity, as reproduced in Calliou (1997: 229–30).

Cultural Racism

On a daily basis in society, the hegemony (dominance) of the dominant group's culture is expressed through various acts of omission or commission that redound to the detriment of those of other cultures. When that dominant group is relatively homogeneous in terms of 'race', the imposition of its cultural norms and standards on people of other 'races', to their systematic detriment, can be called cultural racism.

Perhaps the most unmitigated form of cultural racism in Canadian society is the effort by governments and missionaries to 'civilize' the Aboriginal people. This was especially pronounced in the infamous church-run boarding schools where Indian children experienced corporal punishment for speaking their language, sexual abuse by staff members was rampant, and a conscious effort was made to undermine Indian parents' value system (Miller, 1996). One of the many tragedies of that residential school system is that young children were removed from their parents and the role models those parents provided. As a result, some of those former residential school students now find themselves deficient in parenting skills so that their children continue to bear the brunt of the effects of the now-defunct residential school system.

Society's reluctance to accommodate Sikhs' kirpans (ceremonial daggers) and turbans (e.g., in the RCMP), as manifested in the proliferation of racist lapel pins and T-shirts in 1990, provides a more recent illustration of the clash of cultures to the systematic detriment of members of a visible minority. For Sikhs, the kirpan is a sacred symbol of faith, courage, honour, and commitment, and the baptized Sikh is expected to wear it in public. Similarly, wearing the turban is mandatory for the baptized Sikh male. Hence, to prohibit the wearing of these items would be to exclude systematically the Sikh from full participation in Canadian society, such as from the opportunity to serve in the RCMP.

Schools and universities are a particularly important forum where cultural racism is manifested. For example, requiring certain qualifications, such as a doctorate, for the position of director of a Native Studies program in a university might preclude most of the very candidates (Natives) who can best relate to Native students, while discrimination in hiring produces a shortage of non-white role models. Calliou (1997: 230–1) points out that one of the cultural practices of universities that is particularly inhospitable, and sometimes devastating, to aboriginal students is the multiple-choice format of tests and exams. Many Native students do well in short essay questions but poorly in multiple choice because cultural factors are associated with the multiple-choice format. For instance, the linearity of the format is at odds with the circularity of most First Nation cultures. Second, English is a foreign language to many First Nation individuals. The assumption that the student understands all of the nuances of the vocabulary is often invalid. Third, the Aboriginal student might bring a different interpretive scheme to the assigned reading material, so that he or she derives a different message from that which the instructor assumes when reading the same material. Further, the intricate manipulation of the language (e.g., some combination of a negative or even double negative, an 'all of the above' option, an 'all except b' option, and the fact that the truth or falsehood of an option might revolve around one word or one prefix or even one letter) comes across to some First Nation students as trickery, even when not intended as such by the composer of the question. Such 'trickery' is in marked contrast to Aboriginal cultures, which stress straightforward communication. Having been conditioned to find such 'trickery' in multiple-choice questions, some First Nation students look for it when it is not present, so they misinterpret the question.

Another example of cultural racism is found in officially prescribed school curricula that regularly give short shrift to the vital economic, social, and cultural contributions that racial minorities have made to Canadian nation-building, such as their contributions during World War I and World War II. Kelly (1998: 49) notes:

> The importance of who fights for whom and under what terms they can display patriotism comes to represent part of the construction and racialization of who can be seen as a true Canadian. Whether we like it or not, part of the process of othering surrounding issues such as whether Sikhs should be able to wear a turban in British [sic: Royal Canadian] Legion halls in Alberta is the ability of 'White' groups to construct soldiers 'who gave their all for this country' as White—as one of 'us' rather than one of 'them'.

Not surprisingly, the educational experience for students from racial minorities is often quite alienating and their rate of dropping out or of transferring to vocational streams can become quite high.

The mass media are another central institution that imposes a culturally racist model of Canadian society. This is noteworthy in news, advertising, programming, and other content. Henry and Tator (1985: 327) submit that 'the media create a distorted image of society in which only those with white skin are seen as participating in mainstream activities.' We return to the media below.

'Race' and Crime

Part of the antagonism some Canadians feel towards immigrants, in general, and non-whites, in particular, stems from an association they make between skin colour and crime.[11] Such antagonism is periodically fuelled when an immigrant, especially a non-white, commits a particularly repugnant crime that, along with demagogic reactions by some politicians, is given intensive coverage by the mass media. Newspapers and radio phone-in shows are often particularly active in this regard. Out of such public frenzy often come calls for data on criminal acts to be collected and published in such a way as to show the skin colour, ethnicity, or country of origin of the accused (and victims). But there are methodological pitfalls to such proposals.

To the extent that such data are valid, they can be used to help assess the extent (if any) of systemic discrimination against certain categories of people. For instance, LaPrairie (1996: 49) reports 1991 data for Ontario and four western provinces showing that rates (per 10,000 population) of sentenced admissions to penal institutions are about 10 times higher (25 times higher in Saskatchewan!) for Aboriginals than for non-Aboriginals. This strongly suggests that Aboriginal people are being treated differently at the earlier stages of the criminal justice processing system.

Some of the problems surrounding 'crime-race' data are statistical. In particular, police records grossly understate the amount of crime that occurs. For instance, victimization studies suggest that only about one-third of robberies and attempted robberies are reported to police. Among those that are reported, not all make it to the occurrence sheets, and among those that do, only a fraction result in charges being laid. Of course, not all of those charges result in convictions. In addition, police arrest data often tell us more about police patrol behaviour and police use of discretionary powers than they tell us about crime. Furthermore, crimes more likely to be committed by whites (e.g., income tax fraud) often do not appear in police records. A further statistical problem resides in the fact that different police departments count crime in different ways. As Mitchell and Abbate (1994) point out, if a person robs a store, stabs the owner, and takes a customer's wallet, Toronto police would count that as one crime, whereas most other Canadian police forces would count it as three crimes. Variations in individual police officers' charging behaviours or in departmental policies on laying charges will also affect arrest rates, as will variations across departments or precincts in an organizational culture of racism.

Other problems with crime data being categorized by race or ethnic origin are definitional. For instance, millions of Canadians reported multiple ethnic origins on the 1996 census. As Mitchell and Abbate (1994) note, if it is not clear how large an ethnic group is, how can anyone say whether or not it is accurately represented in police data? Related to this is the problem of reliability in classifying suspects by skin colour. One witness or police officer might regard a slightly dark-skinned, mixed-ancestry individual as white, while another might consider the same individual to be Aboriginal, and yet a third might consider the same individual to be of Middle Eastern origin, judging by facial appearance alone. Furthermore, different police departments and other parts of the criminal justice system collect these data using different criteria.

Leaders of minority groups point to a separate but not unrelated problem (*Globe and Mail*, 1994). When atrocities are committed by whites—such as multiple murderers Paul Bernardo, Clifford Olsen, and Marc Lépine—politicians and the news media do not focus on the skin colour of the perpetrator. That focus is reserved for non-whites, which leads those leaders to suggest that the underlying text of the media message is one of racism.

In light of the foregoing, it is highly likely that such collecting and publishing of crime statistics according to skin colour, ethnicity, or country of origin would have the effect not only of precipitating what sociologists call 'moral panics', but also of perpetuating and heightening intergroup antagonisms.

Police Interactions with Persons of Colour

Police attitudes towards persons of colour have been roundly denounced by victims of police violence and by many others. Manitoba's Aboriginal Justice Inquiry examined two cases where racism on the part of the police was directed towards Aboriginal people.[12] In their report, Associate Chief Justice A.C. Hamilton of Manitoba's Court of Queen's Bench and Associate Chief Judge Murray Sinclair of the Manitobal Provincial Court concluded that the justice system 'has failed Manitoba's aboriginal people on a massive scale'. That conclusion emerged from their examination of both the shooting death of First Nation leader J.J. Harper (not to be confused with politician Elijah Harper) in a scuffle with a Winnipeg policeman and the handling of the RCMP investigation into the murder of Helen Betty Osborne, an Aboriginal girl who lived in The Pas.

The judges made the poignant observation that 'It is clear that Betty Osborne would not have been killed if she had not been aboriginal.' While they found racist attitudes on the part of some of the police officers, they expressed satisfaction that the 10-year delay in building the case and the RCMP role in contributing to that delay 'were not attributable to racism on the part of the force or any individual within the force'. However, their investigation into the tragic Harper incident, which bore striking similarity to the racism in the Marcelus François incident in Montreal, found racism literally from start to finish. For instance, they concluded that the original decision by Constable Robert Cross to approach Harper, ostensibly in connection with a car theft, was unnecessary and racially motivated: 'He stopped the first aboriginal person he saw, even though that person was a poor match for the description in other respects and a suspect had already been caught.' Then, in the ensuing Firearms Board of Inquiry, inquest, and police department internal investigation, 'the effort to protect Cross and to shift the blame to Harper took precedence . . . and precluded any objective determination of the facts.' Said the judges: 'We conclude that racism exists within the Winnipeg Police Department and that it was expressed openly the night that Harper was killed.'

Other examples of mistreatment of Aboriginal people by the justice system are legion and include the case of Donald Marshall Jr, a Mi'kmaq Indian from Nova Scotia who spent 11 years in jail for a murder he did not commit, and Wilson Nepoose, a Cree Indian from Alberta who was convicted of murder after police withheld from the Crown prosecutor evidence that further weakened what the prosecutor described as 'one of the weakest cases' he had ever taken to trial.

While Symons (1997) neither denies nor condones racist attitudes among police, her qualitative research in the ethnically diverse Côte-des-Neiges neighbourhood of Montreal yields important insights into the mutuality of stereotyping, the complexity of racial attitudes, and the interaction of those attitudes with attitudes held by ethnic group members other than the dominant group (in the case of Montreal, the *pur laine* Québécois or *francophones de souche*).

Symons found that the subculture among Montreal police in Côte-des-Neiges defines ethnic groups (*communautés culturelles*) in 'we-they' terms. Thus, ethnic groups are subjected to an 'othering' process at the hands of the Montreal police, who themselves are predominantly white Francophones. Police tend to see ethnic group members as complicated, complex, and difficult people with whom to deal. Symons's police interviewees seek to be respected and they expressed the strongly held view that ethnic group members (especially those who come from police states) do not accord the police due respect.

Simultaneously, the police are also stereotyped ('a cop is a cop is a cop') and perceived as 'The Other' by members of the ethnic groups. To them, the police embody the authority of the state and are the keepers of an order created by and for the dominant, white, Francophone, Québécois society. Montreal police are stereotyped by ethnic group members as racist, incompetent (e.g., unable to distinguish one black from another), irresponsible with their firearms, and lacking in linguistic skills (inability to speak English or languages other than French).

Interestingly, while the ethnic group members criticize the police's lack of linguistic capacity (ability to carry on a conversation in a language other than French), the police focus on what might be called the 'linguistic attitude' of the ethnic group members—their spoken French is perceived by the police as not carrying a respectful tone. Thus, the Montreal situation reminds us that language is not merely a means of communication. It is a means of defining one's total identity—'the mirror of the soul'—and a clash of identities is one part of the complex sociology of minorities' encounters with police.

Race, Social Class, and Feminism

In recent years, a major concern of social scientists and of advocates of social change has been the interrelations of race, class, and gender as bases of social inequality in society and as impediments to social change aimed at reducing social inequality.[13]

Among theorists, sweeping claims have been made for one or the other as being the primary source of inequality. Marxist scholars have tended to view social class as primary and to regard race as a social construct that is merely a product of the ideology that supports the class system. Other theorists regard race and class as standing in some sort of a mutual relationship, while yet others regard all three factors—race, class, and gender—as intrinsic to the day-to-day experiences of 'women of colour'. They hold the view that it is neither possible nor desirable to single out one factor as the primary cause of the oppression experienced by women of colour.

Adding to the diversity of theoretical perspectives, some others stress the need to take into account the macroeconomic context (e.g., the national and global restructuring of capital) of intergroup relations as well as the power and autonomy of capitalists and central state authorities. Some Canadian analyses emphasize the fact that racial or ethnic *communities* often play a crucial role in shaping individuals' identity and in binding together individuals, sometimes with others of similar class and ethnicity, but sometimes with co-ethnics from different social classes (Stasiulis, 1990).

Among practitioners seeking social change, black and Native women have been especially critical of white, middle-class feminists for their frequent insensitivity to the role that race plays in their oppression. Such women of colour have often found that they have little in common with white liberal feminists. As a result, among these potential allies we sometimes find a fragmentation that is counterproductive to social change that would reduce oppression.

This fragmentation has been exacerbated by the feminist movement's ideology that 'the personal is political.' The slogan not only separates women into different and isolated realities by accentuating the differences in the personal life experiences of white women compared to women of colour; it also leads to the inadvertent creation of 'hierarchies of oppression' whereby some women say 'I'm more oppressed than you because I've got more labels and oppressed status' (Adamson et al., 1988: 210). Such invidious comparisons within a social movement can have demoralizing and demobilizing effects that sometimes outweigh the solidarity produced by another slogan of the feminist movement: 'Sisterhood is powerful.' Indeed, the latter slogan, with its inherent bias against coalitions with other male-dominated social movement organizations pursuing similar class interests, stood in the way of women's organizations developing an effective strategy for social change. Furthermore, by glossing over differences among women in search of an undifferentiated sisterhood, the slogan made the concerns of women of colour seem invisible (ibid., 221, 224).[14]

Feminist analysis by women of colour calls into question some of the basic tenets of middle-class, white, feminist analysis, such as the specific role of the state in perpetuating women's oppression. New insights and orientations, sometimes distinctively Canadian, are emerging from such analysis of structures, discourse, and relationships. For instance, this strand of research is correcting the failure of white feminism to recognize women's concerns in immigration issues. It is also drawing our attention both to the special burden of colonialism borne by Aboriginal women in Canada and to the fact that racist ideological notions about the essence of the femininity of women of different 'races' play an important role in assigning those women to different occupations. Of particular benefit to sociology as a discipline has been the realization, emerging from the feminist analysis by women of colour, that different oppressive systems (class, racism, patriarchy) work in different ways, so that no simple explanations or political strategies will suffice when these systems intersect.

First Nations' Resistance to Racism

An important development of the late twentieth century in academic approaches to racism was a setting aside of victimization perspectives in favour of a focus on resistance to racism. This was a natural outcome of theorizing, such as that by Parkin (1979) and others, which has stressed the reciprocal nature of power relations. An anti-racism literature and practice, led by such sociologists as George J. Safa Dei, blossomed in the 1990s. However, with the exception of discussions of the residential school experience (e.g., Haig-Brown, 1988; Miller, 1996: 343–74), that literature paid scant attention to resistance by First Nations. A major purpose of this section is to demonstrate the breadth of resistance strategies exhibited by First Nations collectivities and individuals. The discussion is organized by considering those strategies in the context of both the locus of resistance and whether the resistance was conducted within the bounds of norms approved by the larger society. First, though, a definition of 'resistance' is needed.

Resistance to racism is not as straightforward a matter as one might imagine. Questions arise as to whether mere mitigative behaviours would qualify as resistance, or conversely, whether the behaviours in question must promote social change or, in the case of First Nations, seek to restore some elements of a *status quo ante*. For our purposes, Allahar's (1998: 338) definition will suffice, albeit with one caveat. He defines resistance to racism as 'any action, whether physical, verbal or psychological, and whether individual or collective, that seeks to undo the negative consequences of being categorized for racial reasons'. The caveat is necessary because his definition permits him to consider assimilation as a form of resistance. In the case of First Nations, where an important form taken by the dominant society's racism was attempted cultural genocide, Allahar's classification of assimilation as a form of resistance is not appropriate. Furthermore, behaviours that are 'mere' coping strategies should not be confused with resistance.

Resistance to racism can occur at the international level, at what might be called the domestic or national level, or at the level of the victimized individual or community. It might take a form that falls within the norms of the dominant society or it might fall outside those norms. Combining these two dimensions produces the classification shown in Table 2.1. Admittedly, some of the classifications are somewhat arbitrary. For instance, boycotts such as the international boycott of Daishawa products by the Friends of the Lubicon can occur and have occurred in Canada, but they are listed in the 'International' column in Table 2.1. Each entry in the table refers to actual behaviours that have been exhibited by First Nation individuals or organizations in Canada.

The 'isolationist' form of avoidance, shown in the first column, refers to deliberate attempts to minimize contact with the culture and institutions of the dominant society through spatial separation. Examples include back-to-the-land movements (such as the Smallboy camp in Alberta), resistance to road construction into isolated First Nation communities, individuals' choices to limit their circle of friends to other First Nation individuals, and individuals' decisions to reside on reserve. 'Institutional pluralism' refers to the creation of parallel institutions (e.g., schools) in First Nation society to enable First Nation individuals to avoid coming under the cultural onslaught of the larger society's institutions.

A particularly important form of 'reclamation of pride and culture' is the revival of Aboriginal spirituality. Although there is overlap between Aboriginal spiritualities and the dominant religions of the larger Canadian society, Aboriginal spiritual beliefs also challenge the dominant society's ideologies on some fundamental dimensions (see Ross, 1992).

Table 2.1   Classification of First Nations' Resistance to Racism

| | Locus of Resistance | | |
	Personal/ Community	Other Domestic	International

Normative	Avoidance
	• isolation
	• institutional
	  pluralism
	Expressivism
	• art
	• literature
	• humour
	• drama
	• music
	Reclamation of
	  pride and culture
		Opting out of
		  Indian Act
		Negotiation
		Litigation
		• land claims
		• injunctions
		• other
		Lobbying
		Incorporation
		Demonstration
		  and hunger strike
		Coalition formation
		Persuading and
		  educating others
		Academia
		Use of formal
		  complaint
		  mechanisms
		Devolution
			Boycott
			Intervening with
			  foreign regulatory
			  agencies
			Lobbying interna-
			  tional financiers
			European Parliament
			United Nations

*Extra-
Normative*
	Escapism
	• substance abuse
	• suicide
	• welfarism
	  (opting out)
	Community
	  distrust
	Cultural imposition
		Obstructionism
		Wilful non-
		  compliance
		Vandalism, theft,
		  and desecration
		Engage in own
		  racism
		Gangs
		Assault
		Unilateral assertion
		  of jurisdiction
		Insurrection
		Sabotage
			International
			  embarrassment

*Note: I am grateful to colleague Cora Voyageur for feedback on, and input to, this table.

'Cultural imposition' is illustrated in Denis's bluntly titled book, *We Are Not You*. He examines a case in which, with the guarded approval of the elders, some Vancouver Island First Nation individuals abducted and forcibly detained another Aboriginal, beat him, and initiated him into the Coast Salish culture, which, in their estimation, he had lost to assimilation by the larger society. Cultural imposition is also illustrated by the negative sanctions (e.g., being derided as an 'apple'—red on the outside but white on the inside) brought to bear on some people by their peers because they have pursued 'whiteman's education' beyond the high school level.

'Community distrust' is widespread in many First Nation communities, as Crowfoot (1997) attests. On the one hand, this is counterproductive to community development that could be attained through the building of community social solidarity. On the other hand, when directed at the leadership, as it commonly is, that distrust can serve as a brake on the co-optation of the leadership by the federal government's assimilative Indian Act regime.

In the 'domestic' column the first form of resistance is listed as 'opting out of the Indian Act'. Reference here is to legislated agreements (e.g., the Sechelt Indian Government Act; various provisions of land claims agreements) that replace Indian Act provisions with some other arrangements negotiated by the First Nation and the federal government. Conversely, 'incorporation' refers to attempts to penetrate the larger society's governmental structures to ensure that First Nation interests are taken into account in decision-making. Examples include participating at first ministers' conferences, taking jobs in the Department of Indian Affairs and Northern Development, and participating in environmental impact assessment or social impact assessment hearings.

'Academia' is used here to refer to taking positions in one of the main institutions responsible for perpetuating the hegemony of the dominant society. Faculty positions are particularly important, to the extent that they are accompanied by power (e.g., the power to set curriculum and sanction students). However, one should not underestimate the considerable power held by First Nation students who are prepared to adopt a confrontational style in class in an effort to hold professors and students accountable for the racism that creeps into texts, courses, and classrooms.

The 'use of formal complaint mechanisms' refers to lodging complaints with such institutions as human rights commissions, police commissions, media councils, and university grievance bodies.

'Devolution' mainly refers to First Nation governments entering agreements with the federal government to take back powers that the federal government had arrogated unto itself. This contrasts with 'unilateral assertion of jurisdiction' in that the latter is done without the prior consent of the federal government.

'Insurrection' refers to the taking up of arms against a government of the dominant society or against the band council elected under the Indian Act. An example would be the Oka crisis of 1990. 'Sabotage', on the other hand, is more covert and might be directed at corporations rather than government. It is illustrated by the destruction of logging equipment on certain lands claimed by First Nations.

Finally, foreign countries and international bodies have served as a forum for First Nation resistance to racism. For instance, in seeking to block what they called the 'environmental racism' of the proposed James Bay II project, the James Bay Crees lobbied international financiers of the project and intervened at New York state regulatory hearings. Ponting (1990) and Ponting and Symons (1997) discuss various other forays into the international arena by First Nations from Canada. Since their writing, an important additional action in this arena has been Canadian First Nations' work on the United Nations Draft Declaration of the Rights of Indigenous Peoples.

From the above it is evident that First Nations in Canada have not passively accepted the racism inflicted by Canadian society. Instead, resistance has been multi-faceted and ongoing. It has ranged from the subtle to the blatant and has spanned a variety of institutional forums. Sometimes, as in the case of numerous suicides, the impact of that resistance has been tragically disempowering (insofar as life on earth is concerned). Yet, in other cases, such as some land claim litigation and Elijah Harper's obstruction of the Meech Lake Accord, the resistance has been highly effective at leveraging significant gains for First Nation peoples.

Other Societal Responses to Racism

In modern industrial society, the state not only governs, redistributes wealth, and produces goods and services; it also produces symbolic output. To date, the state's response to racism has been largely, although not entirely, symbolic. Examples are numerous and include the federal government's establishment of a parliamentary task force on the participation of visible minorities in Canadian society, the creation of a Department of Multiculturalism in the federal bureaucracy, and the incorporation of non-white reporters on the team of on-air television journalists at the Canadian Broadcasting Corporation. These actions, although rather limited, are important, for as Breton (1986: 31–2) notes, *individuals expect to be able to recognize themselves in the symbolic outputs of the state*—in public institutions and in the values and meanings incorporated in those institutions. In the absence of such recognition, as is often the case for visible minorities, the individual is likely to feel alienated and to withhold or withdraw legitimacy from those institutions and from the broader state itself. Unfortunately for Canada, that very act of granting symbolic recognition to some is interpreted by others as a loss to themselves and particularly to the identity they built (in part) around those old symbols. Such a reaction leads to resistance to the symbolic revamping that is required to accommodate the non-white minorities who are an increasingly large part of Canadian society.

Admittedly, the state at both the federal and provincial levels has moved beyond the merely symbolic to implement some key changes in the social structure. For instance, human rights commissions have been formed and legislation enacted outlawing discrimination based on race, creed, colour, national origin, and other grounds. The first such legislation was Ontario's Racial Discrimination Act of 1944. However, the legislative mandate of such commissions tends to be weak and highly constrained in the sense that it requires an individual to lodge a complaint before the commission can take action, rather than permitting a more aggressive, proactive investigative stance (e.g., entrapment) by the commission. Procedures for the processing of complaints tend to be cumbersome, very protracted, and in their early stages without significant incentive for the respondent to comply. Similarly, penalties are usually mild. Taken together these factors serve as a deterrent to potential complainants lodging complaints at all. As a result, only a minuscule fraction of the racism in society comes to the attention of such commissions.

Another main response by the state has been the inclusion, in the Canadian Charter of Rights and Freedoms, of protections against racial (and other) discrimination. However, the Charter protects individuals against actions of the state and its agencies, rather than against actions by private individuals not affiliated with the state. Furthermore, it offers mainly negative or proscriptive protections against restrictions that prevent an individual's full participation in society's institutions, rather than positive or prescriptive rights that would recognize a group's collective interest in survival as a distinct group and require the state to be proactive in providing certain resources towards that end. Also, the Charter is primarily concerned with individual rights rather than the collective rights of social groups, such as Aboriginals' right to self-determination. Indeed, even in the recommendations of the federal Royal Commission on Aboriginal Peoples, an Aboriginal right to self-government would be explicitly limited by the Charter with its individualistic bias (RCAP, 1996: 163).[15]

Evelyn Kallen's (1988) critique of the Meech Lake Accord alerts us to several perspectives that can be useful measuring sticks against which to assess future proposals for constitutional reform insofar as their implications for racism are concerned. Her concern is that in Canada we are developing a hierarchy of minority rights, whereby some sectors of society (e.g., official-language minorities) have positive,[16] defined,[17] specified[18] rights, while other sectors of society (e.g., Aboriginal people) have only negative, undefined, and in some cases unspecified rights, and yet other sectors (e.g., gays) have little or no legal recognition of their rights at all. Thus, the rights of the two 'charter groups'—French and English—take precedence over the rights of others, such as visible (non-white) minorities. Furthermore, some rights (such as those found in section 15 of the Charter) are subject to provincial override, while others are not.

Potentially of more benefit to individual members of visible minority groups are two other measures. The first is the Charter's s. 15(2) protection of affirmative action programs from being struck down as unconstitutional 'reverse discrimination', such as happened in the United States. The second is the federal state's employment equity legislation and associated contract compliance program, both of which are protected under s. 15(2). The employment equity legislation requires more proportional hiring and promotion of Aboriginals, other visible minorities, the handicapped, and women on the part of organizations regulated by the federal government (e.g., banks) or doing business with the federal government (e.g., universities). Under the employment equity legislation the penalties for not submitting annual reports on the progress of the organization's employment equity program are significant, but there are no penalties for making no progress or for regressing. Not surprisingly, minority rights advocacy groups have been highly critical of the effectiveness of the legislation, and Voyageur's (1997) empirical analysis of its first nine years of operation generally tends to support those criticisms insofar as Aboriginal people are concerned. The enforcement provisions of the contract compliance program are much more significant and include the possibility of an organization losing its eligibility for all grants and contracts from the federal government. However, initial indications are that the prime beneficiaries of these measures might well be white, middle-class women rather than a broader spectrum of people from the other three target populations. Furthermore, even though employment equity and contract compliance might be an effective attack on institutional racism, many of the minority individuals involved will continue to be subjected to individual racism on the worksite and will continue to be plagued by 'last hired, first fired' (seniority-based) personnel policies during periods of economic downturn.

A final development to be mentioned here is a very important one in the criminal justice area. It is the Supreme Court of Canada decision rendered in the 1998 *Williams* case. There the Court ruled that prospective jurors may be questioned about their racial views in order to root out those whose prejudices could destroy the fairness of a criminal trial.[19]

Racism and the Reform/Canadian Alliance Party

By changing the terms of the public discourse on racial and ethnic issues in the 1990s, the Reform Party of Canada succeeded in getting the federal government and certain provincial governments to step back from some earlier anti-racism, anti-discrimination initiatives. How successful the new Canadian Alliance, born of the merger of the Reform Party with certain other conservative elements, can be electorally or at influencing government agendas is anybody's guess. Also up in the air is how different the new party will be from the Reform Party of the 1990s on issues pertaining to racism and minority rights. Certainly, the Reform Party's stance on minority rights issues acted as an impediment to its electoral success outside the West, so it is reasonable to expect a moderation of those stances in the new party, especially since the Canadian Alliance was created with the purpose of gaining more electoral support, especially in Ontario. What is clear, though, is that many of the state's responses to racism and systemic discrimination would be in grave jeopardy if a rump Reform Party of Canada or others of similar ilk were to form a government or hold the balance of power in a minority government. For that reason, and because of its considerable past influence, a brief retrospective look at the Reform Party of Canada is in order here.

The Reform Party was driven by a simplistic ideology of radical equality—an ideology based on the assumption that *uniformity* of treatment is the only acceptable form of equality. The Reform Party can be considered radical not only because it dismissed equity (the principle that people in quite different situations with quite different abilities to compete should be treated differently) as a desirable goal, but also because it was largely unwilling to act effectively on the existence of systemic discrimination. Furthermore, Reform policy favoured the abolition of many accommodations that have been made in an attempt to improve intergroup relations in Canada.

I have elsewhere described the Reform Party as 'nothing short of an enemy of the empowerment of First Nation peoples' (Ponting, 1997: 143). Consider, first, the party's 1997 election platform plank calling for the cutting of $1 billion from the budget of the Department of Indian Affairs and Northern Development. Second, Reform policy was that Aboriginal rights in the constitution should be abolished, albeit with compensation. Third, consider the Reform stance on comprehensive land claims agreements. In advocating 'affordability to the governments of Canada and the provinces' as a principle to govern land claims negotiations, the party was saying, in effect, that instead of justice being determined by principles of fairness and morality and restitution, justice must take its place amid the transient political priorities of the day. A fourth way in which Reform earned its status as an enemy of First Nations was its position that federal funding of First Nation political organizations should cease, which would emasculate those advocacy organizations. Fifth, the party came out in favour of the privatization of land tenure on Indian reserves. That policy, which was implemented with highly deleterious consequences in the US, would fragment the reserves into a checkerboard mix of non-contiguous First Nation lands interspersed among non-Native owners. Sixth, with its disdain for collective rights, Reform espoused highly assimilationist goals for all minorities.

The list of Reform Party policies inimical to First Nations' collective interests goes on (ibid., 126–8). One concrete example of the party's fundamental challenge to contemporary attempts to bring justice to First Nations is its role in opposing the 1998 treaty signed by the Nisga'a Nation and the governments of British Columbia and Canada. Reform politicized this treaty to an extent that Aboriginal issues had never before been politicized in Canada. In the House of Commons the party even went to the extent of introducing about 470 motions pertaining to the treaty. That, of course, was an attempt to delay passage of the bill and to score political points with right-wing supporters at the expense of justice for the Nisga'a.[20]

Immigrants were another target of the Reform Party. Kirkham argues that, as a movement of the 'new right',[21] Reform used code words to rearticulate a racist discourse. That is, the explicit racial discourse of an earlier era was abandoned in favour of a vocabulary that appears to be race-neutral but is actually merely a disguise for racial issues. For instance, Reform's devaluing of family reunification as a goal of immigration policy and the party's policy statement that 'Immigrants should possess the human capital necessary to adjust quickly and independently to the needs of Canadian society and the job market' can be construed as opposition to immigration by persons who do not speak English. These would include the relatives of many immigrants from Asia and the Indian subcontinent, for a majority of all family class immigrants to Canada now come from Asia. In this regard, Kirkham (1998: 252) asks, what cultural backgrounds are assumed to have the greatest or least potential for 'adjustment'? As Simmons (1998) points out, even a non-racist immigration policy, not to mention a neo-racist one, should not be confused with an anti-racist immigration policy.[22] In addition, considering the bigoted public remarks of some Reform members of Parliament, even a disinterested observer might well ask whether the party's emphasis on 'border control' and on stopping 'bogus refugees' was really code for a preference for drastically curtailing immigration now that a majority of immigrants are non-white.

Yet other targets of the Reform Party were multiculturalism, affirmative action, and collective rights. The party maintained that the federal multiculturalism policy is not only a waste of taxpayers' dollars, but is also inimical to national unity because, in Reform's view, it promotes 'hyphenated Canadianism'. The policy's goals of eradicating racism and removing discriminatory barriers were largely downplayed and sometimes even opposed by Reform on the grounds that they involve excessive government intrusion in the lives of Canadians (Kirkham, 1998: 258–9, 263). Affirmative action, the policy designed to eliminate barriers of systemic discrimination, was roundly denounced by the party. Furthermore, operating under the sociologically naïve yet tenaciously held belief in the equalizing effects of a free-market economy, Reform rearticulated the meaning of racial-ethnic group equality as a matter of individual, rather than group, concern. Said Preston Manning, then leader of Reform: 'It is true that not everyone starts from the same position, but these inequalities are not necessarily cumulative and inherited. A market economy, open society, and democratic polity are great engines for the destruction of privilege' (Kirkham, 1998: 263).

Collective rights were an anathema to Reform Party ideologues, for they regarded such rights as conferring 'special status' on some sectors of society to the detriment of others. Instead of collective rights, Reform championed uniform individual rights, while wrapping itself in a discourse of 'colour-blindness'. In raising the bogeyman of 'special status', Reform Party ideologues engaged in emotional appeals that play upon the insecurities many Canadians feel in their economic situation or even their personal identity. That increases the possibility of a status preservationist backlash against refugees, other immigrants, and Aboriginal people. Indeed, right-wing extremists (e.g., from the Heritage Front) assessed the ranks of Reform to be potentially fertile ground for recruiting others to their 'cause', and some anti-Aboriginal extremist organizations (e.g., BC FIRE) are built around a core of Reform Party supporters. To its credit, the Reform Party formally disassociated the party from the Heritage Front infiltrators. However, such repudiation did little to alter, and might well have functioned as a cloak for, the fundamental direction of the party's broader discourse. That direction was indistinguishable from what Simmons calls 'neo-racism' and Henry et al. (1995) define as 'democratic racism'.[23]

Conclusion

We Canadians can no longer afford to indulge ourselves in the myth that Canadian society is relatively free of racism. Racism is structured into the major institutions of society and members of some visible minorities, subordinated because of their physical appearance, are reaching the limits of their patience with the larger society. As one Native student told me shortly after a First Nation woman was fatally shot by an RCMP officer on a reserve adjacent to Calgary, 'I can't come to class. I've got to go join the revolution.' Interracial violence is becoming more common and racial tensions are mounting to alarmingly high levels, especially in the cities and among First Nations. People are getting killed because of racism in Canada.

The tragedies of Shidane Arone, of Oka, of Marcelus François, of Betty Osborne, of Nirmal Singh Gill, and of others are profound. Yet, other facets of racism are also taking an alarming toll on Canadian society. First, racism hinders economic competitiveness, because the most qualified workers are often being denied the job (or the advancement opportunity) simply because they are not white. This emerged as a major problem in the information technology sector late in the twentieth century, as Canada developed a reputation for racism among skilled computer industry personnel from India and Asia (Stackhouse, 2000). In large numbers they eschewed immigration to Canada in favour of the United States and its truly multicultural 'Silicon Valley'. For instance, Stackhouse reports that during the 1990s, the US attracted over 1,000 graduates from India's prestigious Indian Institutes of Technology (IIT), while Canada attracted just nine IIT graduates! Economic competitiveness can also be hampered because racism can result in talented individuals not getting the opportunity for education and training, so they do not even attain the qualifications necessary for the job. Second, the legitimacy of the existing political institutions (the political regime) is being called into question due to the inability of those institutions to make much tangible progress towards eradicating racism. Third, a new and growing problem of national unity is emerging as many members of racially subordinated groups, such as blacks and First Nations, withdraw the legitimacy they had attached to the political community itself. In other words, their experience with having been excluded from the mainstream of Canadian society for racial reasons has left many to think of themselves first and foremost as blacks or Indians, rather than as Canadians. With that orientation, they see themselves as having little stake in the status quo in Canada. As a result, they feel little compunction about engaging in obstructionist strategies and tactics, even on matters of the utmost importance to the power élite in Canadian society, as illustrated by Elijah Harper's obstruction of the Meech Lake Accord and the James Bay Crees' obstruction of the James Bay II project. Many prison gangs and youth gangs are yet another manifestation of the same phenomenon of racialized minorities coming to see themselves as having little stake in the status quo. Furthermore, issues of racism in Canada are increasingly being drawn into the international arena (e.g., the behaviour of Canadian troops abroad; see also

Ponting, 1990) where the impact is to embarrass Canada and to undermine Canada's influence and attractiveness abroad.

Racism is an inherently political phenomenon and, to a significant degree, race relations are group power contests. To diminish racism in Canadian society, and in response to the politicization of 'race' by the Reform Party, non-whites must politicize their response to a greater degree than has been the case to date among non-white non-Aboriginals. They must vest their interests not only in political parties, as they have started to do, but also in state institutions themselves through consolidating and demonstrating their political power. That, rather than strategies of changing whites' attitudes, is the key to achieving the profound structural change necessary to break the grip of racism on a wide range of Canadian institutions.

Notwithstanding the difficulty of implementing a politicization strategy in the face of class and ethnic divisions within the non-white population, such a strategy is especially important in the present era. That is, despite a slight softening of neo-liberalism at the edges around the turn of the century, the neo-liberal, *laissez-faire* agenda of contemporary capitalist states remains dominant. It bodes ill for effective state involvement in ameliorating race relations unless intense political pressure is applied by minorities.

Another feature of the present era reinforces the necessity of political action. Consider the fact that multiculturalism is under attack as Canadians seek to define and redefine the Canada that we want for the twenty-first century. There is a high probability that, despite their growing demographic importance, visible minorities other than Aboriginals will be the big losers who receive no more than tokenistic redress of their concerns. As Canadians grapple with the demands of Quebec and of Aboriginals, the already shallow reservoir of 'tolerance' and policy creativity might be quickly depleted, such that there is no sense of urgency or political will to combat racism effectively. Traditionally, non-whites have occupied the bottom rungs of the 'pecking order' in Canada. In the absence of a strategy of intense politicization of 'race' in Canada, there is every reason to believe that that tradition will continue.

Questions for Critical Thought

1. Do you believe that a fundamental feature of Canadian society is that we are and should remain predominantly white? Why or why not? If you answered 'Yes' to the first question, where does that leave 'people of colour' (including those whose families have been Canadian for generations) and Aboriginal people ('the First Canadians')? What, if anything, would be lost or gained if the demographics of Canada shifted so that non-whites became the majority in Canada?

2. What are the strengths and unintended negative consequences of government policies based on assumptions of: (a) equality as uniformity; and (b) equality as equity? Over the long term, how viable are policies based on each of these respective models of equality?

3. Consider your first or most formative encounter with racism or ethnic discrimination, as victim, perpetrator, or witness. What was its effect on you? How did you process it in your own mind (e.g., denial vs radicalization vs acceptance)?

4. How would your parents feel if you were to marry a person of a different 'race'? How did they respond when you were young and reflected some aspect of the larger society's racism in your words or actions? Did your parents warn you about playing or hanging out with any particular children, and if so, was their race or ethnicity a visible trait? In your family, was/is poverty among First Nations defined in individualistic or psychological (e.g., laziness) terms that ignore colonialism, discrimination, and systemic racism?

Glossary

Activated prejudice: Feelings of hostility towards members of an out-group, based on presumed attributes of members of that group, and reinforced by a sense of conflict with that group, such that the bearer of the prejudice is likely to oppose public policies intended to improve the life situation of members of the group.

Cultural racism: The negative depiction of the people, art, and other cultural objects of a racially defined out-group and the imposition of ethnocentric standards in the valuation and recognition of the cultural practices and products of people of that group to their detriment.

Dormant prejudice: Feelings of hostility towards members of an out-group, based on presumed attributes of members of that group, but without any sense of conflict with that group.

Economic liberalism: A political philosophy characterized by a positive regard for private enterprise, competition to foster efficiency, profit-making, and private property rights, and a negative regard for government intervention that regulates 'free-market forces' in the economy.

Institutional (systemic) racism: Outcomes of the operation of institutions where those outcomes differ systematically for people of different 'races', regardless of the intentions of the individuals staffing those institutions.

Quondam complex: A set of attitudes and beliefs involving a preponderance of symbolic investment (e.g., one's own identity) based on the past, and hostility towards members of groups believed to be responsible for causing changes to that preferred past state of affairs.

Racialization: The process whereby categories of individuals sharing some physical or cultural attributes are deemed by others to constitute a 'race' and are therefore kept at a social distance and made the object of discrimination.

Radical right: Persons who define themselves as racists, fascists, and anti-Semites, and who are prepared to use violence to achieve their objectives.

Web of institutional interdependencies: A structure of interconnected institutions wherein the output from one institution shapes the input to another institution. This is of special relevance to the study of racism when the output from an institution located near the beginning of a chain of institutions is discriminatory.

Suggested Reading

Barrett, Stanley R. 1987. *Is God a Racist? The Right Wing in Canada.* Toronto: University of Toronto Press. The most comprehensive examination yet of the radical right in late twentieth-century Canada.

Denis, Claude. 1997. *We Are Not You: First Nations and Canadian Modernity.* Peterborough, Ont.: Broadview Press. A brief and controversial case study that offers a thought-provoking examination of cultural racism in the Canadian justice system.

Kelly, Jennifer. 1998. *Under the Gaze.* Halifax: Fernwood. A brief and easy-to-read account of black students' acquisition of identity in the racist environment of Edmonton-area high schools.

Ross, Rupert. 1992. *Dancing With a Ghost.* Markham, Ont.: Octopus Publishing. A non-Native Crown prosecutor's richly descriptive and widely acclaimed account of Native and non-Native cultures' clashing values and perspectives that render the non-Native criminal justice system foreign to most Natives.

Sunahara, Ann. 1981. *The Politics of Racism: The Uprooting of Japanese Canadians During the Second World War.* Toronto: James Lorimer. An account of the dynamics of one of the most outrageous and bigoted state attacks on Canadian citizens in the twentieth century.

Notes

1. Calgary, at 16 per cent, had the third highest proportion of visible minorities among Canadian cities. The figures for selected other cities are: Edmonton, 14 per cent; Montreal, 12 per cent; Ottawa-Hull, 12 per cent; Winnipeg, 11 per cent. Statistics Canada classifies persons from the following national origins as visible minorities: Chinese, South Asians, blacks, Arabs and West Asians, Filipinos, Southeast Asians, Latin Americans, Japanese, Koreans, and Pacific Islanders (Statistics Canada, *The Daily*, 17 Feb. 1998).

2. Some Chinese are now seeking compensation from the government of Canada for these discriminatory payments.

3. R.B. Bennett, *House of Commons Debates*, 7 June 1928, 3925ff., cited in Palmer (1973: 119).

4. William Lyon Mackenzie King, *House of Commons Debates*, 1 May 1947, *c.* 2645, cited ibid.

5. Perceptions of conflicting group interests were measured in terms of such dimensions as the belief that Natives already receive excessive financial assistance from government and the belief that Natives already exercise considerable power and influence with the federal or provincial government.

6. Although my earlier work followed popular usage in referring to this phenomenon as 'economic conservatism', the technically correct term is 'economic liberalism', for it involves the values of classical liberal economic theory.

7. These include Tamil refugees from Sri Lanka who arrived off Newfoundland in December 1985, Punjabi immigrants who came ashore in Nova Scotia in August 1987, and Chinese immigrants who were intercepted on the British Columbia coast in the summer of 1999.

8. In the documentary film *Canadian Harbinger* (University of Calgary, 1997), sociologist Raymond Breton points out that the Anglos of Toronto have been displaced by immigrants, such that the Anglos no longer 'set the rules of the game'. They are, in Breton's words, no longer the definers of the cultural situation.

9. This section draws heavily from Barrett (1987).

10. CBC news, 20 Mar. 1988.

11. For a more detailed discussion of these issues, including the observations of criminologists and sociologists, see Mitchell and Abbate (1994); *Globe and Mail* (1994).

12. The account below is taken from the *Globe and Mail*'s publication of excerpts of the Hamilton and Sinclair report on 30 Aug. 1991.

13. This section draws heavily on the work of Adamson et al. (1988) and Stasiulis (1990).

14. Adamson et al. (1988: 6) provide an excellent and detailed analysis of the strengths and limitations of the 'sisterhood is powerful' and 'the personal is political' slogans of the women's movement, including their impact on collective action that crosses racial, class, and gender lines.

15. The Royal Commission did recommend, however, that Aboriginal governments be able to invoke the so-called 'notwithstanding clause', which would enable them to pass temporary legislation that would have effect despite the fact that it might violate certain provisions of the Charter of Rights and Freedoms.

16. A positive right places obligations on the state to provide resources, whereas a negative right merely guarantees non-interference by the state.

17. A defined right is one for which the meaning and content are spelled out.

18. A specified right is one for which the particular target group holding the right is identified, whereas an unspecified right is one that applies generally and no target population is named.

19. For a journalistic account of this decision, see Makin (1998).

20. Reform's criticisms of the treaty included such points as the claim that the treaty is too generous in the benefits it provides the Nisga'a, that non-Natives living in Nisga'a territory do not have the right to vote in Nisga'a elections, that the Nisga'a government should be reduced to a mere municipal-style government, that certain preferential economic rights are conferred upon the Nisga'a, and others. At the time of writing, Reform's critiques of the Nisga'a treaty could be found at: http://www.reform.ca/duncan/nisgaa.html#TOC

21. Kirkham defines the 'new right' in terms of the presence of a neo-liberal economic philosophy (e.g., belief in unfettered market forces) combined with an authoritarian social conservatism that seeks to uphold traditional authority and morality.

22. Simmons defines a neo-racist immigration policy as one that reveals significant racist influences and outcomes within a framework that claims to be entirely non-racist. A non-racist immigration policy eliminates all signifiers of race from immigrant selection procedures but yields intended or unintended outcomes that put certain groups at a disadvantage while making it easier for other groups to gain admission. Simmons (1998: 99–109) also reminds us that immigration policy refers to more than just the selection of immigrants and the number of immigrants admitted. It also refers to access to immigration services (e.g., the placement or absence of Canadian immigration officers in different countries), the economic role (e.g., farm labourer, domestic) to which immigrants are assigned after entering Canada, and the selective deportation of 'visible minorities'. The Reform Party's policies should be assessed on these dimensions, too.

23. Henry et al. (1995: 21) describe democratic racism as an ideology in which commitments to democratic principles—such as justice, equality, and fairness—conflict with but coexist alongside negative feelings about minority groups and discrimination towards them. Those who hold democratic racist views regard state intervention to ameliorate the situation of people of colour as being a threat to liberal democracy's basic tenets. For instance, anti-racism initiatives are discredited as 'racism in reverse'.

References

Abella, Irving, and Harold Troper. 1982. *None Is Too Many.* Toronto: Lester & Orpen Dennys.

Adachi, Ken. 1976. *The Enemy That Never Was.* Toronto: McClelland & Stewart.

Adamson, Nancy, et al. 1988. *Feminist Organizing for Change.* Toronto: Oxford University Press.

Adorno, T.W., Else Frenkel-Brunswick, D.J. Levinson, and R.N. Sanford. 1950. *The Authoritarian Personality.* New York: Harper and Row, 1950.

Allahar, Anton. 1998. 'Race and Racism: Strategies of Resistance', in Satzewich (1998a: 335–54).

Anderson, Alan B., and James Frideres. 1981. *Ethnicity in Canada*. Scarborough, Ont.: Butterworths.

Angus Reid Group. 1998. *Canadians' Views and Attitudes [sic] Regarding Issues Associated with Aboriginal Peoples: Perspectives, Options and Implications for Canada—A Syndicated National Public Opinion Survey.* Toronto.

Baron, Harold M. 1969. 'The Web of Urban Racism', in Louis L. Knowles and Kenneth Prewitt, eds, *Institutional Racism in America*. Englewood Cliffs, NJ: Prentice-Hall, 134–76.

Barrett, Stanley R. 1987. *Is God a Racist? The Right Wing in Canada*. Toronto: University of Toronto Press.

Bercuson, David, and Douglas Wertheimer. 1985. *A Trust Betrayed: The Keegstra Affair.* Toronto: Doubleday.

Blumer, Herbert. 1961. 'Race Prejudice as a Sense of Group Position', in J. Masouka and Preston Valien, eds, *Race Relations—Problems and Theory*. Chapel Hill: University of North Carolina Press, 217–27.

Bobo, Lawrence. 1983. '"Whites" Opposition to Busing: Symbolic Racism or Realistic Group Conflict?', *Journal of Personality and Social Psychology* 45, 6: 196–210.

Bolaria, B. Singh, and Peter Li. 1988. *Racial Oppression in Canada*, 2nd edn. Toronto: Garamond.

Breton, Raymond. 1986. 'Multiculturalism and Canadian Nation-Building', in Alan Cairns and Cynthia Williams, eds, *The Politics of Gender, Ethnicity and Language in Canada*. Toronto: University of Toronto Press, 27–66.

Calliou, George. 1997. 'Urban Indians: Reflections on Participation of First Nation Individuals in the Institutions of the Larger Society', in Ponting (1997: 222–43).

Cernetig, Miro, and Robert Matas. 1998. '5 men linked to racists held in slaying', *Globe and Mail*, 22 Apr., A1.

Cobb, Chris. 1998. 'Immigration: Welcome becomes forced, says study', *Calgary Herald,* 11 Sept., A10.

Crowfoot, Strater. 1997. 'Leadership in First Nation Communities: A Chief's Perspectives on the Colonial Millstone', in Ponting (1997: 299–325).

Denis, Claude. 1997. *We Are Not You: First Nations and Canadian Modernity.* Peterborough, Ont.: Broadview Press.

Dunk, Thomas. 1991. *It's a Working Man's Town: Male Working Class Culture in Northwestern Ontario.* Montreal and Kingston: McGill-Queen's University Press.

Frideres, James, and William J. Reeves. 1989. 'The Ability to Implement Human Rights Legislation in Canada', *Canadian Review of Sociology and Anthropology* 26, 2: 311–32.

Globe and Mail. 1994. 'Five angles on the crime-race maze', 11 June.

Gregg, Allan, and Michael Posner. 1990. *The Big Picture: What Canadians Think About Almost Everything.* Toronto: Macfarlane, Walter, and Ross.

Haig-Brown, Celia. 1988. *Resistance and Renewal*. Vancouver: Tillacum.

Henry, Frances, and Carol Tator. 1985. 'Racism in Canada: Social Myths and Strategies for Change', in Rita Bienvenue and Jay Goldstein, eds, *Ethnicity and Ethnic Relations in Canada*, 2nd edn. Scarborough, Ont.: Butterworths, 321–35.

Henry, Frances, et al. 1995. *The Colour of Democracy: Racism in Canadian Society*. Toronto: Harcourt Brace.

Jones, J. 1972. *Prejudice and Racism*. Menlo Park, Calif.: Addison-Wesley.

Kallen, Evelyn. 1988. 'The Meech Lake Accord: Entrenching a Pecking Order of Minority Rights', *Canadian Public Policy* 14 (Supplement): 107–20.

Kelly, Jennifer. 1998. *Under the Gaze*. Halifax: Fernwood.

Kirkham, Della. 1998. 'The Reform Party of Canada: A Discourse on Race, Ethnicity, and Equality', in Satzewich (1998a: 243–67).

Kluegel, James R. 1990. 'Trends in Whites' Explanations of the Black-White Gap in SES', *American Sociological Review* 55, 5: 512–25.

——— and Eliot R. Smith. 1986. *Beliefs About Inequality: Americans' Views of What Is and What Ought to Be*. New York: Aldine De Gruyter.

Langford, Tom, and J. Rick Ponting. 1992. 'Canadians' Responses to Aboriginal Issues: The Roles of Prejudice, Perceived Group Conflict, and Economic Conservatism', *Canadian Review of Sociology and Anthropology* 29, 2: 140–66.

LaPrairie, Carol. 1996. *Examining Aboriginal Corrections in Canada*. Ottawa: Supply and Services Canada, Cat. no. JS5–1/14–1996E.

Li, Peter S. 1988. *The Chinese in Canada*. Toronto: Oxford University Press.

———, ed. 1990. *Race and Ethnic Relations in Canada*. Toronto: Oxford University Press.

Lipset, Seymour M., and Earl Raab. 1970. *The Politics of Unreason*. New York: Harper & Row.

Makin, Kirk. 1998. 'Jurors' racial views can be questioned: Bigots must go, Supreme Court says', *Globe and Mail*, 5 June, A1.

Miles, Robert. 1989. *Racism*. London: Routledge.

Miller, J.R. 1996. *Shingwauk's Vision: A History of Native Residential Schools*. Toronto: University of Toronto Press.

Mitchell, Alanna, and Gay Abbate. 1994. 'Crime-race data laden with hazards', *Globe and Mail*, 11 June, A1.

Palmer, Howard, ed. 1973. *Immigration and the Rise of Multiculturalism*. Toronto: Copp Clark.

———. 1982. *Patterns of Prejudice*. Toronto: McClelland & Stewart.

Parkin, Frank. 1979. *Marxism and Class Theory*. London: Tavistock.

Ponting, J. Rick. 1987. *Profiles of Public Opinion Toward Canadian Natives and Native Issues, 1986: Module 3—Knowledge, Perceptions, and Attitudinal Support*. Calgary: University of Calgary Research Unit for Public Policy Studies.

———. 1990. 'Internationalization: Perspectives on an Emerging Direction in Aboriginal Affairs', *Canadian Ethnic Studies* 22, 3: 85–109.

———, ed. 1997. *First Nations in Canada: Perspectives on Opportunity, Empowerment, and Self-Determination*. Whitby, Ont.: McGraw-Hill Ryerson.

——— and Gladys L. Symons. 1997. 'Environmental Politics and the New World Order: Cree Empowerment, La Grande Baleine, and Hydro-Quebec', in Ponting (1997: 206–21).

——— and Richard Wanner. 1983. 'Blacks in Calgary: A Social and Attitudinal Profile', *Canadian Ethnic Studies* 15, 2: 57–76.

Reitz, Jeffrey, and Raymond Breton. 1994. *The Illusion of Difference: Realities of Ethnicity in Canada and the United States.* Toronto: C.D. Howe Institute.

Ross, Rupert. 1992. *Dancing With a Ghost.* Markham, Ont.: Octopus Publishing.

Royal Commission on Aboriginal Peoples (RCAP). 1996. *Report of the Royal Commission on Aboriginal Peoples. Volume 5—Renewal: A Twenty Year Commitment.* Ottawa: Supply and Services Canada.

Satzewich, Vic. 1990. 'The Political Economy of Race and Ethnicity', in Li (1990: 251–68).

———, ed. 1998a. *Racism and Social Inequality in Canada: Concepts, Controversies, and Strategies of Resistance.* Toronto: Thompson Educational Publishing.

———. 1998b. 'Race, Racism, and Racialization: Contested Concepts', in Satzewich (1998a: 25–45).

Sher, Julian. 1983. *White Hoods: Canada's Ku Klux Klan.* Vancouver: New Star Books.

Simmons, Alan. 1998. 'Racism and Immigration Policy', in Satzewich (1998a: 87–114).

Snow, David A., et al. 1986. 'Frame Alignment Processes, Micromobilization, and Movement Participation', *American Sociological Review* 51: 464–81.

Stackhouse, John. 2000. 'Brain dead: Why Canada just doesn't cut it anymore for the world's best and brightest', *Globe and Mail*, 18 Mar.

Stasiulis, Daiva K. 1990. 'Theorizing Connections: Gender, Race, Ethnicity, and Class', in Li (1990: 269–305).

Sunahara, Ann. 1981. *The Politics of Racism: The Uprooting of Japanese Canadians During the Second World War.* Toronto: James Lorimer.

Symons, Gladys. 1997. 'Le contrôle sociale et la construction de l'"Autre": la police dans un quartier multiethnique', in Deirdre Meintel, Victor Piché, Danielle Juteau, and Sylvie Fortin, eds, *Le quartier Côte-des-Neiges à Montréal: Les interfaces de la pluriethnicité.* Paris: l'Harmattan, 173–89.

Vancouver Sun. 1999. 'Racist killers deserve long sentences, judge rules', 18 Nov., A23.

van den Berghe, Pierre. 1967. *Race and Racism.* New York: John Wiley.

Voyageur, Cora J. 1997. 'Employment Equity and Aboriginal People in Canada', Ph.D. dissertation, University of Alberta.

Wagg, Dana. 1991. 'Supremacist Gets 4 Years: "You'll have to pin a medal on me"', *Windspeaker* 9, 3 (26 Apr.): 1.

chapter three

The Growth in Poverty and Social Inequality: Losing Faith in Social Justice

Ann Duffy and Nancy Mandell

Introduction

By the middle of the twentieth century, there was growing optimism in industrialized countries that poverty and social inequality could be simply eradicated. In the postwar boom years, many increasingly affluent families were indulging in the burgeoning consumer market, the children of working-class and immigrant parents were heading off to university, and the social possibilities seemed endless. The media speculated on how we would learn to cope with the leisure and prosperity that promised to be our destiny. The second half of the twentieth century saw much of this promise falter. Despite the 'wars on poverty' launched in the 1960s by both Canada and the United States, as the new century dawns the prospect of prosperity for all seems increasingly a fool's dream (Davies, 1997). Canadian society remains marred by growing homelessness, increasing numbers of poor children, and entrenched social inequities. Rather than historical anachronisms, poverty and inequality have become centrepieces of social research and social activism and seem destined to be foundational to the history of the twenty-first century.

The Dimensions of Poverty

Few Canadians are completely untouched by poverty. Many of us, or our parents, grandparents, or great-grandparents, immigrated to North America because of the hunger, want, and economic marginalization in our countries of origin. Our family values are rooted in this knowledge and fear of impoverishment—'a penny saved is a penny earned'; 'waste not, want not'. For many of us, poverty is also a personal experience. As children, as single parents, as female heads of households, as Native Canadians, as immigrants, as disabled, as minimum-wage workers, and as elderly women and men, we experience first-hand the realities of living with too little money, too little food, clothing, and shelter, and too little hope.

The statistics bear testimony to the many Canadians living through poverty at some point in their lives. About one Canadian in six, one child[1] in five, almost 60 per cent of female single parents, almost one-half of unattached elderly women, more than one-quarter of the disabled, and almost one in seven Canadian families are currently 'poor'[2] (National Council of Welfare, 1999a; Ross et al., 1994). In the course of their working lives, about one in three Canadians will be poor at some point (Economic Council of Canada, 1992: vii). Even the efforts to combat poverty speak to its onerous dimensions. Toronto food banks operate the largest food drives in all of North America. In 1997, 12 million pounds of food were distributed. Each month in Metropolitan Toronto alone 125,000 people turn to food banks (Freid, 1998). By the late 1990s, the amount of money needed to lift poor Canadians out of their poverty had reached $18.6 billion (National Council of Welfare, 1999a).

As plants close and governments cut spending, it seems likely that, on a personal and societal level, poverty will continue to be a key issue for the foreseeable future. Indeed, many researchers fear that poverty rates will worsen under the continuing impact of international economic restructuring (Economic Council of Canada, 1992; Hurtig, 1999). The prediction, for example, that many graduates from community colleges and universities will face primarily peripheral, low-pay, dead-end jobs in the new service economy has been all too frequently accurate (Marquardt, 1998). Unemployment and underemployment are translating into poverty or near poverty for many. Further, this economic malaise is only part of the picture. Alarmingly, for the first time in the twentieth century, poverty rates continued to increase in the late 1990s despite an upturn in the economy (National Council of Welfare, 1998b: 10). Many fear the emergence of an increasingly embedded and intractable polarization of inequalities. The net result may be a country more and more firmly divided between the haves and have-nots.

Evidence continues to suggest that the gap between the rich and non-rich[3] in Canada is both significant and widening. In 1973, according to the Centre for Social Justice, the wealthiest 10 per cent (decile) of the Canadian population earned 21 times more than the poorest 10 per cent. By 1996, they were earning 314 times more (Carey, 1998b). Other research indicates that the average earned income of the wealthiest 10 per cent of Canadian families increased from $122,000 in 1981 to $138,000 in 1996, while the earned incomes of the poorest 10 per cent of families remained relatively unchanged (Federal, Provincial, and Territorial Advisory Committee, 1999: 49). Even conservative analyses from Statistics Canada indicate that the bottom one-third (30 per cent) of the population earns only about 10 per cent of aggregate income in Canada, while the top third earns more than half (56 per cent). Further, between 1970 and 1995, the richest 10 per cent of income-earners increased their income by $4,200; over the same period, those in the middle and bottom lost ground. In total, the bottom 70 per cent of Canadian income-earners lost about $8 billion, which the top 30 per cent gained. Particularly hard hit were female lone-parent families, which increased from 25 to 40 per cent of the poorest decile of income-earners and young[4] families whose 'real' income actually declined between 1970 and 1995 (Rashid, 1999, 1998; see also Zyblock and Lin, 1997).

Significantly, this transfer of national wealth occurred despite the efforts of both governments and individuals to counter the growing inequality. During this period, families engaged in a variety of efforts to increase their income and decrease their expenditures. Notably, multiple-earner families, particularly dual-earner families, became the norm as increasing numbers of wives, mothers, and youth took paid employment, and at the same time families typically decreased their numbers of dependent children. Further, government interceded with dramatic increases in transfer payments (welfare, disability payments, old age pensions). Between 1970 and 1995, transfer payments went from 8.7 per cent of total family incomes to 20.0 per cent. Taken together, transfer payments and personal income taxes effected a redistribution of wealth so that the bottom 50 per cent of the population increased their income share from 18 per cent of total aggregate to 29.2 per cent (Rashid, 1999).[5] However, these efforts were only able to respond partially to the polarizations in income trends. Between 1993 and 1996, for example, the average Canadian chief executive officer saw his/her salary increase by 39 per cent while the average worker's wages increased by 2 per cent or less[6] (Carey, 1998b; see also Wright, 1998).

Of course, this is not a situation peculiar to Canada. Indeed, the economic polarization is most acute in the United States, where the top 1 per cent of the population owns 42 per cent of the national wealth (up 100 per cent since 1970 and the highest rate since 1929).[7] Predictably, social-economic inequalities are growing in this context. In 1983 median US white families were 11 times wealthier than their black and Hispanic counterparts; by 1995 this had increased to 20 times wealthier. Further, globally it appears that the rich are getting richer (and, by implication, the poor are losing ground). According to the 1998 *World Wealth Report* by Merrill Lynch, 'high net worth individuals' around the world (individuals with investable assets of more than US $1 million), from 1996 to 1997, had increased their global net worth by 5 per cent, to $17.4 trillion. The report predicted that the global rich would increase their wealth by 10 per cent annually to the year 2000, at which point they would hold $23.1 trillion (*Toronto Star*, 1998a).

While the rich become richer, critics argue that our traditional social assistance programs are now being gutted to respond to the 'deficit crisis'. Deficit-minded provincial and federal governments are in no way inclined to respond with significant new strategies or monies. Indeed, a United Nations report in 1998 castigated Canada for its poor response, relative to other comparable countries, in responding to human poverty. Out of 17 industrialized countries, Canada placed tenth in terms of the 'human poverty index'. Sweden, the Netherlands, Germany, Norway, Italy, Finland, France, Japan, and Denmark all do a 'better job of spreading around the wealth', of reducing social inequality and avoiding the enormous social costs of widespread impoverishment (*Toronto Star*, 1998b). Sweden, for example, while far from perfect, is not plagued by extreme poverty or homelessness and only one child in 20 is poor (see, e.g., Rosenthal, 1990).

The successes in other countries underscore the fact that poverty is not an intractable social problem.[8] It is not necessarily the case that 'the poor are always with us.' Tackling poverty in Canada requires a realization that it is woven through Canadian history and rooted in our social and economic order. It also means breaking through us-them notions of the poor and understanding who the poor are. This means abandoning our comfortable beliefs that 'they' are poor because they are lazy, uneducated, unintelligent, or, at least, different from 'us'. Almost all of us—by being born into the 'wrong' family, by living in the 'wrong' region, by becoming parents, by getting divorced, by being immigrants, by being disabled, by being laid off or unable to find a job, or, simply, by growing old—are at risk of being poor. Indeed, given that the principal reasons individuals end up on social assistance are lack of work (45 per cent of cases), disability (27 per cent), and being a single parent (14 per cent), few individuals are completely exempt from the possibility of poverty (National Council of Welfare, 1998c: 15).

Clearly, as individuals and as a society, we need to understand how poverty is changing and what the current hot spots are. Further, we need to know what poverty means both to the individual and to our society. Finally, armed with this understanding of the issue, we need to consider critically our policy responses to poverty. If our future, not only as a nation but as individuals, is not to be impoverished by social inequality and social unrest, we must commit ourselves to solving poverty.

The Roots of Poverty

> The beggar and the tramp are becoming only too familiar to Toronto streets, the girl mendicant and the girl outcast are in our midst, and the question of organizing, or rather of controlling the regulation of our public charities, is only too pressing. (Mulvany, 1884: 62)

Poverty is not a new problem. It has been a persistent feature of Canadian life. In the years prior to 1800, when a pre-industrial economy predominated, the poor were mostly rural. The majority of Canadians lived on farms and engaged in agriculture, fishing, lumbering, and the fur trade. Cities like Toronto, Montreal, and Quebec, while primarily administrative and commercial centres, did have craftsmen with shops in their houses. The pre-industrial economy was relatively small-scale, labour-intensive, and domestically focused (Gaffield, 1984).

While daily life focused on the land, production was based in households. Age and gender roles were fixed by custom and no one lacked useful work. However, many early inhabitants struggled to make a living and were required to survive on relatively little. Harsh winter conditions, problems of new settlements, infectious diseases, prairie droughts, disabilities, infirmities, widowhood, and, for the lucky few, old age all conspired to keep the majority of settlers in the seventeenth and eighteenth centuries battling daily with hunger and want. Poverty, in the sense of not having 'enough' and being forced to do without, was seen as a natural condition, affecting almost everyone at some time during life. As it was thought to arise inevitably from environmental conditions, misfortune, or character defects, poverty was generally accepted.

By the 1850s, industrialization produced profound social and economic trans-formations in Canada. The steady shift in the workforce from farmers and inde-pendent craftsmen towards wage labourers in the emerging industrial economy restructured community relations and the meaning of work. The reorganization of economic life eroded the status and power of independent journeymen and arti-sans. Rather than remaining as independent craftsmen who owned their own raw materials and tools and sold their products directly, they increasingly became wage labourers. Work came to mean employment for wages.

Wage labour introduced a new set of work problems. As paid employees, workers tended to lose the flexibility that marked artisanal manufacture and they lost any skill monopoly they may have enjoyed. While skilled workers were able to form workers' organizations to protect somewhat their privileged position, the large numbers of unskilled workers were increasingly compelled to accept what-ever work and wages employers offered. From the employers' perspective, prof-itability depended on decreasing costs, which meant keeping wages as low as possible. In short, industrialization worked to create a class of highly mobile employees subject to irregular, seasonal, dangerous, unhealthy, and usually poorly paid work. The resultant 'reserve army of labour' provided a much needed pool of cheap, flexible workers to be called on by employers during periods of economic expansion and pushed aside during periods of recession or depression.

Not surprisingly, this highly volatile and competitive economic situation, rela-tively unfettered by laws and policies to protect and assist the weakest members of society, tended to produce patterns of widespread urban poverty. Tenacious poverty, which grew along with industrialization, became a constant feature of working-class industrial life. By the mid-1800s slums, shantytowns, and slabtowns (built from discarded lumber) were to be found in Hamilton, Toronto, Montreal, and other urban centres. Here, newly arrived immigrants, many from famine-stricken Ireland, and the urban poor scraped by in conditions of extreme impoverishment (Duncan, 1974). By the late nineteenth century in Canada's largest city, Montreal, the *typical* family was living in a small, cold-water flat in a densely populated urban area. The family's bare subsistence depended on the husband working 60 hours a week, 52 weeks a year. But winter usually brought shortened hours or layoffs and the family had to rely on the wife earning wages at whatever jobs were available and the children working from the earliest possible age (Copp, 1974: 29). In this manner, families struggled along until illness, accident, disability, death, or recession pushed them into destitution.

The rate of poverty in the country was reflected in high disease and death rates. For example, in the 1890s Montreal enjoyed the dismal distinction of having the highest infant death rate in the industrialized world. Inadequate housing and unsanitary conditions (unsafe water, communal taps, outhouses, poor ventilation and heating, inadequate or non-existent health care) translated into illness and death. Between 1899 and 1901 a staggering 27 per cent of all newborns in Montreal died before they reached one year of age, an infant death rate topped only by Calcutta (ibid., 25–6). Predictably, most of this toll of disease and death was extracted from the poorer wards in the city (Bradbury, 1982: 112), and children who did survive often could not be cared for by their parents. Reflecting the dire poverty of their families, tens of thousands of children were turned over to orphanages, apprenticed out as servants, placed as factory workers, or left to the streets (ibid.; Houston, 1982).

Then, as now, Canadian poverty resulted not from a lack of national wealth but from its unequal distribution (Ross et al., 1994: 1). In many respects, this pattern of systemic poverty resulted from the very nature of capitalist development. A primary feature of capitalism is its inclination to depress wages and benefits (thereby reducing costs) and to pour resulting profits into ever-expanding and more competitive business ventures. Capitalist economists encourage the resultant élite concentration of wealth by arguing that such an accumulation produces a 'trickle-down' effect for the rest of the population, raising the living standards for everyone in the process. This notion remains contentious since for over 100 years most Canadian wage labourers have rarely received a 'family wage', that is, an income sufficient to support the worker, his spouse, and dependent children. As a result, many working-class women and children from the nineteenth century to the present have had to supplement the uncertain and/or insufficient wages of men, especially those in poorly paid, unskilled work. By taking in boarders, laundry, and sewing, by working as servants and apprentices, and, today, by working at fast-food outlets and convenience stores and by taking part-time or seasonal work, women and youth struggle to maintain a stable and acceptable standard of living (Katz, 1975; Rashid, 1989). As recently as 1965, John Porter revealed that only about 10 per cent of Canadian families could actually afford the middle-class lifestyle then considered average (Nett, 1990: 55; see also Coulter, 1982: 149).

Historically, female and visible-minority wage labourers have received even lower wages than male labourers. Since 1900, two types of industrial jobs have emerged: (1) capital-intensive jobs—those requiring a stable workforce, skilled and experienced with expensive machinery; and (2) labour-intensive jobs—those demanding less skill, involving less investment in machinery, and filled by low-paid, easily trained, and disposable employees. This second group of jobs has tended to be filled by women, the young, minority groups, and immigrants.

Even these low wages have often been unreliable. Irregular, seasonal, and unsteady employment has frequently characterized working-class experience. In the early years of industrialization, much unskilled labour took place outdoors—unloading ships, building railroads, digging canals, constructing offices, harvesting crops. Irregular work was common and relief rolls always grew in the winter months. At the same time, capitalist development was also characterized by an unpredictable boom-and-bust cycle that left masses of workers stranded during recurring periods of economic depression. Despite the persistent myth that there is always work for any able-bodied person who really wants a job, work was no more universally available in the 1800s than it is today (Katz, 1986: 6).

In addition, the often dangerous working conditions, unstable and unhealthy diets, inadequate medical care, and poor sanitary conditions in which employees lived day and night escalated their rates of illness, morbidity, and mortality. Unable to save money from the low and irregular wages and without a social welfare net, a male wage labourer who became ill or was injured on the job often plunged the family into dire poverty. Similarly, desertion, widowhood, and old age quickly depleted family resources and often forced families headed by women to seek relief from charitable organizations (which had been organized and funded by religious groups and the well-to-do). Without savings, pensions, social security, or social assistance, and with few real employment opportunities for women, single and widowed women were particularly likely to be left permanently destitute (Bradbury, 1991: 113).

Further, as capitalism developed it was associated with an 'ever-accelerating pace of technological change' (Hale, 1990: 231–4). The competition for profits translated into competition for a competitive edge, which in turn led to continual, escalating technological improvements. Throughout the nineteenth and twentieth centuries, mechanization and technological innovation transformed work and production. In the process, hundreds of thousands of workers were displaced and dislocated. For example, in the 1880s Montreal's independent hand laundresses found themselves displaced by steam laundries. Messenger boys were displaced by telephones. Today, as the pace of technological change quickens, word processors, fax machines, and electronic mail are transforming office work while robotics transforms heavy industry (Pfeiffer, 1999).

From the past to the present, the structure of our economy and its patterns of prosperity, recession, and depression have functioned to generate social inequality. While the life conditions of the less advantaged improved over time, they never kept pace with the dramatic improvements in quality of life experienced by the well-to-do. In particular, inadequate public responses to poverty failed to challenge patterned inequities. The colonial welfare system was based on the Elizabethan Poor Laws (established in England in 1601), which enshrined the notion that while the poor were a public responsibility, this responsibility should be discharged by local communities, and, wherever possible, family and kin must take responsibility for their poor relatives. The principal victims of poverty—the 'deserving poor'—were seen to be the children of the poor; poor adults—the 'undeserving poor'—were often felt to owe their impoverishment to immorality and sloth. These punitive notions underlay the delivery of relief to Canadian poor from the 1600s to the mid-twentieth century (Guest, 1980). Local communities established poorhouses to shelter the poor and indigent. In return, much like indentured servants, children and adults alike were expected to work for their keep. For example, the Nova Scotia Orphan House, opened in 1752, contracted out orphan children to work for adults requiring labourers. In other locales, such as Prince Edward Island, no provision was made for the poor, who were expected to rely instead on private and religious charities (Rooke and Schnell, 1982).

Until the mid-1850s the poor, along with other societal 'deviants', were cared for in a haphazard, local manner under the auspices of religious institutions. Most jurisdictions relied on a mixture of private and public charity. Newfoundland, for example, by 1861 had a provincial poorhouse, the Catholic St Vincent de Paul Society, an Irish Benevolent Society, St John's Dorcas Society, and the Society for Improving the Condition of the Poor (ibid.). Since attitudes towards the poor were, at best, ambivalent, poor relief often seemed aimed more at punishing than helping the poor. Certainly, despite any notions of Christian charity, there was no free ride for the poor, who were often expected to pay back whatever meagre assistance they received.

Not uncommonly, the poor were forced to choose between either outdoor relief or being auctioned off as labourers to local farmers (Katz, 1986: 10). In 1851 in Dalhousie and Perot in the Maritimes, all paupers, including children, were advertised in local papers for public auction to the lowest bidder. In return for room and board, the successful bidder would receive five to 12 months of service, unsupervised by the local authorities and with only a verbal agreement to treat his or her 'employees' fairly and reasonably (Rooke and Schnell, 1982).

As capitalism developed and urbanization, industrialization, and immigration swelled the ranks of the urban poor, it became clear that a more systematic and efficient system of dealing with the poor was needed. Increasing efforts were made to remove the abysmally poor (along with other 'deviants') as potential contaminants from society. This pattern of institutionalization was often combined with increasing discrimination. During periods of unemployment, bereavement, or misfortune, children of the 'worthy poor' were housed in fee-paying orphanages where their parent(s) paid a nominal monthly fee for their care. Children of 'unworthy' parents (such as women defined as prostitutes) who were unable to pay the monthly fee were placed instead in public orphanages where they became wards of the orphanages. Unworthy parents lost any rights over their children's treatment or 'binding out' as cheap farm labour (ibid.). Distinguishing among the poor, as well as the resultant provision of specialized institutions to respond to mental illness, juvenile delinquency, the blind, deaf, and dumb, crime, and pauperism, was given an enormous boost by the new social sciences. By the nineteenth century the American federal census distinguished seven types of morally, socially, and physically inferior people, who together 'constituted a "morphology of evil", a malignant growth, spread of defective types of humanity, threatening to overwhelm the social body': the blind, insane, prisoners, deaf-mutes, idiots, paupers, and homeless children (Katz, 1983: 134). The line between 'us' and 'them' was not only physically maintained by the institutional segregation of the indigent, it was also acquiring scientific legitimacy.

This belief that the poor were biological degenerates who were flooding the world with children often led to efforts to sterilize the 'undesirables'. There was an often stated concern that since the 'poor get children', soon the superior classes—white, financially secure, and well-educated families—would be overwhelmed by their inferiors. Not surprisingly, this belief supported the popular eugenics movements of the early 1900s, which sought to restrict the procreation of undesirables. The Alberta Sexual Sterilization Act, for example, targeted in particular the poor, women, and minorities for forced sterilization. These efforts to restrict the growth of undesirable populations would reach their apogee in Nazi Germany.

The social climate was, of course, not completely bleak. Certainly many of the social activists, social reformers, social scientists, and settlement and charity workers who emerged in the late 1800s and early 1900s promoted a more enlightened and sympathetic approach to the problems of social inequality. Increasingly, religious and private involvement gave way to a centralized state-run system of social assistance. Recurring economic downturns, persistent and extensive unemployment, and, in particular, the Great Depression of the 1930s underscored the need for a more extensive social net if extreme social inequalities and attendant social unrest were to be avoided. As new legislation such as workmen's compensation (Quebec, 1909), mothers' allowance (British Columbia, 1920), old age pensions (1927), pensions for the blind (1937), unemployment insurance (1940), Family Allowances (1944), allowances for the disabled (1954), and medical care (1966) was gradually introduced, more and more individuals were covered by the social assistance umbrella and the old 'charity' and 'punishment' approaches were gradually eroded (Guest, 1980). Social assistance was seen, increasingly, as an entitlement (Katz, 1983: 228; Pupo, 1988).

Inevitably, as coverage expanded, a massive social welfare bureaucracy at the federal and provincial levels grew to administer the new social support net. In 1866 total public welfare expenditures amounted to only $500,000 (3.2 per cent of all government expenditures). By 1939 Canadian governments were spending $317.2 million on public welfare, or 27.1 per cent of all government expenditures (Guest, 1980: 102). By the mid-1980s, Health and Welfare Canada spent $29 billion annually on transfers to provincial health services, the Canada Assistance Plan (welfare), Family Allowances, Old Age Security, and Guaranteed Income Supplements[9] (Waddell, 1989: D1). It was, of course, precisely these burgeoning expenditures that spurred the federal government to reduce its commitments to the provinces in 1990—the famous 'cap on CAP' that cut federal support under the Canada Assistance Plan to Ontario, Alberta, and British Columbia, followed by the 1995–6 extension of this policy to all the provinces with a freeze on federal support for welfare and social services.

Through the course of our history we have moved from a piecemeal approach to the indigent, which was often reliant on religious institutions for funding and service provision, to an extensive, highly bureaucratized, and costly social welfare system. The progress is evident but also precarious. Today, few Canadians starve; few die of exposure or malnutrition; few ragged children beg in our streets or work in our factories or are warehoused in orphanages. Yet, many would argue that any real solution to poverty has eluded us. The myriad welfare programs have smoothed the harshest edges of Canadian social inequality, have kept the reserve army of labour reasonably healthy and available for work, and have controlled and regulated the poor (Johnson, 1972: 30). Evidence, however, suggests that the core of poverty remains untouched and the political will to seriously challenge poverty seems to be failing.

We live, as analysts point out, in a two-thirds society, where two-thirds (or less) enjoy reasonably secure and prosperous lives while one-third exist precariously on the economic margins. These people—female single parents, unemployed and underemployed youth, children in single-parent homes, the elderly (especially unattached and female), immigrants and visible minorities, Native Canadians, the disabled, unskilled/displaced workers—despite their contributions as parents, workers, and citizens, have been peripheralized by our economy and society. When employed at minimum-wage jobs they become the 'working poor'; when they receive social assistance their impoverishment is assured (and perpetuated) by the low level of benefits. This portion of the population suffers first and longest when-ever the economy experiences a recessionary period; these individuals also often suffer during periods of prosperity as inflation, spiralling housing costs, and so on eat away at any hard-won improvements in their income levels. Despite our progress away from the workhouses and orphanages, we have not been able to shed the fundamental inequalities that have plagued us for generations.

Poverty in Canada Today

This is a rich, rich, rich country. The trouble is, it's too rich at the top and too poor at the bottom. (Senator David Croll in Goar, 1990)

Any discussion of poverty inevitably must confront the contentious issues of defi-nition and measurement. It is easy to see that homeless, starving children in nine-teenth-century Montreal (or modern Somalia) were poor; it is more difficult to identify those contemporary Canadians who have too little to get by and who are unable to participate in any meaningful fashion in the social, political, educational, or spiritual life of the nation.[10] While these individuals are not (necessarily) starv-ing or homeless, they are 'relatively deprived' in the nation and community in which they live. For years, government agencies, social researchers, and advocacy groups have struggled to arrive at meaningful standards of impoverishment—level of family income, costs of housing, food, clothing, fuel, etc.—that distinguish the poor. To date Canada has not arrived at an 'official' definition of poverty and relies, uneasily, on Statistics Canada's low-income cut-offs (LICOs) to identify the poor. This resolution has been far from satisfactory and in recent years the definitional debate has greatly intensified, with, for example, some advocates weighing in with a much more restrictive conception of poverty (Sarlo, 1992; National Council of Welfare, 1999a; *Toronto Star*, 1999; Burman, 1996: 19–23).

In particular, 'a market basket approach' is currently the centre of heated debate. In this approach, analysts determine the necessities the average Canadian family needs for economic and social existence—transportation, shelter, clothing, personal care, household needs, furniture, telephone, reading, recreation, school supplies, and so on. Families unable to afford the market basket are considered 'poor'. The net result has been a much more conservative approach to poverty. For example, the poverty line according to the market basket measure (1997) for a family of four in a large city is $25,647, in contrast to the low-income cut-off of

$32,377 (pre-tax) (National Council of Welfare, 1999a: 5). Critics argue that the market basket approach is just as arbitrary and clumsy as the LICOs. For example, in some versions of the market basket approach, tea, coffee, eyeglasses, and dental care are not included on the grounds that the former two are optional and the later two can be obtained through private charities (Crane, 1998; National Council of Welfare, 1999a). Clearly, there are important political implications attached to definitions that produce either a more or less restrictive notion of the numbers of poor (National Council of Welfare, 1998a: 6).

Since any definition of poverty that goes beyond simple physical human survival is relative, defining poverty always involves drawing a somewhat arbitrary line below which live the 'poor'. As a result, definitions of poverty are always subject to political pressures and agendas. A stricter definition may, at the stroke of a pen, dramatically reduce the numbers of poor (and, of course, vice versa). For governments seeking to respond painlessly (and inexpensively) to pressures for social reform, this is always and everywhere a tempting alternative.[11]

In the midst of these definitional debates, the best-known and most widely used measure continues to be the Statistics Canada definition (adopted in 1973; reset in 1992) that establishes income cut-offs below which people are considered to live in 'straitened circumstances'.[12] The cut-offs are based on the notion that poor families are those whose size of income requires them to spend more than 54.7 per cent of their gross income on food, clothing, and shelter, leaving few or no funds for transportation, health, personal care, education, household operation, recreation, or insurance. These income cut-offs vary in terms of the size of the household and the size of the area of residence (more than 500,000, 100,000–499,999, and so on), resulting in 35 separate low-income cut-offs. For example, a single person living in Regina in 1998 on less than $14,468 was considered 'poor' by the Statistics Canada definition (1986 base), while a two-person family living on less than $15,202 in a rural area was deemed poor (National Council of Welfare, 1999a: 109).

While the Statistics Canada parameters provide us with a revealing portrayal of poverty in Canada, this portrait has serious limitations. It leaves out all Natives living on reserves, institutional inmates, residents of Yukon, the Northwest Territories, and Nunavut, and the homeless. It tells us nothing about the duration of poverty, that is, how long any one individual is poor. There is also considerable debate about the locational adjustments. According to Statistics Canada calculations, it is 31 per cent less expensive to live in rural areas. While research does suggest that shelter costs are lower than in the city, transportation costs are, in fact, higher. Further, access to subsidized public services such as child care, health services, and education, as well as to competitively priced goods, is likely restricted in many rural areas. The Canadian Council on Social Development, for example, calculates that rural costs are probably about 88 per cent of those in large urban centres, but also points out that there are considerable differences between cities. In short, locational adjustments are likely both inaccurate and imprecise. Others argue that with the large tax bite, income cut-offs should be based on after-tax income.[13] In addition, the measures ignore differences in the actual level of need in the household. For example, severe disability and lack of access to subsidized services may significantly increase household economic needs (Ross et al., 1994: 26–31).

Finally, there are general problems attached to the Statistics Canada measures of poverty. Like many measures, they reinforce the notion that there are two kinds of people: the poor and the non-poor. This is a split that is too easily translated into 'us' and 'them' and sustains stereotypes of the poor as somehow different and, possibly, defective. In fact, poverty is a very porous identity.[14] Within the course of a year or two, low-income Canadians may drift in and out of 'official' poverty. Recent research examining low-income patterns between 1982 and 1993 found that most people had only one spell of low income within this time period and it lasted on average two years. Indeed, the chances of a period of low income ending after one year were better than 50 per cent and for the clear majority of individuals (60 per cent) a period of low income was a temporary setback, not a chronic and persistent problem (Laroche, 1998). Unemployment, illness, accident, or disability may, even in the course of a month, tip the balance. Similarly, in the course of a lifetime, an interplay of key factors (notably, gender, age, marital status, and number of children) may trigger a slide into low income and poverty. Given these patterns, the problem of poverty needs to be understood as encompassing a broad continuum of individuals and families both below and above the designated 'poverty line'.[15]

Further, the poor are far from a homogeneous group. For example, the sources of income for the poor vary considerably. Many are 'welfare poor' because the social assistance they receive is below the low-income cut-offs. In 1998, basic welfare assistance for a single parent with one child ranged from $11,300 in Saskatchewan to $13,695 in Ontario, but in each instance this benefit would place the individual well below the Statistics Canada low-income cut-offs (National Council of Welfare, 1999–2000: 40–1). In British Columbia (1998), for example, total welfare income provided only 38 per cent of the poverty-line income for a single employable individual and 61 per cent for a single parent with one child (ibid., 41). Being reliant on welfare for economic survival means living in poverty.

Many poor Canadians are termed 'the working poor' because, although they have paid employment, their earnings from work are below the low-income cut-offs. Of 1,108,000 poor heads of families under age 65 in 1997, 21 per cent were employed full-time and 35 per cent were employed part-time—leaving 36 per cent who did not work and 8 per cent who were unable to work (National Council of Welfare, 1999a: 86). Paid employment is no guarantee that poverty will be avoided. When the worker is a single parent, when only one parent in the family is employed, when the work is part-time, contract, short-term, irregular, low-wage, unskilled (young, immigrant, and/or poorly educated workers), and when there are dependent children in the home, employment frequently fails to provide an escape from poverty (Kazemipur and Halli, 2000; Ross et al., 1994: 76–9; Gunderson et al., 1990: 68–71).

Taken as a whole the portrait of poverty in Canada today is sobering. In 1997, 5.1 million Canadians—17.2 per cent of children, women, and men in Canada— were poor. Among unattached individuals,[16] 36.3 per cent (1,496,000 Canadians) lived below the low-income cut-offs; among families, 14.3 per cent (1,203,000 families) did so (National Council of Welfare, 1999a). Predictably, these poverty rates are patterned by a variety of social factors. For example, there is a distinct regional dimension to Canadian poverty. In 1997, only 12.9 per cent of Alberta families were poor, while poverty was a fact of life for 18.9 per cent of Newfound-land families. Youth is also a critical determinant of poverty rates. One in three (34 per cent) families (couples with children) headed by young people (under 25 years of age) is poor. Families and individuals with low levels of education[17] are more likely to be poor, as are families with only one wage-earner. Not surprisingly, participation in the paid labour force is directly related to poverty rates, with 'a good job [being] the best insurance against poverty for Canadians under the age of 65' (ibid.; Lawton, 1998). Finally, as discussed in more detail below, a complex intersection of factors such as gender, age, family structure and composition, race, ethnicity, and current social policies conditions poverty rates (Kazemipur and Halli, 2000; National Council of Welfare, 1999a; Ross et al., 1994).

The Feminization of Poverty

Canadian women are particularly at risk of being poor. This 'feminization of poverty' refers to the fact that women in many industrialized Western nations, as well as in developing countries, are more likely to be poor than men (Pearce, 1978; Goldberg, 1990). Though Canadian women continue to be better off than their American counterparts (as a result of lower rates of single parenthood and more expansive social policies), the poverty rate for women (1997) was 18.3 per cent and for men 14.3 per cent. As a result, women comprise 57 per cent of Canadian adults who are poor (National Council of Welfare, 1999a: 99). Further, at every age level adult women have higher poverty rates than men (National Council of Welfare, 1998a: 85, 36, 19). Nor is this a new problem; the ranks of the poor have long been populated by women who were deserted, widowed, or orphaned (Katz, 1975: 60; Simmons, 1986). Evidence suggests, too, that women figure among the poorest of the poor. For example, until recently the largest poverty gap for poor families (how far below the poverty line an individual or family lives) was found among female-headed single-parent families (under 65 with children under 18) (National Coun-cil of Welfare, 1998a: 53, 60; 1998b: 12). Their situation improved marginally in 1997, when couples under 65 with children under 18 averaged $9,822 below the poverty line and headed the list of the poorest of the poor, followed closely by single-parent mothers at $9,337 below the poverty cut-off (National Council of Welfare, 1999a).

While the reasons behind women's impoverishment are complex they have much to do with traditional gender ideologies, inequities in the labour force, and flaws in our family law and responses to marriage breakdown. For generations, women have been expected to devote their lives to their unpaid duties in marriage and motherhood. Although many wives and mothers also worked for pay, this was generally seen as undesirable. Lower pay rates for women, rules against the employment of married women, and the peripheralization and stigmatization of 'women's work' all reinforced the notion that women's place was in the home (Duffy and Pupo, 1992: 13–40).

Throughout the twentieth century, however, these notions came under increasing attack. The first and second waves of the women's movement, advanced education for women, and the reduction in family size, among other factors, undermined the traditional sexual division of labour. In particular, increasing numbers of Canadians have found that they simply cannot survive on the uncertain income of a single male (or female) breadwinner. The failure of wages to keep pace with inflation, increases in taxation, high rates of unemployment, and the loss of high-paying industrial and resource-extraction jobs have made the male-breadwinner family increasingly anachronistic. In 1997, 66 per cent of married women with children under age 16 and 59 per cent of women with children under age three were employed (National Council of Welfare, 1999b: 12). Indeed, the poverty rate among husband–wife families would double (to 22.1 per cent of Canadian families) if these wives and mothers were not in the paid labour force (National Council of Welfare, 1999a: 100).

While much has changed, much remains the same. Women are still encouraged to focus their energies on marriage and motherhood; women's employment is still less well paid than men's, with full-time women workers earning about 73 per cent of male wages; patterns of sexual and gender harassment continue to maintain female job ghettos (Statistics Canada, 1999: 27). Women are still occupationally segregated into work with lower wages, less prestige, and less opportunity for advancement (Statistics Canada, 1998: 53). These employment inequities are likely to be further exacerbated if a woman is a recent immigrant or disabled or a member of a visible minority. For example, only 58 per cent of recent immigrant women aged 25–44 and holding a university degree were employed in 1996, in contrast to 86 per cent of comparable non-immigrant women (Badets and Howatson-Leo, 1999: 17). Similarly, the poverty rate for disabled women over 15 years of age is 29.5 per cent (Ross et al., 1994: 41). In short, a variety of factors intersect in a complex manner to compound some women's vulnerability to impoverishment.

Finally, almost all women, regardless of race, ethnicity, or disability, are still considered responsible for most child care, family caregiving, and housework. In the absence of adequate child-care and parental leave policies, juggling the conflicting demands of child care, housework, and paid work often means costly interruptions in labour force participation and/or peripheral employment as a part-time, casual, or contract employee (Marshall, 1993; Fast and Da Pont, 1997). Being employed in 'women's work' or taking several years off to care for young children can translate into disaster when marriages end in divorce, when women face long years of widowhood, or when women become single parents.

Single parenthood, typically the result of divorce, can have devastating effects on women's economic well-being. An astounding 57.1 per cent of single-parent mothers are poor (1997), in contrast to a poverty rate of 11.9 per cent for couples with children (National Council of Welfare, 1999a). Without a male breadwinner in the family and with inadequate or non-existent support payments, many women cannot provide sufficient income for their families. For example, research on low-income patterns between 1982 and 1993 found that lone-parent women were particularly susceptible to long-term impoverishment, often spending between 5.1 and 6.9 years out of 10 in low income in contrast to the average of two years (Laroche, 1998). Further, as noted above, they are likely to sink deep into poverty.

Single parenting is a particularly potent combination when combined with youthfulness or young children. Single-parent mothers under age 25 have a staggering poverty rate of 93.3 per cent and single-parent mothers with children under age seven have rates as high as 80.2 per cent (National Council of Welfare, 1999a). However, contrary to powerful stereotypes, single mothers are not primarily teenagers having numerous babies so they can live off welfare payments. Teenage mothers comprise only 3 per cent of all single parents on welfare and almost half (49 per cent) of single mothers have only one child and another one-third (31 per cent) have only two children (National Council of Welfare, 1998c: 33).

For many of these women, low income is a direct consequence of marriage breakup. The Economic Council of Canada's five-year survey of Canadian incomes found women's incomes (adjusted for family size) dropped by about 39 per cent when they separated or divorced and thereafter rose only slightly. Three years after the marriage breakup, women's incomes were still 27 per cent below their earlier level. Men's income (adjusted for family size), in contrast, increased by an average of 7 per cent. Along with the labour force inequalities discussed above, inadequate support payments produce the inequity. Only 68 per cent of divorces involving dependent children (1989) resulted in a child-support order, and those orders averaged a scant $250 per child per month (Economic Council of Canada, 1992: 49). Further, as repeatedly explored in the media, problems persist in the successful collection of child-support payments from non-custodial parents.

Despite the clear neediness of single mothers, recent social policy initiatives have tended to exacerbate their plight. For example, in Ontario, single welfare mothers of school-age children are required to sign up for workfare,[18] and these mothers, along with other welfare recipients, are now required to get by on substantially lower rates of social assistance. This push to any form of paid employment is often coupled with inadequate child-care provisions. To further compound their plight, single mothers must also confront the persistent tendency to stigmatize mothers on welfare as somehow less worthy of social support than, for example, low-income two-parent families. Popular ideology suggests that single mothers who receive social assistance are simply being encouraged to have more children[19] and these children are perceived as growing up troubled and disruptive.

Growing old provides little promise of relief to women. While policy initiatives between 1980 and 1996 have successfully eased much of the poverty burden for the elderly, it has by no means eliminated it. Unattached elderly women (65 and over)—typically, those who are widowed, divorced, or separated—face high rates of poverty. In 1997, 42 per cent of unattached women over age 65, compared to 27.2 per cent for unattached elderly men, lived below the low-income cut-offs.[20] Another 25 per cent of unattached older women are only slightly above the poverty line (earning 100 to 125 per cent of the poverty line) (National Council of Welfare, 1999a). Increasing age exacerbates the problem. Unattached women aged 75–9 have a poverty rate of 48 per cent, and the rate rises to 53 per cent for unattached women 85 or older. Women are particularly at risk[21] because they are less likely to receive income from occupational pension plans, the Canada/Quebec Pension Plan, and investments. The traditional patterns of women's lives, with work interruptions to take care of family responsibilities, work in low-paying, poorly benefited jobs, and high rates of part-time and contractual work, contribute to high rates of female impoverishment whenever women find themselves without a spouse (McDonald, 1997).

Based on current trends in marriage, divorce, and life expectancy, an estimated 84 per cent of all Canadian women can expect to spend some portion of their adult lives without a male breadwinner in the home—as pregnant teens, single mothers, divorced middle-aged workers, and/or elderly widows (National Council of Welfare, 1990: 17). Today, as marriage is increasingly postponed, almost every woman will be self-supporting at some point. Yet, few Canadian women live with these expectations, and fewer still plan their work and marital lives to bring them financial independence and solvency (Duffy et al., 1988). In a society that perpetuates unrealistic notions of romantic love, marital life, and parenting, and in an economy premised on the peripheralized, low-wage, ghettoized work of women, many women continue to be set up for poverty.

Predictably, certain groups of women—immigrant women, the disabled, minority women, and Native Canadians—are at greater risk. Native women, for example, have lower than average labour force participation rates, lower than average earnings, and substantially higher rates of unemployment, partly because of the remote, rural areas in which many live (Federal, Provincial, and Territorial Advisory Committee, 1999: 47; Abella, 1984). Visible-minority and immigrant women frequently find that racial and ethnic discrimination, along with language difficulties and inadequate government policy, translate into long hours of low-wage work (Kazemipur and Halli, 2000; National Council of Welfare, 1990: 118–27). Foreign-born elderly women, in all marital categories, have lower average incomes than their Canadian-born counterparts. Elderly women who are recent immigrants and/or who come from less-developed countries receive particularly low incomes (Boyd, 1989). Although the majority of disabled adults live on low incomes, disabled women are, generally, worse off than their male counterparts (Ross and Shillington, 1989: 28; Barile, 1992).

The Poverty of Children

Interwoven with the impoverishment of women and families is the poverty of children. More than a million children[22] (or 19.6 per cent of Canadian children in 1997) are growing up poor (Crane, 1999). Young children (aged 0–11 years) have even higher poverty rates, with one-quarter (Ontario) to one-third (Newfoundland) living below the Statistics Canada low-income cut-offs (Cheal et al., 1997). Despite a unanimous vote in the House of Commons in 1989 to eradicate child poverty by the year 2000—the highly publicized Campaign 2000—Canadian child poverty rates grew from 1989 to 1996 and remain high today (National Council of Welfare, 1999a). Indeed, although the number of Canadian children increased by just 6 per cent between 1989 and 1997, the number of 'poor' children rose by 37 per cent, and since the mid-1980s Canadian children have had a consistently higher rate of poverty than adult Canadians under age 65 (Crane, 1999; National Council of Welfare, 1999a). Children constitute more than one-quarter of our poor and the child poverty rate in Canada is, with the exception of the United States, the United Kingdom, and Australia, the highest in the industrialized world (National Council of Welfare, 1999b: 7; Hurtig, 1999: 320).

Simple explanations for the expansion of child poverty, such as the dramatic increase in single-parent families, provide only part of the puzzle. While children in families headed by single mothers have extremely high poverty rates (60.4 per cent in 1997), most (56 per cent) poor children in Canada are growing up in two-parent families (National Council of Welfare, 1999a: 91). These children are poor because their parents are poor and their parents' poverty often stems from unemployment, underemployment, inadequate minimum-wage levels, and reduced social welfare supports (ibid.; Baxter, 1993).[23]

The Changing Face of Poverty

> How is it that, as our country's economy has expanded, as our gross domestic product (GDP) has increased year after year, there have been growing numbers of poor men, women and children in Canada? (Hurtig, 1999: xiii)

Poverty patterns are far from static or monochromatic. Over time there have been important changes in poverty and, depending on where you look in the population and in the country, there are significant variations in the nature of impoverishment.

In the 1960s and early 1970s, there were significant reductions in the rate and depth of poverty (Economic Council of Canada, 1992: 2). Progress slowed during the 1970s, and since 1973 the poverty rate has tended to fluctuate with the health of the economy (Ross and Shillington, 1989: 21; National Council of Welfare, 1988: 1). This is reflected, for example, in the marked decrease in the numbers of Canadians, from all types of families, living on low incomes during the 1970s.

From the early 1980s to 1995, however, there was little evidence of decline in low-income rates and indications of increases of low income among some types of families (Zyblock and Lin, 1997). Most recently, poverty rates have been less inclined to mirror the ups and downs of the economy, suggesting that a more or less permanent underclass is emerging.

Among the general Canadian population, single parents are at a distinct disadvantage in terms of impoverishment, but this is also true for individuals living on their own. Among unattached (unmarried) individuals poverty rates have shown relatively little improvement. From 1980 to 1997, poverty rates for this population fluctuated from 41.4 per cent in 1980 to a low of 34.1 per cent in 1990 and back up to 36.3 per cent in 1997. Further, the depth of poverty experienced by unattached men and women under age 65 has remained alarmingly high from 1980 to the present. In 1997, unattached men and women under age 65 were earning on average only slightly more than half (54 per cent and 55 per cent respectively) of the poverty line. In other words, these individuals were living almost $7,000 below the low-income cut-offs (National Council of Welfare, 1999a).

Similarly, there has been considerable regional variation in poverty rates. Although in the last several decades Ontario and Quebec have fairly consistently held their claims to having, respectively, among the lowest and highest provincial poverty rates, other provinces have been less consistent. Prince Edward Island has moved from above to below the national average in terms of poverty rates, while Alberta and British Columbia's poverty rates moved from below the national average to above or at the national level (ibid.). Amid these changes, poverty has also increasingly become an urban phenomenon.

The Lost Generation: The Poverty of Young Adults

Among the alarming trends has been the growing vulnerability of young adults. Certainly, the appearance of food banks on campuses signalled a dismal deterioration in the lives of many Canadian university and college students (McGrath, 1998). Young people who marry and have dependants are in a particularly difficult economic position. Although in 1997 young families (those headed by someone under age 25) comprised only 4 per cent of all Canadian families, they accounted for 11 per cent of poor families, and almost half (42.8 per cent) of young families were low income (Crane, 1999). As high rates of unemployment and underemployment continue to plague young workers, not surprisingly, the rates of poverty grow among families with young parents (under age 35).

From 1973 to 1986 there was also an increase in the number of poor families with two or more earners. This reflects, in part, the failure of real family wages to keep pace with rising costs, along with a failed commitment to maintain an adequate minimum wage. In 1973 minimum-wage legislation meant that someone who worked 40 hours a week over 52 weeks could earn a yearly income 20 per cent over the poverty line. By 1991 the same worker would have to work 50 hours a week for 52 weeks simply to reach the poverty line (Kitchen et al., 1991: 36).

During this same period, education has become less of a barrier to impoverish-ment; by 1997, 7.7 per cent of heads of poor families and 23.4 per cent of poor unattached individuals held a university degree (National Council of Welfare, 1999a). Although these rates are the lowest among all educational categories and confirm the partial protection from poverty provided by higher education, the pattern also indicates that poverty may be 'more a result of lack of job opportuni-ties rather than a lack of education' (National Council of Welfare, 1997: 48; Hurtig, 1999: 133–4).

Homelessness

Another important shift in poverty patterns has been the dramatic emergence of urban homelessness in Canada and other industrialized countries. By the late 1990s, activists and analysts were pointing to homelessness as a 'national disaster' and 'national crisis' (James, 1999). Toronto, 'a magnet for the homeless', provided shelter for an estimated 5,000 homeless each night during the winter of 1998 (Gillespie, 1998). Research on shelter patterns suggests that one-fifth of those using shelter beds are children (under 18 years of age). Shelters and hostels, once consid-ered stop-gap solutions, seemed increasingly entrenched as a long-term response to the homeless. Yet, even as the numbers of shelters and food banks burgeoned, there were not enough available beds or services (Orwen, 1998). Toronto front-line workers estimated that two to four homeless died each week and analysts suggested that, nationally, the number of Canadian homeless was approaching 200,000 (Crowe, 1998).[24]

The Elderly: The Success Story

Despite the unrelenting advance of homelessness in our urban centres, there is nothing immutable or inevitable about poverty. As dramatically evidenced by the fight against poverty among senior Canadians, it is possible to reverse established patterns of income inequality. Policy changes, including the creation of the federal Guaranteed Income Supplement in 1967 for low-income seniors, the creation of the Canada/Quebec Pension Plan in 1966, and the implementation of provincial supplements, have meant that instead of one-third (33.6 per cent) of all seniors being poor (as in 1980), a near-record low of less than one-fifth (17.0 per cent) are now living below low-income cut-offs (1997). Similarly, the poverty rate for poor senior couples went from 22.2 per cent in 1980 to 7.0 per cent in 1997 (National Council of Welfare, 1999a: 19, 20). Although the number of Canadians aged 65 and older has increased from 2.2 million in 1980 to 3.5 million in 1997 (a 59 per cent increase), the number of seniors living in poverty has actually decreased over this time period (ibid.).

The exception to these cheery developments is the continuing plight of unattached (unmarried) seniors. As with other segments of the population, living on one's own leads to higher overall rates of poverty. This is particularly true of

Canadians 65 and older. In 1980, more than two-thirds (68.7 per cent) of unattached women 65 and older and more than half (57.8 per cent) of comparable senior men were living below the low-income cut-offs. Since that time there has been marked improvement. However, much remains to be done—in 1997 almost half of senior unattached women (42 per cent) and more than one in four senior unattached men were poor (ibid., 22).

Struggling with Poverty: The Personal Experience

No part of our lives is untouched. (Women for Economic Survival, 1984: 21)

Being poor has always meant much more than getting by at some arbitrary level of income, and understanding poverty demands more than a statistical overview. Poverty often affects people's lives, their sense of self, and their most important relationships with others. Although the toll of poverty is most apparent in the lives of children, few adults survive impoverishment unscathed (Benner, 1998). For children and their families, poverty still generally translates into inadequate housing. In Calgary, Edmonton, Vancouver, and Toronto, poor children are likely to live with substandard heating, too little hot water, improper ventilation, generally unsafe conditions (exposed wiring and electrical outlets and so on), and too little space in which to play or study (Bragg, 1999). Even inadequate housing in large metropolitan areas may gobble up social assistance benefits, leaving little left over for necessities, let alone for emergencies (Spears, 1999). Housing problems are frequently compounded by neighbourhoods plagued with high rates of crime and vandalism, inadequate play facilities, and/or hazardous traffic conditions (Marsden, 1991: 8; Kitchen et al., 1991: 6). Echoing nineteenth-century Montreal, recent research indicates that New Brunswick children were living in developing world conditions in dwellings with mud floors, leaking roofs, and no running water (Spears, 1991).

Housing problems combine with inadequate nutrition. Poor families often lack the income to maintain a nutritious diet. High housing costs and the spectre of homelessness mean that food budgets are stretched to the limit: 'Juice wars we have at our place. "You can't have that extra glass of juice." They bring somebody in the house and the three of them are having a glass of juice and that's all the juice there is for the rest of the week. And there they are just drinking it down, and you're going, "Oh my God, don't they understand anything?"' (Women for Economic Survival, 1984: 13). While Canada's food banks and soup kitchens provide a stop-gap solution for many families, many poor children clearly get by on too little or low-quality (high fat and sugar content) food (Kitchen et al., 1991: 7).

Predictably, poor housing and inadequate nutrition frequently combine to jeopardize the health of the poor (Hyndman, 1998a). Repeatedly, research has demonstrated a relationship between poverty and poor physical health. For example, surveys report that low-income Canadians are four times more likely to report their health as only fair or poor and two times more likely to have a long-term activity limitation and one-third as likely to have dental insurance (Federal, Provincial, and Territorial Advisory Committee, 1999: 43). While national health care in Canada mitigates some of the worst health consequences, the poor often lack access to many important health services and certainly, contrary to a popular stereotype, do not 'get it all free'. Poor families in Alberta, whether on social assistance or working low-wage jobs, routinely lack access to dental and optical services as well as prescription medication (Williamson and Fast, 1998). Welfare recipients are particularly hard hit. For example, children in Ontario whose parents are on welfare are not covered for root canal procedures. If they need this kind of dental work, their teeth are simply pulled (Hudson, 1999: A1).

Not surprisingly, the poorest of the poor, the homeless, are frequently plagued with physical health problems, including malnourishment, chronic respiratory or ear infections, gastrointestinal disorders, sexually transmitted disease, and chronic infections. Indicative of the health concerns of the homeless, 38 per cent of Toronto homeless screened recently had been exposed to tuberculosis, in contrast to only 10 per cent of the general public. Even a relatively simple medical problem, if left untreated, may inflict misery on the homeless. In a recent report, a Toronto dentist describes referring a homeless man with a severely abscessed tooth who was 'in excruciating pain' and 'hadn't eaten in days' to a hospital emergency department. The next day, the man returned to the drop-in centre, still untreated and 'still an obviously very sick man' (Hudson, 1999: A4).

The psychological health of the poor, in turn, reflects the painful social and emotional environment in which many live.[25] The pressure of poverty contributes to family breakdown and dislocation. Life often becomes unpredictable and insecure. Being poor means not knowing whether you will be able to continue living in your old home, whether you will retain custody of your children, whether your children will have to change schools and make new friends. In these and numerous other ways, the foundations of one's life may be shattered. Living with this profound uncertainty inevitably takes a toll on self-confidence and hopefulness.

Upheaval may permeate family life. Some evidence suggests that poorer families are more subject to family violence, including child abuse and neglect (MacLeod, 1987: 20–1; Gelles and Cornell, 1990: 14–15). Growing up poor often means coping with a parent or parents who are themselves struggling with fear, anger, frustration, isolation, and despair. The emotional and psychological realities of poverty are complex, and reactions to poverty reflect the particular personal circumstances and history of each individual. Many poor adults and children cope with courage, resourcefulness, and a sense of humour, and many poor children grow up with positive adult role models and a strong sense of family loyalty. However, most poor children do not live on Walton Mountain and the adults in their lives are also often deeply troubled by their economic straits. Poverty typically means more than doing without; it means feeling cut off from the mainstream of our consumer society. With a few exceptions, the lives and experiences of the poor are not reflected sympathetically on television or in the movies; the advertisements in magazines and on subway trains simply underscore the insufficiencies of their lifestyle. Life becomes an observer sport: watching other people get new jobs, buy new houses, or take their families to Disneyland. A 50-year-old woman, on her own, who had been looking for work for five months, voiced the alienation felt by so many: 'I need a job. I want to work. I want to be able to pay my bills. I want to be solvent. I want to live!' (Burman, 1988: 54).

Each day small and large events underscore the poor person's marginalization in society. When the school organizes a bike hike, any children without bikes have to sit in the classroom and do worksheets. Frustrated parents see their children left out and humiliated: 'It visually stamps them as poor. You can hide many things, but when visually you're made poor, then something's bloody wrong' (Women for Economic Survival, 1984: 16). A woman buys food with a food voucher at her local grocery store and when change is owed, the cashiers engage in a loud conversation about whether 'you're supposed to give them any money'. Not surprisingly, the woman ends up feeling 'like they were talking about somebody who wasn't a person. I just wanted to tell them to forget about it, keep the damn change' (Carniol, 1987: 90). Day by day and incident by incident, the chasm grows between poverty and 'normal life', leaving poor adults and their children feeling more isolated, stereotyped, and rejected:

> I could read their mind, right, so that I know what they're saying, 'Well he's unemployed, he's getting nowhere', right? Because that's what I'm doing right now, getting nowhere. (Burman, 1988: 204)

> People never really think of what it's like to be poor until they are poor themselves. It's a sad fact but it's true. They have to live it. My husband is not one of those 'welfare bums'. He tries; he tries really hard. (Baxter, 1988: 41)

When people become poor themselves, it comes as a shock that the negative stereotype now applies to them:

> When I went down there, I felt that I just stuck right out. I thought, 'Oh my God, people think I'm on welfare.' Typical stereotype I guess you're led to believe. You used to think, 'It's those people who are on welfare,' and now you discover you're one of those people. (Burman, 1988: 86)

Being one of those people often means living with a stigma. Many poor are ashamed of their identity as poor, seek to hide it whenever possible, and feel there is something 'wrong' with them:

> At the beginning [of being unemployed] I was feeling so good about myself that that was a lot easier. . . . Towards the end I was feeling like such a loser. . . . You portray this, it's written all over your face. (Ibid., 196)

> I need to move to a better place. There are so many losers living around me but being on welfare people think you're a loser anyway. (Baxter, 1988: 165)

Coping with stigmatization may mean being filled with anger at the injustices of a social system that seems to benefit so many other people:

> I walked down the street one day. God, how do people buy their clothes, where are they getting their money, how come they have a job? . . . Like, I just thought SHIT! (Burman, 1988: 203)

For some, when the impoverishment seems to grind on endlessly or when their personal situations deteriorate, anger and frustration give way to despair and depression. A recent national health survey of self-reported levels of self-esteem, sense of mastery, and sense of coherence predictably finds that larger percentages of those occupying the lowest income levels report low levels of all three measures of psychological well-being (Federal, Provincial, and Territorial Advisory Committee, 1999). Not surprisingly, poverty activists report that poor people often talk of periods of hopelessness and of suicidal depression.

Being poor and being on welfare can be a double whammy. Many of the poor, who must rely on social assistance for all or part of their income, report that dealing with the social work apparatus compounds feelings of stigmatization and vulnerability. Even when individual welfare workers are helpful and supportive, the relationship between worker and client is structured to erode the autonomy, power, and privacy of the poor. The negativity of some welfare workers merely exacerbates a bad situation: 'Social assistance is based on the notion that women need help and can't make decisions. The system makes you feel like you failed at your role in life' (Blouin, 1992).

> My worker is very strict. It's like being with my parents when I was younger. The worker controls my life. I hate it. (Ibid.)

> They have a real looking-down-on-you attitude, and my back just gets right up. I don't find them very pleasant people. I keep thinking how people less assertive than me deal with that. I bet there's a lot of people that cry. (Burman, 1988: 85)

Home visits by welfare workers, personal questions from workers, and the constant fear of being 'reported to welfare' for having not followed all the rules tend to undermine clients' sense of personal power and self-confidence:

> I never want to go back on welfare. Self-esteem while you are on welfare is really low. You end up being dependent on somebody you don't want to be dependent on. You don't have any say or any control over your own life. When I was a single parent on welfare and my kids were here, welfare was always checking up on me,

social workers were pulling these short-notice visits, like five minutes notice, to see who was living at my house. (Baxter, 1988: 31)

Problems with the welfare apparatus are further complicated by the negative reactions of the general public to welfare recipients. Commonly, landlords will not rent to individuals on welfare, and women on welfare may find themselves labelled as desperate and available: 'He wants to go to bed with me! I refuse and he says, "You'll be sorry." He figures I'm on welfare, I'm a single parent—I'm fair game' (Carniol, 1987: 86–7). Most commonly, the social assistance recipient has to confront the still popular belief, held by much of the general public as well as many social assistance workers, that people on welfare cheat (Blouin, 1992). Informed by the historical notions that many of the poor are not deserving and/or should be punished for their plight, attitudes towards the provision of adequate social assistance remain ambivalent at best.

As welfare cases soared in the recession of the early 1990s, public preoccupation with welfare fraud intensified. In 1991 the *Toronto Star* ran at least two major stories on welfare cheating, followed in 1992 by a front-page article on welfare abuse. Although a survey of welfare fraud by independent researchers indicated that less than 3 per cent of the welfare caseload involved cheating, prominent members of the community continue to protest that the welfare rules on eligibility are too lax and that penalties for welfare abusers are too lenient (Armstrong, 1992: A18; Sweet, 1991a: B1). The poor, who after all receive welfare benefits that leave them below the low-income cut-offs, must face the knowledge that numerous Canadians (some 20 per cent of whom admit to cheating on their income tax) (McCarthy, 1992) think of them as cheats. Even when the issue of cheating is left aside, many Canadians continue to evidence a harsh and unsympathetic attitude towards welfare recipients (while overlooking government 'handouts' to corporate interests) (Hurtig, 1999). Despite the proliferation of food banks and homeless, a full one-third of the Canadian public think the government spends too much money on welfare, and one-quarter feel that most people on welfare could get along without it if they tried (Sweet, 1991b).

Being poor means living with the knowledge that in many ways one is despised or pitied by our consumer society, or, at best, considered to be irrelevant. Certainly, it typically means living on the far side of an ideological divide in which most non-poor Canadians do not understand or empathize with the day-to-day realities of living in poverty. Not surprisingly, this pattern of social alienation takes a heavy toll on personal and family life:

There are times when I am so scared that I'm not going to find a job, I think, 'What the hell is wrong with me?' I can get scared to death. I'll have periods of insomnia. I'll get very short-tempered with my husband and with the children. (Burman, 1988: 195)

My husband and I are very close. In the past year with the pressure of his job when he suddenly turned 55, he's got very sharp with me. He yelled at me twice and he's never yelled at me in his life. We're fighting for our relationship and we're fighting to survive. What's happening financially can destroy couples that are so close. (Women for Economic Survival, 1984: 14)

If I say 'no' to the children, they feel very depressed when they see other children taking things to school. The children feel very disappointed. They kind of lose love for you. They think that you don't love them. (Ibid., 23)

The children, lacking the life experience and acquired coping skills of adults, are often most deeply wounded by poverty and its personal and familial consequences. Certainly, little is accomplished in terms of ensuring loyalty to social institutions and public values. When the adults in their lives are filled with confusion, frustration, anger, rage, humiliation, and fear, when their lives seem beyond their control and beyond hope, the children grow up truly impoverished.

The burdens placed on many poor children (particularly the poorest of children) serve to perpetuate poverty and economic vulnerability. The fallout often begins before birth with inadequate prenatal nutrition or health care. Poor kids are twice as likely as other kids to suffer low birth weight, death in the first year, death from accidents, poor physical health, physical disabilities, and mental disorders (Reitsma-Street et al., 1993: 7). Predictably, poor children tend not to do as well in school. By age 11, one in three girls from families on social assistance evidences poor school performance (for example, repeating a grade or being placed in a special class). Four of 10 children (aged 12–16) living in subsidized housing have poor school performance (Offord, 1991: 23).[26] Inevitably, children who do not do well in school are more likely to drop out, and dropouts are more likely to come from single-parent, minority group, and/or poorly educated families (Denton and Hunter, 1991: 133). Children from poor families are almost twice as likely to drop out of school as non-poor children. While children of average and low ability from well-to-do families are likely stay in school, even children of high ability from poor families are likely to succumb to the pressures. Without a private place to study, with parents who are preoccupied with their economic plight, and with the ever-apparent need for more family income, students from poor families often see immediate employment as the best option (Kitchen et al., 1991: 10–11).[27] Unfortunately, in the long run their lack of education and skills may simply perpetuate their own and, later, their children's economic and social marginalization.

Addressing Poverty

I believe that poverty in Canada is truly a tragedy and a national disgrace. (Hurtig, 1999: xvi)

Policy initiatives on the national and provincial levels have been the front-line response to poverty. Social welfare provisions, unemployment insurance, disability insurance, national medical care, Old Age Security and the Guaranteed Income Supplement for the elderly, the federal GST credit, the federal Child Tax Benefit, taxation, and many other measures speak to the power of governmental responses to poverty and social inequality. These actions have transformed the face of poverty in Canada and alleviated considerable social suffering. For example, without government transfer payments (social welfare, disability insurance, old age supplements, and so on) income inequalities in Canada would have risen by 7 percentage points between 1970 and 1995 instead of only 2 points.

The clear ability of governmental policy to address poverty is nowhere more evident than in government responses to poverty among the elderly. A generation ago governments made a commitment to fight poverty among seniors and funded programs that dramatically reduced the poverty rates of the elderly. By the close of the 1990s, government transfer payments were providing over 90 per cent of the total income of all three categories of poor seniors (poor unattached women and unattached men over 65 and poor couples over 65) (National Council of Welfare, 1999a: 67). Throughout the 1990s, however, the trend was towards retrenchment and deficit reduction. Poverty policies on the national and provincial levels have been transformed but the impact on the poor has been, at the least, contentious.

The clear failure of government policy to address poverty is nowhere more evident than in government responses to child poverty (Hyndman, 1998b). One of the more momentous events of the 1990s was the elimination of Family Allowances. Instituted in 1949, this universal program provided monthly benefits to virtually all families with children under 18. Tacitly, this policy acknowledged the governmental (and societal) responsibility for all children and the increased expenses incurred by all parents. The policy was eliminated in 1989 and replaced with a Child Tax Benefit that directed governmental support, in particular, to low-income families in the paid labour force. Coupled with other government actions, such as the Ontario government's 21 per cent reduction in welfare payments and the subsequent 'clawback' of federal child benefits by provincial and territorial governments, these developments are seen as demonstrating how hollow 'the rhetoric about children as our future' and 'about ending child poverty by the year 2000' is (National Council of Welfare, 1999a, 1998a).

Understanding poverty in Canada means melding together the statistical picture, the historical record, and the personal realities. Poverty means the reality of more than a million poor families living with the emotional consequences of being stigmatized and marginalized. It means more than a million children learning to do without and learning about shame and anger. It means more than a half-million seniors struggling to live out their lives with some measure of dignity. It means generations of lives that have been damaged by poverty. With these national and historical dimensions, poverty is not simply a personal problem; it is a public issue. In a sense all Canadians live with the costs of poverty—if not the present realities of impoverishment or the future possibility of being poor, then the societal consequences of a widening social and economic gap. Analysts frequently point to poverty as one of the root causes of social problems and social disorder.

Criminologists and police often identify bad economic times and high rates of unemployment as contributing factors in episodes of senseless violence.

For generations social scientists have argued that whenever significant portions of the population are denied an opportunity to share in the benefits of that society and are socially and economically marginalized, the stage is set for social unrest, rebellion, violence, and crime (Hale, 1990: 179–226). While the state may respond by imprisoning those who rebel and offend, this is clearly an expensive and inefficient solution. For example, in the 1990s as the United States dismantled much of its social assistance net and social inequality grew dramatically, its incarceration rate doubled. By the turn of the century, it was building a new prison or jail each week (Hurtig, 1999: 245). America now has (with the exception of Russia) the world's highest rate of incarceration (1.7 million prisoners, or about one in every 235 Americans, are in custody) at a costly $16 billion a year. Predictably, the prison solution to social unrest and social inequality falls disproportionately on the shoulders of the socially and economically disadvantaged. Half of the US prison population is black and 60 per cent are from racial or ethnic minorities. Further, the United States has more prisoners awaiting execution (3,300) than any other industrialized country, and the trend seems to be on the rise (*Toronto Star*, 1998c).

Although overall rates of incarceration are lower in Canada, the economically and socially disadvantaged also bear the brunt of our criminal justice system. While Native people comprise 3 per cent of the Canadian population, 11 per cent of our federal prison population is Aboriginal; in some provinces they make up an estimated 70 per cent of provincial prisoners (Hale, 1990: 211). If we are to avoid escalating social unrest, public disarray, and violence and high rates of incarceration, we must address the realities of poverty and economic disadvantage in Canada. Key factors contributing to Canadian poverty rates, such as high unemployment, the proliferation of low-wage jobs, and the reduction of the welfare net, are likely to persist or worsen. Put simply, more workers are joining the labour force than there are jobs being created, and many of the new jobs in the economy are short-term or part-time. Increased international competition, the decline of manufacturing jobs, the growth of part-time, contract, and other forms of non-standard employment in the burgeoning service sector of the economy, the continuing impact of microtechnology—all these factors are likely to continue to cause economic upheaval.

Many advocate groups and community-based anti-poverty groups are currently urging the federal and provincial governments to adopt simple reforms in order to develop more effective poverty measures. For example, there has been a long-standing plea to increase provincial and territorial welfare incomes so that welfare recipients are not the 'poorest of the poor' and to gather the political will to address child poverty (National Council of Welfare, 1999a, 1991). However, through the 1980s and 1990s federal and provincial governments focused primarily on decreasing the deficit, in part, by reducing social services. Once progress was achieved in this area, policy-makers turned to reductions in income tax—a step that clearly is of little direct benefit to those who have little income to tax.

Others have urged improvements in the human facet of the social welfare apparatus, in particular, a reduction in welfare workers' caseloads so that they can provide more in-depth and detailed assistance to their clients and to reduce complaints that the system is dignity-destroying, beset by arbitrary rules, and hostile.[28] However, governments preoccupied by deficits are making little progress in this area. Other proposals include increases in the minimum wage to protect marginal workers, a more progressive taxation system, provision of affordable, licensed child care, and improvements in the delivery system for court-ordered child-support payments in divorce cases (Kitchen et al., 1991: 35–6; Vienneau, 1991; Duffy, 1992). A wage supplement for welfare recipients is also receiving considerable attention. Under old rules, almost all wages earned by those on welfare were simply deducted from welfare benefits. Currently in Ontario, welfare recipients are encouraged to take employment by regulations that 'tax' back only 80 per cent of their work income so that holding a job does allow some improvement in their economic situation (Sweet, 1991b). The federal government has introduced a test project to examine similar wage supplementation among women welfare recipients in New Brunswick and British Columbia.

A more radical approach to poverty is a guaranteed annual income. According to this measure, poverty would be eradicated since all Canadians would be assured a minimum income. All earnings above a certain level would then be taxed. Such a program would effectively eliminate the need for social welfare programs (Special Senate Committee on Poverty, 1976: 175–92). First presented in the early 1970s, the idea of a guaranteed annual income for all Canadians has been supported by dozens of organizations, including the Canadian Conference of Catholic Bishops, as well as by the 1985 Macdonald Royal Commission on the Economic Union and Development Prospects for Canada (Goar, 1990). Recently, an Economic Council of Canada study came out in support of a guaranteed annual income, reporting that such a program would not significantly reduce the incentive to work (Beauchesne, 1991). Predictably, the proposal has generated considerable criticism in terms of its costs and feasibility.

More broadly focused proposals call for changes in most of our major institutions. For example, the Economic Council of Canada (1992: 53–9) called for enhanced co-ordination between provincial and federal governments, heightened co-operation among labour, business, and government, improvements in education and training, and a complete restructuring of income security programs. While these complex and varied policies are debated, much of the action on poverty has emanated from community groups. Local food banks and clothing drives have picked up the slack of inadequate social assistance. Citizens' groups have frequently taken the lead in providing actual aid to the poor. Further, many low-income Canadians have formed self-help and lobbying organizations, such as Campaign 2000 (to end poverty by 2000), Women for Economic Survival (BC), the Women's

Action Coalition of Nova Scotia, Anishnawbe Health (Native Canadians), Action Canada Network, and the National Anti-Poverty Organization (Dunphy, 1999; Green, 1999; Interfaith Social Assistance Reform Coalition, 1998).

While these grassroots efforts are hopeful, there are other alarming signs of growing social division and the entrenchment of inequalities. As in numerous US communities, there is a noticeable trend among the well-to-do to seal themselves off from the unpleasant realities of poverty and deprivation. Gated communities, security guards and services, 24-hour concierges, and other kindred developments speak to this trend towards middle- and upper-class defensiveness. Combined with ideological campaigns portraying welfare recipients as undeserving cheats, presenting the homeless as both malevolent and lazy, and stereotyping single mothers as irresponsible drains on the economy, these developments are frightening in their implications. Instead of fighting poverty, there is a move to fight the poor.

Whether Canadians in the twenty-first century will be able to transcend our history, with its often punitive, niggardly responses to the poor and disadvantaged, and whether we will have the courage and creativity to opt for a more equitable nation remain to be seen.

Questions for Critical Thought

1. Although poverty is often thought of as a personal problem, it is, in fact, a social problem with societal roots. In what ways is poverty routinely explained as a personal failing and how would you counter this argument with evidence of its social origins?

2. In the chapter, we talk about the ideological divide between the poor and the non-poor. How is that divide created and maintained in both day-to-day interaction and from generation to generation?

3. The plight of single-parent mother-headed families underscores the societal roots of social inequality. In what ways do the prevailing beliefs, values, and norms in contemporary Canadian society guide women into poverty?

Glossary

Low-income cut-offs (LICOs): Employed by Statistics Canada to signify the income level below which Canadians would be considered to be living on 'low' income. A variety of analysts and agencies employ these cut-offs as informal poverty lines for Canada. Statistics Canada determines these cut-offs based on the assumption that families spending more than 54.7 per cent of their gross income on food, shelter, and clothing are low income. Statistics Canada's low-income cut-offs vary by the size of the family unit and the population of the area of residence. There are seven categories of family size and five community sizes, resulting in 35 cut-offs in all.

Poverty trends: Poverty rates in Canada and elsewhere are typically not static. Over time the numbers and characteristics of the poor change. Currently, for example, single-parent mother-headed families are particularly prone to impoverishment while seniors in Canada have seen a decrease in poverty rates.

Feminization of poverty: The tendency, across countries and cultures, for women to have higher rates of poverty than men, regardless of age. Currently in Canada, for example, adult women are more likely than adult men to find themselves impoverished. This pattern reflects entrenched gender inequities both in the family and in the labour force.

Government transfer payments: Funding by the federal and provincial governments to provide support for Canadians who have low incomes. Social welfare, unemployment insurance, disability insurance, national medical care, guaranteed income supplements, the Child Tax Benefit, the GST credit, and so on all represent ways in which governments now attempt to redress some of the economic inequality among Canadians.

Guaranteed annual income (GAI): A once more popular proposal that all Canadians should benefit from a certain basic standard of living simply by token of being Canadian citizens. This proposal sought to eliminate some of the basic inequalities while challenging notions that only the 'deserving' should be supported by society.

Poverty gap: The distance between the poverty line (low-income cut-off) and the actual income of poor people. This measure provides a sense of the depth of impoverishment (how poor are the poor) as well as the amount of funds needed to lift Canadians out of poverty.

Suggested Readings

Burman, Patrick. 1988. *Killing Time, Losing Ground: Experiences of Unemployment.* Toronto: Wall and Thompson. Burman provides a classic sociological analysis of the personal pain and social complexity of inequality in Canadian society.

Federal, Provincial, and Territorial Advisory Committee on Population Health. 1999. *Toward a Healthy Future: Second Report on the Health of Canadians.* Ottawa: Minister of Public Works and Government Services Canada. Although this is a government committee report, it provides a very readable, comprehensive, and up-to-date overview of the relationship between the quality of Canadians' lives (health) and patterns of social inequality in Canada.

Hurtig, Mel. 1999. *Pay the Rent or Feed the Kids: The Tragedy and Disgrace of Poverty in Canada.* Toronto: McClelland & Stewart. If you read only one book on poverty, read this impassioned condemnation of Canada's failure to address poverty.

National Council of Welfare. 1999. *Poverty Profile 1997.* Ottawa: Minister of Public Works and Government Services Canada. Each year the National Council of Welfare, a citizens' advisory body to the federal government, provides an invaluable examination of poverty rates and trends in Canada. (See also publications from the Canadian Council on Social Development.)

Sarlo, Christopher. *Poverty in Canada.* Vancouver: Fraser Institute. In this book, which is one of the definitive conservative texts on poverty in Canada, the author lambasts the National Council of Welfare and Canadian Council on Social Development and mounts an extensive argument to the effect that 'poverty, as it has been traditionally understood, has been virtually eliminated' among Canadians.

Notes

1. A 'child' is defined here as under the age of 18.
2. Poverty definitions will rely on Statistics Canada low-income cut-offs unless otherwise specified.
3. As anyone with a good sociological imagination will immediately recognize, the differences between the rich and poor involve more than differences in the amount and source of income. While income and wealth are often related to one another, wealth is a much broader concept than income and includes ownership of financial and other assets. The wealthy may have enormous assets in terms of stocks, bonds, and other holdings while having a relatively low yearly income. Further, there are, of course, important differences in terms of presentation of self and lifestyle (Federal, Provincial, and Territorial Advisory Committee, 1999; Hale, 1990). In short, difference in income is only one, imprecise, measure of the differences between those who have and those who do not.
4. 'Young' is defined here as an individual between 15 and 25 years of age.
5. Without taxes and government transfers, the top 20 per cent of Canadians would earn $22 to every $1 earned by the bottom 20 per cent. The effect of taxes and transfer payments (by tripling the earned income of the bottom 20 per cent) reduced this discrepancy to $5 to every $1 (Carey, 1998a).
6. In other words, increases in the average worker's wages did not keep up with the rate of inflation.
7. This is the highest rate in the inductrialized world. In Canada, the top 1 per cent owns 25 per cent of all assets, and in Britain, 18 per cent (Goar, 1995).
8. The National Council of Welfare (1998a: 2) points out that in 1996 virtually every poor person in Canada could be brought above the low-income cut-off line (effectively eliminating 'poverty' in Canada) by the expenditure of $17.8 billion. Given that the federal, provincial, and territorial governments spent $386 billion that year, this does not seem an impossible political goal.
9. These expenditures comprised 25 per cent of the federal budget at this time.
10. This definitional problem is compounded by the pervasive ideology in Canadian society that we are a basically 'classless society' (Allahar and Côté, 1998).
11. For example, P. Sainath, noted Indian journalist, recounts the struggles over such competing definitions of poverty. In the late 1980s, the government of India devised a very narrow definition of impoverishment that reduced the poverty rate to just over 19

per cent of the population. When a succeeding government dumped 'this particular piece of dishonesty', the percentage of Indian people living in poverty soared to 39.9 per cent in 1997 (Sainath, 1996: 348–50).

12. Statistics Canada warns against the use of low-income cut-offs as a poverty line. They have also proposed an alternative, simpler measure—the low-income measure—which is 50 per cent of the median income in Canada.

13. Commencing in 1990, Statistics Canada published an appendix that included low-income cut-offs based on after-tax income. Estimating the number of people living in poverty using the after-tax method results in a reduction in the rate (for 1990) from 14.6 per cent to 11.5 per cent (Ross et al., 1994: 28).

14. A recent survey of labour and income dynamics in Canada found, for example, that between 1993 and 1994 over one million Canadians fell into poverty, almost as many climbed out, and slightly more remained poor in both years (National Council of Welfare, 1998a: 9).

15. In addition, historical trends increase or decrease vulnerability to official poverty. As evidenced most dramatically during the Great Depression, impoverishment may touch any individual or family.

16. 'Unattached individuals' are those who are not married and who are not living with family members.

17. Level of education, however, does not dictate likelihood of poverty. Many Canadians who have relatively little education avoid impoverishment and, conversely, there are numerous families and individuals with post-secondary education who are still poor (National Council of Welfare, 1998a: 45).

18. Workfare refers to the increasingly popular policy of requiring able-bodied recipients of social welfare benefits to take some form of state-orchestrated employment. In Ontario, for example, some welfare recipients have been deployed into phone solicitation positions. Refusal to accept such positions may result in loss of welfare benefits. Needless to say, these initiatives have resulted in strong protests from poverty activists.

19. Research indicates that single-parent mothers have fewer children on average than two-parent families (National Council of Welfare, 1998a: 41).

20. However, the poverty gap (the amount of income needed to bring the population up to the poverty line) for unattached senior women (and men) is significantly *less* than that experienced by other parts of the poor population, notably unattached men under age 65 and single-parent mothers (National Council of Welfare, 1998a: 52).

21. Research suggests that the death of a wife actually decreases the risk of poverty for her husband (as cited in McDonald, 1997: 557).

22. Not included in these figures are the 51 per cent of Native children who are poor (Kitchen et al., 1991: 15).

23. In 1999, the average Toronto single mother 'on welfare' received $1,071.70 a month. She paid on average $680.53 in rent, which left $391.17 or $13.03 a day for food, clothing, transportation, a telephone, and other expenses (Hurtig, 1999: 292).

24. The Toronto Mayor's Task Force on Homelessness (headed by Anne Golden) found that 170,000 different individuals had used shelters for the homeless in Toronto between 1987 and 1996 (Golden, 1998).

25. The high rates of suicide among Aboriginal groups in Canada speaks, in part, to the effect of economic and social marginalization (Federal, Provincial, and Territorial Advisory Committee, 1999).

26. Research also indicates that parents' level of education influences the child's school readiness. Children whose parents are well-educated are more prepared for school at ages four and five than children whose parents are poorly educated. Clearly, this suggests a mechanism for the generational impact of poverty (Federal, Provincial, and Territorial Advisory Committee, 1999: 52).

27. Predictably, there is a clear relationship between living in low-income households and having a low level of prose literacy (Federal, Provincial, and Territorial Advisory Committee, 1999: 53).

28. In an ironic development, Ontario recently considered using electronic monitors on provincial social workers to ensure that they were making good use of their work hours.

References

Abella, R.S. 1984. *Equality in Employment: A Royal Commission Report*. Ottawa: Ministry of Supply and Services.

Allahar, Anton L., and James E. Côté. 1998. *Richer and Poorer: The Structure of Inequality in Canada*. Toronto: James Lorimer.

Armstrong, Jane. 1992. 'Is our welfare system being abused?', *Toronto Star*, 7 Mar., A7, A18.

Badets, Jane, and Linda Howatson-Leo. 1999. 'Recent immigrants in the workforce', *Canadian Social Trends* 52 (Spring): 16–22.

Barile, Maria. 1992. 'Dis-Abled Women: An Exploited Genderless Under-class', *Canadian Woman Studies* (Summer): 32–3.

Baxter, Sheila. 1988. *No Way to Live: Poor Women Speak Out*. Vancouver: New Star Books.

———. 1993. *A Child Is Not a Toy: Voices of Children in Poverty*. Vancouver: New Star Books.

Beauchesne, Eric. 1991. 'Income guarantee doesn't discourage work, study finds', *Toronto Star*, 4 July, A12.

Benner, Allan. 1998. 'Report offers real portrait of poverty', *St. Catharines Standard*, 26 Nov., A7.

Blouin, Barbara. 1992. 'Welfare Workers and Clients: Problems of Sexism and Paternalism', *Canadian Woman Studies* (Summer): 64–5.

Bradbury, Bettina. 1982. 'The Fragmented Family: Family Strategies in the Face of Death, Illness, and Poverty, Montreal, 1860–1885', in Joy Parr, ed., *Childhood and Family in Canadian History*. Toronto: McClelland & Stewart.

———. 1991. 'Surviving as a Widow in Nineteenth Century Montreal', in Veronica Strong-Boag and Anita Clair Fellman, eds, *Rethinking Canada: The Promise of Women's History*. Toronto: Copp Clark.

Bragg, Rebecca. 1999. 'Housing top priority for Canada's poor', *Toronto Star*, 26 Mar., E4.

Burman, Patrick. 1988. *Killing Time, Losing Ground: Experiences of Unemployment*. Toronto: Wall & Thompson.

———. 1996. *Poverty's Bonds: Power and Agency in the Social Relations of Welfare*. Toronto: Thompson Educational Publishing.

Carey, Elaine. 1998a. 'Record-high income taxes gobble fifth of family pay', *Toronto Star*, 23 June, A4.

———. 1998b. 'Rich get richer as wage gap widens', *Toronto Star*, 22 Oct., A1, A36.

Carniol, Ben. 1987. *Case Critical: The Dilemma of Social Work in Canada*. Toronto: Between the Lines.

Cheal, David, et al. 1997. 'Canadian Children in the 1990s', *Canadian Social Trends* 4 (Spring): 1–9.

Copp, Terry. 1974. *The Anatomy of Poverty: The Condition of the Working Class in Montreal, 1897–1929*. Toronto: McClelland & Stewart.

Coulter, Rebecca. 1982. 'The Working Young of Edmonton, 1921–1931', in Joy Parr, ed., *Childhood and Family in Canadian History*. Toronto: McClelland & Stewart.

Crane, David. 1998. 'Where do we draw the line on poverty?', *Toronto Star*, 4 Nov., E2.

———. 1999. 'Children are the "sound bite" in productivity', *Toronto Star*, 15 Apr., D2.

Crowe, Cathy. 1998. 'In the calculation of real disasters homelessness has easily won its place', *Toronto Star*, 30 Oct., A21.

Davies, Gareth. 1997. 'Understanding the War on Poverty: The Advantages of a Canadian Perspective', *Journal of Policy History* 9, 4: 425–49.

Denton, Margaret, and Alfred Hunter. 1991. 'Education and the Child', in Richard Barnhorst and Laura C. Johnson, eds, *The State of the Child in Ontario*. Toronto: Oxford University Press.

Duffy, Andrew. 1992. 'Day care need "enormous", study says', *Toronto Star*, 29 Feb., A21.

Duffy, Ann, Nancy Mandell, and Norene Pupo. 1988. *Few Choices: Women, Work and Family*. Toronto: Garamond Press.

——— and Norene Pupo. 1992. *Part-Time Paradox: Connecting Gender, Work, and Family*. Toronto: McClelland & Stewart.

Duncan, Kenneth. 1974. 'Irish Famine Immigration and the Social Structure of Canada West', in Michiel Horn and Ronald Sabourin, eds, *Studies in Canadian Social History*. Toronto: McClelland & Stewart.

Dunphy, Catherine. 1999. 'Aboriginal people look to leave Toronto's mean streets', *Toronto Star*, 27 Mar., A8.

Economic Council of Canada. 1992. *The New Face of Poverty: Income Security Needs of Canadian Families*. Ottawa: Ministry of Supply and Services.

Fast, Janet, and Moreno Da Pont. 1997. 'Changes in Women's Work Continuity', *Canadian Social Trends* (Autumn): 2–7.

Federal, Provincial, and Territorial Advisory Committee on Population Health for the Meeting of Ministers of Health, Charlottetown, PEI. 1999. *Toward a Healthy Future: Second Report on the Health of Canadians*. Ottawa: Minister of Public Works and Government Services.

Freid, Loren. 1998. 'Are we asking the right questions?', *Toronto Star*, 9 Oct., A24.

Gaffield, Chad. 1984. 'Wage Labour, Industrialization and the Origins of the Modern Family', in Maureen Baker, ed., *The Family: Changing Trends in Canada*. Toronto: McGraw-Hill.

Gelles, Richard J., and Claire P. Cornell. 1990. *Intimate Violence in Families,* 2nd edn. Newbury Park, Calif.: Sage.

Gillespie, Kerry. 1998. 'Civilized society feared at risk', *Toronto Star,* 29 Sept., B1.

Goar, Carol. 1990. 'Senator's passionate attack on poverty', *Toronto Star,* 13 Jan., D4.

———. 1995. 'Unequal shares of the American Dream', *Toronto Star,* 14 May, F5.

Goldberg, Gertrude Schaffner. 1990. 'Canada: Bordering on the Feminization of Poverty', in Goldberg and Eleanor Kremen, eds, *The Feminization of Poverty: Only in America?* New York: Praeger.

Golden, Anne. 1998. 'Breaking the cycle of homelessness', *Toronto Star,* 30 Sept., A18.

Green, Sara Jean. 1999. 'Street youth program nets $1.1 million grant', *Toronto Star,* 27 Mar., A9.

Guest, Dennis. 1980. *The Emergence of Social Security in Canada.* Vancouver: University of British Columbia Press.

Gunderson, Morley, and Leon Muszynski, with Jennifer Keck. 1990. *Women and Labour Market Poverty.* Ottawa: Canadian Advisory Council on the Status of Women.

Hale, Sylvia M. 1990. *Controversies in Sociology: A Canadian Introduction.* Toronto: Copp Clark Pitman.

Houston, Susan E. 1982. 'The "Waifs and Strays" of a Late Victorian City: Juvenile Delinquents in Toronto', in Joy Parr, ed., *Childhood and Family in Canadian History.* Toronto: McClelland & Stewart.

Hudson, Kellie. 1999. 'Dentists root out 2nd-class care for welfare children', *Toronto Star,* 28 Mar., A1, A4.

Hurtig, Mel. 1999. *Pay the Rent or Feed the Kids: The Tragedy and Disgrace of Poverty in Canada.* Toronto: McClelland & Stewart.

Hyndman, Brian. 1998a. 'Being poor still means being sicker, dying younger than rich', *Toronto Star,* 8 Jan., A15.

———. 1998b. 'Children paying for war on debt', *Toronto Star,* 10 July, A26.

Interfaith Social Assistance Reform Coalition. 1998. *Our Neighbours' Voices: Will We Listen?* Toronto: James Lorimer.

James, Royson. 1999. 'We can't turn backs on homeless', *Toronto Star,* 31 Mar., B2.

Johnson, Leo A. 1972. *Poverty in Wealth.* Toronto: New Hogtown Press.

Katz, Michael B. 1975. *The People of Hamilton, Canada West: Family and Class in a Mid-Nineteenth-Century City.* Cambridge, Mass.: Harvard University Press.

———. 1983. *Poverty and Policy in American History.* New York: Academic Press.

———. 1986. *In the Shadow of the Poorhouse: A Social History of Welfare in America.* New York: Basic Books.

Kazemipur, A., and S.S. Halli. 2000. *The New Poverty in Canada: Ethnic Groups and Ghetto Neighbourhoods.* Toronto: Thompson Educational Publishing.

Kitchen, Brigitte, Andrew Mitchell, Peter Clutterbuck, and Marvyn Novick. 1991. *Unequal Futures: The Legacies of Child Poverty in Canada.* Toronto: Child Poverty Action Group and the Social Planning Council of Metropolitan Toronto.

Laroche, M. 1998. 'In and Out of Low Income', *Canadian Social Trends* (Autumn): 20–4.

Lawton, Valerie. 1998. 'Plight of the long-term jobless', *Toronto Star,* 7 Nov., B4.

McCarthy, Shawn. 1992. 'Ottawa missing $90 billion a year as cheaters use cash to dodge taxes', *Toronto Star*, 30 Apr., A1, A32.

McDonald, Lynn. 1997. 'The Invisible Poor: Canada's Retired Windows', *Canadian Journal of Aging* 16, 3: 553–83.

McGrath, Paul. 1998. 'Food banks part of life on campus', *Toronto Star*, 23 Feb., F1, F2.

MacLeod, Linda. 1987. *Battered But Not Beaten: Preventing Wife Battering in Canada.* Ottawa: Canadian Advisory Council on the Status of Women.

Marquardt, Richard. 1998. *Enter at Your Own Risk: Canadian Youth and the Labour Market.* Toronto: Between the Lines.

Marsden, Lorna, chair. 1991. *Children in Poverty: Toward a Better Future.* Standing Senate Committee on Social Affairs, Science and Technology. Ottawa: Ministry of Supply and Services.

Marshall, Katherine. 1993. 'Dual Earners: Who's Responsible for Housework?', *Canadian Social Trends* (Winter): 11–15.

Mulvany, C. Pelham. 1884. *Toronto: Past and Present.* Toronto: W.E. Caiger.

National Council of Welfare. 1988. *Poverty Profile 1988.* Ottawa: Ministry of Supply and Services.

———. 1990. *Women and Poverty Revisited.* Ottawa: Ministry of Supply and Services.

———. 1991. *Welfare Incomes 1990.* Ottawa: Ministry of Supply and Services.

———. 1997. *Another Look at Welfare Reform.* Ottawa: Ministry of Supply and Services.

———. 1998a. *Poverty Profile 1996.* Ottawa: Minister of Public Works and Government Services Canada.

———. 1998b. *Child Benefits: Kids Are Still Hungry.* Ottawa: Minister of Public Works and Government Services Canada.

———. 1998c. *Profiles of Welfare: Myths and Realities.* Ottawa: Minister of Public Works and Government Services Canada.

———. 1999a. *Poverty Profile 1997.* Ottawa: Minister of Public Works and Government Services Canada.

———. 1999b. *Preschool Children: Promises to Keep.* Ottawa: Minister of Public Works and Government Services Canada.

———. 1999c. *Children First.* Ottawa: Minister of Public Works and Government Services Canada.

———. 1999–2000. *Welfare Incomes: 1997 and 1998.* Ottawa: Minister of Public Works and Government Services Canada.

Nett, Emily. 1990. *Canadian Families: Past and Present.* Toronto: Butterworths.

Offord, Dan. 1991. 'Growing Up Poor in Ontario', *Transition* (Vanier Institute of the Family) (June): 10–11.

Orwen, Patricia. 1998. 'Food bank use jumps 17% in GTA in just one year', *Toronto Star*, 11 Sept., A2.

Pearce, Diana. 1978. 'The Feminization of Poverty: Women, Work and Welfare', *Urban and Social Change Review* 11 (Feb.): 28–36.

Pfeiffer, J. William. 1999. *Road Kill on the Information Highway: The Future of Work in Canada.* Toronto: Pfeiffer and Co.

Pupo, Norene. 1988. 'Preserving Patriarchy: Women, the Family and the State', in Nancy Mandell and Ann Duffy, eds, *Reconstructing the Canadian Family: Feminist Perspectives.* Toronto: Butterworths.

Rashid, Abdul. 1989. *Family Income.* Ottawa: Ministry of Supply and Services.

———. 1998. 'Family income inequality: 1970–1995', *Perspectives on Labour and Income* 10, 4 (Winter): 12–17.

———. 1999. 'Family income: 25 years of stability and change', *Perspectives on Labour and Income* 11, 1 (Spring): 9–15.

Reitsma-Street, Marge, Richard Carriere, Adje Van de Sande, and Carol Hein. 1993. 'Three Perspectives on Child Poverty in Canada', *The Social Worker* 61, 1 (Spring): 6–13.

Robinson, Patricia. 1986. *Women's Work Interruptions.* Ottawa: Ministry of Supply and Services.

Rooke, Patricia, and R.L. Schnell. 1982. 'Guttersnipes and Charity Children: 19th Century Child Rescue in the Atlantic Provinces', in Rooke and Shnell, eds, *Studies in Childhood History: A Canadian Perspective.* Calgary: Detselig.

Rosenthal, Marguerite O. 1990. 'Sweden: Promise and Paradox', in Gertrude Schaffner Goldberg and Eleanor Kremen, eds, *The Feminization of Poverty: Only in America?* New York: Praeger.

Ross, David, and Richard Shillington. 1989. *The Canadian Fact Book on Poverty.* Ottawa: Canadian Council on Social Development.

———, ———, and Clarence Lochhead. 1994. *The Canadian Fact Book on Poverty.* Ottawa: Canadian Council on Social Development.

Sainath, P. 1996. *Everybody Loves a Good Drought.* London: Review.

Sarlo, Christopher. 1992. *Poverty in Canada.* Vancouver: Fraser Institute.

Simmons, Christina. 1986. '"Helping the Poorer Sisters": The Women of the Jost Mission, Halifax, 1905–1945', in Veronica Strong-Boag and Anita Clair Fellman, eds, *Rethinking Canada: The Promise of Women's History.* Toronto: Copp Clark Pitman.

Spears, John. 1991. 'NB seeks answer to childhood poverty', *Toronto Star,* 31 May, A21.

———. 1999. 'Rent erodes tenants' income, study shows', *Toronto Star,* 23 Mar., A6.

Special Senate Committee on Poverty. 1976. *Poverty in Canada.* Ottawa: Ministry of Supply and Services.

Statistics Canada. 1998. 'Sources of Income, Earnings and Total Income and Family Income', *The Daily,* Catalogue no. 11–001E, 9 June.

———. 1999. 'Social Indicators', *Canadian Social Trends* (Spring): 27.

Sweet, Lois. 1991a. 'Is welfare cheating running wild?', *Toronto Star,* 2 June, BI, B7.

———. 1991b. 'Jobs offer hope as welfare cure', *Toronto Star,* 3 June, A15.

Toronto Star. 1998a. 'World's richest get richer', 29 Apr., E2.

———. 1998b. 'Canada's a fine home . . . for some of us', 10 Sept., A24.

———. 1998c. 'Amnesty report slams U.S. prisons', 7 Oct., A20.

———. 1999. 'Poverty can't be measured away', 5 Apr., A16.

Vienneau, David. 1991. 'Court-ordered child support often too low report warns', *Toronto Star,* 4 July, A2.

Waddell, Christopher. 1989. 'The Debt: Where Does All the Money Go?', *Globe and Mail,* 8 Apr., D1, D8.

Williamson, Deanna L., and Janet E. Fast. 1998. 'Poverty Status, Health Behaviours and Health: Implications for Social Assistance and Health Care Policy', *Canadian Public Policy* 24, 1: 1–22.

Women for Economic Survival. 1984. *Women and Economic Hard Times: A Record*. Victoria: Women for Economic Survival and the University of Victoria.

Wright, Lisa. 1998. 'Big brass earn top dollar', *Toronto Star*, 10 Dec., C3.

Zyblock, Myles, and Zhengxi Lin. 1997. *Trickling Down or Fizzling Out?: Economic Performance, Transfers, Inequality and Low Income*. Ottawa: Statistics Canada.

part two

Institutions
in Crisis

What do we mean by institutions in crisis? An institution is defined as 'a well-established pattern of social relationships that is accepted as a fundamental part of a society' (Spencer, 1996: 221; see also Henslin et al., 2000). The family is commonly viewed as an important institution of society. Another important institution is the state. The state in Canada is changing. Whatever the reason or reasons—globalization, budget deficits, NAFTA, the constitutional crisis over Quebec—the state is not what it used to be. And, inasmuch as the 'established pattern of social relationships', which prior generations experienced as legitimate, is collapsing, we can now speak of a crisis. Moreover, the state, in large measure, sets the agenda for what is and is not important to citizens, especially as we have entered the Information Age where the need for 'new skills' is a powerful mantra repeated by educators and by spokespersons at all levels of government. Crime has become another important concern expressed by Canadians who look to the state for guidance and leadership. These two are among the more important issues facing Canadians.

Norene Pupo, in Chapter 4, introduces the student to the contemporary political setting in Canada. She reviews the strengths and weaknesses of the three major theories of the state—liberal-pluralist, instrumentalist, and structuralist—by pointing out that it does not really matter whether this or that politician will find a future career in a particular Canadian bank or corporation. What truly matters is how the federal and provincial governments are run, what makes them tick. In addition, several examples are given of how the state shapes our individual and collective lives in such a manner that few interstices or social sanctuaries remain between the public and private realms. In recent years, succumbing to pressure from some well-meaning Canadians, the state is encroaching on the private realm by creating a social climate where, for example, 'welfare snitches' are acceptable role models and mistrust of neighbours and strangers increasingly characterizes the treatment of others in our society.

In periods of crisis, past and present, one of the first institutions to be singled out for reform and revitalization is the society's education system. Time and again, it is argued that 'the common people' possess inadequate knowledge and ambition. David Livingstone, in Chapter 5, critically evaluates the three options to the crisis in education: the *market-driven* option, which involves restricting and relating entry to post-secondary education more closely to employment prospects; the *knowledge economy* option, which encourages advanced education at increased personal expense; and the *economic democracy* option, which means supporting public education as a right and reorganizing paid employment to allow more fully for people's learning capabilities.

In Chapter 6, Kelly Hannah-Moffat addresses the nature of crime and the public's fear of and fascination with crime. She points out that our view of crime is often linked to our social definitions of 'deviance' or 'the violation of norms—whether the infraction is as minor as jaywalking, or as serious as murder' (Henslin et al., 2000: 192). In a period of change, the boundaries for what is or is not deviant also shift. Take, for example, spanking a child. Not so long ago, this behaviour was encouraged. It was seen as a way of establishing boundaries, even a way of telling the child that he/she is loved. Today, a very different message is endorsed.

The changes in societal norms can be unsettling. Canadians may feel mystified as traditional practices—spanking, lifelong marriages—are challenged and new standards of behaviour are introduced. Canadians are also concerned and puzzled by the judicial responses to crime, the length and nature of prison sentences. In short, Canadians feel considerable anxieties about crime and deviances. These anxieties about crime can, in part, be situated in the changing social context of what crime is. Hannah-Moffat explains the plastic nature of criminal behaviours such as 'pirating software, speeding, purchasing sexual services'. In effect, she points out the applicability of criminality to all of us to communicate that many of our anxieties about crime and criminal behaviours are ill-founded.

References

Henslin, James M., Dan Glenday, Ann Duffy, and Norene Pupo. 2000. *Sociology: A-Down-to-Earth Approach*, 2nd Canadian edn. Toronto: Allyn and Bacon.

Spencer, Metta. 1996. *Foundations of Modern Sociology*, 7th edn. Toronto: Prentice-Hall.

chapter four

The Role of the State in a Restructured Economy

Norene Pupo

Within Canadian culture, privacy, independence, equality of opportunity, and achievement are highly regarded values. As Canadians, we like to consider ourselves as overseers of our own destinies, as capable of making independent decisions that affect our families, our careers, and our well-being. When we enter the private world of our homes from school, the workplace, or the public realm, we tend to see ourselves as constructing our own courses, particularly when we are involved in intimate relations and in discussions on private family matters. However, even private actions and personal decisions are shaped by the social world. The state plays a large role in setting the parameters in which we act, in providing the latitude in which we may make decisions.

Canadians often debate the question of whether there should be more or less state intervention in social, political, economic, and private matters. Drawing on the notions of free enterprise, independence, and self-sufficiency, some Canadians would prefer a smaller state structure and less state intervention in all affairs. They view the state as too powerful, with too much discretion to act on matters they believe fall within the realm of individual entrepreneurship and private decision-making. This argument is frequently applied to the marketplace, where it is advised that individual players should be left to their own devices and that in this process the stronger, more sound ventures will flourish and the weaker, inappropriate ones will be eliminated. State interference is viewed as contributing to economic stagnation by reducing the competitive spirit and personal ambition. With respect to private matters, critics argue that state intervention in effect obstructs personal freedom.

In contrast, others prefer more state intervention, arguing that the state should adopt a protectionist role, insulating citizens publicly against the effects of volatile or extreme market conditions and international economic and political crises, and privately against problems associated with family breakdown, illness, or other individual predicaments, while ensuring equal opportunity and objectivity in education, in the workplace, and before the courts. Within this framework, the state is viewed as a form of security and as a vehicle of fairness and justice. For example, the state has been called on to intervene in marital disputes over child support by providing payments to the primary caretakers, predominantly women, by means of garnishing wages.

Calling on state action has sometimes been the approach adopted by women attempting to buffer the power of their husbands/partners or employers to counterbalance their own relative powerlessness. Working towards equality through state policy represents a collective resistance to an imbalanced social and political structure. While social programs (family benefits, general welfare) may create or re-create dependency on the state because they are usually not structured to provide opportunities for developing self-sufficiency, they are an alternative to personal dependency on a spouse, partner, or other family member.

Between these two general opinions about the benefits and drawbacks of greater or less state intervention are more moderate approaches to the role of the state. Some Canadians prefer to evaluate each issue with regard to the advantages and disadvantages of expanded or limited state involvement. Nevertheless, this ongoing debate calls into focus two interrelated questions: What are the nature and function of the Canadian state? And, how does the state affect our personal and public lives?

This chapter will examine various theories of the state and will assess their ability to explain the state's role and structure in Canadian society. We will discuss how the state operates in the economy and in the labour market as well as how it responds to individuals' needs. We will consider how the state reacts to various groups' requests for protection, aid, and justice and will consider whether the state promotes equality, as it has been constitutionalized in the Charter of Rights and Freedoms.

The State: Parameters and Power

The state is not a single remote institution, nor is it limited in its activity and dimensions. State policy affects our lives from birth to death. The state mediates in both private and public relationships. State policy is invoked in intimate relations through marriage, the birth of children, adoption, abortion decisions; in family-related matters, such as separation and divorce, custody, child care, and elder care. In the public domain we interact with or through the state in education, in the workplace, in seeking medical care. We are taxed and licensed; we are issued Social Insurance numbers; we are registered at birth; we are served notice; we are enumerated at regular intervals for political and statistical purposes. School records document our successes and failures. Our names may appear on waiting lists for government-subsidized housing or living allowances, for social assistance, for pensions, for research grants, or for hospital beds. There may be files kept about our political activities by central intelligence and police agencies.

The study of the state and political sociology includes the study of *power* and the ways in which our individual and collective lives are shaped. *Power* may be defined as the ability to affect the behaviour of individuals or groups. The power of the state is both *direct* and *indirect*. The state may employ the direct use of force during times of war, in deploying weapons, or in undertaking strategic manoeuvres. In Canada, the Prime Minister may invoke the War Measures Act, which provides police forces with wide-ranging powers of arrest, search, and seizure without warrant and detention without trial in the event of a national emergency (Enright, 1990: 477). Prime Minister Pierre Elliott Trudeau invoked the War Measures Act in October 1970 following the kidnapping of British Trade Commissioner James Cross and Quebec Labour Minister Pierre Laporte in a demonstration of the government's disapproval of the actions of the Front de Libération du Québec (FLQ). In addition to its direct use of force to maintain control over groups or the wider society, the state may curb individuals' behaviour through the criminal justice system and the actions of various levels of police.

Most Canadians experience the state's presence in an indirect rather than a direct manner. The state maintains control through indirect means, providing programs, such as education, health care, and social welfare, maintaining the infrastructure, establishing preventive measures such as policing, public health, and environmental programs, promoting equity through the legal framework surrounding marriage, divorce, custody, marital property, and the family, as well as through employment standards, employment and pay equity, and other policy related to the workplace. Numerous studies have documented how the state maintains control through education, for example, by promoting values, ideas, and beliefs supportive of the ongoing system of social class, economics and power and by preparing people for their future roles within a hierarchically organized society by means of streaming and other selection mechanisms (Freire, 1972; Livingstone, 1985, 1987; Wotherspoon, 1987; Nelsen, 1991).

The state operates within both *public* and *private* spheres. It is difficult to distinguish its various roles within these realms. State policy simultaneously affects our public and private relations and blends private matters with public responsibility. For example, while the decision to marry may be an intimate declaration of love between partners, at the same time marriage is an institution sanctioned by the state and guided by legal contract. A person's marital status in turn affects his/her situation with regard to income tax, pensions, general welfare assistance, and a wide range of other social policies and programs. Although we tend to refer to state policies and institutions as falling within the public domain, in reality they weave an intricate path between the public and private spheres in such a fashion that it is impossible to discuss their operation within these spheres separately. The formal posture we adopt in interaction with public officials masks how social institutions and their policies affect our personal lives.

Although Canadians vary in their opinions on the level of appropriate state intervention, overriding this debate is the popular notion of the *benevolent* state. This notion derives from the material and ideological support for the concept of the welfare state as historically developed within Canada. The system of social welfare is described as providing a *safety net* for families and individuals who experience difficulties generated by financial insecurity and health and interpersonal problems. By promoting the well-being of Canadians and by making a wide variety of social programs universally accessible through the social welfare system, the state maintains the image of working towards the common good.

The state's general support for the safety net is related to its role within the economy, to ensure the well-being of the working classes, while maintaining the structure of social class and power, and to contain criticism directed against that system (Panitch, 1977; Moscovitch and Drover, 1987). Its immediate decisions regarding social welfare are simultaneously shaped by this function within the economy as well as by the reactions and interests of employers, lobbyists, union leaders, and the working classes.

Recently, the public outcry over changes to Employment Insurance legislation, specifically workers' and unions' reactions to the state's suggestion of a crackdown on the system's abusers, forced clarifications over workers' rights to EI particularly when quitting a job. The state was obliged under growing public rage and scrutiny to dispel the rumour that there were plans to institute a 'snitch line' for workers to report anonymously anyone suspected of abusing the system. With the official unemployment rate in 1998 at 8.3 per cent (a significant improvement following the double-digit years between 1991 and 1994), the Canadian working class was painfully aware of the state's cost-saving interest in streamlining aid to the unemployed and strategically raised public discussion over the question of the state's benevolence with regard to its seeming indifference to workers' well-being at a time of such a high level of insecurity. At the same time employers interested in downsizing and adopting corporate policies designed to encourage early retirement and buy-out options were watchful that the government's proposal would neither obstruct their plans for corporate reorganization nor direct public antagonism towards their doors. Mounting public pressure from both employers and workers prompted the state to assure both sides that workers who quit their jobs to accommodate another worker would not be penalized.

The State Defined

The state is most popularly conceived of as the group of elected officials and is often interchangeably referred to as the government. The state, however, encompasses more than this group and while the government in office is an aspect of the state, it does not represent the state in its entirety. Simply to conceptualize the state as the government of the day oversimplifies its context, its roles, and its development. It also overlooks how various groups have struggled for recognition, for alterations in social policy, and for justice, and it ignores the dimensions of economic and political power shaping state policy and programs. We must understand the workings of the state mainly by drawing on the historical context of its development and operation.

According to Miliband (1973) and Panitch (1977), along with the government in office, the state includes the bureaucratic and administrative structures that conduct and manage the state's activities (ministries, departments, regulatory commissions, central banks, Crown corporations); the military, security, and police forces; the system of judges and courts; successive levels of government and administration (provincial and municipal executives, legislatures, and bureaucracies); and the entire group of elected representatives at all levels. Together these bodies constitute the system of *state power*.

Panitch (1977: 7) underscores the importance of recognizing that the elected government and its power are not the equivalent of the state and state power. The degree to which the government controls state power depends, Panitch argues, 'on the balance of forces within the various institutions of the state, such as the bureaucracy, the judiciary, and the military, in terms of the classes *they* represent and the values *they* hold'. In Canada, the election of a New Democratic Party (NDP) government is no guarantee that social democratic principles, programs, and policies in line with the interests of labour will be adopted. When an NDP government was elected in Ontario under the leadership of Premier Bob Rae during the fall of 1990, discussion in the media seemed to be based on the presumption that Ontario would be transformed into a socialist state and that the government's policies would be unsympathetic and even hostile to business. These assumptions rest on the equation of government and state power, exposing the liberal democratic theoretical framework upon which the popular conception of the state is drawn.

To understand the nature of the state, the interaction among the complex of institutions constituting the state should be studied from a historical perspective and within the context of the particular economic and political circumstances. In Canada, the relationship among the levels of the state is very important and has shaped numerous debates and jurisdictional disputes. Canadian history has been riddled with conflicts over the rightful level of authority for decisions regarding resources, the allocation of finances and taxation revenue, and the structure of the welfare state. The continuing controversy over Quebec's status as a distinct society and the struggle by Native Canadians for self-determination embody the question of state power and its intricate political, economic, and socio-historical dimensions. What issues underlie the ongoing debates over Canadian federalism and the structure of the Canadian state? How have important questions of social and economic development affected the provincial and municipal levels and how do these issues directly and indirectly touch the lives of average Canadians?

The Welfare State

Despite the debates over federalism or jurisdiction, most Canadians recognize the contribution of social programs to their overall quality of life and in this regard have welcomed the expansion of the welfare state. The *welfare state* refers to the vast systems of social programs designed to meet the educational, health, and income needs of Canadians. In comparison with the US, where the system of social welfare is less accessible, Canadians regard themselves as fortunate, particularly with regard to universal health care. However, at the same time many resent the state's beneficence towards the impoverished and disenfranchised. They consider these problems to be the result of individuals' lack of motivation or other character flaws and, as such, they argue that taxation revenue should not be diverted to welfare and income security programs to meet the needs of those who may not subscribe to commonly declared values and goals of hard work and success. In embracing the notion of social welfare, many differentiate among the types of programs and benefits offered, separating those developed to meet the needs of people who through 'no fault of their own' experience difficulties from those generated to meet the needs of those who are regarded as less deserving of public expenditure. The conception of the welfare state is double-edged, combining the notion of the state's benevolence and the value of security with its authority to dig deeply into Canadians' pockets to finance public expenditures on social programs.

The existence of the welfare state has generated confusion over the character and function of the state within capitalist society. On whose behalf does the state operate? Is the state impartial? Does the state function to protect particular interests within society? Or does the state operate to enhance the well-being of its citizenry and to meet the 'common good'? Or does the state work to promote the well-being of capitalism in general without minding any particular interests?

Theories of the State

Among the most popular explanations of the state's structure and roles are the *liberal democratic*, the *Marxist instrumentalist*, and the *structuralist*. These theories of the state differ in their assessments of the primary interests met by the state through its economic and social policies. Scholars disagree on what constitutes the common good and indeed whether or not divergent economic, political, or class interests may render this notion a vague and meaningless ideal.

The Liberal Democratic Framework

Within the *liberal democratic* or *pluralist* tradition, the state is regarded as a neutral arbitrator. This position starts with the notion of society as composed of a number of competing political parties and interest groups, including business associations, labour unions, professional organizations, religious groups, and so on. These interest groups function as checks and balances against one another. Overall, no particular group dominates the others, but rather each group works to defend its own interests. According to this theory, the state balances the various demands of competing interest groups and parties and implements impartial decisions.

In making decisions, the state is seen to take into account relevant facts, historical circumstances, the wishes of the majority, the submissions it receives from informed and affected groups, the data gathered through scientific study, the findings of commissions or other such bodies, the arguments of politicians about the needs of their constituents, and the idea of the common good. Liberals argue that once all the relevant information is collected and factors are assessed, an objective decision is made. From this, they conclude that the state is fair: that different positions are equally reviewed and that judgements reflect what is most beneficial to the greatest number and to its overriding concern for the nation's welfare. In establishing that the state is unbiased in its decision-making, liberal democrats point to different issues on which the same group has won and lost (Pupo, 1988: 209). For example, amendments made to the Employment Insurance Act to increase the provision for parental leave upon the birth or adoption of a child may be viewed as a victory for employed parents, whereas the state's refusal to intro-duce a national child-care program may be viewed as a bitter defeat for this same group.

This argument is instructive to some degree on how policy is made, that is, on the number of groups, opinions, informed positions, and interests that may be taken into account in policy decisions. However, the argument rests on three major flaws.

First, liberal thinkers maintain that the state weighs all positions equally before reaching decisions. They assume that political resources, such as wealth, charismatic leadership, strong organization, and the right to vote, are dispersed throughout society and that any particular group does not monopolize the political resources available. Since proponents of this theory do not distinguish among different polit-ical resources, they deny the relationship between wealth and political influence. With regard to the Sunday shopping issue, for example, they would maintain that religious groups' lobbying efforts for a common day of rest are balanced against corporate efforts to pursue business and commercial trade seven days a week. Under this logic, however, it is difficult to explain why there is such an unequal distribution of wealth and power within Canada if all groups' interests are equally taken into account in the decision-making process.

In response to those who argue that the dominant or capitalist class has unequal access to wealth and may therefore dominate the political process, plural-ists respond by pointing to the number of times business interests were absent from the decision-making process or were defeated historically and recently, such as in their campaigns against medicare, unemployment insurance, workers' compensa-tion, and pay equity.

Liberal democrats' focus on actors within the decision-making process misconstrues the essential character of power and disregards the privileged position in the economy and society occupied by owners of the means of production. The fact that one group within society, the dominant or capitalist class, owns and controls the means of production and disproportionately occupies seats of influ-ence within the economy must be seen as indicative of *political power*. Elected government officials and politicians simply cannot ignore concentrated ownership of the economy in their decision-making. In other words, private ownership within the economy and the influence of persons in positions of wealth and economic power constitute the *context* in which political decisions are made.

Politicians and policy-makers do not necessarily seek direct input from members of the dominant class, nor do business interests always need to engage in lobbying or in other direct actions to be taken into account in the political process.

If a decision will create unfavourable conditions and thereby alienate industrial or commercial interests, for example, then it may be carefully reassessed. The possibility that industrialists will move their operations overseas or simply slow down production and investment if they are dissatisfied with state policy, or if they perceive the government as hostile to their interests, may be weighed more heavily in the political arena than labour's dissatisfaction over a particular industrial policy. Economic ownership, therefore, can be tantamount to political power.

The second criticism of the pluralist framework is that it encompasses a very narrow conception of political power and decision-making, focusing primarily on formal channels through which state policies are developed and on the participants involved in policy-making. The main assumption is that political power is only exercised in these formal processes. This overlooks informal channels of political influence and covert pressures applied to political decision-makers. In Canada, for example, a number of writers (Porter, 1965; Clement, 1975, 1977; Niosi, 1981; Carroll, 1986; Marchak, 1979; Newman, 1975) have documented corporate, family, and friendship ties that provide some groups with informal access to decision-makers. Moreover, many politicians have held directorships or other top-level positions within corporate circles before entering politics or once their political careers were over (Olsen, 1980). Prime Minister Jean Chrétien, former prime ministers (Brian Mulroney and Pierre Elliott Trudeau, for example), premiers, and cabinet members have all enjoyed careers within the highest levels of both the political and economic orders. Not surprisingly, then, top-ranking corporate officials may enjoy informal, personal contact with political leaders, and unlike those representing labour or other less powerful interests, they may not have to ascend the political bureaucracy step-by-step to be heard.

Finally, the liberal democratic explanation pays little or no attention to the overall structure of the society and to the nature of economic and political power. The theory is based on the notion of voluntarism, assuming that political officials act on their own accord, at points in time they regard as most appropriate to propose policy and to affect social change to meet the needs of constituents, to raise pertinent issues, and to further the interests of the common good. Employing this theory to explain advancements or improvements in social policy places individual decision-makers in a positive light by underscoring their good intentions and benevolent social goals. Yet, it ignores the context in which these individuals undertake their various social campaigns, providing no indication of how their actions may be shaped or constrained by their locations within social institutions and the social order, by the social structure, and by historical circumstances.

Some of the criticisms raised concerning the liberal democratic framework are answered by Marxist scholars advancing instrumentalist and structuralist theories of the state.

The Instrumentalist Position

Within a Marxist tradition and in opposition to the liberal democratic explanation, the *instrumentalist* or *élite* theory argues that the state primarily functions to enhance profit-making and the accumulation of wealth by individuals and private concerns and that economic and social policy are designed to further the interests of capital and to benefit the dominant class directly.

Proponents of this theory focus primarily on institutional locations. They identify those who occupy the uppermost positions within the political and economic orders as exercising power and as belonging to an élite. The power of this group is enhanced, they argue, by three interrelated factors: (1) members of the élite have similar class and social characteristics, and as a result share similar values and world views; (2) decisions within the political and economic orders are increasingly interconnected and centralized, thereby strengthening the power of those in commanding positions; and (3) co-ordination and formal and informal collaboration among members of the élite are escalating.

Within this general framework, instrumentalists usually maintain that the economic élite, that is, those persons who reside at the 'command posts' (Mills, 1972) within the economic order, tend to dominate the political sphere. Élite theorists often document the numerous formal and informal connections the economically powerful have to the state structure, demonstrating how business persons are integrated into the political structure through advisory boards, standing committees, and other similar bodies, through kinship ties, and through their own career paths. From this wealth of data, they conclude that the economic élite dominates decision-making within the political arena.

Compared to the liberal democratic theory of the state, the instrumentalist position provides a better explanation for the unequal balance of power within society and the continued domination of an economic élite. This position elucidates the nature of inequality, demonstrating the imbalances in wealth and power that are strengthened by numerous interconnections between the political and economic structures. Unlike the pluralist framework, this theory accounts for the institutional context of decision-making by highlighting the increasing centralization and co-ordination of political and economic decisions. This provides a more accurate picture of the major players within the political sphere than the pluralists' notion of numerous associations, voluntary groups, and individual lobbyists counterbalancing the economic élite's power.

Despite its relative strengths, the instrumentalist position suffers from a similar problem as that encountered by the pluralist perspective. Although their underlying arguments stand at opposite poles, both theories define the scope of decision-making rather narrowly and study activities surrounding the policy-making process for evidence of the state's bias or neutrality. Pluralists chiefly scrutinize politicians' promises and actions whereas instrumentalists are primarily concerned with the deliberate actions of people defined as occupying powerful positions. However, there is no explicit explanation within the instrumentalist framework of structural limitations working upon decision-makers. In the long run, does it matter whether or not the Prime Minister once held certain corporate posts or whether or not he will assume similar economic positions once his political career has ended? Within the context of a capitalist economy, would political and social policies be inherently different? Would the same structural conditions not constrain the policy-making process?

Under the logic of the élite theory of the state, it is difficult to explain some of the progress that has been made in social legislation. Policies such as Workers' Compensation and Employment Insurance were rigorously fought against by the dominant class and represent struggle and victory by the working class. To some degree, the instrumentalists conceptualize power as a zero-sum phenomenon. That is, they assume that the élite holds concentrated power and therefore the power of the majority, the working classes, approaches zero. The theory inadvertently disempowers the working class, labour, and disenfranchised groups by disregarding their actions and the forms of resistance they have used in their struggles for equity and fairness. Employing the instrumentalists' conception of political power leads to a static image of society and social change. The influence of class conflict and the struggles of the disenfranchised are not incorporated in the analysis of political power and social change.

The Structuralist Position

According to the *structuralist* position, the state works on behalf of the dominant class, not at its behest as the instrumentalist view maintains (Panitch, 1977). There is considerable overlap between the instrumentalist and structuralist positions. Structuralists generally agree with the instrumentalists' approach that the state serves the interests of the capitalist class. However, the two theories diverge in how they make this argument and understand the process of class domination. While the élite theorists focus on direct relationships between the state and the dominant class and argue that it is because of their close ties that the capitalist class dominates the state, structuralists focus on the organization of capitalism and the limits it places on the operation of the state and the process of policy-making. Within this framework, the main concern is not whether Canadian state officials were all members of the capitalist class or whether the state was comprised of members of your Introductory Sociology class. Rather, the central focus is on understanding the ways in which state officials' actions are limited and policies are shaped by or are developed in reaction to the contradictions and constraints of the economic system.

Structuralists begin their analysis of the state within capitalist society by underscoring its integral relationship to the economy and by examining how the state is constrained by the logic and structure of capitalism (Panitch, 1977; O'Connor, 1973; Cuneo, 1979; Poulantzas, 1973; Walters, 1982; Pupo, 1988). Within this context, they argue that the state has a vested interest in maintaining a healthy capitalist economy or it risks drying up the sources of its own economic renewal (O'Connor, 1973). To accomplish this, the state has three major functions (O'Connor, 1973; Panitch, 1977). Its first and primary role is to aid the process of capital *accumulation* by maintaining or creating favourable economic conditions. To do this, it engages in *legitimization*. This means that the state maintains or creates favourable social conditions. Finally, the state functions as the agent of *coercion* or social control. This means that the state employs direct or indirect means to maintain or impose social order.

The primary constraint under which the state operates is the fact of private ownership of the means of production. Structuralists argue that this constraint drives the state to serve the interests of the capitalist class since the state itself depends on the prosperity of this class and its members' enterprises for its own survival (O'Connor, 1973). The state's actions therefore could only be understood within the context of this constraint. The state may not directly work for capital, but its decisions and policies derive from its need to accommodate the needs of capital. Political decisions carry high stakes. Inappropriate or unacceptable decisions may alienate key members of the dominant class, who may in turn decide not to reinvest in Canada, not to expand their operations, to conduct their business elsewhere, or to adopt plans that in other ways would jeopardize Canada's economic health or impede economic growth.

At the same time that the state must take into account the needs and interests of the capitalist class to avoid risking its own economic health, it must also account for the needs of the working class, its struggle for social and political action, and the conflicts between and among classes. That is, it must provide opportunities for education and training; it must offer services to maintain the health of the labour force; and it must respond to the call for equity and justice. In other words, in order to fulfil its primary function of accumulation, the state must preserve amicable social relations and perpetuate the idea of the system's neutrality and legitimation (Pupo, 1988: 210).

The state's involvement in the development of social welfare, health, and education policy reveals a complex and dynamic process riddled with evidence of class struggle (Moscovitch and Albert, 1987; Dickinson and Russell, 1986; Struthers, 1983; Finkel, 1977; Carniol, 1990; Kirwin, 1990; Jones, 1983; Walters, 1982). In the short run, state policies may appear to be inequitable, providing greater advantages for poor and disenfranchised groups. In the long run, however, legislation maintains existing class relations by fostering the growth of social harmony and by masking the most blatant forms of inequity. The ways in which state policy is a response to and is limited by the logic and structure of capitalism may become evident by examining the questions of how, why, and under what specific historical circumstances particular policies were proposed, defeated, or amended (Pupo, 1988: 210–11).

In a groundbreaking analysis of the introduction of Canadian Unemployment Insurance in 1941, Cuneo (1979) demonstrates that labour organizations had consistently struggled for unemployment insurance since at least 1919. However, in these struggles workers posed no major threat to the social order until the Depression, when the unemployed began to organize and adopted a notably militant posture. At this point the state drafted unemployment insurance legislation. In other words, structural factors, in this case, class struggle, prompted the introduction of state policy.

Political decisions are not abstract, nor are they determined by the free will of state officials or by goodwill gestures of incumbents to their constituents. Rather, political decisions reflect the circumstances within the real world, the context of the economic condition, and the need for balance among social classes. Unemployment insurance legislation was adopted at a particular point in Canadian history not because state officials abstractly thought it was a good idea or because it was a humanitarian courtesy. Rather, the legislation was passed at this particular juncture because working-class militancy around this issue was beginning to threaten the social accord.

If the state simply met the wishes of the dominant class, as Marxists suggest, then it would be very difficult to explain the existence of legislation establishing unemployment insurance, workers' compensation, or pay equity. Although such legislation is far from perfect in labour's view, nevertheless it still represents labour's historical struggles to legitimize the problems of workers and the structural inequalities within which they live and work.

Central to the structuralists' argument is the notion that the state is *relatively autonomous* from the capitalist class. In other words, the state has a degree of independence from the capitalist class and is not directly dominated by it (Panitch, 1977; Niosi, 1981; Brym, 1985; Ornstein, 1986). This relative autonomy is essential for the state to promote the overall, long-term interests of capital and the rights of private property. The capitalist class, like other social classes, has many internal divisions or differences. Each sector or fraction of the capitalist class has similar long-term interests—to maintain the general economic well-being and to preserve the free enterprise system. In the short term, however, the various sectors may adopt different specific objectives or may advance dissimilar interests.

Internal disagreements within the dominant class were apparent, for example, during the discussions over the Canada-US Free Trade Agreement (FTA). Small nascent manufacturers (clothing, textiles) who wished to avoid further competition from US manufacturers fought against the agreement, often joining forces with Liberal Party opponents to free trade. Resource-based exporting companies and international corporations welcomed the Progressive Conservatives' free trade initiative. In this debate, workers, too, were divided, based on their assessments of what would save jobs and what would reduce the escalating cost of living. Without a degree of autonomy, the state would be restrained from operating in the manner its officials view as best serving the capitalist class in general and it therefore would be limited in its bid to maintain broadly defined economic well-being. Rather, it would be compelled to satisfy particular interests, specifically those with the greatest influence over the state at the expense of charges of partisanship from within both capitalist and working classes. As a result of the state's relative autonomy, state policies sometimes counter the interests of sectors within the capitalist class, thereby creating some hostility between sections of the capitalist class and the state.

While the structuralist theory accounts for the state's need to respond to the working class and at the same time to operate on behalf of capital, it is important to recognize that in practice the system does not necessarily operate with such smooth efficiency. The state's actions are neither as calculating nor as mechanistic as structuralist theory in abstract terms may seem to contend. The state is a highly complex institution that is called on to respond to conflicting class interests within the context of its own historical culture and its location within the global political economy. To understand how the state operates and how it affects everyday lives, it is important to examine the discussions and struggles surrounding individual policy decisions, including the state's response to working-class demands and dominant-class interests as well as its reactions to all forms of resistance. While our approach to the state provides a general view on the ways in which the state has operated within the context of Canadian political economy and therefore allows us to project possible future directions, it is important to avoid 'grand theory' that may overlook the historical traditions and circumstances affecting its course, its complexity and location within the global political economy, the specific interests with which it may be most concerned at the time, and the impact of popular resistance.

Despite the mechanistic conceptualization of the state sometimes derived through the structuralist framework, this perspective is most adequate in explaining the organization and functions of the Canadian state. This theory is able to account for criticisms of the state launched by members of the dominant class and for progressive legislation won by the working class. From this general perspective, we will now consider concretely how the state operates by examining briefly its involvement in the economy, its role in maintaining the labour force, and its interest in protecting the individual within the family home.

Understanding the Role of the State

As noted above, structuralists have outlined the three major functions of the state as accumulation, legitimation, and coercion or social control. These roles are performed simultaneously and are interrelated, although many theorists contend that the state's principal role is in accumulation, in maintaining favourable economic conditions to ensure its own survival as well as that of private enterprise. Each of these functions is carried out in a variety of ways through economic and social policy, through the system of courts and justice, and through public institutions and programs. The state's accumulation function may be examined most clearly through its actions in the economy, whereas its roles in legitimization and social control become more explicit by studying its intervention in the labour market and its impact on families is revealed through public policy and social programs.

While the three functions of the state have not changed throughout the course of Canadian history, the ways in which the state may undertake to execute its roles have varied. Currently, in the transformation to a global economic system in which internationalized capital and global organizations dominate, the Canadian state, along with other capitalist states, is repositioning in order to assure Canada's place within the global economy (Teeple, 1995). According to Teeple, this process of globalization has contributed to the transformation and decline of the welfare state in a dramatic shift in economic policy from *Keynesianism* to *monetarism*. Under Keynesianism, popularized in the post–World War II era, the welfare state or public sector grew, and policies and programs in health, education, social welfare, and labour relations expanded. Keynesian policies were designed to complement the unprecedented growth in capital accumulation by stimulating or maintaining healthy market conditions in a number of ways: by alleviating some of the insecurities felt by the working class through social welfare programs and a liberal labour relations agenda; by maintaining vibrant market conditions within the national economy through programs designed to enhance labour market conditions; and by financing the costs of production, particularly through extensive health and education programs.

During the 1970s globalization of production expanded, becoming part of the new economic reality. Within this context, Keynesianism was replaced with the economic practices of monetarism, an approach that was 'required by internationalized capital in a global economy' (ibid., 70). The primary goal of increasing globalization was to reduce the costs of production and this would be accomplished at the expense of one of the main purposes of the Keynesian approach, that is, to create and maintain a reasonably comfortable social, economic, and political climate for the working class in order to achieve its participation within the capitalist labour market. Monetarism promotes the war against inflation in an effort to bring about currency and price stability and, in this way, dismantles the welfare state, which is no longer regarded as necessary but rather is seen as too costly and economically destabilizing. This approach is guided by the goals of central banks and the international organizations, such as the World Bank and the International Monetary Fund, as well as by international treaties and trade agreements.

The Economy

The state works to maintain a healthy economy operating within the international marketplace. To this end, it functions in a number of ways (Panitch, 1977: 14). First, it provides opportune fiscal and monetary conditions for economic growth. Within the context of a global economy, the state works to entice international capital investment while satisfying the needs of national and multinational corporate leaders whose enterprises are already well established within the economy. It must try to balance the conflicting needs of various sectors within the capitalist class. This sometimes involves intricate strategies since, as discussed above, the dominant class is internally differentiated and the state cannot appear consistently to be favouring one fraction as opposed to another. The state negotiates with international powers for oil and other resources. Through its diplomatic relations and its bargaining with foreign state structures, it paves the way for the expansion of Canadian businesses into developing countries and international marketplaces. Moreover, through its adoption of monetarist economic policies and its program of retrenchment and restraint in social welfare and health and education spending, it aligns Canadian policy with the expectations and approaches in effect among the world's economic powers.

As a major consumer of a number of services and a wealth of goods, the state also generates business. It buys an endless list of goods (medical, school, and office supplies, aircraft and military hardware, computers and office software, uniforms) and contracts with numerous landlords and financial institutions, consulting firms and services (office cleaners and general maintenance, construction, movers, food services, secretarial and administrative support). The move towards privatization in health care and the social services, documented during the late 1980s and partic-ularly throughout the 1990s (Brodie, 1996; Ismael and Vaillancourt, 1988), may expand this role.

Second, the state underwrites the private risks of production at public expense through grants, subsidies, forgivable loans, depreciation allowances, corporate bailouts, and other measures. The Canadian state has historically maintained a regressive taxation system (Hunter, 1986; Armitage, 1988; McQuaig, 1992a, 1995). A *regressive* system is one in which the rate of taxation does not increase relative to wealth and income, thereby maintaining levels of inequality. In contrast, under a *progressive* system taxes increase with income levels, thereby narrowing the gaps between higher- and lower-income earners. The Canadian taxation system, one of the most complicated worldwide, includes provisions for a number of tax write-offs, allowances, and incentives and a corporate tax rate that is lower than that for individuals.

Third, the state is responsible for maintaining the labour market through its labour and immigration policies. It also absorbs the social cost of production through policies such as medicare and education and training programs. Immigra-tion policy corresponds to labour market needs and is constantly revised to reflect the dynamics of the marketplace, the demands of new technologies, and the diverse requirements for various types of labour (Foster, 1998). Since 1967 Canadian immigration policy has been based on a 'points system' in which prospective immi-grants are selected on the basis of their scores on a number of criteria, including education, occupation, and language. This specific labour recruitment strategy, together with the classification of immigrants under independent, family, or busi-ness class, has operated to discriminate against immigrant women, who are most often categorized as family class and, accordingly, are granted landed status only through the sponsorship of a spouse or other immediate family member (Ng, 1988). Family class immigrants are usually ineligible independently for a number of social services as well as for subsidies for language and job training programs. Consequently, when they do enter the paid labour force, they are frequently employed in marginalized, low-wage job ghettos, with little security and often without union protection. Moreover, a recent study based on Statistics Canada 1991 data found that visible-minority immigrants are vastly overrepresented among Canada's poor. Nearly 40 per cent of West Asian, Arab, Vietnamese, and Latin and South American immigrants, compared to about 15.6 per cent of all Canadians, live at or below the poverty line (Roberts, 1999; Li, 1998). Hence, the structure of immigration policy satisfies capital's requirement for a cheap, expend-able labour force.

Fourth, the state furnishes and maintains the technical infrastructure, includ-ing roads, highways, transportation systems, airports, and facilities for technological research and development. Maintaining the infrastructure is regarded as too costly and risky for private business.

Among the most contentious economic policies in recent times have been the free trade agreements. These initiatives were promoted for the ways in which they would provide a necessary economic boost for the Canadian economy because of the opportunities they were expected to afford for the expansion of US corpora-tions in Canada and the opening of the vast market in the US and Mexico for Canadian manufactured goods. In an era of the global corporation and the tendency for capital to seek the best price for labour and resources as well as for taxes, one of the overriding purposes of the agreements was to entice US and other foreign capital to invest in or remain in Canada. The discussions surrounding the conditions of the agreement exposed some of the divisions within the capitalist class over their specific needs.

Labour leaders have repeatedly pointed to the long-term devastating conse-quences of free trade (Pupo and White, 1994). Canadian labour cannot compete with the lower-waged labour available in the United States and particularly in Mexico. The rate of unionization in the civilian labour force in Canada was about 31 per cent in 1997, far outstripping the comparable US rate (Lipsig-Mumme and Laxer, 1998). The North American Free Trade Agreement (NAFTA) between Canada, the US, and Mexico has, according to labour analysts, worsened conditions for labour as well as for small Canadian manufacturers, who are forced to compete with the far cheaper Mexican labour market.

The Labour Market

Through labour legislation, union protection, anti-combines legislation, and social welfare measures, the state integrates the working class into capitalist society by gaining its loyalty and support and by diffusing social conflict by appearing to respond to demands for equity and justice.

Over the years there have been numerous calls from labour for action from the Canadian state for fair labour legislation, shorter working hours, union recognition and collective bargaining, unemployment insurance, workers' compensation, health and safety standards, employment standards, equality for women and minorities, and pay equity. Fair and protective labour legislation is not a measure of the benev-olence of the state, but, rather, represents labour's resistance to oppressive work structures and organizational practices. Labour's ongoing challenge is the struggle for democracy and the defence of its rights. This struggle continues, as Panitch and Swartz (1988: 115) note, because 'even reforms basic to liberal democracy are always subject to limits and never guaranteed forever.' The state's concessions to labour derive from its primary role in facilitating capital accumulation. As this role develops and changes in response to national and international market conditions, the state's reaction to labour will reflect this dynamic process.

In strike action, the state often adopts the role of arbitrator and may legislate compulsory arbitration. It also maintains control during strikes by deploying police forces instructed to restrain the strikers. Panitch and Swartz have documented the ways in which federal and provincial governments, through denying the right to strike and increasing intervention against labour rights, transformed capital–labour relations during the 1980s from 'an era of consent' to 'an era of coercion'. This coercive climate, which persisted throughout the 1990s, reflects harsh economic conditions as well as the dispensability of labour in the vast majority of work settings.

The state monitors the rate of unemployment and through the system of social welfare offers programs for workers who are laid off from their jobs or who are unable to find secure employment. Unemployment counselling, job creation strategies, retraining programs, and the funding of pragmatic learning through community colleges and science and technology programs are activities aimed at maintaining the labour market and diverting attention from corporate cutbacks and retrenchment policies (Riches and Ternowetsky, 1990). Little direct action has been undertaken by the state to address the issue of unemployment, even at the depths of recessions when the problem is most severe. During the recession of the early 1980s the government adopted a monetarist strategy, aiming its fight against inflation, which is more costly to capital accumulation, rather than at unemployment, which is most harmful to individuals and families (Burman, 1988: 11; 1996). The fight against poverty and unemployment and the struggle to maintain social benefits have fallen further onto the shoulders of individuals and their families. This struggle has also found its way to the negotiation table as unions find themselves having to play a greater role in dealing with insecurity and in protecting their memberships from harsh economic conditions, diverting attention from their need to address changes in working conditions brought by new managerial strategies, reorganization and restructuring, and technological innovation.

The Canadian economy has been restructuring in response to global trends in markets and industries. Over the past 15–20 years the heavy industrial sector— where relatively well-paying blue-collar jobs are located—shrank, a process referred to as *deindustrialization*. At the same time, the personal, business, and community services sector expanded. Although employment growth has been measured in the services sector, jobs within this sector are typically low-paying and insecure, and frequently part-time, contractually limited, or in other ways 'atypical' (Duffy and Pupo, 1992; Schellenberg, 1997). The trend in Canada has been for 'good jobs' to vanish only to be replaced by 'bad jobs' (Economic Council of Canada, 1990; Duffy et al., 1997). Economic restructuring and the demise of heavy industry are irreversible and therefore will necessitate adjustments in the state structure, in social policy, in the labour movement, and in the systems of social welfare, education, and health as the number of families and individuals unaccustomed to such a degree of insecurity continues to multiply.

Individuals and Families

The state operates directly and indirectly to affect our personal lives. While public and private spheres are usually differentiated, there is significant interrelation between these spheres. It is impossible, in fact, to separate public and private domains since circumstances in one sphere ultimately affect those in the other.

THE SCHOOLS: REPRODUCING INEQUALITY

One of the ways the state maintains harmonious social relations is by providing opportunities for personal development and success through the publicly supported educational system. Of all social institutions, schools are regarded as the great levellers. Theoretically, all children enter the scholastic footrace at the same starting point and have similar chances for success. However, studies indicate that although the educational system may operate under the rubric of equality of opportunity, it is not impartial. High educational achievement correlates with class background. Children from middle-class and upper-class families gain most from a good education (Porter et al., 1979; Macdonnell, 1987). Working-class children are not as likely to stay in school as long nor are they as likely to achieve as high a degree of success as children of higher-income parents. Moreover, educational degrees are not passports to secure or coveted positions in the labour market. Rather than levelling class differences, the educational system re-creates the status quo by reproducing hierarchical and unequal class and social relations (Livingstone, 1985).

Critical analyses of education argue that schooling contributes to the repro-duction of labour power in two ways. First, through the process of sorting and selecting students into various streams and programs, schools function to reproduce the existing pattern of social relationships and inequalities. Second, education fosters the development of particular values, ideologies, beliefs, and behaviours essential for the maintenance of the ongoing social order. In these ways, education does not create inequality but rather facilitates and legitimizes its re-creation. In concrete terms, employers rely on school evaluations of students for their selection of workers.

Through education, and what is often referred to as the *hidden curriculum*, the social and political orders are legitimized. Schools prepare workers for the labour market, equipped not only with the skills and knowledge necessary to perform certain jobs, but with a commitment to the socio-political structure. This is most evident, of course, in business schools where the curriculum, while taught in an 'objective' manner, embraces the ideology and practice of capitalism.

SOCIAL WELFARE: PRESERVING SOCIAL RELATIONS

Under capitalism, social welfare legitimizes the class structure by shielding the most blatant forms of inequality, by promoting the well-being of Canadians within a system based on inequality, and by making a wide variety of social programs universally available, thereby strengthening notions regarding the state's impartial-ity. The welfare safety net represents the state's somewhat enigmatic roles within the economy and society, securing the well-being of the working classes while preserving the structure of social class and power and deflecting criticism directed against the general structure of the social system (Panitch, 1977; Moscovitch and Drover, 1987).

Social welfare programs tend to focus on individuals and their failures to provide for themselves or for their families. Focusing on individuals' shortcomings diverts criticism from the private sector and the structure of class and power. Although social welfare functions to maintain social harmony and to reaffirm values of thrift and hard work, many deplore the system, arguing that the poor are shiftless, overpaid in welfare benefits, and live off the backs of the middle and upper classes. However, the welfare system has neither flattened the class hierarchy nor has it reduced the significant discrepancies in income levels. In comparison to most Western European and Scandinavian countries, Canada's level of social expenditure (as a percentage of its gross national product) is moderate to low, falling substantially below the rates calculated for Belgium, Sweden, Norway, Denmark, Germany, Austria, the United Kingdom, and France, among other countries (McQuaig, 1992b; Armitage, 1988). At the same time, the system affords welfare to the rich in the form of research grants, corporate subsidies, depreciation allowances, and numerous tax loopholes. For example, the Canadian Pacific Railway, a privately owned concern, was largely financed through the public purse by numerous government allowances and land grants (Hiller, 1996: 136). The tax system, as mentioned earlier, provides little to counterbalance the shortfalls in welfare spending and programming and does not alter the overall income structure.

Early social welfare programs were specifically designed to teach thrift, economy, and selflessness and were intended to transform the intransigent into hardworking and responsible citizens (Struthers, 1983). Many modern programs echo these sentiments. For example, provincial governments in Canada have been steadfast in their attempts to promote work incentive policies to discourage long-term social assistance and to encourage self-sufficiency through entry/re-entry to the paid labour market. For many welfare recipients the prospect of a paid job, even one in which they would earn the minimum wage or marginally more or less than they would on welfare once employment costs are calculated, is preferred over the stigma and social isolation of social assistance. However, within the context of a recessionary economy and employment discrimination, work incentive schemes consistently fail to deliver on their promises. Moreover, their underlying objective—to entice recipients to accept low-paying, insecure, and unattractive jobs and to be complacent with that 'privilege'—is highly questionable (Evans and McIntyre, 1987).

Modern programs have come under attack as agents of systemic discrimination based on class, gender, and race/ethnicity (Carniol, 1990). Few traditional programs are derived from a critical practice and are ultimately oriented towards social change. Recently, however, groups of social workers, along with nurses and other front-line workers, fuelled by their dissatisfaction with the conditions of their employment and the insecurity of their jobs, have been criticizing openly the

design and purpose of the programs they administer (ibid.; Jones, 1983). This resistance by social workers and their clients constitutes a significant contradiction
confronting the state's forces of legitimation.

SOCIAL AND FAMILY POLICY: PROMOTING EQUALITY

Changes in the structure of the family and women's roles in the public and domestic spheres have raised important questions about the state's responsibility to address
the numerous dilemmas of the work and family interface. The state has committed itself publicly to the notion of formal equality by incorporating the principle
of gender neutrality within the boundaries of the courts and the policy-making
process (Morton, 1988; Evans and Pupo, 1993; Evans and Wekerle, 1997). The state
defines gender equality in terms of equality of access to opportunities and
resources but ignores the real and profound differences in the lives of men and
women. This refusal to acknowledge and account for the ways in which individual lives are shaped by gender prevents the construction of a truly progressive social
program and entrenches systemic discrimination.

Although policy appears to uphold the tradition of impartiality, a profound
gender bias derived from the state's insistence on an inherent equality in men's and
women's lives pervades family policy, including divorce and child custody legislation, parental leave provision, and family law (Morton, 1988; Pupo, 1988; Boyd,
1989; Delorey, 1989; Evans and Pupo, 1993). The relative costs of divorce, custody
disputes, and other family matters are usually higher for women, largely due to
their unequal access to and share of material resources and their relative powerlessness in the family and society. Defining men's and women's lives as equal, then,
places women at a disadvantage. Rather than starting from the premise of women's
equality, legislation should work towards equality by taking into account at the
outset women's unequal access to resources and power, and women's unpaid and
unrecognized contributions to the family and society (their 'labours of love'), and
should provide for compensation for those contributions.

Because of the time and energy (practical and emotional) women devote to
family and because of the assumptions and demands family members make with
regard to women's caring obligations, women frequently forfeit personal time for
self-improvement, education, and experience and seniority in the paid labour
force. For example, the division of parental responsibilities in Canadian households
is very unequal. Women are absent from their jobs for family reasons far more often
than their male partners; they spend more hours per week in household work and
child care, regardless of the employment status of their spouses; they are usually
responsible for all child-care arrangements; and they report feeling very 'time-
crunched' or stressed due to the conflicting demands of their domestic and paid
work (Pupo, 1997). Although men may tend to under-report days lost due to
family obligations, women nevertheless undertake the greatest share of family caregiving and this tends to undervalue their public roles. The hiddenness of women's
caregiving work spares both the state and capital from the expense of the fundamental and socially necessary work of the renewal and provision of the labour
force. Family policy, then, should begin with the objective of confronting the

structural parameters upholding women's prescribed roles/condition, aiming to rectify rather than to enshrine this measure of inequality.

The state operates as if each individual before the court has a specific claim to justice and equity and that this claim is unrelated to or detached from one's status as a gendered being. Inequality related to gender is denied. Feminists have argued that the state should rethink the meaning of equality by taking into account the reality of gender inequality, the privatization of domestic labour and child care under capitalism and women's collective relationship to that structure (Morton, 1988; Sassoon, 1987). That is, women's unpaid caregiving and family work, as well as their consequent losses in the public domain, should figure prominently in court decisions (Baines, Evans, and Neysmith, 1991). The political and economic reality of women's lives as distinct from men's would constitute the starting point for negotiations.

The State and Social Change

The operation of the state is a dynamic process that simultaneously confronts the constraints of capitalism and the contradictions emerging from its roles in legitimation and social control. The welfare state has provided opportunity for women and other minorities to challenge the meaning of democracy and to struggle for recognition before the courts as well as for an equitable share of political resources. Improved social policy, reforms in labour legislation and family law, and questions raised under the Charter of Rights represent alliances and struggles waged by women, the poor, labour, and disenfranchised groups. While we cannot view the state *per se* as a vehicle of social change or ignore its overriding function to facilitate capital accumulation and maintain the structure of class and power under capitalism, at the same time the state inadvertently provides an avenue for resistance. The tension between the public-sector unions and the government in Ontario in 1996 and again in 1999 exposes the dynamic process of change. The Ontario government, as an employer, has adopted severe measures of cutbacks and restraint, arguing that its program of deficit-cutting and retrenchment of social spending is necessary in light of how the provincial government is constrained by federal government strategies and international economic conditions. The Canadian labour movement, the public service unions, and numerous activist organizations and coalitions, as a result of government policies, have been on a collision course, and this has raised public discussion regarding the state's interests while demonstrating to labour the need to substantiate its power.

We may work towards social change by studying the strategies previous generations of women, workers, and other social activists have used to capitalize on the state's own contradiction: its need to consolidate class struggle and integrate the working class into the socio-political framework by granting some concessions and maintaining an appearance of neutrality, accessibility, and justice. Active political participation by means of demonstrations, rallies, vigorous campaigning, unrelenting criticism, and lobbying state officials and bureaucrats together may provide a structure through which various alliances may be consolidated and social change may eventually result.

Questions for Critical Thought

1. Why have governments cut back on and in some cases privatized social programs despite unrelentingly high rates of unemployment, poverty, and other related problems in Canada?

2. Discuss the effects on health care and education of governments' shifting from Keynesian to deficit-cutting economic policies.

3. Is the state's decision to adopt a monetarist framework reversible? Under what conditions might the state undertake the process of mending the frayed social safety net?

Glossary

Globalization: The current stage of advanced capitalism in which production, distribution, and exchange occur on a global basis, rendering intervention at the level of the nation-state secondary to the decision-making and power of transnational corporations. Under globalization, states function to maintain the infrastructure necessary to support global enterprise.

Keynesianism: Popularized in the postwar period, an economic strategy that enlarges the public sector by increasing spending on education, health, and social welfare in order to buffer the insecurity of the working class and to encourage spending and economic growth.

Monetarism: Economic policy that reduces costs of production by trimming spending on social programs, waging war against inflation, and promoting currency and price stability. Under monetarism, welfare is seen as costly and destabilizing.

Power: The ability to affect the behaviour of individuals or of groups. The power of the state is both *direct* and *indirect*.

Welfare state: The vast system of publicly supported education, health, and social programs that functions to support and aid in the reproduction of the working class. These programs are described as the public's *social safety net*, which is designed to 'catch' individuals when they are unable to meet their or their families' needs due to unpredictable or difficult circumstances (loss of job, ill health, etc.).

Suggested Reading

Armstrong, Pat, and Hugh Armstrong. 1996. *Wasting Away: The Undermining of Canadian Health Care.* Toronto: Oxford University Press. A discussion of the impact of governments' decisions to practice cost-cutting and move towards privatization of health care in Canada.

Clarke, Tony. 1997. *Silent Coup: Confronting the Big Business Takeover of Canada.* Ottawa and Toronto: Canadian Centre for Policy Alternatives and James Lorimer. An exposé of the power of Canada's largest corporations and their takeover of the Canadian economy. The book provides plans for challenging big business through social movements and community organizations.

McQuaig, Linda. 1999. *The Cult of Impotence: Selling the Myth of Powerlessness in the Global Economy*. Toronto: Penguin Books. Dispels the notion that governments are too cash-poor to repair the social safety net and develop financial plans that include provisions to deal with unemployment, poverty, and other social problems.

Shragge, Eric, ed. 1997. *Community Economic Development: In Search of Empowerment*. Montreal: Black Rose Books. An exploration of agency through local communities in their struggles to reclaim control from central powers and re-establish a sense of dignity in the communities.

Teeple, Gary. 1995. *Globalization and the Decline of Social Reform*. Toronto: Garamond Press. An examination of the rise of the welfare state in the postwar period and its collapse under governments' shifting economic strategies within the globalized economy.

References

Armitage, Andrew. 1988. *Social Welfare in Canada: Ideals, Realities, and Future Paths*, 2nd edn. Toronto: McClelland & Stewart.

Baines, Carol, Patricia Evans, and Sheila Neysmith, eds. 1998. *Women's Caring: Feminist Perspectives on Social Welfare*, 2nd edn. Toronto: Oxford University Press.

Boyd, Susan B. 1989. 'Child Custody, Ideologies and Employment', *Canadian Journal of Women and the Law* 3: 111–33.

Brodie, Janine, ed. 1996. *Women and Canadian Public Policy*. Toronto: Harcourt, Brace.

Brym, Robert, ed. 1985. *The Structure of the Canadian Capitalist Class*. Toronto: Garamond Press.

Burman, Patrick. 1988. *Killing Time, Losing Ground: Experiences of Unemployment*. Toronto: Wall & Thompson.

———. 1996. *Poverty's Bonds: Power and Agency in the Social Relations of Welfare*. Toronto: Thompson Educational Publishing.

Carniol, Ben. 1990. *Case Critical: Challenging Social Work in Canada*, 2nd edn. Toronto: Between the Lines.

Carroll, William K. 1986. *Corporate Power and Canadian Capitalism*. Vancouver: University of British Columbia Press.

Clement, Wallace. 1975. *The Canadian Corporate Elite: An Analysis of Economic Power*. Toronto: McClelland & Stewart.

———. 1977. *Continental Corporate Power*. Toronto: McClelland & Stewart.

Cuneo, Carl J. 1979. 'State, Class and Reserve Labour: The Case of the 1941 Canadian Unemployment Insurance Act', *Canadian Review of Sociology and Anthropology* 16, 2: 147–70.

Delorey, Anne Marie. 1989. 'Joint Legal Custody: A Reversion to Patriarchal Power', *Canadian Journal of Women and the Law* 3: 33–44.

Dickinson, James, and Bob Russell, eds. 1986. *Family, Economy and State: The Social Reproduction Process Under Capitalism*. Toronto: Garamond Press.

Duffy, Ann, Daniel Glenday, and Norene Pupo, eds. 1997. *Good Jobs, Bad Jobs, No Jobs: The Transformation of Work in the 21st Century*. Toronto: Harcourt, Brace.

———— and Norene Pupo. 1992. *Part-Time Paradox: Connecting Gender, Work, and Family*. Toronto: McClelland & Stewart.

Economic Council of Canada. 1990. *Good Jobs, Bad Jobs: Employment in the Service Economy*. Ottawa: Minister of Supply and Services.

Enright, Janet. 1990. 'Civil Liberties and Canada's War Measures Act', in Katherina L.P. Lundy and Barbara D. Warme, eds, *Sociology: A Window on the World*, 2nd edn. Toronto: Nelson Canada, 476–8.

Evans, Patricia M., and Eilene L. McIntyre. 1987. 'Welfare, Work Incentives and the Single Mother: An Interprovincial Comparison', in Jacqueline S. Ismael, ed., *The Canadian Welfare State: Evolution and Transition*. Edmonton: University of Alberta Press.

———— and Norene Pupo. 1993. 'Parental Leave: Assessing Women's Interests', *Canadian Journal of Women and the Law* 6, 2: 402-18.

———— and Gerda R. Wekerle, eds. 1997. *Women and the Canadian Welfare State: Challenges and Change*. Toronto: University of Toronto Press.

Finkel, Alvin. 1977. 'Origins of the Welfare State', in Leo Panitch, ed., *The Canadian State*. Toronto: University of Toronto Press, 344–70.

Foster, Lorne. 1998. *Turnstile Immigration: Multiculturalism, Social Order and Social Justice in Canada*. Toronto: Thompson Educational Publishing.

Freire, Paulo. 1972. *Pedagogy of the Oppressed*, trans. Myra Bergman Ramos. New York: Herder and Herder.

Hiller, Harry H. 1996. *Canadian Society: A Macro Analysis*, 3rd edn. Scarborough, Ont.: Prentice-Hall Canada.

Hunter, A.A. 1986. *Class Tells: On Social Inequality in Canada*, 2nd edn. Toronto: Butterworths.

Ismael, Jacqueline S., and Yves Vaillancourt, eds. 1988. *Privatization and Provincial Social Services in Canada: Policy, Administration and Service Delivery*. Edmonton: University of Alberta Press.

Jones, Chris. 1983. *State Social Work and the Working Class*. London: Macmillan.

Kirwin, Bill, ed. 1990. *Ideology, Development and Social Welfare: Canadian Perspectives*. Toronto: Canadian Scholars' Press.

Li, Peter S. 1998. 'The Market Value and Social Value of Race', in Vic Satzewich, ed., *Racism and Social Inequality in Canada*. Toronto: Thompson Educational Publishing.

Lipsig-Mumme, Carla, and Kate Laxer. 1998. 'Organizing and Union Membership: A Canadian Profile in 1997', paper prepared for the Canadian Labour Congress.

Livingstone, David. 1985. *Social Crisis and Schooling*. Toronto: Garamond Press.

————, ed. 1987. *Critical Pedagogy and Cultural Power*. Toronto: Garamond Press.

Macdonnell, Allan. 1987. *Canadian Degree Undergraduates and Their Study Preferences*. Ottawa: Statistics Canada.

McQuaig, Linda. 1992a. 'Canada's Social Programs: Under Attack. How Much Do We Value Equality?', *Toronto Star*, 12 Nov., A23.

————. 1992b. 'The Fraying of Our Social Safety Net', *Toronto Star*, 8 Nov., B1, B7.

————. 1995. *Shooting the Hippo: Death by Deficit and Other Canadian Myths.* Toronto: Penguin Books.

Marchak, Patricia. 1979. *In Whose Interests: An Essay on Multinational Corporations in a Canadian Context.* Toronto: McClelland & Stewart.

Miliband, Ralph. 1973. *The State in Capitalist Society.* London: Quartet Books.

Mills, C.W. 1972. *The Power Elite.* New York: Oxford University Press.

Morton, Mary E. 1988. 'Dividing the Wealth, Sharing the Poverty: The (Re)formation of "Family" Law in Ontario', *Canadian Review of Sociology and Anthropology* 25, 2 (May).

Moscovitch, Allan, and Jim Albert, eds. 1987. *The Benevolent State: The Growth of Welfare in Canada.* Toronto: Garamond Press.

———— and Glenn Drover. 1987. 'Social Expenditures and the Welfare State: The Canadian Experience in Historical Perspective', in Moscovitch and Albert (1987).

Nelsen, Randle W. 1991. *Miseducating: Death of the Sensible.* Kingston, Ont.: Cedarcreek Publications.

Newman, Peter C. 1975. *The Canadian Establishment*, vol. 1. Toronto: McClelland & Stewart.

Ng, Roxana. 1988. 'Immigrant Women and Institutionalized Racism', in Sandra Burt, Lorraine Code, and Lindsay Dorney, eds, *Changing Patterns: Women in Canada.* Toronto: McClelland & Stewart, 184–203.

Niosi, Jorge. 1981. *Canadian Capitalism: A Study of Power in the Canadian Business Establishment.* Toronto: James Lorimer.

O'Connor, James. 1973. *The Fiscal Crisis of the State.* New York: St Martin's Press.

Olsen, Dennis. 1980. *The State Elite.* Toronto: McClelland & Stewart.

Ornstein, Michael. 1986. 'The Political Ideology of the Canadian Capitalist Class', *Canadian Review of Sociology and Anthropology* 23, 3: 182–209.

Panitch, Leo. 1977. 'The Role and Nature of the Canadian State', in Panitch, ed., *The Canadian State.* Toronto: University of Toronto Press, 3–27.

———— and Donald Swartz. 1988. *The Assault on Trade Union Freedoms.* Toronto: Garamond Press.

Porter, John. 1965. *The Vertical Mosaic.* Toronto: University of Toronto Press.

Porter, Marion R., John Porter, and Bernard Blishen. 1979. *Does Money Matter? Prospects for Higher Education in Ontario.* Toronto: Macmillan.

Poulantzas, Nicos. 1973. *Political Power and Social Classes.* London: New Left Books.

Pupo, Norene. 1988. 'Preserving Patriarchy: Women, the Family and the State', in Nancy Mandell and Ann Duffy, eds, *Reconstructing the Canadian Family: Feminist Perspectives.* Toronto: Butterworths, 207–37.

————. 1997. 'Always Working, Never Done: The Expansion of the Double Day', in Ann Duffy, Daniel Glenday, and Pupo, eds, *Good Jobs, Bad Jobs, No Jobs: The Transformation of Work in the 21st Century.* Toronto: Harcourt, Brace.

———— and Jerry White. 1994. 'Union Leaders and the Economic Crisis: Responses to Restructuring', *Relations Industrielles/Industrial Relations* 49, 4 (Autumn): 821–45.

Riches, Graham, and Gordon Ternowetsky, eds. 1990. *Unemployment and Welfare: Social Policy and the Work of Social Work.* Toronto: Garamond Press.

Roberts, David. 1999. 'Some Immigrant Groups Fare Badly, New Study Asserts', *Globe and Mail*, 1 Feb., A4.

Sassoon, Anne Showstack, ed. 1987. *Women and the State*. London: Unwin Hyman.

Schellenberg, Grant. 1997. *The Changing Nature of Part-time Work*. Ottawa: Canadian Council on Social Development.

Struthers, James. 1983. *No Fault of Their Own: Unemployment and the Canadian Welfare State, 1914-1941*. Toronto: University of Toronto Press.

Teeple, Gary. 1995. *Globalization and the Decline of Social Reform*. Toronto: Garamond Press.

Walters, Vivienne. 1982. 'State, Capital and Labour: The Introduction of Federal–Provincial Insurance for Physician Care in Canada', *Canadian Review of Sociology and Anthropology* 19, 2: 157–72.

Wotherspoon, Terry, ed. 1987. *The Political Economy of Canadian Schooling*. Toronto: Methuen.

chapter five

Public Education at the Crossroads: Confronting Underemployment in a Knowledge Society

David W. Livingstone

But our historical situation itself is torn by contradictions, on the razor's edge between the potential 'humanization' of man and 'planetization' of the earth on the one hand and the complete destruction of life or at least of civilization by war and totalitarianism on the other. . . . We only have faith that we are declining and falling; we do not yet have faith in our ability to build a new civilization or to revitalize the old one. . . . We, the newest barbarians, in the midst of this declining civilization, must learn to preserve what we are ravaging. To do so, we must also learn to change it and ourselves in ways that are radical, even utopian, and that, to many, will at first look decadent, or barbaric, or both. (Brantlinger, 1983: 296–7)

Introduction

All prior civilizations have experienced a decline and fall, through ecological and political overextension (Diamond, 1998), loss of faith in shared notions of a good society (Polak, 1967), or the interaction of material challenges and ideological disillusionment. The environmental degradation and the dominant theories and media portrayals of the mediocrity of mass culture in contemporary societies suggest a similar prospect of decline. Conversely, various new social movements and advocates of space-age democratization point to chances for environmental renewal and societal transformation. Whether the changes turn out to be apocalyptic or merely incremental, modern civilization now clearly faces serious questions about the nature of its future existence.

In virtually all periods of economic or social crisis within industrial capitalist societies over the past 200 years, established leaders and associated intellectuals have decried the inadequate knowledge and ambition of the common people as major contributing factors, and have called for the reform and revitalization of educational institutions as a key step to resolving the crisis (e.g., Curti, 1935), while other voices have dismissed such claims as 'blaming the victim' (e.g., Farber 1970) but ignoring root causes of such crises.

In the current period of increased chronic unemployment and industrial restructuring that began in the 1970s, both public educational institutions and various features of mass culture have once again been subjected to concerted attack for contributing to the failings of the economy and social disorder. On the other hand, the popular pursuit of knowledge has never been greater. People generally are spending more time than ever in various learning activities while the gap between their usable knowledge and its actual use in employment widens, a condition increasingly recognized as *underemployment*.[1]

We now face three basic choices in dealing with the education–employment relationship: (1) restrict the flow of people into public education institutions and tie entry more closely to future employment prospects—the 'market-driven' option; (2) continue to encourage the pursuit of more advanced education at increased personal expense in the belief that this investment will generate 'intellectual capital', which leads to a more prosperous economy—the 'knowledge economy' option; or (3) defend the public right to education in relation to growing popular demand while reorganizing paid employment to allow more fully the use of people's learning capacities—the 'economic democracy' option.

The *market-driven* option assumes there is too much irrelevant and inferior provision of public education. After more than a century of continuing expansion of public education, its quality is considered to have seriously declined. More rigorous and restrictive standards are regarded as essential. The key element in this option is increasing reliance on individual market choices through such means as voucher systems and privatization of education. The problem of 'over-education' is addressed by increasingly determining access to education by ability to pay rather than ability to learn.

The *knowledge economy* option is grounded in the belief that human learning capacity is the central productive resource in information-based economies. Since investment in education has been associated with increased economic wealth in the past, it is assumed that this relation will continue. People are generally encouraged to continue to invest in education, even if this leads to great personal indebtedness in a context of government constraint in education spending. The problem of underemployment is generally regarded as either fleeting or irrelevant.

The *economic democracy* option recognizes that continual learning is the most distinctive quality of human beings and that our primary means of expressing ourselves is through our labours. An effective address to underemployment should not deny or divert learning capacities but find better ways to express our knowledge through reorganizing and redistributing valued labour in our workplaces. The basic problem resides not in education but in the lack of decent jobs.

As in prior periods of crisis, most public debate has focused on resolving both social and educational problems by either somewhat more reliance on private market forces or somewhat more state intervention to regulate market forces, 'shareholder capitalism' versus 'stakeholder capitalism'.[2] Either a bit less or a bit more regulation of private market relations is seen as sufficient to resolve the crisis. Reorganization of the education system is seen as imperative, either through market-driven initiatives in shareholder capitalist versions or through greater intellectual capital investments in stakeholder capitalist versions. Serious reform of the economy is not even considered in either dominant perspective. The captains of industry, mass opinion, and government continue to suggest resolutions to the education-jobs gap that amount to either jettisoning ballast from or shuffling deck chairs on education and training ships, while underemployment mounts around them in a sea of 'global competition' they regard as beyond any real human control. Is this really all there is?

The Canadian Case

The general conditions described above apply throughout the advanced industrial societies. What is distinctive about Canada is that it has the least current control over its own economy as well as the most accessible educational system. Among the G-7 countries, Canada has the highest continuing reliance on natural resource extraction and a much higher level of foreign ownership of productive enterprises, and hence relatively less demand for highly skilled managerial, professional, and technical research jobs in value-added industries. At the same time, as a liberal democratic political regime with a well-established tradition of upward social mobility through education, Canada has seen public education authorities respond to growing popular demand by rapidly expanding post-compulsory educational provisions.

In short, Canada has the highest levels of economic dependence on its major trading partners as well as the highest levels of educational attainment among its youth cohorts. Consequently, it also has the highest cumulative levels of underemployment (Livingstone, 1999a). This chapter documents both the extensive lifelong learning and massive underemployment in Canada. The need for addressing the growing problem of underemployment through substantial policy reforms is most pressing in this country.

A Knowledge Society: Schooling, Further Education, and Informal Learning

Three basic sorts of conscious learning practices are commonly distinguished in terms of the context in which they occur: formal education or schooling; non-formal, continuing, or further education; and informal learning. *Formal education* has been defined as full-time study within state-certified school systems. *Further education* is all other organized educational activities, including further courses or training programs offered by any social institution. *Informal learning* is any activity involving the pursuit of understanding, knowledge, or skill that occurs outside or beyond the curricula and authorized instructors of institutions providing educational programs, courses, or workshops. Informal learning may occur in any context, including paid workplaces, households, and local community settings. Explicit informal learning is distinguished from everyday perceptions and general socialization by peoples' own conscious retrospective identification of the activity as significant learning. Its basic terms are determined by the individuals and groups who choose to engage in it (see Selman and Dampier, 1991; Percy, 1997). Informal learning is really the invisible part of the iceberg of adult learning that most people do not recognize unless they are encouraged to reflect on their actual learning practices as a whole.[3] For example, most Canadians have probably learned most of what they know about computers on their own with friends and workmates rather than through school programs or courses (Sawchuk, 1996).

These three types of learning activities overlap and interact. While a lockstep march from the end of schooling into the permanent workforce used to be common, we now see multiple transitions between full-time school and full-time work and frequent combining of part-time paid work with further education (Livingstone, 2000). Informal learners can base some of their learning without a formal instructor on the same curricular materials as formal schooling or continuing education programs. Human learning is a complex and multi-dimensional activity that should never be reduced merely to formal schooling (Illich, 1971). Informal learning is indeed the usually hidden part of the learning iceberg that supports the more visible parts in both positive and negative ways (Brookfield, 1981).

The cumulative body of human information systems and our collective capacity to convert this information into useful bodies of knowledge have increased greatly during the past century (Machlup, 1980). Canadians are now spending more time acquiring knowledge than ever before in our history. I will document the contemporary expansion briefly in terms of schooling, continuing education, and informal learning.

Growth of Schooling

The rate of participation in formal schooling has grown almost continuously throughout the past century. From a tiny minority participating in high school in the early years of the century, the majority of youths were graduating from high school by the end of the 1950s. The high school enrolment ratio has continued to climb to near universality in the 1990s. Over 85 per cent of each age group are now graduating from high school (Statistics Canada, 1996). In spite of these impressive gains in educational participation, 'illiteracy panics' have typically been evoked in periods of high unemployment. The implication is that, rather than the organization of our economy being a problem, the increasing ignorance of the people in terms of the rudiments of reading, writing, and counting is at the root of employment problems. Now once again we hear criticisms of the declining competencies of our youths. However, the most thorough analyses of the evidence on student performance and literacy levels in Canada and elsewhere confirm that neither school achievement nor literacy levels have declined in recent years; in fact, quite the reverse is the case on some measures (Livingstone, 1999a: 42–51, 167–8; 1999b).

Between 1900 and 1980, the participation rate in university doubled every 20 years. In 1980, 14 per cent of the 20 to 24 age cohort were in full-time school attendance. By 1997, participation had grown to over 34 per cent, an increase of more than 250 per cent in 17 years (Betcherman, McMullan, and Davidman, 1998: 29). Canada's post-secondary participation rates now lead the world.

During the past generation, the formal educational attainment profile of the employed labour force has changed substantially. Table 5.1 documents changes between 1978 and 1996 in the formal education attainments of the labour force in the industrial heartland of Ontario (Livingstone et al., 1997). During this period, the aggregate educational attainments of the Ontario workforce have increased significantly. In 1978, high school dropouts made up nearly half of the labour force. By 1996, only about a quarter had less than a high school diploma, while there had been substantial gains in the proportions completing high school, college, and university programs. Similar increases have occurred elsewhere in Canada. Particularly in light of the very rapid development of community colleges since the late 1960s, more workers now have some kind of post-secondary credential than have only a high school diploma. The labour force has continued to become more highly schooled until recent program cutbacks led to some enrolment declines.

Further Education Boom

Since the 1960s, largely voluntary adult participation in further education courses has generally increased even more quickly than formal school enrolments in Canada. Participation has grown from very small numbers. As Table 5.2 summarizes, only 4 per cent of Canadian adults were enrolled in further education courses in 1960, but the participation rate grew to 20 per cent by the early 1980s and to around a third by the mid-1990s (Livingstone, 1999a).

Table 5.1 Formal Educational Attainments, Employed Ontario Labour Force, 1978–1996

Attainments	1978 %	1980 %	1982 %	1984 %	1986 %	1988 %	1990 %	1992 %	1994 %	1996 %
<High school	47	42	40	36	33	33	27	26	25	24
High school diploma	29	32	33	34	36	36	38	38	39	36
College certificate	12	12	13	15	16	15	17	18	18	21
University degree	12	13	13	14	15	15	17	18	19	19

Source: OISE Survey of Educational Issues Data Archive.

Table 5.2   Annual Adult Education Course Participation Rates, Canada, 17+ Population, 1960–1995

	1960 (%)	1983 (%)	1991 (%)	1995 (%)
Canada	4	20	28	38

Sources: Selman and Dampier (1991); Devereaux (1985); Statistics Canada (1995, 1996).

According to a Canadian national survey in 1989, over a quarter of employed workers had plans to begin a major educational program during the next five years (Lowe, 1992: 58–9), while a 1998 survey found that about half of all adults intended to take at least a course in the next few years (NALL, 1998). These increases in both demand and participation in continuing education have occurred across virtually all social groups (Livingstone, 1999a). However, in the past few years adult participation rates may have begun to decline, at least partly because of reduced provision of and government funding for adult certification programs (Livingstone et al., 1999; Livingstone, 2000).

There are also strong indications that workplace-based training programs have generally been growing and broadening their functions since at least around 1980. A number of the most comparable and inclusive Canadian surveys suggest that annual participation in employer-sponsored training programs has increased from around 5 per cent of the labour force in the mid-1960s to between 10 and 15 per cent in the next two decades and to over 20 per cent in the mid-1990s (Betcherman et al., 1997: 4). Other Canadian studies also indicate an increase in the number of workers taking various training courses since the 1980s (Bennett, 1994: 22–5; Crompton, 1992: 30–8).

By any measure, however, North American employers appear to be under-investing in long-term employee training programs relative to employers in most other OECD countries (Betcherman, 1992; Bishop, 1992). The incidence of employer-sponsored training for legislated health and safety provisions, specific job-related computer skills, and encouraging employee teamwork has certainly increased (Betcherman et al., 1997). But there remains little immediate incentive for Canadian employers to invest much more in broader-based and longer-term training programs. Employers continue to complain of immediate training costs and express fears of their competitors poaching well-trained employees (Betcherman et al., 1998), while skill surpluses abound and both current and prospective employees have been making great efforts to get further education on their own. Canadian employers' underinvestment in long-term training, like low spending on research and development, is also probably related to the country's continuing relative status as a staple resources-dependent, branch-plant economy.

The most immediate consequence of the distinctive North American combination of high formal educational attainments, rapidly increased popular demand for adult education, and employers' relative reluctance to pay for more ongoing training programs is the greater growth of general certification and general interest courses than substantial job training programs, as has been the case in Ontario adult education programs since the mid-1980s (Livingstone et al., 1993: 26–7). In the longer term, this trend portends a North American labour force that is even more highly educated, but without some of the specific technical vocational skills that may be immediately required to do some specific jobs.

Informal Learning

The empirical research studies initiated in Canada by Allen Tough in the late 1960s document that *most* adults are regularly involved in deliberate, self-directed learning projects beyond school and training programs. As Tough (1978: 252) summarized the central finding from a wide array of case studies in the 1970s: 'The typical learner conducts five quite distinct learning projects in one year. He or she learns five distinct areas of knowledge and skill. The person spends an average of 100 hours per learning effort—a total of 500 hours per year.' The only previous major country-level survey of informal learning, conducted in the US in the mid-1970s, also found an average of about 500 hours per year (Penland, 1977).

The first Canadian survey of informal learning practices recently found that *people are now spending an average of about 750 hours per year in informal learning, or 15 hours a week.* The vast majority of this informal learning is directly related to our various labours, either paid employment, volunteer community work, or domestic labour. According to this survey, Canadian adults generally are now spending about five times as much time in informal learning activities as in organized education courses (NALL, 1998). All of these studies have found that people with little schooling are doing at least as much informal learning as the highly schooled.

Recent Canadian and US surveys have all found that over 70 per cent of the job training received by employees is informal (Ekos Research Associates, 1993; US Department of Labor, 1994). The most recent in-depth US study of over 1,000 workers (Center for Workforce Development, 1998: 1) again finds this 70 per cent figure and concludes that 'Informal learning was widespread and served to fulfill most learning needs. . . . Workers constantly learn and develop while executing their day-to-day job responsibilities, acquiring a broad range of knowledge and skills.'

So, in spite of the substantial expansion of participation in schooling and continuing education, Canadian adults generally have continued to spend much greater and probably increasing amounts of time on informal learning projects. Certainly the proliferation of information technologies and exponential increases in the production of information have created massively greater opportunities for informal learning beyond their own direct experience by people in all walks of life in recent years. Institutional education programs and courses are indeed the tip of the adult learning iceberg.

The cumulative evidence clearly demonstrates that Canadians have achieved unprecedented levels of formal credentials and these levels have continued to increase rapidly until very recently. The levels of informal practical knowledge attained in the workplace and in everyday life by even the least formally educated people have been both very extensive and generally unrecognized or discounted in public debate and in job-hiring policies. The 'pyramids' of schooling continue to be supported by massive 'icebergs' of informal learning in most spheres of life in our increasingly knowledgeable society. The icebergs are even deeper than the pyramids are high.

The very recently detected declines in adult participation rates in schooling and further education courses appear to be related to restrictions on accessibility through fee increases and program reductions rather than to any decline in popular demand for more advanced education. Certainly, an increasingly large majority of Canadians think that an advanced education is needed to get along in society today (Livingstone et al., 1999). Also, the incidence of informal learning—over which people have more direct personal control than institution-based education—appears to have increased significantly in the past few years (ibid.). Restricting the flow of people into higher education institutions is merely serving to redirect the pursuit of more learning into other more informal channels.

The Myth of the 'Knowledge Economy'

The emergence of a 'post-industrial' workplace dominated by highly educated information service workers has been heralded since the early 1960s (see, especially, Bell, 1973). The theories of post-industrialism have promoted the belief that the prevalence of information processing over material handling in the mode of production would necessitate skill upgrading and greater creativity and critical thinking of workers. In short, post-industrial/knowledge economy theories generally assume or assert that workers increasingly require more skill, become more involved in planning their own work, and increasingly constitute a professional class. But, as I have documented in detail elsewhere (Livingstone, 1999a: 133–226), the image of contemporary society inherent in post-industrial/knowledge economy and human capital theories has proven to be illusory. With regard to the actual skills required to perform current jobs, one of the most extensive recent North American surveys concludes that:

> Most employers do not expect their skill requirements to change. Despite the widespread presumption that advancing technology and the evolving service economy will create jobs demanding higher skills, only five per cent of employers were concerned about skills shortage. (National Center on Education and the Economy, 1990: 3)

The overall weight of empirical evidence suggests that there has been some net upgrading of the technical skill requirements of the Canadian and US job structure since the 1940s. But the most substantial gains occurred prior to 1960 and the slight upgrading that is discernible since then is being far outpaced by our collective acquisition of work-related knowledge and credentials (Livingstone, 1999a).

The Many Faces of Underemployment

'Underemployment' denotes the wasted work-related ability of the eligible work-force, including both job holders and those without paid employment. Six basic dimensions of underemployment have been identified (see ibid., 52–96, for detailed discussion). These dimensions are: (1) the talent use gap; (2) structural unemployment; (3) involuntary reduced employment; (4) the credential gap; (5) the performance gap; and (6) subjective underemployment.

All six of these dimensions now appear to represent very substantial chronic problems. The *talent use gap* refers to the difference in educational achievements between those of higher and lower social origins. A huge gap between learning capacities and job opportunities continues to be set up for many lower-class and visible-minority youths long before they have a chance to enter the labour market. The *credential gap* refers to the relationship between the educational attainments of job holders and the formal educational credentials required for entry into their current jobs. There has clearly been a rapid inflation of the entry credential required by employers for even the most menial jobs during the past generation. But, as we have seen, educational attainments have also increased rapidly. So, around a quarter of the workforce continues to have higher formal qualifications than required for entry, while about the same proportion continue to perform their jobs adequately with less formal education than their employers now require of new entrants. In terms of *subjective underemployment*, around a quarter of the workforce perceive themselves to be overqualified for their jobs, while over two-thirds see themselves as adequately qualified and only a tiny minority consider that they are underqualified. But most of the objectively underemployed continue to blame themselves if they have not been able to find a better job.[4]

I will focus here on the three dimensions on which underemployment has been increasing most rapidly during the current generation: structural unemployment, involuntary reduced employment, and the performance gap.

Structural unemployment refers to a persistent gap between the excess number of job seekers and the scarce number of available jobs. Recent OECD (1994: 9) studies of official unemployment rates have found that 'Unemployment of 35 million, some 8.5 per cent of the OECD labour force, represents an enormous waste of human resources, reflects an important amount of inefficiency in economic systems, and causes a disturbing degree of social distress.' Canada's official unemployment rate has been around 8 per cent since the 1980s. While there have been some downward fluctuations in the official rate, this figure seriously underestimates the actual numbers of people who want jobs. If we include discouraged workers who have given up active job searching because of the absence of jobs, as well as those who want to work but are excluded because of non-legitimate barriers such as lack of accessible dependant care and legislated restrictions on the rights of disabled people and the retired to pursue employment while receiving other state-administered benefits, the actual unemployment rates are now considerably higher (Livingstone, 1999a: 63–9).

The proportion of the Canadian labour force in part-time employment has increased quite rapidly during the past generation, almost doubling since 1976 to about 20 per cent of all jobs. The rate of *involuntary reduced employment* (i.e., those who want full-time jobs but can only obtain part-time ones) has tripled during this period, so that now over a third of part-time employees want full-time jobs (Betcherman, McMullen, and Davidman, 1998: 33–4).

If we include not only official unemployment rates but also discouraged workers and those who have only involuntary part-time employment, the 'subemployment' rates have been greater that 20 per cent since the late 1960s in Canada, as in the US, and have generally been increasing (Sheak, 1994; Carrick, 1996).

To what extent do employees experience a *performance gap* between their achieved levels of skill and knowledge and those needed to actually perform their jobs? The most commonly used indicator of job skill levels in Canada and the US has been the general educational development (GED) scale, which provides estimates of required levels of reasoning, math, and language skills. The estimation of technical skill requirements has been done primarily by government job analysts and published in occasional dictionaries of occupational titles. The basic pattern of findings about the extent of and recent changes in the performance gap is summarized in Table 5.3, which is based on the best available data sources on the employed labour forces for the US and Canada (see Livingstone, 1999a: 78–85) and the most plausible GED-educational attainment equivalencies, developed by Ivar Berg (1970).

The general trends are similar for both countries. The extent of performance underemployment appears to have increased substantially during the current generation. According to this measure, there was a gradual increase from 46 per cent to over 60 per cent of the employed US labour force being underemployed between 1972 and 1990; the comparable figures for Ontario suggest an increase from 44 per cent underemployment to just under 60 per cent between 1980 and 1996, a slightly shorter but more recent period. According to these measures, performance underemployment has now become a majority condition for the North American labour force.

Other studies, not based on GED measures, have found that since the early 1970s almost a third of the employed North American workforce have had work-related skills they could use in their jobs but have not been permitted to do so; this actual underuse appears to have grown to include over 40 per cent of the entire workforce in the 1990s.[5]

In spite of much rhetoric about skill deficiencies of the current workforce, there is little evidence of any general and persistent technical skill deficit among employed workers. The recent US survey by the National Center on the Educational Quality of the Workforce (1995) has found that employers consider over 80

Table 5.3   Trends in Performance Underemployment Levels, US and Ontario (%)

	1972	1974	1976	1978	1980	1982	1984	1986	1988	1990
United States										
Underemployed	46	53	57	55	55	59	59	57	59	62
Matched	31	23	26	30	31	31	29	30	28	29
Underqualified	23	19	17	15	14	11	12	13	13	12
(N=678–1,166)										

	1980	1982	1984	1986	1988	1990	1992	1994	1996
Ontario									
Underemployed	44	43	50	51	52	54	58	55	57
Matched	29	34	28	33	31	30	31	32	27
Underqualified	27	23	22	16	17	16	10	13	16
(N=526–715)									

Sources: Davis and Smith (1994); OISE Survey of Educational Issues Data Archive.

per cent of their employees to be fully technically proficient in their current jobs and that most employers are more concerned with prospective employees' attitudes than their industry-based skills or prior school performance. The basic point is that the performance gap between high educational attainments and lower actual technical job skill requirements in Canada, as well as in the US, is extensive and increasing on all available measures.

Class, Sex, and Ethnic Differences in Underemployment

In general, more powerful groups are less likely to experience underemployment. They tend to be more able to control both the knowledge that gets recognized as legitimate and access to social positions in which it can be used. Detailed analyses of Canadian data confirm that both working-class and self-employed people tend to be more underemployed on most of these six dimensions than those in the employer and professional-managerial classes. Non-European visible minorities are generally more underemployed than those of European origins. While women have made significant progress in general employment conditions during the past generation, they are still more likely to be underemployed than men in the more powerful occupational class positions as they bump into 'glass ceilings'. In addition, unionized workers generally are less likely to be underemployed than non-unionized workers. The longitudinal evidence shows that it is among non-unionized subordinate-class minority workers that underemployment is most rapidly increasing.[6] Those who have the least control over their conditions of employment are also least likely to gain recognition for the work-related knowledge and skill they actually possess. Economic power determines which knowledge counts.

The Massive Scale of Underemployment

An overall estimate of the extent of underemployment cannot simply be additive. In Canada, objective underemployment would affect well over 100 per cent of the workforce! However, it is safe to say that over half of the potential Canadian adult workforce has experienced some of the overlapping dimensions of objective underemployment, and that significantly less have a coherent sense of their underemployment.

The massive scale of the underuse of knowledge and skills in current industrial market economies may still be difficult for most analysts to accept and may well appear incredible to the general reader—in spite of the fact that estimates of similar magnitude have been made by reputable scholars for over a generation now. But this assessment is based on merely applying the array of conventional measures of underemployment to the array of available databases.

Some critics will undoubtedly be able to find empirical grounds for lower estimates on specific dimensions of underemployment. Others have already suggested discarding underemployment as a social problem because underemployed college graduates have not become massively disaffected politically; and, furthermore, with continued post-secondary educational expansion, the marginal economic utility of more education is diminishing and seen to be leading to widespread acceptance of credential inflation (Smith, 1986). There is some support for the political aspect of this argument. Increasing subemployment and performance underemployment over the past decade have been associated with relatively little change in attitudes about job entitlement rather than provoking corresponding increases in subjective underemployment. But there is little credible aggregate-level evidence for declining capacity among college students. Objective underemployment, as estimated by various measures, continues to increase. The growing wastage of knowledge and skills in our workplaces should not be dismissed or relativized just because the highly schooled have not taken to the barricades. Rather than presumptively trivializing the problem,[7] interested researchers should be looking more closely at the actual experiences of those currently living in the education-jobs gap.

Underemployment and Lifelong Learning

If the condition of underemployment were to diminish people's aspirations and enthusiasm for the pursuit of more knowledge, then the education-jobs gap might begin to abate without significant economic reform to create more good jobs. Is there any evidence to suggest this relationship? We will examine here the association between underemployment and both participation in further education and the incidence of informal learning activities.

Underemployment and Further Education Courses

In-depth studies of people in various types of underemployment (see Livingstone, 1999a) find that the underemployed typically continue to see themselves as active agents who aspire to transcend these conditions. The choice most frequently referred to is the pursuit of more work-related knowledge, either in terms of further schooling and continuing education courses or through their own informal learning. As Lowe (1992: 58–9) concluded on the basis of a 1989 Canadian national survey: 'Ironically, many individuals possessing higher credentials than required for their particular job believed that they must obtain even more education to compete effectively for a better job.' According to the 1989 Canadian national survey, further education plans were most common in sales and service jobs where people were most likely to feel overqualified (ibid., 53–9). Further analysis of Ontario survey data indicates that the underemployed have been slightly more likely than others to have such plans, but the majority of those who were underqualified also expect to take further courses (Livingstone et al., 1987).

General Ontario surveys between 1986 and 1996 have similarly found that, as Table 5.4 indicates, those whose educational qualifications exceed the actual performance requirements of their jobs may be slightly more likely than those with underqualified statuses to participate in further education courses, certainly not less likely to do so. The very small numbers of highly underqualified employees with

Table 5.4 Percentage Participation in Adult Education Courses by Performance Gap Status, Ontario Labour Force, 1986–1996

Performance Gap Status	Annual Participation Rates						
	1986	1988	1990	1992	1994	1996	Average
Highly underemployed	32	34	45	38	32	33	36
Underemployed	25	30	34	40	33	32	33
Matched	31	30	34	39	33	36	34
Underqualified	12	22	25	34	32	22	22
Highly underqualified	12	19	24	34	11	11	16
Unemployed	7	16	28	40	32	39	30
Totals	26	30	34	37	32	31	32
N	590	559	581	526	715	610	3,580

Source: OISE Survey of Educational Issues Data Archive.

little schooling probably face the greatest accessibility barriers and are now the least likely to participate in further courses. But it should also be noted that the officially unemployed increased their participation rates in further education programs quite dramatically over the past decade, from relatively low rates of less than 10 per cent in the mid-1980s to around a third in the 1990s, as high a frequency as any other social group. Since the unemployed generally have less personal financial resources to participate in education programs than others, their continuing involvement is most contingent on government funding of adult training programs.

For the underemployed, the equation between more education and better jobs is far from certain in light of the underuse of education in their present jobs. But the apparent necessity to respond to this uncertainty by pursuing yet more formal education also remains largely unquestioned. Among the underqualified, there is a virtually unanimous equation between further educational credentials and either a better job or a fuller life—even if because of lack of resources or entry requirements they are blocked from actually participating in many desired educational programs. So, in spite of their common experience of a superficial connection between their formal educational attainments and the requirements of their current or recent jobs, both underemployed university graduates and underqualified school dropouts continue to believe and act as if more education is the personal solution to escaping the education-jobs gap. There are undoubtedly many motives associated with the popular demand for and engagement in adult education: competition for scarce jobs; the desire to be a more effective consumer or citizen; assertion of the democratic right to equal educational opportunity; a more generic quest for knowledge to cope with uncertain times; or even the joy of learning. But there is now an almost universal general perception that more advanced education is a fundamental imperative for adults in contemporary society (see Livingstone et al., 1999).

Underemployment and Informal Learning

The empirical research on self-directed learning has demonstrated that informal learning outside of organized courses is more extensive than course-based learning among adults. However, this research has paid virtually no attention to the informal learning practices of the underemployed (see Candy, 1993; Adams et al., 1997). Recent surveys of the general adult population of Ontario (Livingstone et al., 1997, 1999) have asked all respondents to estimate the amount of time they typically devoted to informal learning activities outside organized coursework. We have analysed these estimates by underemployment statuses.

Relations between the performance gap and informal learning activities are summarized in Table 5.5. Those who are moderately underqualified on performance criteria average more time in employment-related informal learning than others do—about 400 hours a year. This may reflect their greater need to upgrade their skills for adequate job performance. But the small number who are highly underqualified for their jobs tend to spend less time in both work-related and

Table 5.5   Estimated Informal Learning Activities by Performance Gap Status, Ontario Labour Force, 1996

Performance Gap Status	Average Hours per Year*		
	Work-related[a]	General interest[b]	Total
Highly underemployed	350	325	675
Underemployed	300	275	575
Matched	300	325	625
Underqualified	400	300	700
Highly underqualified	225	200	425
Unemployed	300	325	625
Total	325	300	625
(N=691)			

*Weekly estimates have been multiplied by 52 weeks and rounded to the nearest 25 hours.

[a]'Not counting coursework, about how many hours in a typical week do you spend trying to learn anything related to your paid or household work, or work you do as a volunteer? Just give your best guess.'

[b]'Not counting coursework, about how many hours in a typical week do you spend trying to learn anything of general interest to you? Just give your best guess.'

Source: Livingstone et al. (1997).

general interest informal learning activities than any other group; this pattern is similar to their participation in adult education courses. This group only represents about 5 per cent of the labour force and includes mainly older people with very little schooling; they typically have limited income and limited time for informal learning beyond their low-wage jobs. But even these folks with little schooling and little discretionary time estimate that they devote an average of over 400 hours a year to informal learning.

In-depth follow-up studies with credentially underemployed and underqualified people in Ontario (Livingstone, 1999) have confirmed that both underemployed university/college graduates and underqualified non-college workers spend at least as much time on informal work-related learning as people whose credentials match their jobs. They also spend much more time in informal learning projects than they do in organized course-based learning, generally well over five times as much. Neither underemployment nor underqualification serves to shrink the iceberg of informal learning.

As in prior studies that have compared patterns of informal learning across social groupings, variations in learning time *within* the underemployed college and underqualified non-college groups are much greater than the differences between them. In particular, there is no systemic difference between the underemployed or underqualified and the rest of the workforce in their work-related continuing learning capacities and interests. Regardless of their employment status and in spite of various institutional and material barriers, most people living in the education-jobs gap continue to engage in substantial informal learning activities.

The Irreversible Popular Demand for Knowledge

Overall, these surveys and follow-up interviews indicate an increasing general popular demand for more adult education courses and few significant differences between underemployed and most other employees in their general participation rates in organized adult education courses. The Ontario population survey of informal learning activities and the follow-up interviews with credentially mismatched employees demonstrate that there are also no major differences between underemployed and underqualified employees in the total amount of time they now devote to work-related learning activities. It appears that these mismatched employees are spending more time in informal learning than adult learners generally were in the 1970s. The condition of underemployment has evidently not discouraged people from continuing both their work-related and general learning activities. As for the small numbers of workers who are objectively underqualified in GED terms—most of whom deny they are actually underqualified for their jobs—the evidence suggests that most of them are devoting as much effort to continuing work-related learning activities as matched and underemployed workers. The learning efforts of both the underemployed and the underqualified are much more extensive than the dominant rhetoric about the pressing need for more education would suggest.

It is clear, then, that one of the most common current responses to underemployment is to seek more education and training. This mindset is as common among underemployed university and college graduates as it is among underqualified school dropouts. These people live with a deep-seated recognition of the arbitrariness of the formal educational credential requirements set for the jobs they have had. They understand, more intimately than those living within the current comfort of job requirements matched to their educational attainments, that employers are upping the ante for job entry and that the link between job performance requirements and educational attainments is being loosened in an 'employer's market'.

Those living in the education-jobs gap give no serious indication of giving up on the faith that more education should get them a better job. Indeed, their current situation seems to have provoked in many at least a quiet sense of desperation that somehow they must continue to get more and still more education, training, or knowledge in order to achieve any economic security (Livingstone, 1999a). Such increasingly common learning efforts among the unemployed and underemployed underline just how wide the gulf between the knowledge base of the general population and the limited knowledge required in most jobs has become.

The conviction of these marginalized people that our current economic system can produce the jobs to which they continue to feel at least ambiguously entitled has definitely been shaken severely.[8] In the absence of any economic alternative that seems practical, however, most of those living on both sides of the education-jobs gap (i.e., underemployed or underqualified) are actively engaged in trying to revise rather than reject this conviction. As in the 1930s, the waste of human potential is immense and gut-wrenching. Just as during the 'dirty thirties', the economic polarization between the haves and have-nots has also increased greatly (Yalnizyan, 1998). The difference is that the promise and pursuit of more advanced education are now playing a much larger role than make-work programs in preoccupying the swelling number of outcasts and misfits of the labour market.

Conclusion

The shortage of adequate paid work is a far more profound problem than most political leaders are yet prepared to admit publicly. The real scope of underemployment continues to be underestimated because so much of it beyond official unemployment counts remains hidden in the underground economy, the household, and prisons, among discouraged and involuntary part-time workers, and in the largely invisible credential and performance gaps. Most political leaders persist in focusing on enhancing a 'training culture' for a 'knowledge economy' as the primary policy response, when a continual learning culture is already thriving across the current and potential workforce. In collaboration with corporate business leaders, elected politicians continue to promote partnership programs to try to ensure that specific groups of potential workers obtain better 'employability skills' (Taylor, 1996). Indeed, the focus on education and training solutions has now reached the level of colleges now offering warranties that include taking back their graduates from unhappy employers for retraining (Lewington, 1994). Many educational reforms may be admirable in themselves, but they remain utterly incapable of resolving the problem of underemployment.

If underemployment of peoples' knowledge and skills in the legal labour market economy of advanced capitalist societies is as extensive as the prior analyses suggest, recommendations that stress a growing need for lifelong learning and greater investment in 'intellectual capital' miss the point. Market-driven solutions that propose restricting the flow of people into advanced education are politically unrealistic in light of the strong and unremitting popular demand. The first step beyond passive acceptance of the mantra that Canadians must inevitably obey the dictates of 'global competition' is to recognize that these private market relations are continually socially reconstructed or reproduced through the actions or inactions of our political leaders (see McQuaig, 1998).

Beyond such recognition, our primary emphasis should be on practical and political initiatives to reorganize work to enable more people to apply in legitimate and sustainable ways the knowledge and skills they already possess. As I have argued in detail elsewhere (Livingstone, 1999a), we need to: (1) more deeply understand the full array of past, present, and possible future forms of work; (2) appreciate that unpaid household and community work and informal learning can aid in bridging the gap between paid work and organized schooling and lead to a sustainable knowledge society; (3) further explore the reduction of underemployment in basic economic alternatives to shareholder and stakeholder versions of capitalism, especially in the forms of *economic democracy*[9] that have been emerging in the crevices of profit-driven capitalism; and (4) build on the existing popular support for these alternatives, especially features of economic democracy (i.e., socialized markets, worker self-management, reduced standard workweeks, green work) that can serve to close the education–jobs gap. *Without active public support for economic alternatives related to more democratic visions of work organization, little substantial reduction in current levels of underemployment is likely in the near future* (see ibid.; Quarter, 1992).

Some of the underemployed Canadians who are most critical of capitalism's economic imperatives express explicit hopes that interactive educational and workplace reforms will lead to a more human-centred system (Livingstone, 1999a: 273). As an underemployed middle-aged female service worker with a university degree has said:

We need a society which puts human beings first, not money. The education system needs to be more geared to practicalities. Whatever you learn you should be able to apply to your job. Learning on the job should also be recognized as learning experience by educational institutions. It works both ways. There should be an ongoing process of on-the-job and in-school learning. Education-job gaps are bound to happen, because the economy is changing and types of qualifications don't match, because institutions of learning have different timetables and don't react so fast to the market. . . . There needs to be more coordinated planning among governments, schools/colleges and business. But businesses are not taking that initiative at all. . . . The people who control things need a massive dose of education to bring them down to the human level as opposed to a preoccupation with money.

There is now a good deal of popular support in Canada for democratizing measures such as co-operative forms of ownership, workplace participation, shorter workweeks, and gender equity in unpaid labour (ibid., 258–74). People in general are giving these progressive economic alternatives more serious consideration than is evident in either the mass media or the writings of professional economists. The elements of viable economic solutions to underemployment exist in the 'tacit fore-knowledge' (Polanyi, 1983) of the general public.

Will the popular support among both the fully employed and the growing ranks of the underemployed for progressive economic reforms—such as genuine workplace democratization and a reduced normal workweek—be taken up effectively in local, national, and international initiatives by progressive political movements such as the advocates of the new economics and political ecology? Or can vested economic and political power hierarchies continue to promote the 'education as secular salvation' solution in conjunction with individual internalization of the blame for underemployment, fear of unemployment, and a sense that there is really no economic alternative? The massive systemic extent of underemployment in all of its aspects must be widely recognized and the false claims for a 'knowledge economy' full of 'high-performance learning organizations' must be directly confronted. Otherwise, the wastage of much of our work-related education and training, along with the relative withering of our collective opportunities to use this knowledge in any future workplaces, is likely to continue to grow.

We have to grasp the present as part of history and recognize that economic and other institutions are nothing but sets of behaviour patterns subject to transformation when we identify better alternatives and can convince enough others of their merits. Nelson Mandela, Richard Turner (1980), and many others exercised this form of apparently radical thought and action in leading South Africa to overcome apartheid during the past 30 years. Many North American citizens exercised the same mode of thought and action in helping to end the Cold War in the 1980s (Cortright, 1993). While underemployment is less visible, it is now no less a threat to human fulfilment than apartheid or the arms race. In my view, economic democracy offers the only discernible alternative to this problem that is positively sustainable in the long term, both within the advanced capitalist societies and in terms of their impact on the rest of the world. The combined conditions in Canada of high levels of underemployment, the current branch-plant character of the economy that provides diminishing chances for comparative trade advantages with other advanced capitalist states through conventional market competition, and a deeply ingrained support for political democracy provide a great opportunity for social transformation in Canada. We could lead the world in democratizing economic reforms to reduce underemployment while continuing to provide advanced educational opportunities for people to further develop their learning capacities. But we first have to convince ourselves that such economic change is not merely utopian or barbaric because it has less preoccupation with profit-driven production and competitive consumption of rapidly obsolescent or out-of-fashion goods and services.

As we enter the twenty-first century, there are strong popular sentiments of resistance to government moves to make advanced education less accessible through program cutbacks that restrict entry (the 'market-driven' option) and to policies that maintain access but lead to greater personal indebtedness through higher tuition fees (the 'knowledge economy' option).[10] There is also widespread, if less vocal, interest among an increasingly underemployed Canadian labour force in more opportunities to use their increasing knowledge in meaningful and rewarding work. Sooner or later, the growing gap between the ample rewards and secure lives of executives and top experts and the wasted education and withering work of most of the population could provoke profound social upheaval. The result may be a more authoritarian shareholder capitalist society run by a technocratic élite, the growth of a version of economic democracy, or some other historic compromise. Which road will you choose?

Questions for Critical Thought

1. Have you been underemployed in the jobs that you have been able to find to date? On the basis of your own observations, how common is underemployment on the dimensions identified in this chapter? Have your future job expectations improved, stayed the same, or worsened since you began post-secondary studies?

2. Which of the three basic alternatives outlined at the beginning of this chapter—the market-driven, knowledge economy, or economic democracy options—do you think will dominate future education-employment relationships?

3. Do you know anything about experiments in economic democracy and how it has worked to reduce underemployment in the various places it has been tried (e.g., kibbutzim in Israel, Mondragon in Basque region in Spain, worker co-ops in Canada)?

Glossary

Economic democracy A mode of organization of production and consumption governed co-operatively by and for the members of the effective community.

G-7 The advanced capitalist countries with the largest private market-based economies, the leaders of which meet annually to assess the condition of the global market economy. Members include the United States, Japan, Germany, France, Great Britain, Italy, and Canada.

GED A general educational development index that estimates levels of intellectual function, used by educational authorities to assign grade equivalencies to people without school certification and by census analysts to assign differential technical skill levels to various occupations.

Informal learning Any effort to acquire new knowledge, skill, or understanding that occurs outside the teacher-led curricula of organized educational sites such as school programs, adult education courses, and tutorial lessons.

Underemployment The underutilization of the work-related knowledge of the available labour force in the current array of jobs.

Suggested Readings

Livingstone, D.W. 1999. *The Education-Jobs Gap: Underemployment or Economic Democracy*. Toronto: Garamond Press. Provides extensive documentation for all six dimensions of underemployment in Canada and the United States, explores different theories for explaining this gap, and assesses alternative policy measures to close it.

Marquardt, R. 1998. *Enter at Your Own Risk: Canadian Youth and the Labour Market*. Toronto: Between the Lines. A synthetic account of empirical research on the complex and problematic transitions between school and employment now faced by Canadian youths.

Osberg, L., F. Wien, and J. Grude. 1995. *Vanishing Jobs: Canada's Changing Workplace*. Toronto: James Lorimer. A well-documented overview of the changing job structure of the Canadian economy with solid evidence of extensive net job losses.

Quarter, J. 1992. *Canada's Social Economy: Co-operatives, Non-profits, and Other Community Enterprises*. Toronto: James Lorimer. The most comprehensive account of community-owned and managed businesses in Canada, including general overviews, a wide variety of case studies, and general proposals for expanding this social economy.

Roberts, W., and S. Brandum. 1995. *Get a Life: How to Make a Good Buck, Dance around the Dinosaurs and Save the World While You're at It*. Toronto: Get A Life Publishing House. A thought-provoking potpourri of very practical ideas for individuals and local communities to use their skills to create a sustainable economy.

Notes

I am indebted to Doug Hart for statistical assistance, to Jill Given-King for formatting help with the text and tables, and to the editors and reviewers for comments on a prior draft.

1. Profiles of contemporary learning activities, changing job requirements, and the multiple dimensions of underemployment in Canada, the US, and other G-7 countries, as well as explanations for and alternative resolutions to underemployment, are discussed in detail in Livingstone (1999a).

2. The defining features of these two capitalist alternatives, as well as economic democracy and the relations of all three economic alternatives with several dimensions of underemployment, are delineated in Livingstone (1999a).

3. For a fuller discussion of the dimensions and measurement of explicit informal learning as well as a summary of the first Canadian survey of informal learning practices, see Livingstone (1999b).

4. All three of these dimensions of underemployment are discussed and documented in detail in Livingstone (1999a).

5. Halaby (1994) offers a critique of GED-based measures of skill mismatch. He also presents an analysis of skill mismatch based on an alternative self-report question from the 1973 and 1977 Quality of Employment Surveys in the US. These surveys found a skill underuse rate of about 30 per cent of the workforce. We have replicated the same question in the 1994 and 1996 OISE surveys and found rates of just over 40 per cent in Ontario (see Livingstone et al., 1997: 73).

6. See Livingstone (1999a) for detailed empirical analyses of the incidence of underemployment on all six of these dimensions by class position, ethnic group, sex, and union membership.

7. Canada's leading business magazine, *Canadian Business*, provides a particularly absurd example of this evasive approach. In a cover article on credential underemployment, the authors first describe current conditions, relying partly on some of my own research findings. They then conclude that because such entrepreneurs as the Bank of Montreal's Matthew Barrett and Microsoft's Bill Gates have become successful without college degrees, the solution to inflated credentialism is to focus on performance skills. They conveniently ignore the fact that performance skill underemployment is actually much greater than the credential gap! See Taylor and McGugan (1995).

8. For accounts in the words of underemployed and underqualified people themselves, see Livingstone (1999a: 97–132).

9. Economic democracy refers to the organization of production and consumption by the majority of the people for the majority. It is characterized by collective community ownership of many means of production and distribution, worker self-management of the labour process, distribution of available work for full employment, and recognition of many forms of unpaid labour as valuable and necessary. For fuller discussion of existing forms of economic democracy and their success in reducing underemployment, see Livingstone (1999a: 240–57).

10. See Livingstone et al., (1999) for extensive documentation of these current popular sentiments in the only regularly administered, publicly accessible public opinion survey of educational policy issues in Canada.

References

Adams, M., et al. 1997. *Preliminary Bibliography of the Research Network for New Approaches to Lifelong Learning (NALL)*. Toronto: Centre for the Study of Education and Work, Ontario Institute for the Study of Education at the University of Toronto.

Bell, D. 1973. *The Coming of Post-Industrial Society*. New York: Basic Books.

Bennett, K. 1994. 'Recent information on training', *Perspectives on Labour and Income* 6, 1.

Berg, I. 1970. *Education and Jobs: The Great Training Robbery*. New York: Praeger.

Betcherman, G. 1992. 'Are Canadian firms underinvesting in training?', *Canadian Business Economics* 1, 1: 25–33.

———, N. Leckie, and K. McMullen. 1997. *Developing Skills in the Canadian Workplace: The Results of the Ekos Workplace Training Survey*. Ottawa: Canadian Policy Research Networks.

———, ———, and ———. 1998. *Barriers to Employer-Sponsored Training in Canada*. Ottawa: Canadian Policy Research Networks.

———, K. McMullen, and K. Davidman. 1998. *Training for the New Economy: A Synthesis Report*. Ottawa: Renouf.

Bishop, J. 1992. *The French Mandate to Spend on Training: A Model for the United States*. Ithaca, NY: Center on the Educational Quality of the Workforce, Cornell University.

Brantlinger, P. 1983. *Bread and Circuses: Theories of Mass Culture and Social Decay*. Ithaca, NY: Cornell University Press.

Brookfield, S. 1981. 'The adult education learning iceberg', *Adult Education* (UK) 54, 2: 110–18.

Candy, P. 1993. *Self-Direction for Lifelong Learning: A Comprehensive Guide to Theory and Practice*. San Francisco: Jossey-Bass.

Carrick, R. 1996. 'Jobless rate understated, bank reports', *Toronto Star*, 10 May, E3.

Center for Workforce Development. 1998. *The Teaching Firm: Where Productive Work and Learning Converge*. Newton, Mass.: Education Development Center.

Cortright, D. 1993. *Peace Works*. Boulder, Colo.: Westview Press.

Crompton, S. 1992. Studying on the job', *Perspectives on Labour and Income* 4, 2: 30–8.

Curti, M. 1935. *The Social Ideas of American Educators*. Paterson, NJ: Littlefield, Adams.

Davis, J.A., and T.W. Smith. 1994. *General Social Surveys 1972–1994*. Chicago: National Opinion Research Center.

Devereaux, M. 1985. *One in Every Five: A Survey of Adult Education in Canada*. Ottawa: Statistics Canada and Education Support Section, Secretary of State.

Diamond, J. 1998. *Guns, Germs, and Steel: The Fates of Human Societies*. New York: Norton.

Ekos Research Associates. 1993. *Reskilling Society (Phase I): Industrial Perspectives. The National Survey of Employers on Training and Development Issues*. Hull, Que.: Human Resources Development Canada.

Farber, J. 1970. *The Student as Nigger: Essays and Stories*. New York: Pocket Books.

Halaby, C. 1994. 'Overeducation and Skill Mismatch', *Sociology of Education* 67, 1 (Jan.): 47–59.

Illich, I. 1971. *Deschooling Society*. New York: Harper and Row.

Lewington, J. 1994. 'Nova Scotia plans to offer warranties on grads', *Globe and Mail*, 3 Feb., A1.

Livingstone, D.W. 1999a. *The Education-Jobs Gap: Underemployment or Economic Democracy*. Toronto: Garamond Press.

————. 1999b. 'Exploring the Icebergs of Adult Learning: Findings of the First Canadian Survey of Informal Learning Practices', *Canadian Journal for the Study of Adult Education* 13, 2: 49-72.

————. 2000. *Work and Lifelong Learning in the Information Age: A Canadian Profile*. Ottawa: Canadian Policy Research Networks.

————, D. Hart, and L. Davie. 1987. *Public Attitudes Toward Education in Ontario, 1986: Sixth OISE Survey*. Toronto: OISE Press.

————, ————, and ————. 1993. *Public Attitudes Toward Education in Ontario, 1992: Ninth OISE Survey*. Toronto: OISE Press.

————, ————, and ————. 1997. *Public Attitudes Toward Education in Ontario, 1996: Eleventh OISE/UT Survey*. Toronto: University of Toronto Press.

————, ————, and ————. 1999. *Public Attitudes Toward Education in Ontario, 1998: Twelfth OISE Survey*. Toronto: University of Toronto Press.

Lowe, G. 1992. *Human Resource Challenges of Education, Computers and Retirement*. Ottawa: Statistics Canada.

Machlup, F. 1980. *Knowledge, Its Creation, Distribution and Economic Significance*. Princeton, NJ: Princeton University Press.

McQuaig, L. 1998. *The Cult of Impotence: Selling the Myth of Powerlessness in the Global Economy*. Toronto: Viking.

NALL (Research Network for New Approaches to Lifelong Learning). 1998. 'Lifelong Learning Profiles: Findings from the First Canadian Survey of Informal Learning', (press release, 11 Nov., available at: www.oise.utoronto.ca/depts/sese/csew/nall

National Center on Education and the Economy. 1990. *America's Choice: High Skills or Low Wages*. Washington: NCEE.

National Center on the Educational Quality of the Workforce. 1995. *First Findings from the EQW National Employer Survey*. Philadelphia: National Center on the Educational Quality of the Workforce.

OECD. 1994. *The OECD Job Study: Facts, Analysis, Strategies*. Paris: OECD.

OISE Survey of Educational Issues Data Archive is accessible at: www.oise.utoronto.ca/OISE-Survey

Penland, P. 1977. *Self-Planned Learning in America*. Pittsburgh: University of Pittsburgh Press.

Percy, K. 1997. 'On formal, non-formal lifelong learning: Reconceptualizing the boundaries for research, theory and practice', in P. Armstrong, N. Miller, and M. Zukas, eds, *Crossing Borders, Breaking Boundaries: Research in the Education of Adults*. London: SCUTREA.

Polak, F. 1967. *The Image of the Future*. San Francisco: Jossey-Bass.

Polanyi, M. 1983. *The Tacit Dimension*. Gloucester, Mass.: Peter Smith.

Quarter, J. 1992. *Canada's Social Economy: Co-operatives, Non-profits, and Other Community Enterprises*. Toronto: James Lorimer.

Sawchuk, P. 1996. 'Working Class Informal Learning and Computer Literacy', MA thesis, University of Toronto.

Selman, G., and P. Dampier. 1991. *The Foundations of Adult Education in Canada*. Toronto: Thompson Educational Publishing.

Sheak, R. 1994. 'The chronic jobs problem in the United States: No end in sight', *Free Inquiry in Creative Sociology* 22, 1: 23–32.

Smith, H. 1986. 'Overeducation and underemployment: An agnostic view', *Sociology of Education* 50 (Apr.): 85–99.

Statistics Canada. 1995. *Adult Education and Training Survey*. Ottawa: Employment and Immigration Canada.

———. 1996. *Reading the Future: A Portrait of Literacy in Canada*. Ottawa: National Literacy Secretariat, Human Resources Development Canada and Statistics Canada.

Taylor, A. 1996. 'Education for "Post-Industrial" Purposes: Understanding the Context of Change in Alberta Schools', Ed.D. thesis, OISE/University of Toronto.

Taylor, P., and I. McGugan. 1995. 'Devoured by degrees', *Canadian Business* 68, 9: 26–36.

Tough, A. 1978. 'Major learning efforts: Recent research and future directions', *Adult Education* 28: 250–63.

Turner, R. 1980. *The Eye of the Needle: Towards Participatory Democracy in South Africa*. Johannesburg: Raven Press.

US Department of Labor, Bureau of Labor Statistics. 1994. *Employer-Provided Formal Training*. Washington: US Department of Labor.

Yalnizyan, A. 1998. *The Growing Gap: A Report on Growing Inequality between the Rich and Poor in Canada*. Toronto: Centre for Social Justice.

chapter six

An Introduction
to Crime
in Canada

Kelly Hannah-Moffat

The Social Construction of Criminality

The public fear of and fascination with crime, in particular violent crime committed by strangers, are an integral part of Canadian culture. Stories about crime
appear daily in nearly every major newspaper and on television news broadcasts.
Most popular television dramas, movies, and novels feature story lines that sustain
the public's curiosity and appetite for information about the criminal mind, the
responses of our system of justice, and the plight of crime victims in our society.
Embedded in this cultural preoccupation is the assumption that we 'know' who
criminals are and that they are somehow different from 'us', the law-abiding public.
Everyone has opinions about why individuals commit crime and about how the
criminal justice system should punish those who deviate from societal norms
and/or violate the law. Rarely do we question or think critically about the meaning of crime.

Our understanding of crime is closely aligned with social definitions of
deviance. The concepts of crime and deviance often overlap. 'Crime' is a word that
is used to describe a wide range of behaviours considered by a large segment of
the population to be morally wrong. However, there are behaviours considered by
many to be anti-social or deviant, but that are not legally defined as criminal,
including, for example, excessive consumption of alcohol and certain sexual behaviours. Likewise, a wide range of behaviours considered by many to be acceptable
are actually illegal, such as pirating software, copying videotapes, using illegal drugs,
speeding, purchasing sexual services, and evading taxes. In many instances crimes
have occurred but the individuals involved (victim and/or offender) do not recognize the act is criminal. For example, in some segments of the youth culture
shoplifting is an accepted practice, perceived more as a game than as a criminal act.
Predictably, Canadians often engage in a wide range of illegal activities without
being penalized either formally or informally. Finally, there is not always a clear
connection between the personal or social harmfulness of an act and its social
designation as criminal or deviant. In general, more emphasis is placed on 'street

crimes' like assault, theft, and robbery than on 'suite crimes' or corporate crimes, which many argue do more harm, cost more money, and ruin more lives than street crimes. For example, Snider (1993: 1) argues that corporate crimes (including unsafe or illegal working conditions, dangerous consumer products, environmental destruction due to industrial waste, 'accidents', and price fixing) cause major devastation, causing more deaths per month than all mass murderers combined do in a decade.

The term 'crime' comes from the Latin word *crimen*, meaning 'accusation'. The word 'crime' is a generic term that people apply to a wide range of acts socially, culturally, or legally defined as wrong or anti-social. Acts prohibited by law are crimes. In Canada, the Criminal Code and related legislation define what are deemed to be crimes within our legal system—'any form of human behaviour designated by the law as criminal and subject to penal sanction' (Liden, 1996: 42). Police, lawyers, judges, and correctional personnel use legal definitions of crime to inform their daily activities. Sociologists, however, are more apt to examine the historical, cultural, and social significance of acts and omissions and to challenge our taken-for-granted assumptions about crime and criminals. Critical sociological analyses of crime may even question the appropriateness of the legal regulation of behaviour and the unequal policing of different segments of society.

A study by Chambliss (1973) that examined the behaviours of two high school gangs, the 'Saints' and the 'Roughnecks', found variations in social and criminal justice responses to similar behaviours. The Saints, who were 'bright promising young men—children of good stable, white upper middle class families, active in school affairs, good pre-college students—were some of the most delinquent boys.' They, like the Roughnecks, who were six lower-class white boys, were involved in truancy, drinking, dangerous driving, theft, and vandalism. While none of the Saints were officially arrested, the Roughnecks, whose deviance was more visible, were constantly in trouble with the police and the community. The study suggests that those with the least power are the most likely to be targets of surveillance and to be stigmatized as criminal.

This study also reveals that the definition of individuals as criminals and their processing through the criminal justice system tend to reproduce general assumptions and stereotypes about particular social groups. These stereotypes are gendered, racialized, and class-specific: younger impoverished and marginalized men of certain cultural and ethnic minorities are more often regarded as 'dangerous' or 'suspicious'. Recent government policies, such as the Safe Streets Act in Ontario that attempts to regulate and criminalize the actions of homeless youth who may work as 'squeegee kids' or beg for money in public, further illustrate how marginalized and highly visible populations are disproportionately policed.

The Historical Context of Crime

Crime is a relative and fluid concept. What constitutes crime at any given time is historically, culturally, and situationally specific, therefore, the designation of a particular behaviour as criminal will be historically contingent. Over time the actions and behaviours that constitute crime change. As time passes, the boundaries of behaviours considered appropriate and inappropriate change. In some instances, illegal activities are decriminalized and in others legal activities are criminalized. For example, during prohibition the sale and consumption of alcohol was illegal. For many years attempted suicide, consensual adult homosexual behaviour, and adultery were crimes, yet under current Canadian law these activities are not illegal.

On the other hand, several acts and behaviours that previously were unregulated are now illegal. At one time spousal abuse and child abuse were not matters subject to state intervention and legal regulation. Prior to the nineteenth century, 'customary law proclaimed a husband's right to use physical chastisement to correct his wife (along with his children, his servants and his animals)' (Strange, 1995: 295). The home was conceptualized as a 'haven'—a private space free from state regulation and legal interventions. As Strange (1995: 296) notes, 'the civil and criminal law upheld the deeply patriarchal character of marriage, both by granting husbands enormous latitude in exercising their power and by severely limiting married women's ability to extricate themselves from violent partners.' The abuse of children and women became a case for state concern only if the abuse was extreme and publicly visible. However, over the last 30 years Canadian policy-makers have argued in favour of stricter laws around the policing of domestic violence. Family violence intervention has expanded to the extent that some are now advocating for the criminalization of 'spanking'.

Other areas of law reform that resulted in the criminalization of a new range of behaviours include the regulation of environmental and white-collar crimes, such as the computer-related crime of software piracy. In the eighteenth and nineteenth centuries there were virtually no laws governing pollution or other types of environmental hazards. There were (and continue to be) many actions that result in serious injuries and even death that are not regulated by law. For instance, corporate executives have knowingly marketed unsafe products to consumers and companies have placed workers in dangerous environments and contaminated the biosphere with toxic pollutants. Until recently, there were no laws forbidding these actions (Gomme, 1998). Today, we have several complex laws to govern the sale and consumption of consumer products, to protect the environment, to regulate the marketplace, and to safeguard the interests of employees. Most of the laws regulating corporate crime are less than 100 years old, and the majority of these were passed in the last 50 years (Snider, 1993: 92). The recent criminalization of environmental and white-collar crimes clearly expands our definition of crime and criminal behaviour.

These examples of the criminalization and decriminalization of behaviours show how the concepts of crime and the criminal changed over time. A historical analysis of the criminalization of certain behaviours and not others also illustrates how the regulation of crime is linked to gender, class, and racial characteristics. For example, several authors argue that the development of Canada's first piece of narcotic drug legislation—the Opium Act of 1908—was a part of an international movement to stop the opium trade from China, but also reflected the hostility of Canadians towards Chinese immigrants (Giffen et al., 1996; Boyd, 1995; Comack, 1986). Research suggests that there is an inescapable connection between the legislation aimed at the 'immoral' habit of opium smoking by the Chinese, the need to create a productive workforce, and the ideology that an 'alien' element was responsible for the deterioration of British Columbia society in the early twentieth century (Comack, 1986). Vigorous enforcement of narcotics laws against the Chinese led to numerous convictions and deportations. This narcotics law, like many subsequent drug laws, was used to criminalize and regulate some of the least powerful members of our society. The law singled out the Chinese opium–smoker and the Chinese opium factories and left relatively untouched Caucasian-owned pharmaceutical companies that manufactured several opium–based products (ibid.). The application and effect of the law can be uneven.

Generally, those members of society with the least power suffer the most severe stigma of criminalization. Canadian Aboriginal people are disproportionately overrepresented at all stages of the criminal justice process (Griffiths and Yerbury, 1996). Aboriginal people are not more criminal than non-Aboriginal people. However, some of their activities, like the consumption of alcohol or political protest, are more likely to be criminalized than the same behaviour in non-Aboriginals. Some research suggests that the police and other criminal justice officials behave in a discriminatory fashion towards Aboriginal people, resulting in higher arrest, conviction, and imprisonment rates (ibid.). Aboriginal people are overrepresented in the Canadian federal and provincial prison populations. Rather than improving, this trend towards over-incarceration appears to be getting worse. Aboriginal people accounted for 11 per cent of admissions to federal custody in 1991–2, 15 per cent in 1996–7, and 17 per cent in 1997–8. Yet, they represent only 2 per cent of the adult population (Canadian Centre for Justice Statistics, 1999: 45; for discrimination against non-white offenders, see also Commission on Systemic Racism, 1995; Canada, 1998; Mosher, 1998). The findings of recent task forces and commissions and such well-publicized cases as those of Donald Marshall, who was wrongfully imprisoned for a murder he did not commit, and Helen Betty Osborne, a young Aboriginal who was assaulted and murdered by whites who were never convicted, suggest that the racism and discrimination experienced by Aboriginal people play a major role in the difficulties they encounter with the criminal justice system.

Similar concerns emerge regarding racial, cultural, and ethnic discrimination. The Report of the Ontario Commission on Systemic Racism clearly documents the occurrence of systemic and direct discrimination in the criminal justice system. Systemic discrimination refers to 'the social production of racial inequality in decisions about people and in the treatment they receive' (Commission on Systemic Racism, 1995: 39). For example, some members of visible minorities are overpoliced in that they are more frequently stopped and questioned by the police, and some are denied access to interpreters, other culturally relevant services, and special needs during court processes and while incarcerated. There is an underrepresentation of racialized persons among criminal justice professionals and a perception among racialized people that the system treats white and non-white persons differently. The Commission on Systemic Racism clearly supports this perception. The Commission found that visible minorities experience discrimination at each stage of the criminal justice process, that black men and women disproportionately experience imprisonment, and that discretion is rarely exercised in favour of racialized people as frequently or as significantly as for white people (ibid.).

Crime Is Culturally Specific

Crime is also culturally specific. Actions or activities considered to be criminal are generally designated as wrong, based on certain cultural values, norms, or mores. Different cultures have different conceptions of which behaviours should be regulated through criminal law. For example, in certain Scandinavian countries, the laws governing the so-called 'victimless crimes', such as drug use and prostitution, are more lenient. Conversely, certain non-crimes in Canada, such as spanking, are considered criminal acts in Sweden. In some Middle Eastern countries, the law is closely aligned with religious doctrines. In the United States, there are different laws and different techniques for punishing those who violate the law from those in Canada. For example, several American states endorse the use of capital punishment. The acceptance or rejection of a given punishment or behaviour is highly contingent upon cultural sensibilities or beliefs.

Crime Is Situational

The word 'crime' means different things to different people. In other words, the definition of an act as criminal depends on the perceptions of those involved in the act and how they define the behaviour under consideration. There is a great deal of slippage between law-abiding behaviour and criminal behaviour. Furthermore, since the situational context in which an act occurs also influences our definition of that act as criminal, crime is situationally specific. For example, if an individual strikes another without consent, then legally an assault may have occurred. But what if the act occurred in the context of a sport or was the result of a playful struggle between siblings? The context or circumstances surrounding an act of violence shape our understanding of it as criminal. Much, if not most, violent behaviour is not considered criminal. Although certain sports such as boxing and wrestling and some medical interventions (for example, surgery or shock therapy) could be characterized as violent, they are not deemed so under ordinary circumstances.

Another example of a violent behaviour only considered a crime under certain circumstances is the act of killing another individual. The state-sanctioned killing of individuals that occurs at times of war, or in police action, or when someone is sentenced to death is not legally defined as murder. If a police officer or prison guard kills an individual in his or her line of duty, this action is not automatically considered criminal. In other instances of intentionally inflicted death,

Box 6.1: NHL Goons on Skates

It's good that Thursday night's brawl between the Toronto Maple Leafs and the Chicago Blackhawks broke out late in the hockey game: fewer kids probably saw it on TV.

Hawk defenceman Steve Smith's bloodied and pulpy face and the pile of writhing bodies on the ice were, of course, nothing new for the National Hockey League.

But the sight of Hawk Stu Grimson, a thug on skates if ever there was one, running amok—with the home crowd roaring approval—was unforgettable.

As the fight subsided on the ice, Grimson, glassy-eyed and stripped down to his sweat-soaked undershirt, simply came unglued.

Suddenly, his own coach, Mike Keenan, couldn't hold him back at the bench.

Breaking from Keenan's grasp, Grimson first tracked down, then grabbed one of the linesmen by the head as if hoping to dash his brains out against the glass.

When Grimson finally went to the showers, there was a telling moment when teammate Ed Belfour gave him a congratulatory send-off tap on the rear with his goalstick.

It was disgusting.

And someone could have been seriously hurt.

A night of half-decent hockey—a couple of pretty goals by the Hawks, classic goaltending by the Leafs' Grant Fuhr in a losing cause—ruined by 40 minutes of mayhem.

Starting with this episode of goonery, the NHL must clamp down on the violence that gives hockey a bad name.

Sitting in the comfort of their living rooms, Don Cherry-types may covet this kind of rock-'em, sock-'em stuff on skates.

But if it ever happened in a bar or a back alley somewhere, there'd be criminal charges—and maybe even a trip to the cooler.

Source: *Toronto Star* editorial, 18 Jan. 1992, D2. Reprinted with permission—The Toronto Star Syndicate.

such as euthanasia or in cases where a death was the consequence of an act of self-defence (for example, a battered woman who kills), there are long-standing moral and political debates about whether or not the behaviour should be deemed criminal. One of the major roles of the legal system and more specifically the court process is to determine what behaviours are criminal and what behaviours are perhaps inappropriate or deviant but not crimes in the legal sense.

In summary, when thinking about the concept of crime and of those who are officially labelled criminal, it is important to remember that crime is historically, culturally, and situationally specific. For someone to be labelled criminal he or she must be caught and the law must be enforced. If a crime is detected, there is a great deal of discretion involved in deciding what is and is not a crime, and even more

Box 6.2: Latimer sentence too harsh, poll told

Tolerance shown for mercy killing

Jeff Sallot
The Globe and Mail, Ottawa

The Tracy Latimer homicide case in Saskatchewan exposes strong public dissatisfaction with the current state of Canada's law on mercy killing, a new poll suggests.

Seventy-three per cent of Canadians believe Saskatchewan farmer Robert Latimer's mandatory life sentence for the killing of his severely disabled daughter is too harsh, pollsters found.

Only 23 per cent said Mr Latimer, as the killer of an innocent child, should pay the full legal penalty. (Four per cent said they had no opinion.)

The Angus Reid Group poll also found significant public support for legalizing euthanasia. Forty-one per cent of respondents said mercy killing should not be illegal.

Another 38 per cent said mercy killing should remain illegal, but those convicted should be treated by the courts with leniency and compassion. Only 16 per cent said mercy killing should be treated like any other murder.

The apparent sympathy felt by an overwhelming number of Canadians for a father who said he couldn't stand to see his daughter suffer any further stands in sharp contrast to the strong support for a return to the death penalty that opinion researchers regularly find in other polls.

The mercy-killing poll was conducted for the *Globe and Mail* and CTV last month in the wake of a Saskatchewan Court of Appeal decision to sentence Mr Latimer to the Criminal Code's mandatory penalty for second-degree murder: life imprisonment with no chance of parole for 10 years.

In light of the tragic circumstances, the judge at the original murder trial in 1997 imposed only a two-year sentence.

Twelve-year-old Tracy Latimer suffered severe cerebral palsy and was in pain awaiting surgery for a displaced hip when her father administered a lethal dose of carbon-monoxide gas as she slept.

Mr Latimer has asked the Supreme Court of Canada to overturn the appeal court's decision.

Meanwhile, the federal government has been steering clear of any attempt to rewrite the law on mercy killings despite recent high-profile cases, including the assisted suicide in 1993 of Sue Rodriguez, a terminally ill woman in BC.

The Angus Reid telephone poll of 1,501 Canadians was conducted Dec. 10 to 20 and is considered accurate to within 2.5 percentage points.

On the first question, people were asked whether they believe Mr Latimer acted out of compassion for his daughter and should receive a more lenient sentence or whether the murderer of an innocent child should pay the full legal penalty.

On a followup question, people were given three possible options regarding mercy killing:

- Treat it like any other kind of murder;
- Keep it illegal but treat it with leniency;
- Make it legal in appropriate circumstances.

Older respondents were more likely than younger people to favour leniency.

Attitudes About Euthanasia

Question: *Some people say that, given the pain that Tracy Latimer lived through on a daily basis, Robert Latimer was acting out of compassion and should receive a more lenient sentence. Other people say that he murdered an innocent child who was not able to protect herself and, therefore, Robert Latimer should pay the full penalty for second-degree murder.*
Which of these two opinions is closest to your own?

■ Acted out of compassion. Should receive more lenient sentence.　■ Murdered innocent child. Should pay full penalty for second-degree murder.　□ Don't know/ refused to answer

	Compassion	Murdered	Don't know
TOTAL	73%	23	4
AGES			
18-34	69	29	3
35-54	75	21	5
55 plus	78	18	4
MALE	73	22	5
FEMALE	73	23	3

Question: *Now, some people say that 'mercy killing', like in the Latimer case, should be treated like any other murder. Others say that 'mercy killing' should remain illegal, but people who do it should be treated with leniency and compassion. Still others say that under the appropriate circumstances, 'mercy killing' should not be against the law.*
Which of these three statements is closest to your own point of view?

■ Should be treated like any other murder.　■ Should be illegal. Those who do it treated with leniency and compassion.　■ Should not be against the law under appropriate circumstances.　□ Don't know / refused to answer

	Like murder	Illegal/leniency	Not against law	Don't know
TOTAL	18%	38	41	2
AGES				
18-34	22	33	48	2
35-54	17	36	43	3
55 plus	14	46	37	3
MALE	19	36	42	3
FEMALE	17	41	40	2

Note: Figures may not total 100 per cent because of rounding.

Source: Angus Reid Group and *Globe and Mail*, 11 Jan. 1999.

importantly, in trying to determine how to enforce the law. Thousands of crimes, occurring on a daily basis, are not reported to or detected by the police. Because these events are not being reported, for whatever reason, they are never officially labelled as crimes. The line between what is and what is not labelled a crime is quite fluid.

Measurement of Crime: Attitudes and Misconceptions

What does the public think crime looks like? Although the risk of victimization is real and caution is warranted, most people tend to overestimate the amount of violent crime and of crimes committed by those unknown to the victims. Reports of increased crime rates, especially of violent crime, are highlighted often in the media. Hence, it is not surprising that a large portion of the Canadian public believes that crime in their neighbourhoods has increased and that many citizens feel unsafe walking alone at night in their communities (Doob and Gartner, 1996: 100). Fear for personal safety is more acute among women and the elderly. In spite of these perceptions, recent research indicates that Canadians are not at a higher risk for violent victimizations today than they were in 1988 (ibid., 103–4). Although women feel particularly vulnerable to violent stranger crimes, the primary threat to women's safety does not come from strangers (Johnson, 1996: 91). Instead, research indicates that most women are violently victimized by relatives, partners, friends, and/or acquaintances (ibid.).

Nonetheless, the stereotype of the violent predatory criminal is perpetuated in a number of discourses. Politicians, the media, crime control agents, women's groups, academics, and many others participate in producing particular images of crime. Although sensationalist crimes represent a small portion of the crimes committed, not surprisingly they tend to receive a disproportionate amount of media and public attention. In fact, research repeatedly indicates that you are more likely to be assaulted or killed by someone you know than by a stranger or serial killer.

How is crime measured and where do we get information about crime? All numbers have meaning and they tell us something about crime and perceptions of crime. The measurement of crime is laden with assumptions about crime and criminality. Understanding the meaning and purposes of crime statistics enables us to dispel many common misunderstandings about the nature and extent of crime in Canadian society.

Crime statistics are quite difficult to collect properly. When the number of reported crimes are properly and responsibly collected and interpreted they can improve our knowledge of crime and our ability to make informed policy decisions. Crime statistics are used to make decisions about funding the police and related agencies and to make decisions about the deployment of police resources. For example, if crime statistics indicate that youth or specifically gang-related crimes are on the increase then police divisions may decide to deploy additional

Table 6.1   Examples of Public Misperceptions of Crime-related Statistics

Public Misperception	Reality
Crime rates constantly increasing	Crime rates decline or stable over period 1990–1995
Violent crime rate increasing faster than any other kind of crime	Violent crime rate increasing no faster than property crime
Murder rate increasing	Murder rate stable or declining in Canada, Australia, and US
The murder rate increased in Canada after abolition of death penalty	Murder rate has declined since abolition of death penalty
Violent crime accounts for approximately half of all crime recorded by the police	Violent crime accounts for approximately 10 per cent of crimes recorded by police; smaller percentage of all crimes committed
Crime committed by a small, easily identifiable part of population	Crime committed by a wide range of offender
Most offenders re-offend, and commit same kind of crime over and over again	Most offenders not re-convicted. Little specialization in terms of criminal careers
Most offenders on parole re-offend	Most parolees do not re-offend
Burglary rates increasing faster than other crimes	Burglary rates stable or declining

Source: Roberts and Stalans (1997: 33).

police resources in this area. Some of these police activities may include increased intervention in the high schools, foot patrols in high schools, parks, and community centres where youth gather, the introduction of diversion programs, and crime prevention programs in primary schools.

Crime statistics are used by academics to generate information about the types of crimes committed and to explain criminal activity. Crime statistics help us learn certain 'social facts' (race, class, gender) about the types of people caught breaking the law and about victims of crime. Commercially, crime statistics are used to sell and promote a wide range of personal safety devices, including car alarms, home security systems, and self-defence courses, and to support crime prevention programs, such as campus 'walk safe programs', child identification kits, and neighbourhood watch programs. When crime statistics are decontextualized or used irresponsibly they can artificially inflate the public's fear of crime. Given that crime statistics have such significance it is important to think about what they actually represent and how they are generated.

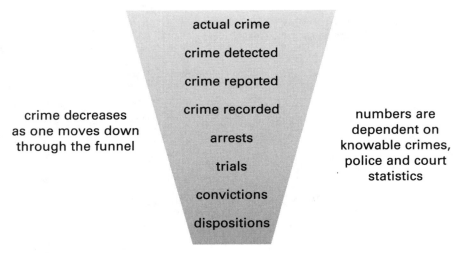

actual crime

crime detected

crime reported

crime decreases   crime recorded   numbers are
as one moves down   dependent on
through the funnel   arrests   knowable crimes,
                                                    police and court
                             trials   statistics

                           convictions

                           dispositions

Figure 6.1
The Crime Funnel

Theoretically, crime statistics can be represented as a funnel with the number of crimes decreasing as we move through the funnel. This funnel is useful in that it shows that not all crime is detected, not all detected crime is reported, not all reported crime is recorded, not all recorded crime results in arrests, not everyone arrested is brought to trial, not everyone tried is convicted, and not everyone convicted is sentenced. Most importantly, the crime funnel illustrates that the actual amount of crime is unknowable and that any given measurement of crime represents a partial picture.

Presently, there is no way of learning about and recording all of the crime that occurs. Criminologists commonly accept that statistical representations of crime have an 'unknowable relationship to the actual volume of crime and morphology of criminal activity' (Stoddart, 1996: 119). In other words, social scientists do not and cannot accurately quantify the amount of crime that exists in a given society at any given time. There are, however, several imprecise measures of crime that provide researchers with some knowledge of the nature and extent of criminal acts. These include police statistics, self-report data, and victimization surveys. The point to remember is that the meanings of the numbers are attached to the systems that collect them. They do not provide an accurate or perfect indication of how much crime there is in society. Many official crime statistics, for example police statistics, actually reflect organizational decisions.

Official Police Statistics

The police are the first to become aware of crimes through their own policing and reporting. Police awareness of crime, however, often depends on the reporting of the crime by a victim. If the victim does not report the crime, it is not likely that it will ever appear in official statistics. It is estimated that 84 per cent of crimes known to the police are reported versus 14 per cent that are discovered. For example, only one-quarter of battered women report their criminal victimization to the police (Johnson, 1996: 205). Similarly, research indicates that 80 per cent of serious violent sexual attacks by strangers were not reported to the police (Statistics Canada, 1994).

The police also have some discretion as to which crimes they will discover. This discretion is sometimes local to the individual officer and at other times it is not. For example, the 'discovery' of crimes depends on the deployment of resources in the areas of morality (prostitution), vehicle traffic, and drugs. The police appropriately pay more attention to violent crimes, such as murder, robbery, and rape, than to non-violent crimes like auto theft, break-and-enter, and tax evasion. The discretion of an individual police officer can also affect police statistics. For example, an officer may decide to allow a first offender to go with a warning, giving that person a second chance and not 'officially' recording the offence. If no paperwork is done on the offence, it is not likely ever to be counted.

With respect to police statistics there is also an issue as to how much crime and which crimes are reported to the police. A change in policing practices can obscure statistical representation of a particular crime. The number of official crimes recorded may increase even though there is no change in the amount of crime committed. For example, the police may be under pressure to 'clean up' the streets in a particular area of the city. In some large cities there is often a lot of pressure from residents of unofficial red-light districts to get rid of the prostitutes and drug dealers working in their neighbourhoods. As a result the police might increase the level of enforcement in that area and the number of prostitution- and drug-related charges increases. Although there were more charges laid by the police, it is unlikely that this apparent increase reflects a real increase in the number of prostitutes, drug dealers, or clients frequenting the area. Another example of the same phenomenon is the number of charges for driving under the influence of alcohol. Often the number of alcohol-related driving charges are said to increase during the holiday season. The number of people going out and drinking may very well increase. However, it is also likely that the statistics collected at these times reflect the fact there are also more spot checks and RIDE (Reduce Impaired Driving Everywhere) programs operating. These programs proactively stop and question individuals who might otherwise remain undetected.

Self-Report and Victimization Survey

Dissatisfaction with official measures of crime have led many researchers to seek alternative ways of measuring crime, in particular, self-report surveys and victimization surveys. Researchers began using victimization and self-report crime surveys in the 1960s to learn about hidden crimes, that is, unreported and undetected crimes. These surveys ask individuals to report anonymously their own law-violating behaviours and their experiences of victimization. The following is an example of a self-report survey.

Take a minute to review the following questions. For each item, answer 'yes' or 'no' as to whether or not you have engaged in the stated activity and estimate the number of times you did the task.

- Have you ever taken something from a store without paying for it?
- Have you ever driven a vehicle even mildly intoxicated?
- Have you ever used marijuana or any other illegal drug?
- Have you ever given a person an illegal drug?
- Have you ever offered a prescription drug to someone whose prescription it was not?
- Have you ever consumed alcohol as a minor?
- Have you ever given, sold, or served alcohol to a minor?
- Have you ever struck someone in anger?
- Have you ever threatened anyone?
- Have you ever made an anonymous call and hung up?
- Have you ever damaged public property, i.e., writing on a desk, restroom wall, library book?
- Have you ever taken anything from someone with force?
- Have you ever carried a weapon?
- Have you had a fist fight with another person?
- Have you ever taken office supplies for personal use?
- Have you ever brought goods into Canada without declaring them?
- Have you ever not declared some income from tips or odd jobs on your income tax or social assistance forms?
- Have you ever written a cheque when you did not have enough money in your bank account to cover the cheque when it was written?
- Have you ever known about someone else committing an offence and not reported that person?
- Have you ever taken something from a hotel room?
- Have you ever photocopied a book instead of purchasing the book?
- Have you ever copied computer software?

If you have answered 'yes' to any of these questions you likely have violated the law.

Most people have at some time or another violated a law. The overwhelming majority of individuals who break the law are not caught or prosecuted. The discrepancy between who gets caught and who does not is important. For example, when we look at data on self-reporting we often learn that men and women, racial majorities and minorities, and various social classes exhibit similar patterns of both offending behaviour and victimization. When the data from self-report studies are compared with official police statistics we find that police statistics tend to overreport crimes committed by male youth, people of lower social classes, and minorities. Although most people have committed some crimes and delinquencies—and some of them serious—the police are often unaware of these activities and most of these events go unnoticed and unpunished.

Victimization surveys are similar to self-report surveys. Victimization surveys ask individuals whether or not they were victims of crimes in a given period of time and they may explore some of the circumstances of the crime, including whether or not the victim reported the crime to the police. These studies generally reveal that even when people 'know' that they have been victimized, they do not report the crime to the police for a variety of reasons. Reiterating the earlier point about the inadequacy of police statistics, it is estimated that only 42 per cent of these crimes were reported (Cunningham and Griffiths, 1997: 39). Like the self-report survey, victimization studies verify that the majority of crimes committed are not known to the police and, further, they tell us a bit about who is likely to report a crime to the police.

Self-report and victimization data, like official statistics, are limited. Some of the problems associated with these techniques include biased sampling (self-reports are often given to young people), dishonesty or selective recall on the part of respondents, and the use of general terms that avoid serious offence categories. In spite of these flaws, these studies are useful in that they tell us something about the behaviour of average people and they can offer valuable information about under-reported crimes like domestic and sexual assault.

In general, there is a lack of consensus among professionals on how to count crime. It is important to look not only at what is being counted but also how it is being counted. For example, an offender enters a house and hits three people. Since these offences each are counted as separate offences, there are three victims. However, if the same offender enters the same house and steals items from three members of the same family, this is counted as one offence of break-and-enter with one victim. Counting is an important problem, not because different methods come up with different estimates, but because different methods have embedded in them different assumptions and implicit theories about what the crime problem is all about and how to solve it. The media in particular promulgate an inaccurate representation of crime because they tend to emphasize sensational cases and generalize about the extent of crime.

Being defined a criminal is also contingent upon the enforcement of the law. In other words, one must be caught and prosecuted for violating the law. We know from self-report and victimization studies that many individuals who break the law are never caught or officially prosecuted. Criminal involvement is often a matter of degree. Those committing crimes or engaging in anti-social acts range from career or habitual criminals to ordinary people who respond unacceptably to temptation or stressful circumstances. Although the former group tends to fill prisons and accounts for a disproportionate amount of serious crimes, a large portion of 'ordinary' people account for a non-trivial portion of assaults (often on partners), sexual assaults, thefts (such as stealing on the job or shoplifting), tax evasions, and frauds. These individuals are not as easily recognizable.

Crime and Its Management

There is no single accepted explanation for the causes of crime, and the popularity of individual theories shifts over time (Jackson and Griffiths, 1995). In spite of decades of study, we still do not definitively know what causes either crime or conformity. Traditional theoretical criminology of both past and present has unduly focused on distinguishing 'them' (the lawbreakers) from 'us' (the law-abiding). Most criminology theories are concerned with the 'etiology of crime' and thus focus on factors related to offending, primarily male juvenile offending. This is what noted criminologist David Garland (1994) calls the Lombrosian or governmental project. This governmental project has involved a long series of empirical inquiries, which have sought to enhance the efficient and equitable administration of justice by charting patterns of crime and monitoring the practices of police and courts and prisons.

While it is difficult to simplify and categorize the range of theoretical explanations of criminality, for our purposes the history of criminological thought falls into three areas: classical, positivist, and critical approaches. The classical school of criminology marks the beginnings of a rational and bureaucratic response to the problem of crime. This approach is premised on the ideas of two eighteenth-century writers, Cesare Beccaria and Jeremy Bentham. Bentham and Beccaria were concerned about the arbitrary and capricious nature of the criminal justice system of their time and they argued that the law and the administration of justice should be based on rationality and human rights, neither of which was commonly applied (Williams and McShane, 1999: 14). Both of these Enlightenment thinkers argued that human beings were free-willed and rational beings, and as a result they viewed crime as a rational choice. Beccaria and Bentham were most concerned about the legal definition of crime and the administration of the criminal justice system. For example, they argued for the codification of laws, the preservation of human rights, and the reform of punishment (Beccaria, 1963; Bentham, 1995). They were not particularly concerned about the causes of criminal behaviour. Instead, they argued that crime was an immoral and irrational activity that most people would choose to avoid provided that the costs of engaging in crime outweighed its benefit. Given that crime was seen as a product of a calculated rational choice, classical theorists argued that deterrence should be a guiding principle of punishment. Penalties arguably were harsh so as to discourage both individual lawbreakers and the general public.

The main premises of classical criminology continued to be popular with the Canadian public and policy-makers in the late twentieth century. The public generally finds it easier to blame the offender for his/her crimes than to recognize society's creation of conditions that leave some people with little choice other than crime (Williams and McShane, 1999: 23). If crime is a rational and calculated choice, then those who violate the law deserve to be punished because they choose to break the law. According to the classical theorist, this punishment should be swift, harsh, and timely so as to deter the offender and other potential offenders from committing future crimes. In the contemporary context, classical ideals are used to support political campaigns to 'get tough on crime' by increasing sanctions. Some examples of this approach include California's 'three strikes and you're out' law, which incarcerates repeat offenders indefinitely after being convicted for the third time, and Canada's recent reforms of the Young Offenders Act, which propose increased penalties for violent youthful offenders.

In contrast, positivist theories of crime are more concerned about the causes of criminality than with the administration of justice. Positivist approaches to crime advocate 'objective' empirical analyses of human behaviour. The purposes of these systematic observations are to uncover the abnormalities that cause an individual to commit a crime and to propose a method of curing or rehabilitating the offender. These theories of crime are deterministic in that they do not view criminal behaviour as the product of free will and rational choice. Instead, the cause of criminal conduct is linked to some combination of predetermined biological, psychological, and social factors (poverty, alcohol, drugs, abuse, and so on). The notion of a 'born criminal' originates with the positivist school. Contemporary positivists construct the offender as reformable and as a result they advocate rehabilitation. From this perspective, treatment of offenders is necessary to treat the abnormalities and to return the offender to a state of normalcy. In order to protect society, the primary purpose of punishment and criminal sanctioning should be to provide treatment for the offender. In contemporary systems of punishment, positivist ideas are used to promote therapeutic programs for convicted offenders, such as substance-abuse treatment, employment training, or specialized treatment for sex offenders, including chemical castration.

The third general category of criminological theories is a critical approach, which ranges from labelling theory to more recent feminist theories of crime and its management. Critical analyses of crime and the criminal justice system, unlike classical and positivist theories, question the power of the law to differentiate in its criminalizing of different segments of the population. Critical theories examine the gendered, racialized, classist, and heterosexist basis of the law and its application. They argue that crime is primarily a function of how criminal law is written and enforced. As discussed earlier, they argue that no act is inherently criminal and that what constitutes a crime is historically, culturally, and contextually specific. The critical theorist, by and large, argues that society creates crime and that criminals are not abnormal or irrational. Critical theorists examine the processes by which activities and individuals are criminalized and decriminalized. They are particularly interested in power relations and how these relations shape our understanding of crime and its management. As noted, there are several diverse critical theories. Some of the issues examined by such theorists may include: the gendered, racialized, and class-defined aspects of criminological theory and the administration of justice; the impact of discretion; the relationship between morality and the law, particularly as it applies to drug legislation, pornography, and prostitution; and the techniques of limiting the state's power. Critical feminist research on the policing of domestic violence illustrates that police discretion plays a central role in the implementation of mandatory charge policies (Hannah-Moffat, 1995). For several years Canadian feminists and advocates have struggled with the problem of how to police effectively the abuse of women. Public pressure on this issue led to demands for greater police accountability and for the police to treat the issue of domestic abuse as seriously as non-domestic stranger assault that occurs outside of a personal relationship. Recent reform initiatives adopt this approach and favour the criminalization of domestic abusers through the use of mandatory arrest and pro-charge policies. Although these policies attempt to aid women in danger by encouraging police officers to lay criminal charges and arrest suspected abusers, one study found that police discretion plays a critical role in determining whether the policy is actually enforced. The findings of this study clearly indicate that many police officers disagree with government-mandated, pro-charge policies (ibid.). Most officers were anxious about having their discretionary power limited. In terms of their role in domestic cases, most police officers felt that it was their duty to enforce the criminal law, not to mediate familial conflicts. Police officers often had negative attitudes towards domestic cases and they were often reluctant to become involved in what they perceived to be family matters. Police discretion, in particular police attitudes towards a policy, can play an integral role in how the criminal law is enforced. This illustrates a wider concern of critical criminologists with the inequitable enforcement of the law and with the discrepancies between formal criminal justice policy and the everyday enforcement of the law.

Each of the theoretical approaches adopts a different approach to the study of crime and criminality and each asks different questions about crime. For example, consider the situation of murder. For a classical criminologist the issue of importance would be how to prevent murder from occurring by looking at different punishments and methods of enforcement that would ensure an offender is caught. They would look at the costs versus benefits. For example, how certain was this person that she/he would be caught? What might have deterred the offender? Would different punishments make a difference—capital punishment versus life imprisonment? For a positivist criminologist the focus could be an examination of the biological, psychological, or social characteristics of the person to determine what causes her/his behaviour. Did the person suffer from a hormonal imbalance? Did she/he have an abusive childhood? Did she/he have a mental illness? Is she/he curable and what is the best method of rehabilitation for this offender? In contrast, a critical criminologist will ask questions like what types of killings are defined as murder under the law. They may also study how the police, courts, and correctional officials define and respond to criminal behaviour by scrutinizing the evidence used to construct the person who kills as dangerous. Critical criminologists are concerned with public policy and with the criminalization and decriminalization of different behaviours. They are also concerned with the unequal and discriminatory application of the law and the limited ability of the law and criminal justice systems to protect certain segments of the population.

The Criminal Justice System

Another area of concern for sociologists and criminologists is the operation of the criminal justice system and the agencies and processes that constitute this 'system'. The criminal justice system has three central components: police, courts, and corrections. Each of these components includes several subsystems that involve both private and public sectors. Corrections, for example, includes federal penitentiaries, provincial correctional centres, halfway houses, community corrections (probation, community service, fines, restitution), treatment programs, youth facilities, boot camps, electronic monitoring, and parole. The description of the criminal justice process as a 'system' is more of an analytical tool than a reality. The word 'system' implies a greater degree of co-operation, co-ordination, and integration than is actually often the case. There are considerable differences in the organizational and policy objectives of courts and corrections. For example, the police, in investigating the accused, are collecting evidence to show that the person is guilty. The courts, however, operate on a presumption of innocence and in theory provide an impartial check on police evidence and decisions. The courts are expected to serve as a check and balance against the potential excess of other components of the criminal justice process. As Schmalleger et al. (2000: 15) note, there are conflicts among and within agencies, the immediate goals are often not shared by individual actors in the system, and the system tends to move in different directions depending on political currents, informal arrangements among agencies, and personal discretionary decisions. The diversity of objectives and mandates has led some observers to characterize the justice system as a 'network of inter-related, yet interdependent, individuals and agencies, rather than a system per se' (Griffiths and Verdun-Jones, 1994: 9).

There are two general explanations of the formulation of criminal law and the operation of criminal justice: *the value-consensus model* and *the conflict model*. The consensus model argues that in a given society there is widespread agreement on social norms and on the acts considered illegal or immoral. It assumes that the components of the criminal justice system work towards a common goal to reaffirm the consensual interests and values of society. This view, however, has been challenged by critical scholars who adopt the conflict model. The conflict model states that there are a plurality of competing interests and values in society and that the criminal justice system tends to represent and reinforce the values of more powerful segments of society at the expense of the least powerful. A central concern of conflict theorists is the role played by the criminal justice system in social control and in the maintenance of the status quo. The conflict theorists examine the unequal treatment of some segments of society (namely women, minorities, and the poor) under the law and before the courts.

Concerns about the operation of the criminal justice system range from wider philosophical questions about the meaning and operationalization of the ideals of justice, fairness, and equality before and under the law to pragmatic concerns about the policing of crime (drug trade, sex trade), police discretion, sentencing, prisoners' rights, the role of victims, parole, and various other institutional issues. Increasingly, observers are questioning the privatization of several components of the criminal justice system. The past 10 years have seen an expansion of private police and of privately run correctional facilities.

Most debates about policing and decision-making at all levels of the criminal justice system involve the issue of discretion. Most official agents of the criminal justice system hold a broad range of discretionary powers, which are used to make decisions about who to arrest, prosecute, convict, sentence, and release. Police, judges, and correctional officials make decisions that directly affect both public safety and the individual's rights to autonomy and freedom. They are expected to satisfy competing demands, such as the needs of victims and the public versus the rights of the offender/accused. The criminal justice system is an elaborate system of checks and balances that attempts to mediate the conflicting demands of various segments of society. A considerable amount of criminological research is devoted to analysing the strengths and weaknesses of this 'system' (e.g., Griffiths and Verdun-Jones, 1994; Roberts, 2000; Schmalleger et al., 2000).

Conclusion

In spite of the commonness of crime, there remains a tendency to think about criminals as either psychologically or biologically different from the rest of 'us'. There is an attempt to develop an explanation for crime based on the premise that criminals are somehow different from non-criminals in ways that can be determined scientifically. One important contribution of self-report and victimization statistics is that they help defuse the myth of a criminal type. Too often, criminals are thought of as vicious characters, inclined towards heinous acts inconceivable to the rest of us. The view that the world can be divided into good and evil or the dangerous and the endangered is a popular one. However, the reality of 'crime' is that by and large it is not committed by inherently evil and easily identifiable monsters but rather by your co-workers, acquaintances, friends, and family members. The formation of criminal law and the administration of justice are not based on a simple consensus of values and not everyone is treated equitably in the criminal justice process. The criminal justice system is an imperfect process designed to deal with the very complex and fluid problem of crime.

Questions for Critical Thought

1. Discuss the historical, cultural, situational, and enforcement characteristics of crime.

2. What are the key elements and differences between classical, positivist, and critical theories of crime?

3. Describe three measures of crime and outline the strengths and weaknesses of each measure.

Glossary

Classical theories of crime: Viewed crime as a product of a calculated rational choice; thus, deterrence should be a guiding principle of punishment.

Crime: Often overlaps with deviance; however, any act prohibited by law is a crime.

Crime funnel: Demonstrates that the actual amount of crime is unknowable because not all crime is detected, not all detected crime is reported, not all reported crime is recorded, not all recorded crime results in arrest, not everyone arrested is brought to trial, not everyone tried is convicted, and not everyone convicted is sentenced.

Critical theories of crime: Question the power of the law to differentiate in its criminalizing of different segments of the law.

Positivist theories of crime: Concerned with the causes of criminality rather than with the administration of justice that guided classical theories of crime.

Suggested Reading

Bouchard, J., S. Boyd, and E. Sheehy. 1999. 'Canadian Feminist Literature on Law: An Annotated Bibliography', Special Issue of *Canadian Journal of Women and the Law* 11, 1–2. Toronto: University of Toronto Press. An annotated bibliography on women and crime and on feminism and the law.

Griffiths, C., and J. Verdun-Jones. 1994. *Canadian Criminal Justice*, 2nd edn. Toronto: Harcourt Brace. An excellent overview of the structure of the Canadian criminal justice system and of the issues that emerge at each stage of the criminal justice process.

Maguire, M., R. Morgan, and R. Reiner. 1997. *The Oxford Handbook of Criminology*. Oxford: Oxford University Press. An excellent and comprehensive collection of review essays on general theories of crime and control, the social dimensions of crime and justice, forms of crime and criminality, and criminal justice structures and processes.

Ontario Commission on Systemic Racism in the Ontario Criminal Justice System. 1995. *Report of the Ontario Commission on Systemic Racism in the Ontario Criminal Justice System*. Ontario: Queen's Printer. Addresses the issue of systemic racism as it pertains to various segments of the criminal justice system.

Roberts, J. 2000. *Criminal Justice in Canada: A Reader*. Toronto: Harcourt Brace. A collection of articles on current issues in the Canadian criminal justice system.

References

Beccaria, C. 1963. [1764]. *On Crimes and Punishment*, trans. Henry Paolucci. Indianapolis: Bobbs-Merrill.

Bentham, J. 1995. *The Panopticon Writings*, ed. M. Bozovic. London: Verso.

Boyd, N. 1995. 'Legal and Illegal Drug Use in Canada', in Jackson and Griffiths (1995: 361–79).

Canada. 1998. *Task Force on Aboriginal Peoples in Corrections*. Ottawa: Ministry of the Solicitor General.

Canadian Centre for Justice Statistics. 1999. *The Juristat Reader*. Toronto: Thompson Educational Publishing.

Chambliss, W. 1973. 'The Saints and Roughnecks', *Society* 11, 1: 24–31. Reprinted 1999, in E. Rubington and M. Weinberg, eds, *Deviance: An Interactionist Perspective*. Toronto: Allyn & Bacon.

Comack, E. 1986. 'We Will Get Some Good Out of This Riot Yet: The Canadian State, Drug Legislation and Class Conflict', in Comack and S. Brickey, eds, *The Social Basis of Law*. Toronto: Garamond Press, 67–89.

Commission on Systemic Racism in the Ontario Criminal Justice System. 1995. *Report of the Commission on Systemic Racism in the Ontario Criminal Justice System*. Toronto: Queen's Printer.

Cunningham, A.H., and C. Griffiths. 1997. *Canadian Criminal Justice: A Primer*. Toronto: Harcourt Brace.

Doob, A., and R. Gartner. 1996. 'Trends in Criminal Victimization', in R. Silverman, J. Teevan, and V. Sacco, eds, *Crime in Canadian Society*. Toronto: Harcourt Brace, 90–104.

Garland, D. 1994. 'Of Crimes and Criminals: The Development of Criminology in Britain', in M. Maguire, R. Morgan, and R. Reiner, eds, *Oxford Handbook of Criminology*. Oxford: Clarendon Press.

Giffen, P.J., S. Endicott, and S. Lambert. 1996. 'The Social Origins of Canadian Narcotic Drug Prohibition', in R. Silverman, J. Teevan, and V. Sacco, eds, *Crime in Canadian Society*. Toronto: Harcourt Brace, 14–24.

Gomme, I. 1998. *The Shadow Line: Deviance and Crime in Canada*. Toronto: Harcourt Brace.

Griffiths, J., and C. Verdun-Jones. 1994. *Canadian Criminal Justice*. Toronto: Harcourt Brace.

Hannah-Moffat, K. 1995. 'To Charge or Not to Charge: Front Line Officers' Perceptions of Mandatory Charge Policies', in M. Valverde, L. MacLeod, and K. Johnson, eds, *Wife Assault and the Canadian Criminal Justice System*. Toronto: Centre of Criminology.

Jackson, M., and C. Griffiths. 1995. *Canadian Criminology: Perspectives on Crime and Criminality*. Toronto: Harcourt Brace.

Johnson, H. 1996. *Dangerous Domains: Violence Against Women in Canada*. Toronto: Nelson.

Liden, R. 1996. *Criminology: A Canadian Perspective*, 3rd edn. Toronto: Harcourt Brace.

Mosher, C. 1998. *Discrimination and Denial: Systemic Racism in Ontario's Legal and Criminal Justice System, 1892–1962*. Toronto: University of Toronto Press.

Roberts, J. 2000. *Criminal Justice in Canada: A Reader*. Toronto: Harcourt Brace.

Roberts, J., and L. Stalans. 1997. *Public Opinion, Crime and Criminal Justice*. Boulder, Colo.: Westview Press.

Schmalleger, F., D. MacAlister, P. McKenna, and J. Winterdyk. 2000. *Canadian Criminal Justice Today: An Introductory Text for the Twenty-First Century*. Toronto: Prentice-Hall, Allyn & Bacon Canada.

Snider, L. 1993. *Bad Business: Corporate Crime in Canada*. Toronto: Nelson.

Statistics Canada. 1994. *Violence Against Women Survey*. Micro data file. Ottawa.

Stoddart, K. 1996. 'It's Easier for the Bulls Now: Official Statistics and Social Change in a Canadian Heroin Using Community', in R. Silverman, J. Teevan, and V. Sacco, eds, *Crime in Canadian Society*. Toronto: Harcourt Brace, 111–20.

Strange, C. 1995. 'Historical Perspectives of Wife Assault', in M. Valverde, L. MacLeod, and K. Johnson, eds, *Wife Assault and the Canadian Criminal Justice System*. Toronto: Centre of Criminology, 293–306.

Williams, F., and M. McShane. 1999. *Criminological Theory*. Toronto: Prentice-Hall.

Yerbury, C., and C. Griffiths. 1991. 'Minorities, Crime and the Law', in M. Jackson and C. Griffiths, *Canadian Criminology*. Toronto: Harcourt Brace Jovanovich.

part three

Movements Towards Social Change

Periods of uncertainty have also been moments when social movements surface to claim a measure of social space and legitimacy for themselves. In the beginning, change is welcomed by a few, but most feel threatened by the new 'upstarts'. Struggles for inclusion are always a messy business. Those in the forefront of change are reviled by detractors but embraced by true believers. This is understandable. Only after the 'dust has settled', when the movement is no longer a movement but part of the social fabric, can the human qualities of the participants be celebrated.

The chapters in this section of the book illustrate the stages social movements pass through on their journey to legitimacy. The Canadian women's movement has reached one of the final stages, becoming part of the established order. The gay and lesbian movement in Canada has achieved begrudging acceptance, while 'youth' appear to be in the initial stages of a social movement grounded, as is not uncommon, in a feeling of being among society's disinherited.

Much has been written about the women's movement in Canada and in the world economy. Its history and leaders are well known and their stories have been well documented. What has not been heard about in Canada is the academic arm of the women's movement. This is the contribution of Huguette Dagenais and Peta Tancred, who help us to understand not only the role played by academic feminists but the crucial differences between academic feminists in Quebec and the rest of Canada. Theirs is an exposition of the Quebec and Anglophone work in the field. They also assess the strengths and weaknesses of the Anglophone and Francophone academic programs in Canada.

The progress made by the gay and lesbian movement in Canada and the struggles that remain are the focus of Chapter 8. Gary Kinsman outlines the history of the gay and lesbian movement in Canada, from the bathhouse raids in Toronto in the 1970s to the present victories in the struggle for legal recognition. Drawing on support from the women's movement, the trade unions in Canada, and anti-racist and other social movements, gays and lesbians have won important steps in the struggle for equality and eventual social acceptance.

James Côté and Anton Allahar, in Chapter 9, examine how youth today are the 'new losers in the struggles among the giant corporations and other societal interests'. They detail the necessary link between today's corporate and government agendas and their consequences for the present generation of young people. While it is true that some young people have found a home in today's workplace, many others feel disinherited, and while some believe they are making a contribution to society, many others have not been called upon to make productive improvements to their communities and societies. Although the career expectations of some are being satisfied, many others feel trapped. Côté and Allahar's analysis argues for an intergenerational quid pro quo if we are to avoid sustaining large segments of the present population, while condemning future generations to a state of idleness and a reduced sense of obligation to other members of society.

chapter seven

Women's Studies, Feminist Studies, Gender Studies: The Academic Arm of the Women's Movement

Peta Tancred and Huguette Dagenais

In Canada, as in other Western countries, the women's movement has been a driving force in the complex social transformations that have affected women's lives over the last three decades. At the forefront of that large and diverse movement, and often understood as a synonym for it, is 'second-wave feminism', whose rebirth in the 1960s owes much to the energy and political convictions of well-educated young women, a large number of them already involved in leftist political movements. Many of these new feminists were university students of the time. It is easy to forget that Kate Millett's *Sexual Politics* (1971) and Shulamith Firestone's *The Dialectic of Sex* (1970), two of the most influential theoretical texts of Western feminism, were the doctoral theses of their authors. Since then, many more theses have been written, some finding their way into the lists of numerous books and articles that inspire our analysis today. Without these academic works, what would we know today of the isolated fights of remarkable women from the past centuries? Of our feminist godmothers' struggles for recognition? Or of the courageous suffragists of the 'first wave' of feminism, at the turn of the century, who ensured the enfranchisement of Canadian women at the federal level (1918) and, eventually, in the various provinces?

Despite a conceptual division between the first and second waves of feminism, the latter was clearly not completely cut off from the former. As Naomi Black points out:

> Feminism and women's groups had not simply died off at the successful end of the suffrage campaigns. . . . After enfranchisement, organized women were engaged in fewer concentrated campaigns, had less publicity and less success, but their activities never stopped. (1993: 153–4)

As of the 1960s, however, certain developments ensured that this activity became more visible, more widespread.

First of all, there was a general context of significant social protest, nationally and internationally—for example, the civil rights movement, the student movement, and the Black Power movement, to name only a few movements of the sixties with their general call for economic and social justice. The way that women perceived their treatment within these movements galvanized them even further towards the rearticulation of the women's movement, i.e., that it was necessary to demand social justice for women as well (Hamilton, 1996: 48). But this was not the only factor, for there were also significant changes in women's lived experiences. As data on women's labour force participation show quite clearly, over the 1960s the labour force participation of women increased significantly and this was particularly marked among married women (ibid.). Thus, a significant group of Canadian women were no longer confined to the home and were active participants in the public sphere. Concomitant with this was the growth of the proportion of women in the higher educational system, which climbed from one-fifth in 1950 to over one-third by 1970 (Gaskell et al., 1989: 84). Thus, the 'interrelated patterns of women's education and work' (Black, 1993: 159) and the general context of claims for social justice more than legitimated women's demands for a whole range of transformations in their societal position during the 1960s.

This context was encouraging for the appointment of the Royal Commission on the Status of Women in 1967, an initiative that was wrenched from the federal government by some of the early feminist groups and activists that had emerged over the 1960s, both in Quebec and the other Canadian provinces. While there may be some differences of opinion concerning the Commission's 167 recommendations, they were remarkably modern for the period. Their implementation was taken on by the strong emerging organizations of the 1970s, particularly the National Action Committee on the Status of Women (NAC), the umbrella organization that has come to regroup more than 570 of the women's organizations that exist across Canada.

Following this propitious start, second-wave feminism has become increasingly diversified, including a wide range of groups centred on race, ethnicity, and sexual orientation. This 'multifaceted and enriched' movement (Hamilton, 1996: 80) has known numerous achievements, including the 1988 Supreme Court ruling supporting women's right to access to abortion; change in the blatantly misogynist Indian Act granting Native women the same treaty rights as Native men; recognition of the prevalence of violence against women; and recognition of the necessity for affirmative action to ensure women's equal treatment in the workplace (1986), to mention only a few examples (Wine and Ristock, 1991: 2).

However, there is the other side of the coin, for the increasingly conservative tendencies of the 1980s have led to significant cuts in grants to such national organizations as the NAC and to provincial feminist groups so that the dependence on state funding has returned to haunt the women's movement; contemporary Canadian women still live in a society in which poverty is predominantly female; women are still highly subject to violence; women are underrepresented in authority positions; and education is still under male control (ibid., 2–3). Thus, the glass is both 'half-empty and half-full' (Tancred, 1994: 12). It has been an eventful three decades for second-wave feminism; but progress has not proceeded in a straight line and has been subjected to frequent regression.

It is in this context that we examine the academic arm of the women's movement. As we will see, there are inevitable parallels between women's activism and Women's Studies—or to put it in another way, feminist praxis implies a close relationship between theory and application. But, as we shall also note, praxis is more or less divisible in different contexts. With this in mind we turn to an examination of Women's Studies in the academy since the 1960s.

Women's Studies courses have existed in Canada at least from the late 1960s.[1] The first program in Women's Studies was founded at the University of Toronto in 1974, followed closely by a program at Concordia University in 1977 (WSAC, 1993: 2). By the late 1980s, nearly half of all Canadian universities offered some kind of program (mainly Anglophone) in Women's Studies and 75 per cent provided at least some courses in the field (Eichler and Tite, 1990: 8). Interdisciplinary graduate programs at the MA level exist at several universities[2] and one doctoral program (at York University) was founded in 1992. Over a 30-year period, Women's Studies has achieved a significant presence within Canadian academia.

The main thrust of this chapter is to delineate the kinds of approaches that characterize Women's Studies[3] programs in our country. To do this, we look at three approaches that have been considered for academic work on women, specifically (1) Women's Studies; (2) Feminist Studies; and (3) Gender Studies. Equipped with some reference points for these three approaches, we will discuss an apparent contradiction between title and content in Anglophone universities and important contrasts between Anglophone and Francophone scholars. In both discussions, we will make reference to links between scholars and activist groups within the field.

Benchmarks for the Field

Women's Studies appears, at first glance, to be the easiest term to define—after all, we are merely discussing studies of or about women or, if we wish to be slightly more elaborate, 'work with a major focus on women, which draws both on research carried out by the traditional disciplines and on the new interdisciplinary scholarship in the area' (WSAC, 1993: 2). However, on further reflection, the term is not totally clear. What does the apostrophe indicate? Are these studies *by* women and therefore part of our heritage? Or, are they studies *for* women and therefore addressed to us? Is the term Women's Studies saying something more than merely studies *of* women?

Fortunately, we have some specifically Canadian material that bears on these questions.[4] When surveyed by the Canadian Women's Studies Project in the late 1980s, those teaching Women's Studies in universities could achieve consensus on several dimensions of their field, specifically that:

1. it covers a subject area: women;
2. it excludes men's studies;

3.   studies are *by* and *about* women;
4.   studies are non-political or neutral;
5.   studies describe and add women to extant knowledge;
6.   the field uses existing methods and theories;
7.   the field is perceived to be 'institutionally safe'. (Eichler, 1990: 44)

As to 'Feminist Studies', the relevant reference points are less obvious. As we know, the term has 'been fiercely contested since its introduction a century ago' (Caine, 1995: 2). Caine provides an interesting account of varying emphases from the 1890s forward, including the interwar period when the term 'feminist' allowed those engaged in the women's movement to differentiate themselves from the suffragists. In the contemporary academic context, however, feminist studies is perceived to 'represent the most important paradigmatic change that has occurred in our times' (Eichler, 1988: 38). The points on which most scholars in the field would agree is that feminist work transforms frameworks of analysis and is not defined by a field of study. The same Canadian Women's Studies Project delineates the consensus concerning 'Feminist Studies' among scholars in the field as including:

1.   studies from a perspective applicable to *all* subject areas;
2.   'Men's studies';
3.   studies *for* women (and not necessarily by or about them);
4.   work that is self-consciously political and committed;
5.   studies that are transformative rather than additive;
6.   studies that develop new methodological and theoretical approaches;
7   work that is 'institutionally unsafe' (Eichler, 1990: 44).

In sum, Feminist Studies constitute the opposite of Women's Studies on practically all dimensions; is it any surprise that the rubric is perceived to infer a major change in paradigm?

Finally, 'Gender Studies' as a denominator floats between a traditional 'gender role' definition of the field and a more contemporary 'gender relations' stance. Under the first heading, gender is sometimes used as a euphemism for women, while simultaneously profiting from the gentler aura surrounding the term, linked as it is to its promise of an even-handed treatment of both women and men. This early meaning of 'Gender Studies' also explains the strong reaction of some Women's Studies scholars who argue that 'women still contribute as much a subject for study as they ever did' while gender 'seems to suggest that the interests of the sexes have now converged' (Evans, 1991: 68, 73).

However, as we understand the contemporary meaning of the term 'Gender Studies', the emphasis is on a field of study that could be circumscribed as 'women in their relations with men'. Instead of emphasizing gender as a dichotomy, scholars seek to emphasize the complexity of gender relations and the importance of including men in an understanding of women's oppression. Under this heading would be subsumed not just men's studies, but particularly the new studies of masculinities that unravel their processes of construction and recognize the oppressive aspects, for both women and men, of traditional forms of masculinity. While the Canadian Women's Studies Project does not address the topic of 'Gender Studies', a rubric that dates from a period following their survey, the relevant definition might be formulated as follows:

1. focuses on women in their relations with men;
2. includes the new studies of masculinities;
3. is *for* and *about* women (but not necessarily by them);
4. is political and committed;
5. is transformative for *both* women and men;
6. employs new methodological and theoretical approaches;
7. is perceived as 'institutionally safe'.

As can be seen, 'Gender Studies' combines aspects of both women's and feminist studies; however, as the rubric suggests, men are much more present within this framework through the study of both their traditional roles and transforming masculinities.

Anglophone Work in the Field

In Anglophone universities, it should be underlined that the development of 'Women's Studies' has proceeded from the introduction of a few courses to the foundation of programs that, as mentioned earlier, now exist in a significant majority of Anglophone institutions. This route is a well-travelled one, at both the undergraduate and graduate levels, and contrasts strongly with the Francophone tradition, to be discussed later. What is salient here is that Anglophone scholars have felt the need for an institutional base for their scholarship and have not been discouraged by any ghettoization implied by program status. Their main priority up to this stage has been to develop the field rather than to disseminate research results throughout the academy. There is hope that the structure represents some degree of continuity—though one of us has argued elsewhere that program status is not sufficient and that we should aim for departmental standing if we are to continue to be included as a recognized and dignified part of the university (Tancred, 1994: 19–20). But institutionalization has been a definite leitmotif of developments in Anglophone Canada.

As to approach, if we were to be guided by title alone, Anglophone studies of women are located firmly under the 'Women's Studies' rubric. The national association goes under the title of the Canadian Women's Studies Association. There are now four federally endowed chairs of Women's Studies in Anglophone Canada as well as a new university chair of Women's Studies at the University of Northern British Columbia. As indicated earlier, the last three decades have witnessed a veritable flowering of offerings and the isolated courses of the late sixties and early seventies have been transformed into Women's Studies programs, a title in use in almost 100 per cent of Anglophone universities.[5]

Any exceptions occur in the titles of periodicals based in university settings, or of research centres. As to the former, the long-standing *Resources for Feminist Research* deliberately changed its title in 1979 to include the word 'feminist', but the other Canadian university-based journals retain 'women' or 'woman' in the title.[6] Among the eight research centres in Anglophone universities,[7] two use the term 'feminist' in their title.[8] Thus, the general image is of Women's Studies undertakings across Anglophone Canada with small islands of feminist work.

However, this is indeed an *image*, for if we dig a little deeper, there is evidence that the Women's Studies rubric covers a plethora of feminist work. On this topic, the ever-helpful Canadian Women's Studies Project provides specific data. Of the respondents who reached the consensus outlined above about differences between Women's Studies and Feminist Studies and who teach in these quasi-uniformly named Women's Studies programs, an overwhelming majority (91 per cent of the women and even 58 per cent of the men)[9] define themselves as feminists (Eichler, 1990: 48, Table 1). Even more impressive, 97 per cent of women and 90 per cent of men state that some or all of their work is informed by a feminist perspective (ibid., Table 2). In effect, only a small minority of instructors teach from a non-feminist perspective.

Thus, Anglophone Canada is characterized by the strong presence of Women's Studies programs that are overwhelmingly taught from a feminist perspective. Or, to express the matter succinctly, there is significant overlap, for many respondents, between the two fields, despite any abstract distinction. But if we push even further, there is a particular kind of overlap between the two terms—an academic overlap rather than one of external political involvement—for these feminist scholars do not appear to be highly politically motivated in their work, particularly post-1975 entrants to the field. Only about 15 per cent of these latter entrants were mainly motivated by their wish to improve conditions for women in teaching their first course in the area (in contrast to about 29 per cent of pre-1975 entrants), and proportions are even lower for post-1975 entrants when asked about their most recent courses (Lenton, 1990: Tables 1 and 2, 61–2). In addition, the majority of all women, and particularly of later entrants to the field, had prior contacts in the academic community with someone in women's/feminist studies, whereas a minority[10] had contacts with political or grassroots organizations external to the university (ibid., Table 3).

On the other hand, while the overall pattern of *current* involvement among Women's Studies scholars is the same (higher for earlier entrants), nearly 50 per cent of the overall group answered positively to more than half of the questions designed to measure 'the political involvement of professors' (ibid., 59), thus suggesting a fairly high level of activism, though admittedly this index of involvement in women's groups could include political activity within the university. It is certainly possible, however, and personal knowledge would so indicate, that many academics teaching Women's Studies courses are also involved in community activism, but the overall proportion does seem to decrease with successive cohorts. Because of this, Lenton suggests that women's/feminist studies has become institutionalized and that scholars are concerned with strengthening their positions within the academic community (ibid., 67).

From our point of view, the meaning of Feminist Studies for Anglophone scholars fragments into its academic and non-academic aspects. Anglophone scholars are very open to the theoretical and methodological contributions of feminism and they certainly manifest contacts across the academy, but they were not necessarily politically involved outside the university before teaching Women's Studies courses. At the same time, many would argue that what bell hooks calls 'feminist movement' (hooks, 1984: 22) can take place in many arenas and that political involvement should not be limited to non-academic or grassroots activism. This distinction will become significant as we discuss the Francophone community, for it provides an important contrast between the approaches of the two language groups.

It remains to speculate on the reasons for this fragmentation.[11] One can suggest that the very small proportion of feminist scholars in the universities[12] are overwhelmed by the feminist project, such that they have invested more time in accessible causes within the academy, leaving non-academic activism to their community sisters. This argument is not very cogent for, as we shall see, their Francophone colleagues, equally burdened with the never-ending academic round, still manage to engage in community activism, and this certainly exacerbates contrasts between the two communities.

A more cogent argument is that the Women's Studies rubric is a mere façade for a wealth of feminist work that is taking place within the academy. For example, many Women's Studies collections are, in fact, totally feminist works; and as indicated earlier, a lot of Women's Studies courses are taught from a feminist perspective. Feminists are using an 'institutionally safe' label that in practice they modify towards a feminist definition.[13] There is a certain basis for this argument. Many Anglophone universities have a strong conservative tradition linked to a non-interventionist stance and this was exacerbated by the neo-conservatism of the 1980s when a number of Women's Studies programs were developed. Maynard (1993: 730) suggests that, rather ironically, Women's Studies initiatives have benefited from the tight budgetary times because they were 'consumer led but . . . also entrepreneurial'. For Anglophone universities, the welcome accorded Women's Studies programs often depended on a separation from overt political action, defined mainly as grassroots activity. University administrators would know little about the argument of 'feminists moving' in a variety of arenas!

It is perhaps, in part, for this 'institutionally safe' reason that the rubric of Gender Studies has started to be discussed in Canadian universities. There is some enthusiasm, particularly among scholars in the humanities, but to our knowledge there is only one program in Anglophone Canada, at the moment, with this title and only one research centre that uses the rubric.[14] There is also considerable resistance because of the halo cast by the gender-role meaning of the term; feminists are just not interested in going back to the sex-gender role research of the 1930s with its strong conservative implications (Connell, 1990: 157).

Despite the great difficulty involved in translating 'Gender Studies' into French, it is probably inevitable that, as the new gender relations meaning of the term becomes widely accepted, the rubric will be adopted in Anglophone Canada. It has the great advantage of both being institutionally safe and designating the kind of work that many feminists want to undertake. It has the additional advantage of including the new work on masculinities, which is presently not easily housed within the university. And finally, it designates a less-marginalized status for feminist work, which may imply the greater integration of feminist scholarship into the academy.

In Quebec: Different Choices on the Francophone Side

The situation among Francophone Canadian feminists is quite different, at least in Quebec. Three aspects characterize these academic feminists: their past attitude towards institutionalization, which explains in part the present situation of feminist studies; their insistence on designating themselves as feminists and defining their feminist teaching, research, and activism in the university as political action; and finally, the importance they attach to maintaining links with women's groups, unions, and 'state feminists', in other words, with other segments of the women's movement.

There is no doubt that some aspects of the ensuing presentation could apply equally to Francophone Canadian academic feminists working outside Quebec, where they have developed original courses in French in different disciplines and in literature in particular, as well as full Women's Studies bilingual programs—in Ontario, for example. However, writings on Ontario women's studies by Michaud (1998), Gauthier (1991), Garceau (1997), and the authors writing in the fall 1997 issue of *Reflets* underline better than we can the specific difficulties, resistance, and successes that have been encountered in the institutionalization of *'études sur les femmes'* by feminist academics working in a minority situation outside Quebec. In the following discussion, we emphasize developments within Quebec as illustrating the major thrust for contemporary Francophone feminists.

Strategic and Political Evolution towards Institutionalization

In the 1970s and 1980s, Quebec Francophone feminists were somewhat ambivalent towards the institutionalization of Women's Studies. On the one hand, like many feminists around the world, and in France in particular, they feared a depoliticization and an attenuation of feminist goals and analysis. On the other hand, university professors among them knew very well that, without a relatively solid niche in university programs and departments, their feminist work had no chance of survival

in the academy. At the time, the opposition from their colleagues was too spontaneous and too systematic to be ignored; strangely, the sacrosanct principle of academic freedom did not seem to apply to feminist work. This is why contemporary
feminist studies in Quebec Francophone universities are much more institutionalized than in France,[15] with which intellectual communication is constant,[16] but less
and differently institutionalized than Feminist/Women's Studies in Anglophone
provinces, which have followed a path more similar to that of the United States.

Indeed, in the seventies and eighties, Quebec Francophone feminist university
professors *deliberately* opted for a multiplication of courses rather than programs *per
se*. This consensus, which persisted till a few years ago, reflected a preoccupation
with the professional future of students: what would happen to them when they
entered the labour market with a Feminist Studies diploma? But this choice also
corresponded—and still does—to the political goal of transforming androcentric
knowledge and androcentric conditions of knowledge production, a long-term
process that requires both that feminist perspectives be disseminated and applied as
broadly as possible in university curricula and that a maximum of students be made
critical of and willing to change existing sexist paradigms in as many disciplines
and departments as possible.

At the root of this strategic choice is a political conception of feminist analysis shared by most Francophone Canadian intellectual feminists we know today
and well summarized in the following quote from the editorial collective of *Questions féministes* in the very first issue of this French journal. The authors write
(Collectif, 1977: 4; authors' translation):

> When one analyses women's oppression, one necessarily examines both their
> material, real condition and the ideology that justifies it. Science (especially human
> sciences) is one of the main locations for the expression and development—since
> it is not produced once and for all—of this ideology. Therefore, feminist analysis
> includes a critique of scientific discourse, the discourse on women and the alleged
> 'general' one. We wish for the advent of a feminist science that could modify the
> global analysis of society.

The dissemination strategy has proved partially successful in Quebec Francophone
universities: most social sciences and humanities disciplinary departments now
offer, in their regular graduate and undergraduate programs, one or more feminist
courses every year, some compulsory. However, a few hundred feminist courses
among tens of thousands of university courses can hardly be considered successful
'mainstreaming'; feminist scientific production is still very marginal and even
ignored in most conventional scientific fields. Also, as colleagues from small universities could testify, while a strategy of diffusion might be efficient in large universities, it is unrealistic in small establishments where one often finds only a few
courses and a few teachers in a given discipline. In such cases, putting together an
interdisciplinary program on women is a better alternative.

In spite of some success, Quebec Francophone academic feminists partly revised their positions a few years ago. Some formally organized 'concentrations' of feminist courses inside existing disciplinary programs (at UQAM)[17] and a few multidisciplinary feminist programs *per se* were put together (at Laval and Sherbrooke) in response to what was felt by professors and students as a need for better integration and less superficial training in feminist theory, methodology, and epistemology, especially for those preparing for feminist research or action. To do so, each feminist group acted according to its own tradition in feminist studies, taking into account the particular power dynamics and local administrative constraints within its university.

If the concentration of a few feminist courses inside an existing program may seem, at first glance, an easier form of institutionalization than separate programs—after all, it does not disturb existing structures and requires almost no money—UQAM colleagues can testify that it is far from easy, even in disciplines whose members consider themselves to be to the left of the political spectrum. As for the introduction of new programs, in Laval University, after years of intensive work that resulted in the proposal of a full interdisciplinary Master's degree program in Feminist Studies, GREMF[18] had to retreat for strategic reasons and accept a graduate 'diploma' (30 credits rather than 45, no thesis) because its feminist Master's degree project was rejected by the university council.[19] The *Diplôme de 2e cycle en études féministes* is now in its seventh year and is still very fragile because of its mainly part-time student body and budgetary constraints and in spite of its coherent, interdisciplinary content.

These experiences illustrate another point that needs to be taken into account if one wants to understand fully the way feminist studies have evolved in Canada. If GREMF had retained its initial political position and stuck to its initial project, it might have been left with nothing, because, over the last five years, the economic situation of Canadian universities has worsened dramatically. Key words nowadays are 'rationalization' of resources and 'budget reduction' resulting in course and program cuts, not expansion or creation of new courses and programs.[20] This general stagnation did not keep the University of Sherbrooke from creating a minor/certificate in *Études sur les femmes* (Women's Studies) (Dumont, 1991). As the co-ordinator explained, resistance to a program on women was already strong; it was impossible to ask for *feminist* studies. Since then, colleagues from this university have worked on a proposal for a *feminist* program at the graduate level. However, registration in the minor/certificate in *Études sur les femmes* (and in other programs at the University of Sherbrooke) has been suspended for budgetary reasons since the 1998 winter semester (Doré, 1998: 255).

In general, even if Women's Studies and feminist programs are successful in attracting students, and even if academics easily pay lip service to interdisciplinarity, it remains very difficult in Quebec universities to organize multidisciplinary teaching, especially at the undergraduate level, and even more so if one is looking for *inter*disciplinarity, as is the case in feminist studies. However, all the activities of the fifth federally endowed chair in Women's Studies, the Chaire d'étude

Claire-Bonenfant sur la condition des femmes at Laval are, in spite of its name, openly feminist and interdisciplinary and, most of the time, inter-university as well.

What's in a Name?

Many feminists in Canada might agree with Françoise Collin, who considers that the designation of our activities (*Études féministes, Études des rapports sociaux de sexe, Études de genre,* etc; Feminist Studies, Women's Studies, Gender Studies, etc.) is generally 'more strategic than epistemological or methodological' (Collin, 1990: 82). However, most women teaching courses on women or feminism in Quebec universities define themselves as feminists. Francophones, in particular, consider, with Margrit Eichler, that 'Naming ourselves as what we are—and the vast majority of us are feminist scholars—seems not only honest but also smart' (1990: 54). This is why the two main Francophone feminist research centres in Quebec, IREF[21] at UQAM and GREMF at Laval, decided almost 20 years ago on the term 'feminist', and they succeeded in imposing this title on their respective administrations. Even the Canadian government acknowledged the principle at stake since it gave differing titles, in French and English, to its guide (CRIAW/ICREF, 1993) to resources in Canadian women's/feminist studies.

Quebec Francophones' openly feminist strategy has not been without professional risks. Those risks are well known to the women involved: disdain and more or less subtle discrimination on the part of colleagues, marginalization, denigration, and even ignorance of their writings. Francophone feminist academics are also conscious that the term 'genre' has an aura of seriousness, as suggested earlier; it looks more scientific and neutral than feminist (Scott, 1988). Using 'études de genre' rather than 'études féministes' would have made their lives much easier since there is little opposition to this term among their colleagues. There would also have been less opposition if they had decided to continue using 'études sur les femmes', as was the case at the time of the very first courses and initial research. Women would then be identified as the object of teaching and research, one scientific object among others, while 'feminist studies' are definitely perceived as being (too) inclusive and openly political.

However, the current strategy has some advantages. Because of the risk involved in the feminist label, there is a high probability that anti-feminists or undecided individuals will hesitate or desist from association with such groups and actions. Few men, for example, seem ready to take such a risk. This kind of forced ghettoization[22] of feminists thus facilitates cohesion and solidarity among like-minded people, sharing the same political goal and working together towards equality between the sexes, even though their theoretical analysis, methodological approach, professional experience, and degree of involvement might differ very much.

In addition, using the feminist label did not preclude some outstanding accomplishments, such as *Recherches féministes,* an international interdisciplinary journal published in French by GREMF at Laval University since 1988, with grants from the federal Social Science and Humanities Research Council and its Quebec equivalent. The twenty-fourth issue of *Recherches féministes* came out late in 1999. Another achievement contributing to the recognition of feminist research as a legitimate scientific field was the large international conference held in September 1996 at the same university under the title: 'La recherche féministe dans la francophonie—État de la situation et pistes de collaboration'. More than 450 people from 30 Francophone countries attended this five-day conference.[23]

At the theoretical and epistemological level, most Francophone feminist professors in the social sciences and humanities in Quebec use a terminology emphasizing *social relations* between women and men. Like French theoreticians, many refer to *rapports sociaux de sexe*, sex being defined as a socially constructed category (Mathieu, 1971), not a fixed biological given. This approach does not negate biological differences between women and men; it merely says that biological dimensions are always socioculturally and historically interpreted. For this reason, there is no theoretical or epistemological need for these feminist researchers to use the term 'genre'.[24]

Also, after years of struggle to be designated and accepted as feminists, some (although limited) measures of recognition of feminism in the academy resulted. Now that the validity of feminist research has been demonstrated (even if this is still not acknowledged by all), most Francophone feminist academics in Quebec would consider it a backward step on their part to use a euphemism and a less political term to designate themselves and their feminist work.

Feminist Studies as Political Involvement

Most Francophone academic feminists in Quebec consider their feminist work in academia, with the professional risks it involves, an integral part of the women's movement. They agree with Renate Duelli Klein (1991) when she speaks of Women's Studies as 'the intellectual arm of the women's movement'. Without this essential limb, the movement could not, as effectively as it does, ground and sustain its political positions and its public interventions in an era when questions have become very complex and require sophisticated analysis (Dagenais, 1996). For Francophone feminist academics, feminist analysis is political analysis because it recognizes and deals with power relationships and inequalities between the sexes in all avenues of life, including the academy. Working to change the mode of production and the content of scientific knowledge is a necessity that requires feminist action on the part of those who have the appropriate intellectual and practical means. This is what makes this field, and the daily life of feminist intellectuals, very different from other fields, and from the daily life of their non-feminist colleagues.

Not surprisingly, in Quebec where all professors in Francophone universities are unionized, and in Canada in general, many if not most feminist university professors have been, one way or another, involved in projects having to do with women's situation within universities (sexual harassment, affirmative action, etc.)

and several continue to play active roles in unions, including executive committees and other central union bodies. This is a kind of feminist militancy that has important consequences for present and future generations of women in the academy, and it is a form of feminist involvement that is particularly strong among Francophone academic feminists.

But more important still, especially in Quebec, as Renée Dandurand explains, 'feminist thought has been fed by demands from militant individuals and groups, demands that feminist researchers themselves had often supported and channelled to decision-makers' (Dandurand, 1996: 36). Not only are research topics closely linked to the women's movement's preoccupations but many feminist professors have been doing research in collaboration with autonomous women's associations and women's caucuses within union structures. This is clear in a recent assessment of feminist research in Quebec over the last three decades (Dagenais, 1996).

Also, one is struck by the strategic 'complicity' that can be put into action between feminists working for the state and university professors in Quebec and in Canada in times of crisis or dire circumstances. As Francine Descarries (1999) explains, since the *Révolution tranquille* of the 1960s and particularly under the social democratic governments of the Parti Québécois, the women's movement in Quebec has developed a specific relation of co-optation and co-operation with the state, which is considered to be a potential ally in the promotion of social justice and equality. Thus the critical distance that feminist researchers have nonetheless rightly maintained towards the state and its initiatives[25] does not mean, for them, ceasing to maintain dialogue with those working for women's interests within the state apparatus, but rather developing original and useful means of planning and collaboration with them as well as with feminist non-governmental associations. One significant example of co-operation between academic and state feminists is the 12-year-old Réseau Québécois des chercheuses féministes (RQCF). The Réseau's 112 members come not only from universities (professors, lecturers, graduate students) and colleges, but also from government bodies and women's groups. From the very beginning, RQCF has benefited from the technical support of Laval University's endowed chair in Women's Studies. First among the RQCF's current activities is the development of a strategic network on the 'social economy'[26] and the fight against women's poverty. The goal of this strategic network is for women's groups and feminist researchers to work together to influence government decisions affecting women's living conditions and social policies. On other issues, RQCF's seven directors were invited during the fall of 1997 to participate in the consultation held by the Québec Conseil du statut de la femme on its orientation for the years 1998–2001. Members of RQCF, as a group and individually, are kept informed and will participate in the Marche mondiale des femmes de l'an 2000, a project put together by the Fédération des femmes du Québec, following its 1996 Marche des femmes contre la pauvreté. These actions have not precluded RQCF's interest in research *per se*; it is now a tradition for the Réseau to hold a colloquium during the annual congress of the Association canadienne-française pour l'avancement de la science (ACFAS).

This is why, for most Quebec Francophone academic feminists, opposing 'academic feminism' to the grassroots women's movement is only, as one of us (Dagenais, 1996) has put it, creating a false dichotomy whose divisive consequences can only serve those who want to preserve the status quo. The same can be said concerning the recent insistence on 'discourse', on difference and differences, and on the 'deconstruction' of the 'woman' category. Indeed, renouncing idealistic or naïve expectations of unanimous sisterhood constitutes a sign of maturity as well as of enrichment for feminism. For the recognition of differences among women and among feminists to be useful to women, especially those who are poor, and to feminism as a social movement, such recognition must be constantly grounded in a social, historical, and political analysis geared towards social change in gender relations and within society. Otherwise, the deconstruction remains precisely that: a discourse accessible to only a small audience of initiated (and intellectual) theoreticians. This discourse may result in the imprisonment of others in their differences, for only 'the others' are 'different'; it could also result in a paralysing relativism where common political positions and collective action would be impossible (Dagenais and Piché, 1994: 67).

Conclusion

As we argued at the beginning of this chapter, the 'academic arm' of the women's movement is a privileged way of grasping developments within the movement. We are convinced that this will be as true of the twenty-first century as it has been of the previous decades, for the women's movement will always be influenced by feminist research that reveals the historical and contemporary contours of women's condition. There are clearly certain commonalities, in both Anglophone and Francophone universities, for the provinces are suffering from severe budgetary cuts at the moment and these are manifested in both academia's resistance to new programs and new courses within the universities—particularly Women's/Feminist Studies initiatives—as well as in severe cuts in the budgets of women's community groups. Initiatives are fragile, requiring all the more commitment and dedication on the part of academic feminists as they train their feminist students—'la relève de demain'—in pursuing the unfinished feminist transformations of knowledge and knowledge production. In such circumstances, language is not a barrier among Canadian feminists. The previously mentioned initiative on the part of all directors of Feminist and Women's Studies programs in Quebec and the formation of their Réseau des études féministes du Québec (REFUQ) illustrate that, in emergencies, co-operation across the languages is easily effected—in this instance, when it is a question of supporting the continuing development of feminist studies within the academy. At the same time, Francophone and Anglophone feminists are rooted in very different intellectual traditions. The intellectual networks, based mainly on language, provide strong contrasts in the literature and academic practices that are familiar to feminists of each language group. What is taken for granted in one group—for example, the particular form of institutionalization of Women's/

Feminist Studies adopted in Anglophone universities—can be regarded askance by the other. Familiar texts for feminists of one language group are sometimes unknown to the other—though it must be admitted that Francophones are still much more active in acquainting themselves with the literature in their second language than are their Anglophone colleagues, despite the increasing degree of bilingualism of the Anglophone community of Quebec.

Activist traditions provide the strongest contrast between the two feminist communities. The left-wing politics of Quebec are, quite naturally, expressed in the feminist movement, with a high level of commitment on the part of feminist academics to participation in the grassroots movement and to radical change (e.g., Collectif Clio, 1987). While many Anglophone feminists would consider that they, also, are activists in the movement in general, their participation might well be more personal ('feminists moving') or confined to the university. Furthermore, the left-wing politics of Quebec also explain the near absence of an organized right-wing response to feminism; despite expressions of traditional feminine values from time to time in the political arena (for example, the Yvettes), Quebec feminists are not constantly fighting rearguard action and against right-wing values. On the other hand, Anglophones are preoccupied to varying degrees with such groups as REAL Women, whose claim to represent a wide spectrum of Canadian (and American) women challenges feminist praxis. Thus, it is not so much the break between academic reflection and activism that differentiates the two groups, but rather the extent of such activism, the ways that it manifests itself, and the varying need to respond to challenges from the right that characterize each language community.

This said, it must be acknowledged that there are moments of total disagreement between Francophone and Anglophone feminists, which are linked, quite frequently, to constitutional issues reflecting differing 'nationalisms', whether Canadian or Québécois. Thus, political stances that appear almost self-evident to certain Anglophone feminists find little support among their Francophone colleagues and vice versa. The classic example, of course, is the disagreement concerning the Canadian Charter of Rights (1982); Anglophone feminists were strong supporters of entrenching equality rights in Sections 15 and 28 of the Charter, while Quebec feminists argued that they were already well ahead of such provisions within their own province. Disagreements also arose around the Meech Lake and Charlottetown Accords; the Fédération des femmes du Québec (FFQ—umbrella organization for many Quebec feminist groups and individuals) supported the former with its inclusion of the distinct society clause, whereas the National Action Committee objected to this apparent weakening of the uniformity of the accord. The Charlottetown Accord was negatively viewed this time by the FFQ, but supported by many women's groups within the NAC (Hamilton, 1996: 77). In effect, in the intertwining of nationalism and gender, there are certain contexts in which the former dominates over the latter, thus opposing feminists who would usually work together with no difficulty.

There has, indeed, been significant collaboration, within Quebec but also at the national level, between Anglophone and Francophone feminists. The FFQ was, in fact, a member of the NAC from 1972 to 1981 and again from 1984 to 1989 (ibid.), both withdrawals occasioned by the constitutional disagreements mentioned above, and the two organizations continue to co-operate on various issues, including the Marche mondiale des femmes en l'an 2000. Perhaps even more important, there are a great number of personal links among academic feminists of both language groups, though this does require, in Quebec, the bilingualism of Anglophones, thus weaving together cross-national groupings, both formal and informal. These groups can work together very effectively on concrete projects (e.g., the editorial boards of journals, joint applications for grants, etc.). The splintering, if present, tends to take place at the provincial or national level where political choices must be made.

However, the current tendency within feminism, both to recognize differences and to cherish the enrichment these differences contribute to the feminist movement, constitutes a valuable direction for Canadian feminism. In some ways, our differences are muted when we think of the international diversity of feminism; if we can survive internationally as a movement—though this may sometimes be arguable—surely the contrasts that have been outlined can be viewed as contributions to the movement rather than as points of fragmentation. The parallel roads of Anglophone and Francophone feminism will sometimes diverge, sometimes overlap; thus, the bridges between them are all the more important to sustain and, for this reason, all the more precious for feminists.

Questions for Critical Thought

1. What do you understand to be the main contrasts between Anglophone and Francophone feminism in Canada?

2. Please provide some everyday examples of how academic feminism can influence the actions of feminists.

Glossary

Praxis: Activist practices in living and behaving that inevitably infer a link to intellectual analysis.

Francophone/Anglophone: A grouping of individuals by mother tongue, i.e., the first language learned by an infant; in practice, those of other language groups are included according to whether French or English dominates their experience.

Multidiscipinarity/interdisciplinarity: Used to refer to either the parallel use of two or more of the traditional disciplines or the complete integration of such disciplines.

Suggested Readings

Dagenais, Huguette, dir. 1999. *Pluralité et convergences. La recherche féministe dans la francophonie.* Montréal: Remue-ménage. Twenty-nine Francophone feminist researchers from different regions of Canada and the world (Quebec, New Brunswick, Ontario, France, Morocco, Senegal) illustrate the common goals and diverse preoccupations and contexts that characterize contemporary feminists having French as a common language.

Hamilton, Roberta. 1996. *Gendering the Vertical Mosaic.* Toronto: Copp Clark. A Canadian feminist reflects on society through the lens of feminist theory, covering the women's movement and the way it challenges Canadian society.

hooks, bell. 1984. *Feminist Theory: From Margin to Center.* Boston: South End Press. An early, classic analysis from an American black feminist of the diversity characterizing the women's movement and the need to integrate women from 'the margins' into the movement.

Recherches féministes. 1998. 'Éducation et émancipation', Vol. 11, no. 1. A few articles in this thematic issue of *Recherches féministes*, the only Francophone feminist research journal in Canada, deal with Feminist and Women's Studies in Quebec and Canada.

Notes

1. There is some disagreement about the date of the very first course, which is either reported to have taken place at Concordia University, Montreal, in 1968 (Descarries, 1992: 24) or at the University of Montreal in 1963–4 (Marie-Andrée Bertrand, personal communication).

2. Depending on how one counts, the most recent listing indicates about a dozen programs in the field.

3. The use of this term already suggests a particular approach, though we will argue that the situation is more subtle than appears true at first glance. Nevertheless, the great majority of programs do, in fact, carry the Women's Studies title; hence, the use of this term in a generic sense.

4. We will be making reference, on several occasions, to the Canadian Women's Studies Project (CWSP), undertaken by Margrit Eichler and her colleagues at the Ontario Institute for Studies in Education and UQAM in the late 1980s; researchers studied those involved in Women's Studies and the results provide a wealth of information on the field.

5. The one exception, interestingly, is the recent MA in 'Gender Studies' at the University of Northern British Columbia.

6. Specifically, *Atlantis: A Women's Studies Journal*; *Canadian Woman Studies*.

7. Carleton, Concordia, McGill, Mount Saint Vincent, Ontario Institute for Studies in Education of the University of Toronto, Western Ontario, York, and Osgoode Hall Law School at York.

8. The Centre for Women's Studies and Feminist Research at the University of Western Ontario (note the compromise) and the Institute for Feminist Legal Studies at Osgoode Hall of York University.

9. The project uncovered a surprising proportion of men (13 per cent) who had ever taught a course in women's/feminist studies.

10. The actual proportion varied from just over one-third for the most recent cohort to nearly one-half for the earliest entrants to the field. It should be noted, also, that the data deal with contacts *prior* to teaching the first course; thus it is a question of original motivation for teaching in the field.

11. As Lenton (1990: 60) points out, the very reasonable hypothesis that the differences in political involvement between early and late entrants to the field might be linked to respondents' general level of activism is not supported by the data. But it is not so much the distinction *between* activists and non-activists that is salient, but rather the particular conjuncture of political involvement characteristic of *all* scholars.

12. Calculated as 1.5 per cent of all faculty members for the whole of Canada (Tancred, 1994: n.17).

13. For example, when questioned about the 'Women's Studies' title chosen for the 'McGill Centre for Research and Teaching on Women', those involved in its establishment explain that the title symbolized the maximum that the university could tolerate. And this was in 1988!

14. The program is the above-mentioned MA in Gender Studies at the University of Northern British Columbia. From the same province comes the 'Centre for Research in Women's Studies and Gender Relations' at the University of British Columbia; note the emphasis on *relations* in the title and, once again, the compromise.

15. In France, to this day, there are very few possibilities for university students to take feminist courses, to work with feminist professors, or to do research from a feminist perspective.

16. This close link with France does not preclude Quebec Francophone academic feminists, most of them bilingual, from having links with Anglophone feminists and using their works, as is clear to anyone who looks at the references they make to English as well as to French authors.

17. UQAM: Université du Québec à Montréal.

18. GREMF: Groupe de recherche multidisciplinaire féministe.

19. Contrary to what one might think, the strongest opposition to the program came from professors, not from Laval administrators, who had been able to judge the seriousness of GREMF's work over the years.

20. As we write, a provincial commission on education is evaluating, among other targeted programs, those in Feminist and Women's Studies. The directors of these programs in the different Quebec universities, English as well as French, are jointly preparing a report on points in common, to be presented during the commission's hearings.

21. IREF: Institut de recherches et d'études féministes.

22. This can only be called *forced* ghettoization of feminists by other academics because, as we have seen, Francophone academic feminists' goals are, on the contrary, to penetrate thoroughly all disciplines and scientific fields by working *inside* institutions of higher learning.

23. A second conference has been held at Dakar University (Sénégal) in May 1999 under the title: 'La recherche féministe dans la francophonie plurielle'; a third one will be organized in Toulouse (France) during 2002.

24. Another, more practical, reason for not using *genre*, the literal French translation for 'gender', is that, in contemporary French usage, this term has about 10 different meanings, in addition to the meaning attributed to it by feminists. For example, in a multidisciplinary setting, there is a high risk of confusion since *genre* means very different things for a linguist, a literary professor, and a sociologist. No doubt also some people use genre in order to maintain distance from feminists, for gender has a scientific aura still largely denied the term 'feminist' (Dagenais and Piché, 1994).

25. For example, feminist research and teaching groups united in 1996 and presented a report, *La souveraineté du Québec: jamais sans ses filles*, to the commission on Quebec sovereignty.

26. The expression 'social economy' has been forged in the present context of unemployment and crises related to the disengagement of the state in the area of certain public policies and services. It refers to activities and groups working collectively, democratically, and in solidarity, to solve socio-economic problems identified by communities themselves. For more detailed definitions and to learn what is at stake, see AFÉAS, Côté, et al. (1998) and Lamarche (1997).

References

AFÉAS (Association féminine d'éducation et d'action sociale), Denise Côté, et al. 1998. *Who Will be Responsible for Providing Care? The Impact of the Shift to Ambulatory Care and Social Economy Policies on Québec Women*. Ottawa: Status of Women Canada.

Caine, Barbara. 1995. 'Women's studies, feminist traditions and the problem of history', in Caine and Rosemary Pringle, eds, *Transitions: New Australian Feminisms*. St Leonards: Allen and Unwin.

Collectif. 1977. 'Variations sur des thèmes communs', *Questions féministes* 1: 3–19.

Collectif Clio. 1987. *Quebec Women: A History*. Toronto: Women's Press.

Collin, Françoise. 1990. 'Ces études qui ne sont "pas tout". Fécondité et limites des études féministes', *Les Cahiers du GRIF* 45: 81–94.

Connell, R.W. 1990. 'The Wrong Stuff: Reflections on the Place of Gender in American Sociology', in Herbert J. Gans, ed., *Sociology in America*. Newbury Park, Calif.: Sage.

CRIAW/ICREF. 1993. *Études féministes au Canada. Canadian Women's Studies/Feminist Research in Canada*. Ottawa: Minister of Supply and Services Canada.

Dagenais, Huguette. 1994. 'False Dichotomy, Real Consequences: Feminist Activism in the Academia', paper presented at the Congress of the International Sociological Association, Bielefeld, July.

———, dir. 1996. *Science, conscience et action. 25 ans de recherche féministe au Québec*. Montréal: Remue-ménage.

——— and Denise Piché, eds. 1994. 'Concepts and Practices of Development: Feminist Contributions and Future Perspectives', in *Women, Feminism and Development/Femmes, féminisme et développement*. Montreal and Kingston: McGill-Queen's University Press, 49–73.

Dandurand, Renée. 1996. 'Entre la quête de l'autonomie et le maintien des liens familiaux', in Dagenais (1996).

Descarries, Francine. 1992. 'Les études féministes: Leurs raisons d'être . . . et leurs enjeux', *Bulletin de l'Association d'Études canadiennes* 14: 22–6.

———. 1999. 'Partenariat féministe . . . pouvons-nous encore rêver de "changer le monde"?', in Huguette Dagenais, dir., *Pluralité et convergences. La recherche féministe dans la francophonie*. Montréal: Remue-ménage, 494–506.

Doré, Chantal. 1998. 'L'enseignement féministe universitaire au Québec', *Recherches féministes* 11, 1: 253–60.

Dumont, Micheline. 1991. 'Un certificat en études sur les femmes à Sherbrooke', *Documentation sur la recherche féministe* 20: 37–8.

Eichler, Margrit. 1988. 'Women's Studies in Canada: A Personal Glimpse', in Dawn Currie, ed., *From the Margins to the Centre: Selected Essays in Women's Studies Research*. Saskatoon: Women's Studies Research Unit, University of Saskatchewan.

———. 1990. 'What's in a Name? Women's Studies or Feminist Studies', *Atlantis* 16: 40–56.

——— and Rosonna Tite. 1990. 'Women's Studies Professors in Canada: A Collective Self-Portrait', *Atlantis* 16: 7–23.

Evans, Mary. 1991. 'The Problem of Gender for Women's Studies', in Jane Aaron and Sylvia Walby, eds, *Out of the Margins: Women's Studies in the Nineties*. London: Falmer Press.

Firestone, Shulamith. 1970. *The Dialectic of Sex: The Case for Feminist Revolution*. New York: Bantam Books.

Garceau, Marie-Luce. 1997. 'Visibles et partenaires; recherches et pratiques féministes', *Reflets* 3: 10–22.

Gaskell, Jane, Arlene McLaren, and Myra Novogrodsky. 1989. *Claiming an Education: Feminism and Canadian Schools*. Toronto: Our Schools/Our Selves Education Foundation.

Gauthier, Lorraine. 1991. 'L'intégration du savoir féministe: la question de l'établissement des programmes d'études sur les femmes', *Resources for Feminist Research/Documentation sur la recherche féministe* 11: 83–93.

Hamilton, Roberta. 1996. *Gendering the Vertical Mosaic: Feminist Perspectives on Canadian Society*. Toronto: Copp Clark.

hooks, bell. 1984. *Feminist Theory: From Margin to Center*. Boston: South End Press.

Klein, Renate Duelli. 1991. 'Passion and Politics in Women's Studies in the Nineties', *Women's Studies International Forum* 14: 125–34.

Lamarche, François. 1997. 'A propos du modèle québécois d'économie sociale', *Nouvelles pratiques sociales* 10: 215–21.

Lenton, Rhonda. 1990. 'Academic Feminists and the Women's Movement in Canada: Continuity or Discontinuity', *Atlantis* 16: 57–67.

Mathieu, Nicole-Claude. 1971. 'Notes pour une définition sociologique des catégories de sexe', *Épistémologie sociologique* 11: 19–39.

Maynard, Mary. 1993. Review of Hilary Hinds et al., eds, in *Working Out: New Directions for Women's Studies* in *Sociology* 27: 729–30.

Michaud, Jacinthe. 1998. 'Les programmes d'études des femmes et l'intervention féministe en Ontario français', *Recherches féministes* 11, 1: 83–93.

Millett, Kate. 1970. *Sexual Politics*. New York: Avon Books.

Scott, Joan. 1988. '"Genre": une catégorie utile d'analyse historique', *Les Cahiers du GRIF* 37–8: 125–53.

Tancred, Peta. 1994. 'Into the Third Decade of Canadian Women's Studies: A Glass Half-Empty or Half-Full?', *Women's Studies Quarterly* 22: 12–25.

Wine, Jeri Dawn, and Janice L. Ristock. 1991. *Women and Social Change: Feminist Activism in Canada*. Toronto: James Lorimer.

WSAC (Women's Studies Advisory Committee). 1993. 'Proposal for the Creation of a Bachelor of Arts—Major in Women's Studies'. Montreal: McGill University, Faculty of Arts.

chapter eight

Gays and Lesbians: Pushing the Boundaries

Gary Kinsman

Introduction: Progress and Contradictions

Gay men, lesbians, and bisexuals have been pushing social, political, gender, and sexual boundaries in the fight for our rights since at least the 1960s in Canada. We have made remarkable strides forward. From a despised, outcast, 'deviant' group, we have struggled to gain support from the feminist movement, the union movement, and human rights supporters to establish some of our basic human rights and, in some cases, to win spousal benefits and even some recognition of our families and support networks (see Kinsman, 1996a).

Hundreds of thousands of people join in Lesbian and Gay Pride parades and celebrations every year in Toronto, Montreal, Vancouver, Ottawa, Halifax, London, Sudbury, Windsor, Kelowna, St John's, and many other cities and towns across the country. There are now even companies that market products to gay men and sometimes to lesbians. Openly gay and lesbian professionals (doctors, lawyers), managers, business people, and politicians have emerged in many cities.

At the same time we face major opposition. There are still those who believe that gays and lesbians are sick, perverted, and criminal. There are still those who blame gay men for AIDS and for child sexual abuse. There has also been the growth of a vociferous, minority, right-wing, anti-gay opposition that has significant influence on official politics. Young lesbians, gay men, and bisexuals, struggling to come to terms with their sexualities, still face a denial of images of their lives in popular culture and are denied knowledge about their sexualities, bodies, and history. Lesbian and gay materials are still being seized by Canada Customs as they come into the country. People still face violence on the streets simply because they are perceived to be lesbian or gay. Lesbians and gay men still face major problems regarding the custody and adoption of children. Lesbian mothers can still be deemed to be 'unfit' mothers by the courts (Arnup, 1995). Males who engage in consensual sex with other males can still be arrested for their activities under 'indecent act' and 'bawdy-house' legislation.[1] In addition, lesbians face all the problems that women face in Canadian society; gays and lesbians of colour face all the problems of racism and discrimination that face other people of colour in a racist society; and working-class lesbians and gay men face all the problems of class exploitation that other working-class people face.

A contradictory situation exists today. On the one hand, our individual and abstract human rights are now increasingly recognized. On the other hand, our relationships still often remain stigmatized and sexualities and our desires are still censored and criminalized. Since relationships and sexualities are central to people's lives, there are profound limitations to the rights and the level of equality that lesbians and gays have won. While individual rights have been achieved in some instances, gay/lesbian sexualities and relationships are not recognized as being equal to or as valid as heterosexual ones. Witness the controversy still generated in popular culture whenever there is even the mildest representation of lesbians and gay men.

While more social spaces have been opened up for our communities and for the expression of our desires, heterosexuality still dominates in this society. Heterosexuality is still constructed as the 'normal' and 'natural' sexuality, even though lesbians, gays, and bisexuals might now be seen as having some human rights. Heterosexual hegemony consists of the ideologies and practices organizing a male-dominated form of heterosexuality as the taken-for-granted norm while portraying lesbianism and homosexuality as some form of deviance, abnormality, or disadvantage. Heterosexism is the ideology that justifies heterosexuality as normal while invalidating lesbian and gay sexualities (see Kinsman, 1996a: 1–47). While the struggles of gays, feminists, men against sexism, and others have altered heterosexual hegemony since the 1960s, it remains with us. Heterosexual hegemony is sometimes portrayed as being 'compulsory' (Rich, 1980; Ferguson, 1981; Martindale, 1995), especially for women, and as a social institution (Bunch, 1975), yet there is also an active construction of consent to heterosexual desire as the 'normal' desire in this culture through the mass media, advertising, and popular culture. This hegemony lies at the social root of gay and lesbian oppression and marginalization. The staying power of heterosexual hegemony creates the barriers and problems that gays and lesbians continue to encounter.

For heterosexual readers, an exercise from American lesbian feminist Charlotte Bunch can help in grasping the social differences between heterosexuals and lesbians and gay men. Bunch pointed out that the knowledge produced from the social location of lesbian oppression is of relevance not only to lesbians but to all women. She once explained to heterosexual feminists that the best way to understand the social practices of 'heterosexual privilege' was to go about for a few days as an open lesbian. The same can apply to a heterosexual man presenting himself as an openly gay man.

> What makes heterosexuality work is heterosexual privilege—and if you don't have a sense of what privilege is, I suggest that you go home and announce to everybody that you know—a roommate, your family, the people you work with—everywhere that you go—that you're a queer. Try being a queer for a week. (Ibid.)

A heterosexual woman or man can easily imagine the discomfort, ridicule, fear, and even violence that she or he might experience, how her or his 'coming out' would disrupt 'normal' relations at work and with his or her family. Such experiences are the substance of gay and lesbian oppression in this society and are also the substance of the social practices of heterosexual privilege and hegemony. Lesbian and gay oppression and heterosexual hegemony exist in relation to each other.

To grasp how gays and lesbians have pushed the boundaries and the contradictory situation in which we now find ourselves it is important to understand how we have come to be here. This also helps set the stage for discussing how the gay/lesbian community can move beyond the current impasse that we face. This requires a historical and sociological investigation of the oppression of gays and lesbians in the Canadian context. How has the historical present (Weeks, 1985: 5–10) we live in come into being—through what social struggles and social processes?

But before getting into this, I should explain briefly who I am and where I am coming from. I am both a sociologist in a university setting and a long-time activist in the gay liberation, AIDS activist, and socialist movements. In my work I try to bring theory and the intellectual world into close relation with the movements and activists trying to transform the world to bring about gay and lesbian liberation and social justice. I have been a gay activist since the mid-1970s so some of the activism and changes that I write about here I have also directly participated in. I therefore do not adopt the standpoint of a disinterested academic observer but instead believe that much can be learned from trying to change the social world and bringing theory and practice together. In my writing and research I adopt the social standpoints of oppressed people to interrogate the ruling social ideologies and institutions that create problems for people in their everyday lives (see D. Smith, 1987; G. Smith, 1990). Such research, it is hoped, creates knowledge for liberation rather than for continuing oppression.

In taking up the social standpoints of gay men and lesbians in my research I do not start with an assumption that lesbians and gay men are 'deviant' or that we comprise a social problem that stands in need of explanation. Instead, by starting from the standpoints and experiences of gay men and lesbians to undertake a historical and sociological investigation, I can see how the oppression we face has been socially organized and therefore how it can be undone. The problem becomes not lesbians and gay men but the social relations that organize the oppression of gay men and lesbians. The problem becomes heterosexual hegemony itself (Kinsman, 1996a: 23–47; Kinsman, 1998).

The Emergence of Heterosexual Hegemony and Lesbian and Gay Oppression

There has been no constant heterosexual or homosexual across all of history. Despite recent claims to the contrary homosexuality is not 'caused' by hormones or genes (Kinsman, 1996a: 32–3). In fact, the heterosexual and the homosexual are contemporary social creations. Anthropological and cross-cultural investigations show that there has been a dramatic diversity of gender and sexual practices across history and in different cultures. While both same-gender eroticism and different-gender eroticism have existed in some form in all cultures, how these practices have been socially organized and made sense of differ widely.

In some cultures there has been no contradiction between engaging in sex with men and sex with women. There was no social space for the heterosexual and homosexual—there was no polarization between same-gender and different-gender desires as creating the basis for distinct sexual beings. In some patriarchal societies compulsory sex between men and younger males was seen as a necessary part of preparation for manhood and sex with women. Among the Sambia of Papua New Guinea, for instance, same-gender sex for males between 7 and 19 was mandatory. Boys fellated men on a daily basis so that they would grow into masculine adults. According to this culture males cannot produce sperm on their own; they can only recycle it from one generation to another. In their adult lives, these males engage in sex with women (Harry, 1982: 3).

In ancient Greece, which was a slave-owning and patriarchal society with a different social organization of gender than our contemporary society, educational and sexual relations between an older male and a younger male were often seen as necessary for the younger male to become a male 'citizen'. These erotic relations were regulated along age and activity lines and the male 'citizen' was never supposed to adopt the 'passive position' in sexual interaction. The crucial dividing line in the regulation of sexual activities was whether one was active or passive and not whether sexual activity was engaged in with males or females. The adult men who had sexual relations with younger males also engaged in reproductive and other sexual relations with women (Dover, 1980; Foucault, 1985; Halperin, 1990). Our contemporary notions of the heterosexual/homosexual dichotomy make no sense in cultures like these. It is impossible to hold onto any universal notion of homosexuality or heterosexuality in the face of these diverse erotic practices and social meanings.

Diversity in social forms of gender life also created different contexts for sexual interaction. Among the Igbo people in what is now Nigeria and in other African cultures it was possible for women to take female husbands and for men to take male wives, and in some cultures there were erotic relationships between older and younger women modelled on mother/daughter relations (Amadiume, 1987; Murray and Roscoe, 1998; Kendall, 1999). Not all cultures have been defined by a two-gender (male/female) system in which there was no possibility of transfer from one gender to another.[2]

Among the Aboriginal peoples of North America before the coming of white 'civilization' there was generally more social, political, and sexual equality for women than in Europe at that time. Although it varied among the different Aboriginal nations there was also a great deal of toleration and acceptance for sex between men and between women. In some cultures there were more than two gender groupings. Alongside what could be described as 'men' and 'women' there would be third- and sometimes fourth-gender groupings made up of individuals born as male or female who took up some of the work and clothing of the 'other' gender. The French called these people 'berdache', mostly referring to those born as male, although in some Aboriginal nations there were also gender groupings for biological females who adopted some of the work, activities, and dress of men (Blackwood, 1984; Williams, 1986; Gay American Indians and Roscoe, 1988; Roscoe, 1991, 1996; Lang, 1999; also see Nanda, 1996).

In some of these cultures gender was seen as a social process that was often viewed as being similar to cooking. To become a 'man' one had to go through a series of social rituals. If you only went through some of them you could become a 'berdache'. Gender was assigned on the basis of an individual's preferences in the division of labour. These mixed or cross-gender groupings were a regular part of how gender was produced in these cultures and many of these third- and fourth-gender groupings were seen as having special spiritual or healing qualities as well as being able to bridge some of the divides between men and women (Kinsman, 1996a: 92–7).

Sometimes a biologically male 'berdache' would become the sexual partner of a 'normal' male or a physiologically female fourth-gender person would take a 'normal' woman as her sexual partner. Reading through our current constructions of sexuality we might view such relationships as being 'homosexual' in character, but in the context of these indigenous cultures they were seen as a form of different-gender sex since there were more than two gender groupings.

When French and British explorers, fur traders, missionaries, and the military encountered Aboriginal cultures they were shocked and horrified by the power that women often had in these cultures, by these third- and fourth-gender groupings, and by the openness and respect often shown to sex between males and between females. They interpreted these as 'barbaric' practices and sometimes as 'sodomy' (sexual practices that were prohibited under religious law because they did not lead to reproduction). They attempted to stamp out these practices through state and Christian missionary practices. A crucial part of the attempted colonization and marginalization of the Aboriginal nations was the destruction of their indigenous sexual and gender practices (Katz, 1976: 281–334; Katz, 1983: 23–8; Duberman et al., 1979). It is these earlier practices of gender and sexual diversity that are being reclaimed currently by two-spirited and lesbian and gay First Nation activists.[3]

The European colonizers brought with them a very different way of sexual and gender life. There were only two genders—men and women—and sexual interaction was largely organized in relation to reproduction and the family as an interdependent household economy based on the land. While same-gender sex did take place among the fur traders and early military men stationed in what would become Canada, there was no social space for people to organize their lives as homosexuals *or* as heterosexuals (Katz, 1983, 1994; Kinsman, 1996a: 48–81, 98–147).

The emergence of heterosexuality and homosexuality is rooted in a profound social process of transformation that the new social relations of industrial capitalism brought about. Capitalism, which is based on the private ownership of the means of production (factories, offices) and the employment by business owners of wage labour, created a new and different social context for sexual expression and identification. The protracted transition from feudal types of land-based relations to capitalist ones removed the labouring population from the means of production (from the land), increasingly separating the 'public' realm of profit and business from the increasingly 'privatized' realm of the family and household that was no longer seen as part of the 'economy'.

Market processes developed unevenly, but began to provide for meeting some daily needs outside the household economy. Previously these needs would have been met for most people only through family relations. The separation of paid work from the household economy and the employment of wage labour meant that some men with money in their pockets could now live outside or on the margins of the family/household system, earning wages and living in boarding houses and, later, eating in taverns and restaurants and renting rooms in inns, hostels, and hotels. In these contexts in the cities some men began to organize their lives around their same-gender erotic desires and seized social spaces for themselves (D'Emilio, 1983; Kinsman, 1996a: 48–81).

The impact on men and women was not the same because capitalism was also a patriarchal society. While many men were 'liberated' from the private realm of the family and household, many women were trapped within it. It would only be later, with the first wave of feminism at the end of the nineteenth century and the opening up of some social and economic spaces for women separate from men, that women would begin to establish more open and visible erotic networks with other women (Faderman, 1981, 1991; Ferguson, 1981). Not only were there gender differences between men and women who were interested in exploring their same-gender erotic desires, but there were also differences of class, race, age, and ability that defined the different experiences of same-gender lovers.

By the mid- to late-nineteenth century, and earlier in some places (Bray, 1982), there were emerging same-gender erotic cultures in the larger urban centres of Europe and later in North America. These were created both through the possibilities opened up by capitalist social relations and through the active agency and resistance of those who engaged in same-gender passions (Kinsman, 1996a: 48–81). Those who came to call themselves lesbians faced a greater social invisibility and the denial of their independence and autonomy in a patriarchal society. This is why distinct cultures of women loving women generally emerged later than those for men.

In response, medical professionals sought to diagnose the new 'sex perverts' as part of the medical profession's expanding 'expertise' on and authority over people's lives. New laws were generated to criminalize all sexual activity between men. New categories of homosexuality and lesbianism emerged through the interaction between these new erotic cultures and official medical, psychiatric, psychological, and eventually sexological (the 'science' of sexuality) knowledge that informed state and policing policies. State and professional agencies responded to these same-gender erotic cultures by labelling them as 'deviant', 'perverted', and 'criminal' (ibid.). While isolated outbreaks of non-reproductive sex (sodomy) had been in defiance of church and state law in the past, the homosexual now emerged as a category of social definition and surveillance. 'The sodomite had been a temporary aberration; the homosexual was now a species,' Michel Foucault (1980: 43) writes.

In response to these 'queer' threats, a social norm of male-dominated hetero-sexuality was institutionalized in state social, family, and criminal policies. Hetero-sexuality emerged as a medical and popular term after the emergence of homosexuality—in response to the demarcation of the deviant anti-norm (Katz, 1995; Adams, 1997). Heterosexuality became the sexuality of the new capitalist ruling and middle classes and was then enforced on the working class and poor as the only approved and normal sexuality. Class struggles were fought not only in factories and offices but also in relation to families and sexualities. Unfortunately, large parts of the male-dominated labour movement ended up joining with the state, business owners, and the 'respectable' middle class in adopting the image of the middle-class heterosexual family as its own. A cross-class alliance bringing together the emerging middle class and the 'respectable' sections of the working class was formed in opposition to the 'bestial' sexual practices of the outcast poor and unrespectable working class. Key to this 'respectable' sexuality was a form of heterosexuality. At the same time, this meant incorporating the oppression of women and gay men and lesbians into the heart of working-class life and culture.[4]

Heterosexuality was defined not simply by different-gender or reproductive sex but by the production of a new sexual being who was defined by erotic inter-est in the 'opposite sex'. As Katz (1983: 661) points out:

> The word and concept 'heterosexual' was produced and distributed in late nine-teenth and early twentieth century America to express and to idealize qualitatively new relationships between men and women in which eroticism was defined as central and legitimate.

This meant that if one was not erotically interested in the other gender then there was something wrong. In relation to spinsters (women living independently of men) and lesbians there was what has been characterized as a 'heterosexual counter-revolution' against feminism and women living autonomously from men. Forms of women's friendship, intimacy, and support networks were transformed in professional discourse and media accounts into the 'perversions' of lesbianism (Faderman, 1981; Chauncey, 1982–3; Simmons, 1979; Freedman, 1979).

While there had been earlier laws against some of the sexual activities that males could engage in with each other, all sex between males was criminal-ized with the entry of the offence of 'gross indecency', based on earlier British legislation, into the Canadian Criminal Code in 1892. This criminalized all sexual acts between males not already covered under buggery. Gross indecency was an offence that only males could commit and it specified a distinctly male homosexual offence. The law directed the police against sexual activities between men and led to the criminalization of all male homosexual sexual activities (Kinsman, 1996a: 128–34). The police and the Criminal Code became major instruments of the oppression that homosexual men faced, and this became central to gay oppression (G. Smith, 1988).

In contrast, women having sex with other women remained largely uncriminalized. This was in part because of the lesser visibility of lesbian erotic networks but also because of fears that any publicity given to lesbianism would allow more women to find out about it (Valverde, 1985: 78–9; Jagoose, 1996: 13–15; Kinsman, 1996a: 51, 65, 69–71). This was also rooted in the denial of women's sexual autonomy from men. Criminal legislation against women's sexuality tended to be defined by laws against prostitutes and against access to birth control and abortion. Lesbians also faced the general stigmatization and censorship of positive information about same-gender sexualities. Lesbian oppression has been organized less directly through the Criminal Code and more through general social and family policies as they relate to women and the enforcement of heterosexual hegemony. Women's social, economic, and sexual dependence and institutionalized heterosexuality became cornerstones of state social policies, so that the heterosexual family unit became the only legally and socially sanctioned way of life (Kinsman, 1996a: 134–7). This has a major impact in the lives of gay men as well.

A mass heterosexual culture emerged beginning in the 1920s. The mass media, advertising, the entertainment industry, and the opening up of new consumer markets all led to proliferation and eroticization of heterosexual images. Products and the new social norm were sold at the same time. The new heterosexual culture was also produced socially in dance halls, movie theatres, ice cream parlours, and later in the back seats of automobiles, and among young women and men in factories, offices, and schools.

Professional disciplines that produced the knowledge that state policy relied on generated various ideologies regarding homosexual perversion and deviation. The psychiatric profession classified homosexuality as a form of psychopathic disorder. This entered into the Criminal Code of Canada when gay men who engaged in consensual sex with other males could be sentenced indefinitely as 'criminal sexual psychopaths' in the 1950s and early 1960s. Such sentences were imposed partly on the basis of psychiatric testimony (ibid., 183–92). During World War II Canadian gay men and lesbians could be discharged from the military as 'psychopathic personalities' with 'abnormal sexuality' (ibid., 148–54). Psychologists often portrayed gay men and lesbians as neurotic and mentally ill. These views led to forms of psychiatric and psychological terrorism that included aversion therapy, lobotomies, and partial lobotomies, as well as electroshock treatment of homosexuals to try to cure them of their homosexuality (Riordan, 1982; Blackbridge and Gilhooly, 1985; Duberman, 1991). Sociologists, too, played their part in portraying gay men and lesbians as epitomizing the classic form of deviance from social norms (Kinsman, 1998: 265–6). Until the late 1970s and continuing in some ways to the present, 'deviance' was the only topic under which homosexuality was ever discussed in many sociology classes.

There was always resistance to these ideologies and practices of oppression. Until the 1960s such resistance took a largely individual form in Canada. The World War II mobilizations created the basis for this to begin to change. Large numbers of men and women were thrown together in gender-segregated contexts in the military and, for women, in war industry, and were separated from their families of origin, thereby creating new possibilities for the exploration of same-gender desires (Kinsman, 1996a: 149–57; Berube, 1990). At the same time, during and especially after the war, those identified as homosexuals were discharged from the military. Following the war these early networks of same-gender lovers found themselves stranded and isolated as heterosexual-patriarchal hegemony was reconstructed.

These early postwar groups responded by seizing some space (often a corner or a few tables) in a largely heterosexual bar or coffee shop and by developing a network of house parties, and gay men developed some 'cruising' areas where they could meet other men. In the postwar years the criminalization of gay male sexuality was intensified. As noted above, men engaging in consensual sex with other males could be sentenced to indefinite detention, first as 'criminal sexual psychopaths' and later as 'dangerous sexual offenders'. These were also the years when the mythology associating gay men with child molestation, which we still often face today, was put in place—even though sexual danger was usually much closer to home (Kinsman, 1996a: 192–200).

In the Cold War years the McCarthy campaigns in the United States targeted not only Communists, socialists, trade unionists, peace activists, and immigrants but also 'sex perverts'. Homosexuals were deemed to be a threat to 'national security', initially because homosexuals were associated with communism and later because they were seen as suffering from a character weakness that made them 'vulnerable' to blackmail by Soviet agents. In Canada the national security campaigns against gay men and lesbians began later than in the US but came to affect the lives of thousands of Canadians in the public service, the military, and other walks of life. Hundreds (and probably thousands) of gay men and lesbians lost their jobs and livelihood as a result, and many more were demoted, spied upon, and forced to inform on their friends because all homosexual acts were technically illegal. By 1967–8 the RCMP had a list of 9,000 suspected homosexuals in the Ottawa area (DSI, 1967–8: 33).

The RCMP even developed a 'fruit machine' based on the assumption that there was a scientific way to detect a gay man or a lesbian by monitoring responses to a series of tests. One of these tests was a pupillary response test. As male and female test subjects were shown images that included semi-naked men and women, the pupils of their eyes would be photographed to record their responses. It was assumed that there would be common and different responses for homosexual men and women and for the heterosexual men and women in the 'normal' control group. If the tests determined an individual to be a homosexual, that person would be denied work in the public service or purged from his or her position if already in government employment. The name 'fruit machine' was given to the research project by RCMP officers who feared that even though they were recruited to be part of the 'normal' control group for the research they would be found out to be 'fruits'. This research never did and never could work, but the government of Canada put money into this project for more than four years (Kinsman, 1995; Kinsman and Gentile, 1998). Such national security campaigns were part of a social process that forced many lesbians and gay men into hiding their sexuality for fear they would be fired or suffer other negative consequences. This was part of how the relations of 'the closet' were created in many people's lives (Chauncey, 1994).

At a lower level of intensity these national security campaigns, especially in the military and in the RCMP itself, continued until relatively recently. It was only in 1992 that lesbians and gay men were officially allowed to be in the Canadian armed forces (Kinsman, 1996a: 359–60). And still in 1998 a Canadian Security and Intelligence Service (CSIS) spokesperson stated that a security clearance could still be denied to a closeted homosexual, which could mean they would lose their position (B. Smith, 1998).

Emergence of Organizations and Movements

In this social and historical context one gay man, Jim Egan, emerged to become Canada's pioneering gay activist. From 1949 on he relentlessly and passionately wrote to newspapers and magazines defending the rights of homosexuals (Champagne, 1987; Kinsman, 1996a: 167–9; Egan, 1998)—Jim Egan died on 9 March 2000.

During the immediate postwar years there was a reassertion and reconstruction of heterosexual hegemony, but other social tendencies began to undermine some of the ways that lesbians and gay men had been oppressed. The development of capitalism by the 1960s was less directly tied up with the heterosexual family than it had been previously (Kinsman, 1996a: 157, 288–9). This began to allow gay men and lesbians to open up more social space for themselves.

By the late 1950s reform of the Criminal Code relating to homosexual acts began to be discussed. The 1957 Wolfenden Report in England argued that homosexual acts between two consenting adults (defined as 21 or over) in private (basically behind bedroom doors) should be decriminalized, while policing of all homosexual expression in public and involving young people under the age of 21 should be intensified (ibid., 213–24). This helped to open a limited space for early homosexual rights activists. In 1964 in Vancouver, Canada's first gay rights group, the Association for Social Knowledge, was established. Unlike early gay rights groups in the US, it was a mixed men's and women's group and engaged in popular education, social activities, and lobbying for law reform (ibid., 230–48).

During the 1960s in Canada a conflict developed between the growing criminalization of homosexuality, which had been derived from developments in the
US, and efforts towards homosexual law reform and partial decriminalization of
homosexual acts, which were largely drawn from England. The partial decriminalization strategy was supported by early homosexual rights activists, who also
wanted more popular education about homosexuality, as well as by liberal elements
in the United and Anglican churches, by some social commentators, and, by 1967,
by leading politicians in the NDP and Liberal Party (ibid., 230–78). In 1967 a legal
decision brought the decriminalization issue to a head. The Supreme Court of
Canada, in a decision regarding the sentencing of Everett George Klippert as a
'dangerous sexual offender' to indefinite detention simply for engaging in consensual homosexual acts, upheld the sentencing decision of a lower court (ibid.,
257–64). This decision came after the British enactment of the proposals of the
Wolfenden Report regarding homosexual law reform. Where the Canadian
Supreme Court defended the expanded criminalization of homosexuality, British
law had moved towards partial decriminalization of homosexual activities.

It was in this context that then Justice Minister Pierre Trudeau made his
famous statement that 'the state has no place in the bedrooms of the nation.'
Trudeau introduced a Wolfenden-type reform of the criminal law relating to
homosexual offences in Canada. In 1969 reforms were adopted that provided for
the partial decriminalization of homosexual acts performed in private between two
individuals of age 21 or over. At the same time the reforms called for escalated
policing of homosexual acts in public and involving young people (under the age
of 21). In effect, most Liberal and NDP supporters of the bill (and some Conservatives) argued that since homosexuals were sick or mentally ill they should be
under a doctor's or therapist's care and should not be designated as criminal and
locked away in prison (ibid., 264–78).

This legal shift opened up social spaces for gay and lesbian community formation, but it also maintained heterosexual hegemony in an altered form. The popular education about and acceptance of homosexuals that early gay and lesbian
rights activists had hoped would come out of law reform were submerged in
notions of homosexuality as a sickness and the distinction between 'private' and
'public' sex, which has became central to the regulation of a series of sexual issues
in Canada since the 1960s. This regulatory distinction constructed the legitimate
realm of 'queer' sex as being in the 'private' realm (behind bedroom doors), thereby
mandating police action when gay and lesbian sex moves into the 'public' realm.
At the same time, while allowing heterosexual sex and desire to have a much more
'public' social presence, this distinction has defined the familial realm as being
'private', which has made it all the more difficult to deal with pervasive forms of
gendered and sexual violence that take place there.

In the late 1960s and early 1970s in Canada, as in many other countries, new
gay and lesbian liberation movements emerged. These movements came out of the
ferment of the social movements of the 1960s—the new left and student movements, the peace (anti-Vietnam War) movement, the feminist movement, and the

black civil rights and liberation movements. In June 1969 at the Stonewall Inn in New York City lesbians and gay men fought back against the routine police repression that gay bars faced. This led to days of rebellion and the emergence of gay liberation fronts in a number of countries, including in Canada (ibid., 288–93).

Gay liberation activists viewed the liberation movement of gays and lesbians as part and parcel of a broader liberation movement of all oppressed people. They saw the lesbian and gay struggle as intimately tied up with the feminist movement against gender and sex roles. Central to the movement were the affirmation that 'gay and lesbian are just as good as straight' and the importance of gays and lesbians coming out of the closet to fight their oppression. The early movement targeted the psychiatric and psychological professions for their position that homosexuality was a form of mental illness and disrupted psychiatric and psychological meetings, leading the American Psychiatric Association in 1973 finally to drop its classification of homosexuality as a mental disorder (Bayer, 1981; Gay Flame, n.d.).

Although gay liberation groups during this time attempted to adopt a feminist perspective, problems soon erupted. Sexism among gay men did not disappear and many gay men did not understand that the lesbian and gay liberation movement had to address all the forms of oppression that women face in this society, since lesbians are also oppressed as women. As a result, many lesbians left the gay movement, which they saw as being dominated by gay men. Many lesbians also joined and were involved in the re-emergence of the feminist movement, although they faced heterosexism from many heterosexual women involved in this movement. A distinct lesbian feminism emerged out of the social experiences of lesbians and criticized the social practices of heterosexual privilege and the social institutionalization of heterosexuality (Bunch, 1975; Ross, 1995; Stone, 1990; Khayatt, 1992). Lesbian activism has had to relate to both the gay and the feminist struggles.

Ironically, even though the early gay liberation movement had critiqued the oppressive character of gay establishments and the 'gay ghetto', the expansion of this ghetto was one of its major gains. Gay bars, restaurants, bookstores, and bathhouses proliferated, and distinct gay neighbourhoods in several larger cities across the country (the East End in Vancouver, the Church–Wellesley area in Toronto, the Gay Village in Montreal) emerged. Given that women in patriarchal society have less access to money and to social space, there were always more establishments available to gay men than to lesbians.

The early liberationist groups fell apart because of their own internal tensions and contradictions. By the mid-1970s the main political current in the movement focused on gaining the human rights of gay men and lesbians. The central focus of this campaign was establishing that discrimination against people on the basis of their sexual orientation was prohibited under human rights legislation. This would mean that lesbians, gay men, and bisexuals who faced discrimination on the basis of their sexual orientation would now have redress through human rights commissions. This provided a public and political organizing focus for gay and lesbian rights. The first major victory of this movement was in 1977 in Quebec, when the Parti Québécois government added sexual orientation protection to its human rights legislation. This early organizing helped lay the basis for human rights victories in the 1980s and 1990s.

The Empire Strikes Back

The growing public visibility of gay community formation led to major police campaigns against gay establishments and gay sex in the late 1970s and early 1980s that, in more limited forms, continue to this day. The Criminal Code continued to criminalize consensual gay sex in public (defined broadly as any place involving more than two people and any place open to public access or view) or involving people under the age of 21, and to call forth the police against the growing visibility of gay men.

Under the Criminal Code gay sex was still classified as 'acts of indecency'. This meant that the police could use the bawdy-house legislation that had originally been designed to deal with houses of prostitution against gay men's establishments. With no evidence of prostitution, they raided gay bars and bathhouses claiming that these were 'common bawdy houses' that were 'habitually resorted to' for 'acts of indecency' and rounded up everyone they found there as 'found-ins' or 'keepers' (if they were employees) of a common bawdy house (G. Smith, 1988). In 1977, 146 men were charged as found-ins during a raid on the Truxx bar in downtown Montreal. This provoked a large demonstration of gay rebellion in downtown streets that helped to push the Parti Québécois government into enacting human rights protection for gay men and lesbians. Similar raids also took place in Ottawa and Edmonton.

The largest series of police raids started in Toronto in 1978. On 5 February 1981, 150 police officers descended on the city's four main gay baths; 289 men were charged as found-ins and 20 as keepers of a common bawdy house. At that point it was the largest mass arrest in Canada since the declaration of the War Measures Act in 1970. The police thus transformed the intimate sexual activities of two men in a private cubicle into a crime under the Criminal Code. In response the gay and lesbian communities defended these men's right to privacy and defined gay bars and baths as community spaces that should be off limits to police raids (ibid.; McCaskell, 1988).

Thousands of gay men and lesbians viewed these raids as an attack on the entire community. The night after the raids more than 3,000 gays, lesbians, and supporters joined a demonstration organized by the Right to Privacy Committee that took over Yonge Street in Toronto and marched on police headquarters. A few weeks later more than 4,000 people marched against police harassment and violence from Queen's Park down Yonge Street. The city was turned on its ear and the plans of the police backfired as the gay demonstrations received the support of the trade union movement, the feminist movement, the black and South Asian communities, and many other community groups. Rather than leading to a decrease in the visibility of the gay scene, the raid led to an explosion of gay and lesbian community formation. The number of gay and lesbian groups in the city and their size increased phenomenally.

The Right to Privacy Committee (RTPC) also fought the case on the legal front: eventually the vast majority of those charged were acquitted. At the same time the RTPC was unsuccessful in repealing the bawdy-house law, which has continued to be used, as in the raid on Katacombes in Montreal in 1994, when 175 men were charged as found-ins, and in the raid on the Remington's bar in Toronto in 1996.[5]

As a result of the unprecedented gay resistance and popular opposition that the raids produced, the Toronto police were forced to shift tactics. The police began regularly to lay overcrowding charges against gay bars in 1981–2. Surveillance, entrapment, and the arrest of men allegedly engaged in sexual acts in washrooms and parks increased significantly. In 1982–3 more than 600 men were arrested in washrooms for homosexual 'offences' and more than 600 'indecent act' arrests took place in Toronto in 1985,[6] although the men arrested had constructed situations of privacy and intimacy for their activities and did nothing to offend or harass other people. As George Smith (n.d.) points out, they produced their sexual activities as private acts even though they took place in state-defined public places. The criminalization of gay sexual behaviour continues to inform police activity at the beginning of the new millennium.

AIDS: Making Us Sick Once Again

Since the early 1980s the AIDS crisis has had a major impact on the lives of gay and bisexual men and of lesbians and bisexual women. The first medical and media mentions of what would come to be called AIDS homosexualized this syndrome. It was portrayed as a homosexual disease even though other people were also being affected by it. The first medical classification used was 'gay-related immune deficiency'. In 1982 a headline in the *Toronto Star* proclaimed that the 'Gay Plague Has Arrived in Canada' (Canadian AIDS Society, 1991; see also Emke, 1991). This constructed the first forms of knowledge about AIDS and portrayed AIDS as something caused by homosexuality. While gay men and lesbians were already a marginalized and outcast group, the growing AIDS epidemic brought even more discrimination and oppression against gay men and, in a lesser way, against lesbians. As AIDS activists have pointed out from the beginning, AIDS was never a gay disease—although in North America it initially appeared to the medical profession in large numbers among gay men who had some contact with the medical system. HIV, the virus believed to lead to the development of AIDS, is transmitted through a series of sexual and blood-related practices that anyone can engage in. There are risk activities, not risk groups.

At first governments in the US and Canada did little in response to AIDS beyond collecting epidemiological information (the numbers of dead and infected, and the risk activities people engaged in). The Reagan administration in the US thought that AIDS was only affecting 'expendable' populations and did not fund research or educational programs. Valuable years were therefore lost because of this lack of funding. The Canadian government was not much better. It was left up to groups in the gay and lesbian communities, often with some influence from the feminist women's health movement, to provide the first support for people living with AIDS and to do the first educational work regarding AIDS. Across Canada community-based AIDS groups emerged. These groups fought against prejudice and provided care and support for people dying and living with AIDS (see, e.g., Altman, 1986; Patton, 1985, 1990; Kinsman, 1991; Adam and Sears, 1996; Rowe and Ryan, 1998).

These community-based groups developed the notion of safe sex—that there were sexual activities people could engage in that would not lead to the transmission of HIV. Among gay men, early safe-sex organizing campaigns showed that safe sex could reduce the risk of transmission of HIV. It would only be later that safe sex would be sanitized by public health and medical experts and focused only on using condoms and being monogamous or celibate (Patton, 1989, 1996). Having one relationship after another one (what is often referred to as serial monogamy) has never been a safe sex practice. What is important is the activities engaged in (safe versus unsafe) and not the number of sexual partners.

By the mid-1980s the Canadian government began to respond by funding AIDS initiatives and by providing funding for community-based AIDS groups. At the same time there were major problems, as the government and official agencies assumed that people living with AIDS were going to die. As people living with AIDS in parts of Canada started to organize they found that the Canadian government and the medical profession were denying them access to promising drugs and treatments that could help prevent the infections that kill people living with AIDS. This led to the birth of a new AIDS activism that focused on direct action to try to get the government and pharmaceutical corporations to allow people living with AIDS to access these treatments. In Toronto AIDS ACTION NOW! staged disruptions, die-ins, sit-ins, and burned effigies to force the release of these promising treatments. Some important success was reached on these fronts and in 1990 the federal government announced the National AIDS Strategy. While this has provided more funding for AIDS groups it has also been used to manage and contain them and to limit AIDS activism (Kinsman, 1997b). In 1996 the federal government refused to commit itself to renewing the AIDS Strategy. Another round of lobbying and activism was required to renew funding.

People living with AIDS and HIV have also been affected detrimentally by government funding cuts to health care. In the 1990s, problems with treatment access and delivery have drawn the focus of AIDS activists, as have questions of poverty, since many people living with AIDS have to leave their jobs. Thus, problems with access to social services are another focus (Mykhalovskiy and Smith, 1994). Without adequate nutrition, housing, and social support, people living with HIV and AIDS are put in situations where it is very difficult to defend their bodies from infection. The AIDS crisis has presented a condensation of all the different social relations in this society.

It not only raises questions of sexuality and the need to combat heterosexism, but also questions regarding gender, class, race, poverty, and access to health care. An adequate social response to AIDS must address all these questions.

Section 15 and Equality Rights

In the 1980s in Canada there was an important shift in Canadian state legal formation with the coming into effect of the Charter of Rights and Freedoms and its section 15 equality rights provisions in 1985 (Herman, 1994: 26–9; Rayside, 1998: 105–39; M. Smith, 1999). Laws could now be challenged on constitutional grounds if they conflicted with the equality rights section of the Charter and governments were supposed to bring their human rights legislation into line with the equality rights section. At the same time, other sections of the Charter could be used to justify continuing discrimination.

Section 15 prohibited discrimination against a number of groups but did not explicitly mention prohibition of discrimination on the basis of sexual orientation. At the same time it was written in an open-ended fashion allowing gay and lesbian activists and progressive lawyers to argue that sexual orientation protection should be 'read into' the Charter. This opened up important possibilities for lesbian and gay activists to make progress on the human rights front, and this potential was seized by activists and by individual gays and lesbians and their lawyers.

The first major success occurred in Ontario following more than a decade of activism when sexual orientation protection was finally added to provincial human rights legislation in 1986 despite the vociferous opposition of the morally conservative 'pro-family' right wing (Rayside, 1988; Herman, 1994: 33–7). This aimed to provide basic protection for lesbians, gays, and bisexuals against discrimination in housing, employment, and services. Other provinces and territories soon began to follow the lead of Quebec and Ontario, including Yukon, Manitoba, and, in the early 1990s, Nova Scotia, New Brunswick, British Columbia, and Saskatchewan.

In 1986, the federal Conservative government, in response to a report from an Equality Rights Committee of Parliament set up to study the impact of section 15, stated that it believed the courts would interpret s. 15 as including sexual orientation protection. Despite this it took another 10 years, until 1996, for sexual orientation finally to be added to the provisions of the Canadian Human Rights Act as first Conservative and then Liberal governments stalled and delayed on this issue. Both governments faced important opposition from within their caucuses and also from moral conservatives to any progress on human rights for lesbians, gay men, and bisexuals. The federal Liberal government only moved to enact sexual orientation in federal human rights legislation after years of gay/lesbian activism, after pressure from the Canadian Human Rights Commission, and after the Supreme Court in the 1995 *Egan/Nesbitt* decision (more on this later) had clearly decided that s. 15 did include sexual orientation protection (Rayside, 1998: 105–39).

In 1997 sexual orientation protection was added to human rights legislation in Newfoundland and Labrador after years of opposition from the Clyde Wells

Liberal government. This followed a decision by the Newfoundland Supreme Court that sexual orientation protection had to be included in the Newfoundland Human Rights Act. In Alberta it took the 1998 Supreme Court decision in the *Vriend* case to get the Alberta Conservative government to include sexual orientation protection in its human rights legislation. Delwin Vriend had been a private college teacher in Alberta who was fired because of his sexual orientation. The provincial human rights commission had refused to take up his case since sexual orientation was not included in the Alberta Human Rights Act. And in 1998 sexual orientation protection was also included in human rights legislation in Prince Edward Island.

At the same time, even the achievement of sexual orientation protection in human rights legislation does not guarantee an end to discrimination. All it means is that if someone has experienced discrimination on the basis of sexual orientation, the person can now take a complaint to a provincial or federal (depending on which government has jurisdiction) human rights commission. In Ontario and other provinces there have been major problems with human rights commissions actually dealing with the cases of discrimination they receive. In the 1990s government cutbacks have left human rights commissions overwhelmed with cases they cannot process and address and they have developed arbitrary criteria for deciding not to pursue cases.[7] Sometimes the bodies set up to 'help' people facing discrimination become another obstacle.

Nonetheless, there has been remarkable progress on basic human rights protection for lesbians, gays, and bisexuals within the Canadian state over the last 20 years. The context for this has been created not only by gay and lesbian rights activists and their allies in the human rights movement, but also by the lessening of the dependence of capitalist and state relations on the heterosexual family. This has led to a certain general moral deregulation of sexuality by state forces and to a limited moral deregulation of lesbian, gay, and bisexual sexualities in particular (Sears, 1998). Gay and lesbian sexualities are now less directly regulated by state laws and policing practices (although these have certainly not disappeared) but more by market forces, professional agencies and policies, and popular culture, which enshrines heterosexuality as the norm while opening up more ghettoized spaces for 'queers'.

From Human Rights to Spousal Benefits and Family Recognition Rights

It did not take long for lesbian and gay activists to realize that basic human rights protection did little to get at some of the major forms of oppression that lesbians and gay men face. Gay men and lesbians in long-term relationships were denied the same type of spousal benefits available to common-law heterosexual couples simply because their relationships were same-gender ones. Most state legislation defined 'spouse' and 'family' to be only heterosexual in character. Activists soon began to contest these state definitions, viewing them as key ways in which heterosexuality was institutionalized as the only relational norm in this society.

One of the first of these struggles was that of Karen Andrews, a library worker and member of the Canadian Union of Public Employees (CUPE). CUPE strongly supported her fight for family medicare coverage for her lesbian partner and the child they were raising together. Although this legal battle was lost in 1988 the Ontario government subsequently abolished health-insurance premiums and moved to individual coverage (Sanders, 1994: 128; Herman, 1994: 27–8, 59–61, 132–3; Andrews, 1995). CUPE and other unions have taken up the fight for same-gender benefits for their members as an important union struggle.

Brian Mossop went to court when he was denied bereavement leave on the death of his partner's father because his partner was male. While he won the case before a human rights tribunal in 1989—where it was recognized that families had changed in character to include homosexual relationships—he lost at the Federal Court of Appeal in 1990 and at the Supreme Court of Canada in 1993 (Sanders, 1994: 123; Herman, 1994: 25–6, 133–9).

In the previously mentioned Jim Egan/Jack Nesbitt case for same-gender pension benefits under the Old Age Security Act, the Federal Court of Appeal in 1993 decided against a spousal benefit for Egan's partner, Jack Nesbitt, on the grounds he was not a 'spouse' (Sanders, 1994: 103, 108, 123, 127; Herman, 1994: 28). In its May 1995 decision, in which the Supreme Court finally recognized that s. 15 of the Charter must be read as including sexual orientation protection, Nesbitt's right to a pension was nonetheless rejected. Four judges argued that there was no discrimination in the denial of the pension benefit to Nesbitt; one argued that there was discrimination but that it was a 'justified' form of discrimination; and four others argued that it was unjustified discrimination.

This decision embodies the ambiguous and contradictory character of the current legal situation facing gay men, lesbians, and bisexuals in Canada. On the one hand, on an abstract and individual basis, our rights are recognized—but not in the context of our actual and substantive relationships and sexualities. This is also the case in other areas of 'social difference' where the individual rights of women and people of colour are supported but not their collective and substantive rights. The discourse of abstract individual rights can actually be used to limit the struggles of oppressed groups for more substantive rights and equality (Herman, 1994; M. Smith, 1999).

At the same time lesbians and gay men involved in raising children, those wanting custody of their children, and those arguing for adoption rights for gay men and lesbians began to argue for family recognition rights for same-gender couples and against the heterosexist legal and social definition of family, asserting that 'we are family' too. In 1989 the Coalition for Lesbian and Gay Rights in Ontario (CLGRO) held a conference to try to develop a common position on the struggle for spousal benefits and family recognition rights, and later established a working group of lawyers to determine the necessary changes in provincial legislation (Wilson, 1989; Ursel, 1995). The CLGRO began to call on the provincial government to change provincial legislation that defined 'family' and 'spouse' as exclusively heterosexual in character.

This led up to the struggle for Bill 167 in Ontario in 1994. Drawn up by the provincial New Democratic Party government after years of pressure and activism from lesbian and gay activists, Bill 167 would have changed 56 pieces of legislation, granting lesbian and gay spousal and family relationships formal equality with common-law heterosexual relationships. While the NDP government was forced to address this question because of pressure from the CLGRO, lesbian and gay activists in the NDP, and other party members, including union activists, its political strategy could only result in defeat. By deciding on a free vote on this legislation, so that caucus members could vote against the party position, the government indicated a lack of commitment to its passage as a fundamental part of its support for human rights. Premier Bob Rae justified his support for a free vote by suggesting that this legislation was a 'moral issue' that raised 'troubling questions' for people. Rather than defining this as an important human rights question, the NDP leadership instead ceded the terrain of argument to those opposed to the bill (Rayside, 1998: 141–77; Kinsman, 1996a: 313–16).

Moral conservative forces across the province mobilized in opposition to Bill 167, which they portrayed as a 'threat' to the family and to children. Roman Catholic priests read letters to their congregations calling on parishioners to write letters against Bill 167. The right wing focused especially on opposition to adoption rights for gay men and lesbians and on family-related issues. The arguments of the political right needed to be addressed head on, but not enough of this was done in 1994. While lesbian and gay organizing to create a broad coalition in support of Bill 167 was the most extensive ever seen in the province, this was not based in mass protests, which is what was needed to sway the politicians and to bring more people on side. In the end Bill 167 was defeated. Every Conservative voted against it, as did all but three Liberals and 12 members of the NDP caucus. This ensured its defeat. Outside Queen's Park that evening more than 8,000 lesbians, gay men, and supporters gathered to express their anger at this defeat for lesbian and gay rights.

Following the defeat of Bill 167 a number of lesbian families pushed for the legal rights of the non-biological mothers, and several second-parent adoption cases proceeded through the courts. In May 1995 in an important legal victory Justice James Paul Nevins of the Ontario Provincial Court (Family Division) decided that the lesbian partners of four women could adopt their partner's biological children. Nevins argued that the provincial Child and Family Services Act was unconstitutional because it restricts 'spouse' to someone of the 'opposite sex' (Lindstrom, 1995). Meanwhile, the BC government changed the provincial Adoption Act in 1995 to allow lesbians and gay men to adopt children (Filipenko, 1995). In 1997 the BC NDP government also passed legislation changing the definitions of 'spouse' in much of its provincial legislation to include gay men and lesbians without the same sort of uproar that took place in Ontario in 1994.

There was a significant legal victory in the 1998 *Rosenberg* case involving two employees of the Canadian Union of Public Employees (CUPE) who challenged the federal income tax regulations that only recognize opposite-sex spouses for survivor benefits. CUPE fully supported the court challenge. The court unanimously ruled that the federal Income Tax Act is unconstitutional and must be read to include coverage for same-sex partners. The federal government has accepted the ruling and is finally looking at amending the law.

In early 1999 the Foundation For Equal Families (one of the groups formed after the defeat of Bill 167 in 1994) announced an 'omnibus' lawsuit against the federal government to challenge 58 laws (including the Canada Pension Plan Act, the Income Tax Act, immigration regulations, the Old Age Security Act, and many others) that discriminate against same-sex couples. This lawsuit is directed at forcing the federal government, which has been stalling on bringing legislation into line with various court rulings, to change legislation that discriminates against lesbians and gay men (Cossman, 1999).

In the spring of 1999 the Supreme Court of Canada handed down a landmark decision in the *M. v. H.* spousal support case. After their relationship ended M. attempted to seek support under the Ontario Family Law Act. She was denied the right to do so due to the exclusively heterosexual definition of 'spouse' in the Act. The Supreme Court found, in an 8–1 judgement, that the Ontario Family Law Act violates the equality rights of lesbians and gay men by defining 'spouse' as someone only of the 'opposite sex'. This decision made it clear that governments cannot continue to deny spousal rights to same-sex couples. The Ontario government was given six months to correct the problem in its legislation (Barnholden, 1999).

On 27 October 1999 Bill 5 ('An Act to Amend Certain Statutes as a Result of the Supreme Court Decision in M v H') was passed by the Ontario legislature. The Tory government was not pleased about this legislation since it was forced into it by the Supreme Court and made it clear that it does not consider lesbian and gay couples to be spouses. This amendment of 67 Ontario statutes to include same-sex partners does not define same-sex partners as spouses or as families but does grant them the same rights as common-law heterosexual spouses in a number of areas. While these changes are an important step forward in the battle for spousal benefits and family recognition rights, many lesbian and gay activists are critical of the legislation for establishing lesbian and gay couples and their relations as separate from heterosexual spousal and family relations (Warner, 1999). M. has announced that she is going back to the Supreme Court of Canada since she feels the legislation violates the spirit of the *M. v. H.* decision.

Responsible versus Irresponsible Queers and the Expansion of the Gay Market

The growth of gay and lesbian community formation has become tied up with the expansion of the 'gay market'. This has led to growing divisions between those identified as being 'responsible' gay men and lesbians and those identified as being 'irresponsible' queers. Within lesbian and gay communities identification is often now organized in reference to 'spouses' and 'families'. This operates to exclude those who do not see themselves as spouses or families. 'Responsible' gay men and lesbians increasingly are seen as emphasizing their *similarities* with 'normal' white middle-class heterosexual couples and families. 'Irresponsible' queers are seen as emphasizing their *differences* from white middle-class heterosexuals through not identifying as spouses or families and through their continuing push for the affirmation of gay, lesbian, bisexual, and queer sexualities and for dealing with sexual censorship and policing (Kinsman, 1996b).

An interesting feature of gay, lesbian, and bisexual activism in the late 1980s and 1990s has been the reclaiming of the word 'queer' so that it can no longer be used as a term of abuse. 'Queer' still sounds very different when uttered by a queer basher against lesbians and gay men than when used by lesbians, gay men, and bisexuals as an affirmation of ourselves in a social world that often tries to deny our very existence. It has also been used as a broader term to include the experiences of transgendered people (people who move in their lives from one gender to another and those who defy gender boundaries) and other sexual minorities (see Jagoose, 1996).

For a long time major corporations stayed away from openly advertising to the gay and lesbian communities because this was considered to be too controversial and because the gay community was not recognized as a potentially profitable market demographic. This has now begun to change. Increasingly, some heterosexual business interests have marketed their commodities to the gay community because they see that this is a consumer market they have been missing out on (Maynard, 1994; Sinfield, 1998: 160–9). This has led in the mass media to increasing discussions of gay capitalism and the 'pink market'.

This image of the gay market largely excludes lesbians, who generally do not have the same economic resources as men in this society, as well as lesbian and gay non-professionals or workers (which is the majority of the gay and lesbian population, as it is of the population as a whole), people of colour, and poor people and serves to drive a wedge between groups within the gay and lesbian communities. Treatment by the heterosexual mass media, and also by much of the gay media, of gay men as a white, middle-class, consumer market is in part a process of class and racial differentiation within queer populations, which excludes working-class people and people of colour from positions of power and influence.

Because heterosexual business interests accept gays as a consumer market does not mean that they support our rights, relationships, and sexualities. We are only accepted because we have money, and because as consumers we can buy commodities and services, but not necessarily because we are perceived to deserve equal rights. While access to consumer goods and services opens up important new social spaces for us, the gay market provides little protection against police repression, nor does it ensure spousal and family rights. As Steven Maynard (1994: 9) writes:

> I think we need to ask ourselves if we are satisfied with the displacement of politics from the streets to the marketplace. How does a politics rooted in consumption speak to the many lesbians and gays who are excluded from the world of queer consumption in the first place? Or, how does a politics of the marketplace tackle such institutions as the police or the legal system?

With the expansion of gay ghettos and communities, openly gay professionals, managers, and business people have risen to the top of the community. Ironically, the street and bar people and the gay and lesbian radicals ('radical' as in getting to the root of the problem) who initiated the gay and lesbian liberation movements, who responded to police repression, and who sustained the movement over the years have not reaped the main benefits. Rather, those who have been able to gain professional and managerial credentials, and who have learned the language of those who manage and rule in this capitalist society, have gained the most. These people within gay communities are able to articulate their concerns to those who rule and to present themselves as the 'legitimate' representatives of the gay (and sometimes also the lesbian) community. This process of class differentiation within gay communities has even led some middle-class gay men to join in 'respectable' campaigns in defence of their property values and against street prostitutes, male hustlers, street people, the poor, the homeless, and even against people who squeegee in some cities.

The social basis for this orientation towards social respectability and responsibility is in part shaped by class formation within gay and lesbian communities. The new middle class that has emerged since the 1969 Stonewall riots in New York has developed class interests they share with the broader heterosexual middle class that dominates in this society. While they want lesbian and gay rights, they basically want to be let into the current definitions of 'spouse', 'family', and 'middle-class society'. They do not want to challenge broader class, racial, or gender relations. This is the social basis for what has been referred to by queer activists as the 'assimilationist' strategy that emphasizes similarities with heterosexual society. This approach argues that gay men and lesbians are the same as heterosexuals except for their intimate relationships. When Queer Nation activist groups in the late 1980s and early 1990s in the US and in Toronto, Vancouver, and Montreal challenged this view with a more militant, grassroots, in-your-face approach, they failed to grasp the class and social basis of this assimilationism and to realize that class relations and divisions also had to be addressed (Kinsman, 1996a: 300).

For those of us who also face oppression on the basis of class, gender, race, ability, or other grounds and who continue to be concerned about the oppressive regulation of our sexualities, the attempt to be let into white 'respectable' heterosexual society largely on its terms does not address the main features of the oppression we face. A strategy for transformation must engage with our continuing sexual oppression as well as with the intersections of our lives with class, race, gender, and other forms of oppression.

We can see some of the limitations of the approach that portrays lesbians and gay men as being as 'respectable' and as 'responsible' as middle-class heterosexuals when we examine some of the ways in which spousal and family benefits have been fought for and justified. 'Family' and 'spouse' are used in legal cases not only in the transformative sense of challenging heterosexual hegemony but also as part of an attempt to 'responsibilize' and 'normalize' a segment of the gay and lesbian communities. Partly, this is bound up with the conceptualization that spousal and family recognition brings with it *responsibilities* as well as rights (Kinsman, 1996b; Barnholden, 1999). This perspective also accepts the individualization of benefits in family/spousal contexts rather than providing social supports in non-familial or non-spousal forms, including social support for children. This is a practice of 'normalization' since these spousal, family regulations are part of a web of relations historically established between families, places of employment, state regulations, and insurance corporations.

We can look at this in relation to spousal benefit plans. These allocate social benefits on the basis of where an individual works (benefit plans are more likely to exist for professional and managerial personnel and in unionized workplaces where unions have fought for them). Clearly, as long as benefits are allocated to hetero-sexual couples on this basis a claim for equal rights for gay and lesbian couples has to be made. But at the same time this is a rather arbitrary way to allocate benefits to people. It does not take into account people's social needs and certainly does not attempt to redistribute wealth to poor people, who are largely denied access to these benefits.

A progressive approach to social benefits would consider questions of social need, poverty, and the redistribution of wealth. Unfortunately, since the mainstream gay and lesbian movement has accepted the social form in which these benefits are allocated and has simply asked for this to be extended to some gay men and lesbians, the possibility to build links with people organizing against poverty (including gays and lesbians living in poverty) and with feminists concerned about new ways to allocate benefits to people and to redistribute wealth have not been pursued. Increasingly, the mainstream gay and lesbian movement has been able to be portrayed as more or less a middle-class movement that is not concerned about the struggles of people living in poverty.

The spousal/family benefits strategy can be used to incorporate some gays and lesbians into familial/spousal classifications as a site for regulation of their lives. These lesbians and gay men, if the strategy is successful, would no longer be portrayed as 'deviant' but instead as some variant of the 'norm'. As a result, a new, albeit limited, social legitimacy would be granted to some gay men and lesbians. Those queers involved in spousal and familial relations would be 'responsibilized' while those who are not would be 'irresponsibilized'.

There is a complementary trend towards the privatization of financial respon-sibility between gay men and lesbians in relationships. For instance, same-sex spouses who obtain state recognition will be liable for each other's support (Dawson, 1994). Some lesbians and gay men who have applied for social assistance have been denied benefits on the grounds that their partners make too much money (Findlay, 1994). Gay men living with HIV/AIDS can lose their access to drugs and treatments covered by social assistance since financial responsibility for them (including very expensive HIV/AIDS drugs) would have to be assumed by their gay spouses if they have high enough incomes. This individualizes and priva-tizes economic responsibility within the spousal relationship. These are some of the reasons why there has been some controversy over the spousal benefits and family recognition strategies.

Sexual Censorship and Policing

Spousal and family recognition strategies, at their best, only deal with one side of gay/lesbian experience. They address discrimination in relation to the official definitions of 'spouse' and 'family' as exclusively heterosexual. Another aspect of the experience of gays/lesbians, sexual censorship and policing of consensual sexualities, must be considered. When right-wing groups and politicians oppose spousal and family benefits for 'queers' they rely on the social construction of our sexualities as 'deviant' and 'criminal' to argue against equal rights. This holds back our progress on human rights and on the spousal and family recognition fronts. But the way spousal and family benefits struggles have been developed and put forward has tended to ignore sexual struggles. This becomes critical in regard to sexual-related struggles that are not defined as being 'responsible' or 'respectable'. The escalation of sexual censorship and policing that gay men and lesbians have faced in the 1980s and 1990s illustrates this problem.

In Toronto, following the resistance to the bath raids, the police focused their attention more specifically against gay institutions. Obscenity charges were brought against Glad Day Bookshop (the main gay bookstore in Toronto) for magazines available at many stores in the city and obscenity charges were laid in May 1982 against *The Body Politic*, a gay liberation magazine, for a column on anal sex. Both legal cases eventually led to acquittals. Obscenity legislation, which censors sexual presentations on the basis of 'the undue exploitation of sex', does not treat all sexual images and texts equally. Given the criminalization of gay sex in 'public' or involving more than two people, the police and courts were able to use the legal notion that gay sex was 'indecent' to construct representations of gay sexuality as more 'obscene' and 'indecent' than similar heterosexual portrayals (see Johnson, 1995; Kinsman, 1985; Valverde and Weir, 1985).

In the mid-1980s Canada Customs escalated its seizure of lesbian and gay materials coming into Canada. Using a new internal memorandum that labelled depictions of 'buggery/sodomy' (often interpreted as referring to anal sex) as 'obscene', they routinely seized materials destined for gay and lesbian bookstores, especially Little Sister's in Vancouver and Glad Day in Toronto. Books and magazines seized included hundreds of titles—sex advice literature, biographies, important works of literature, as well as gay-male erotic writings and lesbian sex magazines and erotic images (Kiss and Tell, 1991, 1994). These seizures did major damage to these smaller community-oriented bookstores and denied many lesbians and gay men access to information about their lives, including safe sex information that often focuses on anal sex. Even though the prohibition on anal sex, which figured prominently in safe-sex education for gay men, had been challenged with partial success in the *Joy of Gay Sex* case in 1987 the Canada Customs memorandum prohibiting the representation of anal penetration was only removed in 1994 just prior to the Little Sister's case (Filipenko, 1994; Fuller and Blackley, 1995).

In February 1992 the Supreme Court of Canada in the *Butler* decision upheld the constitutionality of the obscenity section of the Criminal Code and modified its interpretation (Barclay and Carol, 1992–3; Cossman et al., 1997). This decision was hailed by some feminists as a victory for women since it shifted the definition of obscenity from 'moral' grounds to a basis more on 'harm' to women and other groups. While the focus in interpreting the obscenity section was to remain on 'the undue exploitation of sex' this was shifted from a focus on too much sexual explicitness for 'community standards' to tolerate to a new set of tests based on the relation between sexuality and violence, degradation, and dehumanization. When applied to gay and lesbian materials, however, the *Butler* decision actually led to an intensification of sexual censorship. To some, including many police and some judges, lesbian and gay sex *per se* is degrading and dehumanizing.

It was no surprise, then, that one of the first obscenity charges laid following the *Butler* decision was against Glad Day in Toronto for carrying the lesbian sex magazine *Bad Attitude*. Glad Day was convicted in December 1992 in a decision that relied in part on *Butler* (Ross, 1997). In July 1992 Glad Day, whose proprietors had taken Canada Customs to court regarding 12 books and magazines that had been seized, lost its case, with the judge basing his decision on *Butler* and arguing that depictions of casual gay sex were 'obscene' and suggesting that casual sex and anal sex are potentially harmful to the community (Brown, 1992). In 1994 Little Sister's in Vancouver took Canada Customs to court to try to put an end to the discriminatory seizures it had faced since the mid-1980s. In January 1996 Little Sister's won only a partial legal victory when the BC Supreme Court upheld the constitutionality of Canada Customs censorship powers (Fuller and Blackley, 1995). Some of the practices of Canada Customs were found to be discriminatory but these did not include the constitutionality of the Customs regulations based on 'prior restraint'. In February 1999, however, it was announced that Little Sister's would get a chance to make its case against Canada Customs in the Supreme Court of Canada. In 2000 the Supreme Court heard the Little Sister's case but at the time of writing it had not released its decision.

The power of Canada Customs to seize gay and lesbian materials continues today. This state sexual censorship occurs in the context of broader social and marketplace censorship of images, representations, and knowledge relating to lesbians, gay men, and bisexuals. This is especially a problem for young people who are coming out as lesbian, gay, or bisexual and can find out very little useful and positive information about their lives and sexualities. In the Surrey School Board in British Columbia in 1997 gay and lesbian resource materials were removed from school libraries through the organizing efforts of moral conservative groups. Lesbian and gay students and teachers organized a campaign against this censorship of images and information. In late 1998 the legal case initiated by these groups was successful.

In 1993 the Conservative government rushed Bill C-128 through the House of Commons and Senate (it is now section 163.1 of the Criminal Code). This law was supposed to protect young people by prohibiting child pornography. For the first time it criminalized possession of child pornography, which was in part defined as pictures depicting anyone who appears to be under 18 in explicit sexual activities. This is based on the unfounded assumption that images of sexual acts involving young people incite sexual violence against young people. It also prohibits written materials or visual representations that advocate or counsel sexual activities involving people under the age of 18. The law makes it more difficult to undertake explicit safe-sex education or progressive sexuality education with young people, and many community-based AIDS groups have come out in opposition to it for this reason. The law also does nothing to get at the social roots of sexual violence and harassment against young people, which lie in the social power that fathers have in families over their children, in the aggressive masculine sexuality of some men, and in the eroticization of youth in much of the mass media and popular culture.

The law was used against Toronto artist Eli Langer for his line drawings that explored questions of adult/youth and youth/youth sexuality and child sexual abuse. Langer won in court in 1995 and his art was eventually returned to him. This law has not only been used in sexual censorship but also as a way of criminalizing the lives of young male hustlers (young men who sell sexual services to other men) and consensual sex between men. It has been used against a number of male prostitutes in Toronto, London, and elsewhere, especially those who have participated in sex videos as part of their work or who made home videos. Many of these charges have been associated with male/male sexual activities, and the broad-ranging search-and-seizure provisions of the law have been used to collect evidence that can criminalize consensual gay sex, especially anal sex involving someone under the age of 18. Previously, the police would have had little means of collecting evidence against such consensual sex that occurs in private (Sorfleet and Bearchell, 1994; Forum 128, 1993; Bell and Couture, 2000; Greyson, 1995).

In London, police operations were launched after some sexually explicit videotapes were fished out of a river. The police created still pictures of the local male prostitutes in the videos and showed these photos to school officials, youth-agency workers, and other young people. They were thus making these young men's private and work lives very public, and in the process 'outing' a number of them as gay. Hundreds of young people were interviewed as part of this investigation, named 'Project Guardian'.[8]

As a result of the investigation many men were arrested, some of whom were 21 or younger. Of those convicted, few were convicted of youth-pornography offences. Instead, most were convicted for anal sex with someone under the age of 18, since the age of consent for anal sex remained higher at that point than for other sexual practices, or for buying (or attempting to buy) the sexual services of someone under the age of 18 (see Bell and Couture, 2000). While no doubt there has been harassment and abuse in some of these interactions, the police are not differentiating between consensual and non-consensual activities. Most of the younger people were charged with making obscene material or with having anal intercourse with someone under the age of 18 or both. Most of the young people charged were male prostitutes. The Homophile Association of London Ontario and the Coalition for Lesbian and Gay Rights in Ontario protested the targeting of sex between males and the targeting of male prostitutes under this law. In this instance, a law designed to 'protect' young people was being used against young people themselves and against consensual gay sex. More recently, Ontario and Quebec court decisions challenging the constitutionality of the age of consent for anal sex—when it is 14 for most other sexual acts—have precluded the police from using this section of the Criminal Code in this way.

In early 1999 a BC court decision to strike down the offence of 'possession' of child pornography as unconstitutional led to an attempted 'moral panic' on the part of moral conservatives and some in the mass media to defend all the aspects of the youth pornography legislation (Yeung, 1999). Considerable pressure from the federal and several provincial governments has been mobilized to ensure that this decision is overturned. The case went before the Supreme Court in 2000.

The use of the youth pornography law against gay young people and against gay sex generally, along with continuing forms of censorship against lesbian and gay materials and the continuing use of the 'indecent act' and bawdy-house legislation against consensual gay sex, all point to the ongoing criminalization of important aspects of gay and lesbian sexualities. Since sexual desires and practices comprise a major social difference between gays/lesbians and heterosexuals, this remains an important part of the overall oppression confronting us. Progress in our fight for liberation on other fronts is continuously held back by the ways in which our sexualities are still portrayed as 'criminal' and 'deviant'. Gays and lesbians are now sometimes accepted as people who have human rights, at least on the abstract or formal level, but this does not always carry through into the realm of personal relationships, which are still often stigmatized, and it certainly does not carry through into the realm of sexual lives.

We Need to Keep Pushing the Boundaries

The space opened up by section 15 of the Charter can only take gays and lesbians so far in their quest for equality and freedom. In moving forward to more substantial equality, gay and lesbian communities must return to building a grassroots movement that draws its power from the bottom up and from organized protest. The gains we have won have been based on the activism of our communities, whether in the resistance to the bath raids or in the years of organizing that led up to particular human rights victories. Coalitions and alliances with other oppressed and marginalized groups must also be built anew. Some of the most important gains for gays and lesbians have come with the support of the feminist, union, anti-racist, and other social movements, and we need to return the support that has been given to us.

We also have to move beyond seeing ourselves as only being concerned with narrowly defined gay, lesbian, or queer concerns. We are never just queer (or heterosexual, for that matter)—we also live in the context of class, gender, race, ability, health status, age, and other social relations. These various forms of oppression and exploitation intersect in our lives and it is important that we begin to address these intersections. Queerness is always mediated by or constructed through other social relations, including class, race, and gender (see Bannerji, 1995). To deny this is only to look at the experiences of those gay men and lesbians who do not face class or race (and sometimes gender) forms of oppression. It is to reduce the gay and lesbian movements to a largely white, middle-class, and male movement. Instead, revitalized gay and lesbian liberation movements must address the needs and concerns of the most oppressed and marginalized queers, including those living in poverty and those experiencing racism. Only when all these intersecting forms of oppression are addressed can a much more profound process of social transformation and liberation become possible.

This is not the time to stop pushing the boundaries. Instead, the lesbian and gay movements will keep on pushing the social, political, and sexual boundaries.

Questions for Critical Thought

1. What is the contradictory situation that lesbians, gay men, and bisexuals currently face in Canada?

2. What is the relation between formal, abstract, and individual rights and more collective and substantive forms of rights and equality?

3. What is the social organization of sexuality approach?

4. What is the relation between sexuality and the social relations of gender, class, and race?

Glossary

Heterosexual privilege: The social practices through which heterosexuals gain social benefits from being 'normal' in this society while lesbians, gay men, and bisexuals experience marginalization and discrimination.

Heterosexual hegemony: The ideologies and practices organizing a male-dominated form of heterosexuality as 'normal', 'natural', and taken for granted while portraying lesbianism and homosexuality as some form of 'deviance', 'abnormality', or disadvantage.

Heterosexism: The ideology that justifies heterosexuality as 'normal' while invalidating lesbian and gay sexualities.

Sexual regulation: The various practices, ideologies, and institutions that define and regulate our erotic lives. Key to current forms of sexual regulation is a distinction between 'normal' and 'deviant' sexualities.

Social organization of sexuality: Sexuality is primarily a social and cultural creation. Although our sexualities build on our physiological capacities, these capacities are made sense of and transformed in the social contexts we live in and help to create.

Suggested Reading

Foucault, Michel. 1980. *The History of Sexuality, Volume One: An Introduction*. New York: Vintage. A powerful critical analysis of the hypothesis that our sexualities have been simply 'repressed' by forms of power. Foucault outlines the historical emergence of sexuality and its connections with social power.

Kinsman, Gary. 1996. *The Regulation of Desire: Homo and Hetero Sexualities*. Montreal: Black Rose. A historical-sociological investigation of the relational emergence of homosexualities and heterosexualities in Canada.

Martindale, Kathleen. 1995. 'What Makes Lesbianism Thinkable? Theorizing Lesbianism from Adrienne Rich to Queer Theory', in Nancy Mandell, ed., *Feminist Issues: Race, Class and Sexuality*. Scarborough, Ont.: Prentice-Hall, 67–94. A useful overview of the ways in which lesbianism has been theorized.

Smith, Miriam. 1999. *Lesbian and Gay Rights in Canada: Social Movements and Equality-Seeking, 1971–1995*. Toronto: University of Toronto Press. A good overview of the struggle for lesbian and gay rights in Canada, and especially of how the equality rights section of the Charter of Rights and Freedoms has influenced these struggles.

Stone, Sharon. 1990. *Lesbians in Canada*. Toronto: Between the Lines. A collection of important articles on lesbian experience and struggle in Canada.

Notes

1. It is still technically the case that while most sexual acts can be engaged in at the age of 14, the age of consent is 18 for anal intercourse. This law has been challenged successfully on constitutional grounds in the courts in Ontario and Quebec. On 24 May 1995 the Ontario Court of Appeal released a decision agreeing with a constitutional challenge to the age of consent being set at 18. This decision made it more difficult for the police to arrest and for the courts to convict on anal sex charges in Ontario. The Federal Court of Canada upheld this decision and the Crown did not appeal the decision to the Supreme Court of Canada. Although the section has not been repealed by Parliament, it is now of 'no force and effect'.

2. In our contemporary society the transgendered movement, which attempts to bring together those groups who don't fit into our current two-gender system, also puts in question our current two-gender system. The transgendered movement can include those referred to as transsexuals, transvestites, cross-dressers, and others. See Bornstein (1994).

3. There are now groups such as Two-Spirited Peoples of the First Nations in Toronto and across the country.

4. In the conditions of capitalist exploitation that faced them the male-dominated sections of the working class fought for a 'family wage' to be paid to the male 'breadwinner', to exclude women from the waged workforce, and to construct a heterosexual 'respectable' family. This was also part of building a working-class heterosexual masculinity based on notions of skilled labour that was counterposed to both femininity and any form of male effeminacy. This came to construct particular forms of working-class heterosexism. See Kinsman (1996a: 56–61); D. Smith (1983).

5. All of the charges arising from the raid on Remington's were dropped except for those against the management. In December 1999 Remington's manager, Kenneth McKeigen, was convicted for 'permitting an indecent performance', 'keeping a common bawdy house', and 'knowingly permitting a premise to be used for the purposes of a common bawdy house' (Vincent, 1999). In 1999 the Bijou club was raided and a number of charges were laid by the police. Nineteen men were arrested for engaging in 'indecent acts' (consensual gay sex). After extensive community mobilization the charges were dropped (Pavelich, 1999).

6. These statistics are from Gay Court Watch in Toronto, which was formed to provide support for people arrested on gay-related charges.

7. In Sudbury, Mary Ross was discriminated against on the basis of her being a lesbian by a manager/owner at a Loeb grocery store in the early 1990s. Because of this discrimination she left her job on a disability leave and later filed a complaint with the human rights commission. In the end, even though commission workers had assured Ross that everything was fine with her complaint, the commission decided that the complaint had come in more than six months after the discrimination occurred and decided not to pursue it. Ross then launched other human rights complaints to try to get redress for the discrimination she faced (Kinsman, 1997a). At the time of writing Ross has finally arrived at a satisfactory settlement with the Loeb division of Provigo Distributing, Inc. She has another outstanding human rights complaint proceeding against the former manager/owner of the Loeb store.

8. Julian Fantino was the chief of police in London during Project Guardian. In 2000 he became the chief of police for Toronto despite opposition from many members of the gay/lesbian and other minority communities.

References

Adam, Barry D., and Alan Sears. 1996. *Experiencing HIV: Personal, Family and Work Relationships*. New York: Columbia University Press.

Adams, Mary Louise. 1997. *The Trouble with Normal: Postwar Youth and the Making of Heterosexuality*. Toronto: University of Toronto Press.

Altman, Dennis. 1986. *AIDS in the Mind of America*. Garden City, NY: Anchor Press/Doubleday.

Amadiume, Ifi. 1987. *Male Daughters, Female Husbands: Gender and Sex in an African Society*. London: Zed Press.

Andrews, Karen. 1995. 'Ancient Affections: Gays, Lesbians and Family Status', in Arnup (1995: 358–77).

Arnup, Katherine, ed. 1995. *Lesbian Parenting: Living With Pride and Prejudice*. Charlottetown: gynergy.

Bannerji, Himani. 1995. *Thinking Through*. Toronto: Women's Press.

Barclay, Clare, and Elaine Carol. 1992–3. 'Obscenity Chill: Artists in a Post-Butler Era', *Fuse* 16, 2 (Winter): 18–28.

Barnholden, Patrick. 1999. 'Does the "Straight" Jacket of the Family Fit You?', *New Socialist* 4, 3 (July–Aug.): 22–3.

Bayer, Ronald. 1981. *Homosexuality and American Psychiatry*. New York: Basic Books.

Bell, Shannon, and Joseph Couture. 2000. 'Justice and Law: Passion, Power, Prejudice, and So-called Pedophilia', in Dorothy E. Chunn and Dany Lacombe, eds, *Law as a Gendering Practice*. Toronto: Oxford University Press, 40–59.

Berube, Allan. 1990. *Coming Out Under Fire: The History of Gay Men and Women in World War Two*. New York: Free Press.

Blackbridge, Persimmon, and Sheila Gilhooly. 1985. *Still Sane*. Vancouver: Press Gang.

Blackwood, Evelyn. 1984. 'Sexuality and Gender in Certain North American Tribes: The Case of Cross-Gender Females', *Signs* 10, 1: 27–42.

———— and Saskia E. Wieringa, eds. 1999. *Female Desires, Same-Sex Relations, and Transgender Practices Across Cultures*. New York: Columbia University Press.

Bornstein, Kate. 1994. *Gender Outlaw: On Men, Women and the Rest of Us*. New York: Vintage/Random House.

Bray, Alan. 1982. *Homosexuality in Renaissance England*. London: Gay Men's Press.

Brown, Eleanor. 1992. 'Gay Sex Ruled Obscene: Court Rules Glad Days Porn is Degrading and Harmful', *Xtra!* no. 202 (24 July): 21.

Bunch, Charlotte. 1975. 'Not For Lesbians Only . . .', *Quest* 11, 2 (Fall).

Canadian AIDS Society. 1991. *Homophobia, Heterosexism and AIDS*. Ottawa.

Champagne, Robert, comp. 1987. *Jim Egan: Canada's Pioneer Gay Activist*. Toronto: Canadian Lesbian and Gay History Network.

Chauncey, George, Jr. 1982–3. 'From Sexual Inversion to Homosexuality: Medicine and the Changing Conceptualization of Female Deviance', *Salmagundi* (Fall-Winter): 144–5.

————. 1994. *Gay New York: Gender, Urban Culture and the Making of a Gay Male Erotic World, 1890–1940*. New York: Basic Books.

Cossman, Brenda. 1999. 'Wake Up Call, Activists light a stick of dynamite', *Xtra!* no. 371 (14 Jan.): 11.

————, Shannon Bell, Lise Gotell, and Becki Ross. 1997. *Bad Attitude/s on Trial: Pornography, Feminism, and the Butler Decision*. Toronto: University of Toronto Press.

Dawson, Brettel. 1994. in Mariana Valverde, comp., *Radically Rethinking Regulation Workshop Report*. Centre for Criminology, University of Toronto, 20–2.

D'Emilio, John. 1983. 'Capitalism and Gay Identity', in Snitow, Stansell, and Thompson, eds, *Powers of Desire: The Politics of Sexuality*. New York: Monthly Review Press, 100–13.

Directorate of Security and Intelligence (DSI). 1967–8. *Annual Report*.

Dover, K.J. 1980. *Greek Homosexuality*. New York: Vintage.

Duberman, Martin. 1991. *Cures: A Gay Man's Odyssey*. New York: Dutton.

————, Fred Eggan, and Richard Clements, eds. 1979. 'Documents in Hopi Indian Sexuality: Imperialism, Culture and Resistance', *Radical History Review* no. 20 (Spring-Summer): 99–130.

Egan, Jim. 1998. *Challenging the Conspiracy of Silence: My Life as a Canadian Gay Activist*, comp. and ed. Donald W. McLeod. Toronto: Canadian Lesbian and Gay Archives and Homewood Books.

Emke, Ivan. 1991. 'Speaking of AIDS in Canada: The Texts and Contexts of Official, Counter-Cultural and Mass Media Discourses Surrounding AIDS', Ph.D. thesis, Carleton University.

Faderman, Lillian. 1981. *Surpassing the Love of Men*. New York: William Morrow.

———. 1991. *Odd Girls and Twilight Lovers: A History of Lesbian Life in Twentieth-Century America*. New York: Columbia University Press.

Ferguson, Ann. 1981. 'Patriarchy, Sexual Identity and the Sexual Revolution', *Signs* 7, 1.

Findlay, Barbara. 1994. 'A lesbian's relationship is finally recognized, but only so that the government can deny her a welfare cheque', *Xtra!* no. 257 (2 Sept.): 15.

Filipenko, Cindy. 1994. 'Canada Customs Changes the Rules: Anal Sex Flip-flop Appears Timed to Influence Court Challenge', *Xtra!* no. 260 (14 Oct.): 1.

———. 1995. 'BC Grits Slam Adoption', *Xtra!* no. 276 (26 May): 12.

Forum 128. 1993. 'Young People and Sex', Toronto.

Foucault, Michel. 1980. *The History of Sexuality, Volume One: An Introduction*. New York: Vintage.

———. 1985. *The History of Sexuality, Volume Two: The Use of Pleasure*. New York: Pantheon.

Freedman, Estelle. 1979. 'Separatism as Strategy: Female Institution Building and American Feminism, 1870-1930', *Feminist Studies* 5, 3 (Fall): 512–29.

Fuller, Janine, and Stuart Blackley. 1995. *Restricted Entry: Censorship on Trial*. Vancouver: Press Gang.

Gay American Indians and Will Roscoe, eds. 1988. *Living the Spirit: A Gay American Indian Anthology*. New York: St Martin's Press.

Gay Flame. n.d. [early 1970s]. *Gay Liberation Meets the Shrinks*. Pamphlet no. 6. New York.

Greyson, John. 1995. 'After the Bath', CBC Newsworld, *Rough Cuts*, 5 May.

Halperin, David. 1990. *One Hundred Years of Homosexuality*. New York and London: Routledge.

Harry, Joseph. 1982. *Gay Children Grown Up: Gender Culture and Gender Deviance*. New York: Praeger.

Herdt, Gilbert, ed. 1996. *Third Sex, Third Gender: Beyond Sexual Dimorphism in Culture and History*. New York: Zone Books.

Herman, Didi. 1994. *Rights of Passage: Struggles for Lesbian and Gay Legal Equality*. Toronto: University of Toronto Press.

Jagoose, Annamarie. 1996. *Queer Theory: An Introduction*. New York: New York University Press.

Johnson, Kirsten. 1995. *Undressing the Canadian State: The Politics of Pornography from Hicklin to Butler*. Halifax: Fernwood.

Katz, Jonathan. 1976. *Gay American History*. New York: Thomas Y. Crowell.

———. 1983. *Gay/Lesbian Almanac*. New York: Harper and Row.

———. 1994. 'The Political Economy of Pleasure: Toward a Theory of the Socio-Historical Structure of Erotic Activity with special reference to Homosexuality', unpublished paper.

———. 1995. *The Invention of Heterosexuality*. New York: Dutton.

Kendall. 1999. 'Women in Lesotho and the (Western) Construction of Homophobia', in Blackwood and Wieringa (1999: 157–78).

Khayatt, Madiha Didi. 1992. *Lesbian Teachers: An Invisible Presence*. Albany: SUNY.

Kinsman, Gary. 1985. 'Porn/Censor Wars and the Battlefields of Sex', in *Issues of Censorship*. Toronto: A Space, 31–9.

————. 1991. '"Their Silence, Our Deaths": What Can the Social Sciences Offer to AIDS Research?', in Diane E. Goldstein, ed., *Talking AIDS*. St John's: Institute for Social and Economic Research Press, ISER Policy Papers No. 12, 39–60.

————. 1995. '"Character Weaknesses" and "Fruit Machines": Towards an Analysis of the Anti-Homosexual Campaign in the Canadian Civil Service', *Labour/Le Travail* 35 (Spring): 133–61.

————. 1996a. *The Regulation of Desire: Homo and Hetero Sexualities*. Montreal: Black Rose.

————. 1996b. '"Responsibility" as a Strategy of Governance: Regulating People Living With AIDS and Lesbians and Gay Men in Ontario', *Economy and Society* 25, 3 (Aug.): 393–409.

————. 1997a. 'Lesbian Rights Struggle Continues in Sudbury', *New Socialist* (July): 16.

————. 1997b. 'Managing AIDS Organizing: "Consultation," "Partnership," and "Responsibility" as Strategies of Regulation', in William K. Carrol, ed., *Organizing Dissent: Contemporary Social Movements in Theory and Practice*. Toronto: Garamond, 213–39.

————. 1998. 'Constructing Sexual Problems: "These Things May Lead To the Tragedy of Our Species"', in Wayne Antony and Les Samuelson, eds, *Power and Resistance*. Halifax: Fernwood, 256–82.

———— and Patrizia Gentile, with the assistance of Heidi McDonell and Mary Mahood-Greer. 1998. *'In the Interests of the State': The Anti-Gay, Anti-Lesbian National Security Campaign in Canada*. Sudbury: Laurentian University.

Kiss and Tell. 1991. *Drawing the Line: Lesbian Sexual Politics on the Wall*. Vancouver: Press Gang.

————. 1994. *Her Tongue on My Theory: Images, Essays and Fantasies*. Vancouver: Press Gang.

Lang, Sabine. 1999. 'Lesbians, Men-Women, and Two-Spirits: Homosexuality and Gender in Native American Cultures', in Blackwood and Wieringa (1999: 91–116).

Lindstrom, Jeff. 1995. 'Limited Adoption Rights Granted, But Appeal Could Still Be Filed After Election', *Xtra!* no. 276 (26 May): 12.

McCaskell, Tim. 1988. 'The Bath Raids and Gay Politics', in Frank Cunningham, Sue Findlay, et al., *Social Movements/Social Change: The Politics and Practice of Organizing*. Toronto: Between the Lines/Socialist Studies, 169–88.

Martindale, Kathleen. 1995. 'What Makes Lesbianism Thinkable? Theorizing Lesbianism from Adrienne Rich to Queer Theory', in Nancy Mandell, ed., *Feminist Issues: Race, Class and Sexuality*. Scarborough, Ont.: Prentice-Hall, 67–94.

Maynard, Steven. 1994. 'What Colour Is Your Underwear?: Class, Whiteness and Advertising', *Border/Lines* no. 32: 4–9.

Murray, Stephen O., and Will Roscoe, eds. 1998. *Boy-Wives and Female Husbands: Studies of African Homosexualities*. New York: St Martin's Press.

Mykhalovskiy, Eric, and George Smith. 1994. *Hooking Up To Social Services: A Report on the Barriers People with AIDS Face Accessing Social Services*. Toronto: Ontario Institute for Studies in Education/Community AIDS Treatment Information Exchange.

Nanda, Serena. 1996. 'Hirjas: An Alternative Sex and Gender Role in India', in Herdt (1996: 373–417).

Patton, Cindy. 1985. *Sex and Germs*. Montreal: Black Rose.

———. 1989. 'Resistance and the Erotic: Reclaiming History, Setting Strategy as We Face AIDS', in Peter Aggleton, Graham Hart, and Peter Davies, eds, *AIDS: Social Representations, Social Practices*. London: Falmer Press, 237–51.

———. 1990. *Inventing AIDS*. New York and London: Routledge.

———. 1996. *Fatal Advice: How Safe Sex Education Went Wrong*. Durham, NC: Duke University Press.

Pavelich, Greg. 1999. 'The Bijou Raid: The Battle for Queer Space', *New Socialist* 4, 5 (Nov.-Dec.): 23–4.

Rayside, David. 1988. 'Gay Rights and Family Values: The Passage of Bill 7 in Ontario', *Studies in Political Economy* no. 26 (Summer): 109–47.

———. 1998. *On the Fringe: Gays and Lesbians in Politics*. Ithaca, NY: Cornell University Press.

Rich, Adrienne. 1980. 'Compulsory Heterosexuality and Lesbian Existence', in Stimpson and Persons, eds, *Women, Sex and Sexuality*. Chicago: University of Chicago Press, 62–91.

Riordan, Michael. 1982. 'Blessed Are the Deviates: A Post-Therapy Check-up on My Ex-Psychatrist', in Ed Jackson and Stan Persky, eds, *Flaunting It!* Vancouver and Toronto: New Star/Pink Triangle Press, 14–20.

Roscoe, Will. 1991. *The Zuni Man-Woman*. Albuquerque: University of New Mexico Press.

———. 1996. 'How to Become a Berdache: Towards a Unified Analysis of Gender Diversity', in Herdt (1996: 329–72).

Ross, Becki. 1995. *The House That Jill Built: A Lesbian Nation in Formation*. Toronto: University of Toronto Press.

———. 1997. '"It's Merely Designed for Sexual Arousal": Interrogating the Indefensibility of Lesbian Smut', in Cossman et al. (1997: 152–98).

Rowe, William, and Bill Ryan, eds. 1998. *Social Work and HIV: The Canadian Experience*. Toronto: Oxford University Press.

Sanders, Doug. 1994. 'Constructing Lesbian and Gay Rights', *Canadian Journal of Law and Society* 9, 2 (Fall).

Sears, Alan. 1998. 'Queer Times?', *New Socialist* 3, 3 (June-July): 12–13, 25.

Simmons, Christina. 1979. 'Companionate Marriage and the Lesbian Threat', *Frontiers: A Journal of Women's Studies* 1, 3 (Fall).

Sinfield, Alan. 1998. *Gay and After*. London: Serpent's Tail.

Smith, Brian K. 1998. Interview on CBC radio national news, 14 Apr.

Smith, Dorothy E. 1983. 'Women, Class and Family', *The Socialist Register*. London: Merlin Press, 1–44.

———. 1987. *The Everyday World As Problematic*. Toronto: University of Toronto Press.

Smith, George. n.d. 'In Defence of Privacy', *Action!* 3, 1.

———. 1988. 'Policing the Gay Community: An Inquiry into Textually-Mediated Social Relations', *International Journal of Sociology and the Law* 16: 163–83.

———. 1990. 'Political Activist as Ethnographer', *Social Problems* 37, 4 (Nov.): 629–48.

Smith, Miriam. 1999. *Lesbian and Gay Rights in Canada: Social Movements and Equality-Seeking, 1971–1995*. Toronto: University of Toronto Press.

Sorfleet, Andrew, and Chris Bearchell. 1994. 'The sex police in a moral panic, how the "youth porn" law is being used to censor artists and prosecute youth sexuality', *Parallelograme* 20, 1: 8–21.

Stone, Sharon. 1990. *Lesbians in Canada.* Toronto: Between the Lines.

Ursel, Susan. 1995. 'Bill 167 and Full Human Rights', in Arnup (1995: 341–3).

Valverde, Mariana. 1985. *Sex, Power and Pleasure.* Toronto: Women's Press.

———— and Lorna Weir. 1985. 'Thrills, Chills and the "Lesbian Threat": Of the Media, the State and Women's Sexuality', in Varda Burstyn, ed., *Women Against Censorship.* Vancouver: Douglas & McIntyre, 99–106.

Vincent, Donovan. 1999. 'Gay Club's manager convicted', *Toronto Star*, 14 Dec., B5.

Warner, Tom. 1999. in 'Bill 5: "Same-Sex Partner" Law', *Outwards*, Coalition for Lesbian and Gay Rights in Ontario (Nov.): 1–2.

Weeks, Jeffrey. 1985. *Sexuality and Its Discontents.* London: Routledge.

Williams, Walter L. 1986. *The Spirit and the Flesh: Sexual Diversity in American Indian Culture.* Boston: Beacon Press.

Wilson, John. 1989. 'Spousal Benefits Conference: On Our Own Terms', *Rites* 6, 4 (Sept.): 4, 18.

Yeung, Tom. 1999. 'Why Not Plead Guilty? Pornographer avoided easy "artistic" defence', *Xtra!* no. 372 (28 Jan.): 11.

chapter nine

Youth: The Disinherited Generation

James E. Côté and
Anton L. Allahar

Capitalism in Early Twenty-first-Century Canada

As the unipolar 'New World Order' adjusts to the twenty-first century, a number of economic challenges face the globalization of capital and all the attendant social relations underlying this 'Order'. These challenges include grappling with problems of supply, expanding demand by creating viable consumer markets, securing access to raw materials, and, importantly, maintaining sources of cheap, pliable labour. Corporate survival has meant increased competition among the economic giants, who are doing all in their power to enhance their survivability in an age of cutthroat economic competition. A prime strategy in this regard has been the creation of super trading blocs such as the North American Free Trade Agreement (NAFTA), which appear to be setting the tone and direction of change for the new millennium. These responses to the economic challenges of global capitalism are having a decided effect on both the economic and non-economic spheres in societies around the globe.

This chapter extends arguments in two recent books (Côté and Allahar, 1996; Allahar and Côté, 1998) by examining the socio-economic impact of changes associated with this New World Order on a specific segment of contemporary society—youth. Using Canada as our primary focus, we assess the ways in which young people specifically have become the new losers in the struggles among the giant corporations and other dominant societal interests, each seeking to maximize its advantage and profitability.

The context in which the declining economic prospects of the young can be understood is historical and comparative relative to other exploited groups. In other words, at the same time that progress has been made with regard to the workplace rights of women and minority workers, capital has sought and found in the young a new source of cheap labour—essentially a youth proletariat. Criticisms of and objections to this are generally muted because, as a discrete socio-demographic group in Canada, young people have few legal and political resources and they are without economic protection or spokespersons.

To be competitive both locally and globally, corporations need to be in a position to cheapen their costs of production, to maintain high-quality products, and to gain the upper hand over their competitors in the marketplace. Because of their lack of options, young people constitute an ideal group to meet these corporate needs: they must work for low wages, often with few or no benefits, and they often can find only part-time jobs, thus ensuring that they gain little solidarity as a politically organized labour force.[1] In addition, they provide a much-needed market by spending their hard-earned wages on high-priced products offered by the big corporations. It is important to note, however, that big business could not, and does not, act alone: it is crucial for it to secure the co-operation of the state. And it does.

The state in the New World Order of global capitalism has a dual, though complementary, role to play. On the one hand, it is responsible for safeguarding the conditions under which capitalism is reproduced, that is, to ensure that both capital and labour, and the relationship between them, are not jeopardized. A capitalist can only be a capitalist to the extent that he or she employs wage labour and extracts surplus value from the latter. Without surplus value extraction there is no capitalism. Thus, the second role of the state is that of protecting the interests of the various fractions of the capitalist class. Accordingly, in representing the interests of labour, the state does not grant it the same rights as capital—far from it. The rights of labour and of capital are distinct, though related, and a primary task of the state is to ensure that they remain that way. This is usually accomplished through legislation, for the laws of the land are also responsible for framing the rights of labour and setting limits on its ability to challenge capital.

An examination of the laws passed and enforced in a capitalist society reveal just how the interests of the state and the capitalist class are intertwined.[2] The state has also historically sided with the capitalist class to bolster the dominant institutions (or dominant interests) such as schools, which prepare labour for its role in the society; police, courts, and prisons, which keep labour in check; and the religious institutions and the media, which prepare workers ideologically for fitting into their niches in the society. Thus, both historically and today, the relationship between the state and the youth segment of society has been to the advantage of capital and the dominant interests supporting it.

The Discovery of Youth

At the beginning of the twentieth century, people spent their years between ages 18 and 24 quite differently from the way they did as the century came to an end. For example, around 1900, only a small number of teens attended secondary schools, almost half were employed in the agricultural sector, and the rest were employed in clerical, manufacturing, and service industries—often making a living wage or close to it (Synge, 1979).[3] While many lived with their families, paid work was available (without many of the age prejudices we now witness), and considerable financial contributions were made by these young workers to their household or family unit (see Modell et al., 1976, for a comparable account for the US).

By the 1990s, the vast majority of teens attended secondary schools and over 60 per cent of secondary school graduates went directly to post-secondary institutions (Nobert and McDowell, 1994). However, only a minority in this age group were engaged in employment that was sufficiently well paid to afford them independence from their parents (less than one-third). Those who stayed with their parents rarely contributed much financially, and they made only minor contributions to the household labour (although young females did more housework than young males), leaving them free to pursue various leisure activities (White, 1994; Modell et al., 1976). Instead, their parents often subsidized them with free or cheap room and board, and with allowances, and their mothers often provided 'free domestic services'.

What happened over the twentieth century to transform young people into economic and political dependants of the family, the educational system, and the state? And on what basis were young people denied the opportunity to contribute to the society and economy to their full productive capacities?

As a consequence of industrialization, especially given advances in mass production, the labour of the young was no longer needed in the same way and to the same extent as in the pre-industrial and early industrial eras, when they were integral to the economy and were typically granted semi- to full autonomy during their teen years (Steinberg, 1990). Among other things, the young were victims of 'technological displacement' as techniques of mass production were refined by owners and managers of capital intent on increasing profit (Rifkin, 1995). The tremendous increase in profit that kept the engines of capitalism running during the twentieth century were in large part based on mechanization and computerization. In the manufacturing sector, for example, robots replaced many factory workers, while in the service sector the computer supplanted both clerical and service workers. Although technologies have displaced workers of all ages, the youth segment was particularly hard hit.

The technologization of the labour process, aided by concerted assaults on unions by big business and government, tended to carve the middle out of the labour force. Consequently, workers are now increasingly in greatest demand at either pole of the occupational skills continuum. Rifkin (1995) argues that this polarization is reshaping the class structure of advanced industrial societies (on Canada, see Morissette et al., 1993; Myles et al., 1988). As this happens, current and successive youth cohorts must face the prospect that they will not do as well as their parents financially or occupationally. In fact, the middle-class affluence of the second half of the twentieth century may be beyond the reach of most. Rifkin argues that up to 80 per cent of new workers will be needed in the lower occupational stratum, particularly in the service work that is not worth the cost of mechanization given the available pools of cheap labour. Accordingly, only about 20 per cent of workers may reach the upper stratum, where considerable expertise is needed to design and maintain the technology and to manage complex technical systems. Echoing Rifkin, Picot and Myles (1996: 17) argue that in Canada this 'increased polarization of earnings has been among the most significant economic developments of the past two decades.'

During mid- and late nineteenth century the young were displaced from the workforce by the *first wave* of technological advances in mechanization, and consequently an increasingly idle youth population came to be viewed by many social and political leaders as a problem in need of social control. This development was to affect public policy thereafter. In addition, the misbehaviours among some of the idle youth eventually drew the attention of social scientists and mental health experts, who were looking for objects of study and clients for their fledgling professions. In the spirit of those times, 'misbehaviour' among some young people was defined as a biological problem for *all* young people—'adolescent storm and stress' resulting from the hormonal fallout of puberty (Côté, 1994; Mead, 1928). Thus, the period of adolescence itself was 'discovered' by so-called experts as a distinct and universal period of the life cycle with its own properties and problems. However, the social and economic contexts producing adolescent behaviour were mistakenly downplayed by many, especially in psychiatry and psychology (Proefrock, 1981). These beliefs about adolescence have only recently been debunked as research has exposed purely biological explanations of the (mis)behaviours of teenagers as erroneous (Petersen, 1993).

The images produced by those who reified adolescence as a stage of problematic behaviour, through which all must inevitably pass in the course of 'normal' development, provided the basis of an ideology that was used throughout the century to justify a further *de jure* exclusion of the young from the workforce, as well as their segregation in schools. With this development, the interests of social scientists and mental health practitioners complemented those of educators, who were also trying to legitimate and expand their fledgling profession. The consequence of these combined efforts has been to prolong adolescence in a *de facto* manner so that it extends into the twenties for those who follow newly established institutional routes to the workforce. For example, the expansion of the higher education system during the 1950s and 1960s has produced the period that some now call 'youth', essentially extending the dependencies of teens into their twenties (Keniston, 1975; Klein, 1990).

Now, a significant proportion of the population is denied full participation in mainstream society because of ageist assumptions based in part on faulty beliefs that youthfulness is a form of incapacity. As Melton (1991: 931) notes, 'limitations on adolescents' rights have been premised on unsupportable assumptions about adolescents' competence as decision makers, [and] the vulnerability of adolescents.' The (*de facto*) limitation of the rights of increasing numbers of those in their twenties (now called youth, or young adults) has more recently been justified in terms of the belief that higher education is universally positive as part of a status transition to adulthood.

This institutionalized delay of adulthood undoubtedly has many positive features, but those who would rather not, or cannot, take advantage of it often find themselves having to 'wait' anyway, and this wait often has negative consequences (Petersen, 1993). Thus, a pattern of enforced idleness, or of reduced contribution to the community, now characterizes youth, compelling many to live with their parents as dependants well into their twenties. In Canada, for example, this represents two-thirds of those (unmarried) in their early twenties and one-third of those in their late twenties. The resulting custom whereby parents perform the role of 'safety nets' for their adult children is increasingly taken as a normal and natural sequence of events in Canada.

The Conquest of Youth

Having a large proportion of the population kept in a state of semi- or full dependency may seem like an entirely unintended consequence of social change. Indeed, while it might not have been planned, it certainly complements dominant interests, including bureaucracies, by giving them an army of clients, and big business, by giving them mass markets of identity-hungry consumers. This *disenfranchisement*, or the conquest of youth, has created a virtually powerless social group with few public defenders. Unlike women and racial minorities, it is now legitimate to continue speaking of the young as biologically inferior, with inherent mental problems (ostensibly caused by raging hormones), and to have their biological inferiority used to justify their unequal treatment in society.

The notion of the 'conquest of youth' can be readily illustrated in the following example concerning wage levels. Changes in wages over the past 25 years demonstrate a steady and significant redistribution of wealth in Canada. In the mid-1970s, minimum wage would have put one about 40 per cent *above* the official poverty line; now it puts one 30 per cent *below* that line. However, the telling fact here is that two of three minimum wage-earners are under 24 years of age. Clearly, the state has been on the side of capital in legislating minimum wage rates. Interestingly, few people are aware of this, and many of those who are see no reason to be concerned about it. The idea of 'youth as proletariat' is by no means new, but in the present era it is given a renewed vigour. Left without official spokespersons and personal lobbyists, the youth segment emerges as more vulnerable than traditional labour.

Because their exploitation can produce a sense of alienation and discontent among the young, corporate and government leaders must take care to control or diffuse disaffection so that it does not provoke open revolt. This is not only in terms of preventing open violence, such as rioting by the unemployed and homeless (see Sheridan, 1996, for an analysis of the periodic rioting in Quebec), but also because the youth segment constitutes a large market. According to Palladino (1996), in the US, teenagers constitute 'a red-hot consumer market worth $89 billion', not counting the $200 billion their parents spend on them. This is a tenfold increase over the past 40 years. Astonishingly, this sum is greater than the official US defence budget.

While the low wages paid to youth directly enhance the profits of the corporate sector, so, too, does the consumerism of youth, many of whom appear to have an insatiable drive to acquire a seemingly endless collection of material goods and to purchase myriad services. This makes young people major players in the multi-billion-dollar market of youth 'identity-commodities', and as such they are targeted by the various media that seek to promote the ideology and mentality of consumerism. These media attempt to sell young people some superficial element of an identity that they are missing or have been taught to crave. And while this ought not to be seen as part of some grand conspiracy against youth, it has been made possible precisely because the basis for a viable identity has been denied young people through a series of laws, customs, and institutional practices. With this in place, 'identity packages' are carefully researched, marketed, and sold back to them as commodities that ostensibly provide a means of demonstrating 'individuality' or 'individual identity'.

During the twentieth century mass marketers learned how to feed off young people's agency and resistance by appropriating them at each turn by marketing products as 'hip' or 'cool'. Thomas Frank (1997a) documents these marketing tricks in his recent book, *The Conquest of Cool: Business Culture, Counterculture, and the Rise of Hip Consumerism*. Frank notes how marketers used the concepts of 'cool' and 'hip' to trick the mass consumer into believing that he or she could be set apart from the masses and meaningfully react against a standardizing and exploitative establishment. The chief marketing strategy documented by Frank (1997b) is 'liberation marketing', which tacitly admits that business now rules the world, but its own products or services can liberate consumers from this oppression, if only momentarily (e.g., shampoos that give women orgasms in public or soft drinks that enable impossible stunts). Marketers have also nurtured new brand loyalties that provide models of existential rebellion, in which a product is used as an expression of resistance against, or escape from, the drudgeries of work and urban life. They have also worked to create brand identities, which help consumers to assimilate a product into their own sense of identity (e.g., Apple computers attempt to appeal to those who have a humanistic vision of the future, or Benetton clothing appeals to a libertarian vision, achievable by overthrowing communication conventions).

Frank argues that business culture is replacing civil society and that corporations are the dominant institutions of our time, replacing the nation-state. He refers to the US as the 'Republic of Business' run by a 'corporocracy' that does not 'demand order, conformity, grey clothes, and Muzak; it presents itself as an opponent to those very things.' In fact, for him the 'defining fact of American life in the 1990s is its complete reorganization around the needs of corporations. The world of business, it seems, is becoming the world, period. The market is politics, the office is society, the brand is equivalent human identity' (1997b: 44). He goes on to argue that 'advertising is taking over the cultural functions that used to be filled by the left. Dreaming of a better world is now the work of marketers. We used to have movements for change; now we have products' (ibid., 47).

As a consequence of the above trends, leisure industries such as music, fashion, and cosmetics now have a virtual army of consumers awaiting the next craze or fad. But youth culture is now mostly a fabrication of corporate R&D (research and development) and marketing. Corporations now have the benefit of several cohorts of highly educated business and social science graduates,[4] whom they hire to monitor, imitate, and commodify expressions of youth dissent. Hence, whenever signs of protest emerge, they are skilfully manipulated and made to appear 'chic' and part of mainstream culture, as youth who are looking for validation from their peers adopt these mass-produced 'identity kits' and maintain the illusion that these are a mark of 'individuality'. This process of commodifying dissent and distracting young people with trivial 'identity pursuits' keeps their sense of agency focused on making choices about day-to-day concerns such as how to act and what to wear and, in so doing, diverts them from exercising 'political agency' against the many social, economic, and political injustices that affect their current lives and future prospects.

Complementarity and the Social Control of Dissent

It is politically expedient that the injustices cited above are not perceived as such by those who are most affected. Therefore, the commodification of dissent is directly related to the questions of social order and social control as they serve to channel and redirect potential youth anger. To ensure social control under the conditions described above, it is crucial that the disenfranchised youth of Canada (and elsewhere) not recognize their experiences as apathy and disaffection and that they not see themselves as unwitting pawns in a system that does not have much respect for them. This speaks to the politics of language, for if disaffection with the system could be defined as freedom to disengage, if freedom (personal agency) is defined as the ability to choose to spend their money on an endless array of youth identity-items such as running shoes, compact discs, and designer clothes, and if apathy is defined as freedom *not* to participate meaningfully in the dominant institutions of their society (political agency), then the task of social control is complete. The manipulated (youth) do not even perceive the extent of their disenfranchisement, and those who stand to benefit from such manipulation and disenfranchisement escape unscathed.

But how is this acceptance of the status quo engineered? Aldous Huxley laid out the general formula nearly 70 years ago as he witnessed the early implications of social scientific knowledge informing social control techniques. He could well have been referring to today's Canadian youth when he wrote: 'To make them love it is the task assigned, in present-day totalitarian states, to ministries of propaganda, newspaper editors and schoolteachers' (1932: 12). This form of social engineering is akin to the situation in Western, liberal democratic countries today where newspaper and TV editors censor and sanitize the news; schoolteachers indoctrinate students religiously and politically; and 'ministries of propaganda' package politicians and sell everything from pet rocks to vacation trips to the moon.

The point Huxley makes, then, is valid not only for totalitarian societies everywhere, but also for various Western societies where control and manipulation of the populations are more cleverly disguised (Herman and Chomsky, 1988). That such control and manipulation are not usually seen to be applicable to the Western 'democracies', however, suggests that the process is ideologically masked in those societies.

From the perspective of youth in advanced industrial society, the corporate-consumer 'plan' is clear: disenfranchised and potentially disruptive groups need to be distracted from a clear understanding of their disenfranchisement. And the most efficient form of such distraction is ideological, for a distracted population is beneficial or *complementary* to the interests of those who wish to rule. Force should be used only as a last resort since it produces resentment and could potentially lead to an order that is continually contested, whether in an overt or a clandestine manner. The political challenge for the successful rulers, then, is to secure the consent of the ruled (in this case youth), at the same time ensuring that those who are ruled do not perceive themselves as being controlled or manipulated.

To understand fully the manner in which this type of hegemony (rule by consent) is effected, we invoke the concept of complementarity, as elaborated in the writings of Bernd Baldus (1975, 1977). This concept is closely related to concerns with social control and legitimacy. Baldus argues that social control can be effected in one of two ways: either physically, via the deliberate intervention of some body or agency, or more subtly and ideologically by the manipulation of what he calls 'complementary conditions'. Physical control and ideological control differ in both form and content. Ideological control is slower to effect, more indirect, less easily resisted, but more difficult to escape once it is established. This makes ideological control more effective—it is less likely to produce protest on the part of the controlled, while those in control do not generally suffer the loss of legitimacy.

As a strategy of control, the manipulation of 'complementary conditions' involves either the use of existing patterns of behaviour within the population and society at large or the deliberate creation of such behaviour patterns. Those with power and something to gain seek to discover specific types of behaviour engaged in by the 'target' population, in this case youth, with a view to seeing whether or not such behaviour complements or furthers their interests. Where it is complementary it will be encouraged, used, or exploited; and where such patterns of behaviour do not exist beforehand, vested interests will attempt to ascertain the possibilities of creating them. In the case of 'youth as consumer' this task might be seen as falling to the media and advertising industries. On the other hand, where a pattern of behaviour exists that appears inimical to the dominant interests, steps are taken to modify or eliminate it. This latter option is often more related to the question of physical force: police, courts, prisons. An instance of this might be seen in the case of the so-called 'squeegee kids' in Ontario, whose behaviour is now outlawed and criminalized.

Therefore, the widespread political apathy among the youth segment of the population can be seen as quite complementary to the interests of the dominant class, for the activities of the latter are seldom seriously questioned or challenged. In addition, the rise of the so-called 'me generation', which promotes an ideology of individualism, has been accompanied by a parallel decline in political involvement on the part of young people. Unlike the 1960s when a large segment of the youth culture sought to question authority and to defy the Establishment, the 1980s and 1990s witnessed a progressive disengagement of youth from serious concern with the political processes that govern their lives. Instead, there has been a heightened concern with consumption and acquiring material possessions (Green and Astin, 1985). Canadian youth are not generally schooled or encouraged in the educational system to think critically and beyond the narrow confines of personal materialism and consumerism, from which big business is the principal beneficiary.

We must stress, however, that the young are not to be individually blamed, even though they have the potential to resist. Rather, their political apathy and personal self-interest, which are complementary to the dominant economic and political interests, have been systematically manufactured by the principal institutions in the society: mass education, the mass media, and the mass entertainment industry. The political importance of distracting the potentially powerful masses (youth, workers, unemployed) from a realization of their true sources of oppression is clear. Such distraction is a powerful form of social control, which is indispensable for the securing of social order and also for the preservation of those conditions that enable the reproduction of capital and profits.

But in the same way that political apathy is complementary to vested interests, so, too, is the general level of illiteracy. Illiteracy has reached what some call outlandish proportions (e.g., Hargreaves and Goodson, 1992). In a resource-rich country such as Canada, for example, as many as 40 per cent of those who begin high school either drop out or graduate as functional illiterates (i.e., they cannot perform the basic reading and arithmetic tasks required for independent functioning). The sincerity of governments with recent school reforms is questionable, especially when teachers and other educational professionals argue that the reforms are likely to exacerbate an already bad situation. When class size expands, when teachers are laid off, when overall educational expenditures are drastically cut, and when morale in the institution hits an all-time low, one is only left to wonder on whose 'side' the government really stands: students, or those who benefit from illiteracy, deskilling, and apathy! Moreover, while these so-called reforms have been going on, the education system has degenerated to the point where students are increasingly being bribed just to go to classes where they are increasingly met with armed guards, metal detectors, and/or the risk of violence from belligerent schoolmates.[5]

While many thousands of young males contribute to a multimillion-dollar industry that produces hockey, football, baseball, and basketball cards, and while many can recite the batting, catching, pitching, and scoring statistics of individual players, a significant proportion do not know multiplication tables. And the same applies to those who know the lyrics to the latest popular song but who are seemingly unable to memorize a poem or remember historical events. But there are additional forms of political numbing aimed at the youth and other powerless segments of Western societies. The sports and entertainment industries are able to maintain a level of hype and distraction that is almost perpetual. Quite apart from the whole video revolution in music and interactive arcade-type games, and the compact disc and Walkman gadgets that enable individuals to tune out the rest of the society around them, youth are fed a steady diet of flashy concert tours that are matched in pomp and ceremony only by the highest levels of sporting rivalries: the Super Bowl, the Grey Cup, the Stanley Cup, the World Series, the National Basketball Association (NBA) finals, not to mention the glitzy and enormously popular WWF matches. These are featured year-round and serve as powerful distractions.

With salaries many times higher than the highest-paid politicians and economic actors, movie stars and sports figures assume cult-like stature that the average young person is able to identify with vicariously. It is a sort of make-believe world that the average individual can dream about, taking comfort in the knowledge that he or she could have made it, for the most commonly repeated stories about these popular culture icons stress their 'rags to riches' ascent of the social and economic ladders.

If the people are suitably disinterested and uninformed, the job of managing the population is made that much easier.[6] And because distraction and ignorance among the bulk of the population are complementary to vested interests, it is easy to see why so much emphasis is placed on the entertainment and sports industries: they make billions of dollars for those concerned; they are politically useful as distractions; and they enable non-disruptive dreams even among the least fortunate members of society. This is not to say, however, that such things as sports and movies were designed specifically for this purpose; rather, they are examples of behaviours and practices that become complementary to certain vested interests. Conversely, if such conditions did not exist beforehand, they could be created via the manipulation of such institutions as public education, advertising, and the mass media.

What is important for this type of ideological control is not the personal meanings that youth might attach to their behaviour; rather, it is the political outcomes of that behaviour. For example, if young people *think* that rap music is pointedly critical of the system, and if it provides some release and grants some satisfaction in terms of exercising their sense of personal agency, that is fine. To the extent that their protests go nowhere politically and economically, they are left alone by the authorities, recording companies produce and sell their records, and everyone is content. However, if the young performers of rap music chose to act politically on the message of their lyrics, then it would be a different matter and force might be brought into the picture. In the public's mind, the illusion of 'freedom' contained in the liberal Charter of Rights and Freedoms masks a clear realization of their economic disenfranchisement and political manipulation. In other words, the notion of freedom contained in such so-called rights to free speech, free association, and a free press merely mystifies the powerless by leading them to believe that they are indeed free and equal with all others in the society when in actuality they are not. Freedom thus conceived is ideological.

Complementarity and Mass Society

Corporate capitalism flourishes when tastes and lifestyles spread among a sizeable proportion of the population. When this happens consumption becomes more predictable and, therefore, more manageable and profitable. Goods and services can be mass-produced with a confidence that they will be mass-consumed. As with other generations of the twentieth century, young people today have been targeted as members of a 'mass society'—a large group of people with homogeneous tastes, desires, and opinions. The difference with the current cohort is that, with new technologies, the techniques for producing mass behaviours have become more and more sophisticated, and therefore their impact is more effective and widespread (Côté and Allahar, 1996).

Young people are voracious consumers of various mass media, now absorbing up to 55 hours per week (Strasburger and Donnerstein, 1999). In the early twentieth century, adult concerns over the content of the messages directed at the young emerged with the introduction of low-tech media like pocket novels, comic books, magazines, and movies. Since the 1950s, adults have raised issues over the effects of TV and popular music, and more recently, movie videos, video games, and the Internet. Much of this apprehension has involved the fear that some sort of moral degeneration will take place when young people are exposed to 'adult' themes. Our concern here, however, is not with shielding young people from 'adult' material; to the contrary, our interest is with the indoctrination of the young into an ethos of consumerism, conformism, and immediate gratification. Dominant economic interests have shaped these media to produce such an ethos, at the expense of a critical consciousness among the young concerning larger issues of personal and social responsibility. Following the principle of complementarity, those aspects of youth behaviour that suit dominant economic interests are encouraged, while those that threaten those interests are discouraged.

Fashion magazines directed at young women—teenzines—socialize them to intensify their feminine characteristics with cosmetics and fashionable clothing. One response to these magazines is to argue that they are simply meeting a market demand because young women want them. Another response is that these magazines are specifically designed to *create* a mass consciousness among young women that is only then defined as a need.

Of course, the control of advertisers over the media varies by degree. Yet, few would dispute that advertisers have an interest in producing an ethos of mass consumption (Ewen, 1976; Herman and Chomsky, 1988; Rifkin, 1995). Countless examples of media manipulation of the young could be cited, as is the case with cigarette and beer ads (Schultze et al., 1991); suffice it to say, however, that the various mass media share a vested interest in creating and maintaining a certain mass consciousness among the young. Some of these media do so as agents for other economic interests (e.g., television programs, teenzines, and fashion magazines) while others do it directly for themselves (e.g., the music industry, including MTV in the US and MuchMusic in Canada—TV channels devoted entirely to this task).

In sum, then, these media play an integral role in creating mass consumer demand and also in effecting social control by distracting and stifling dissent among a potentially powerful and disruptive segment of the population.

The principle of complementarity applied to the mass manipulation of youth is also clearly illustrated via an analysis of the public education system. Such an analysis shows that the public system was developed to suit the traditional interests of dominant economic and social groups, which simultaneously resisted and discouraged developments that went counter to their interests. Schools currently contain, shape, and condition young people; this prepares a good proportion of them to be part of a passive and uncritical workforce, which is crucial to the functioning of industrial societies. In Canada, there is a tendency to accept mass education as inevitable and necessary, but such a view clearly plays into the hands of those managing the status quo, for if mass indoctrination and mass processing can pass for education, then the indoctrinators and processors will encounter little real challenge to their authority.

Furthermore, Canadian society has unmistakably become one in which most occupational roles require credentials formally granted by specially designated bureaucracies. Except in a few surviving apprenticeships, it is no longer considered appropriate that workers acquire their qualifications and skills in the workplace. At the same time, the primary reason for keeping students in school for longer periods of time *is not* to ensure that they are better trained in terms of advanced skills, except for the minority who go on to highly specialized fields. It is just as much for the sake of others, namely, schools and their employees, professional associations, and dominant economic interests. Moreover, the sequestering of young people in schools protects the community from disruptions that might occur if young people were idle and legitimately keeps them out of the labour force as potential competitors with older workers.

In brief, Canada's modern mass education system has benefited big business and big government far more than it has benefited the so-called 'masses' who have been subjected to it. This educational monopoly has produced an education inflation by which the value of lower levels of education decreases as more individuals obtain higher levels. Consequently, as more university degrees have flooded the market, the value of these degrees has decreased and increasing numbers of graduates have become underemployed (almost 50 per cent of university graduates in Canada find themselves in jobs that do not require university-level credentials). Thus, professions have required increasingly higher qualifications for entrance without a proportionate increase in direct skill acquisition. In addition, the growing costs associated with entering professional programs have kept their enrolment levels low and have enabled the professions to maintain their high prestige and income levels as more individuals are competing for educational credentials with less chance of success. This is particularly true for those not from middle- or upper-class backgrounds (Allahar and Côté, 1998: 23–59; de Broucker and Lavallée, 1998).

Those who scramble for credentials must endure years of socialization to qualify as workers who are suited for jobs over which they have little or no control (i.e., they are prepared for alienated labour). Hence, the emphasis on rigid training for the requirements of the industrial and business workplace, which often require punctuality, self-discipline, and an uncritical willingness to do whatever is required, no matter how demeaning, mind-numbing, or unethical. Such training also requires of students the suppression of independent, critical thinking about corporate-capitalist society. Those who resist this socialization in educational settings generally find themselves excluded from all but the most menial work.

The Manufacture of Dissent

The strategy of distraction does not always work as part of the attempt to manufacture consent. Indeed, when attempts to manufacture consent backfire, dissent can be inadvertently manufactured. This is especially the case when those targeted are insufficiently rewarded for their conformity, as Aldous Huxley wrote in *Brave New World*. The more serious and threatening forms of youth dissent that have emerged in acts of both individual and gang violence bear testimony to this. Rates of violent youth crime have risen steadily since the mid-1980s, at twice the rate of rise of violent adult crime (Frank, 1992). Since the 1980s, American-style youth gang violence has been spreading through Canadian cities.

In the past decade, therefore, we have seen unintended consequences of the 'discovery and conquest of youth' in their dissent and resistance. This dissent is increasingly externalized in violence and riots, but it has more often been internalized in drug use, gang membership, and dropping out of school or displayed through shocking hairstyles, body piercing, and tattoos, effectively locking them out of the adult labour force. This latter form of dissent may be seen as a non-violent protest and resistance by which the young refuse to co-operate in their own subjugation.

In addition to not providing sufficient rewards for conformity, the attempt to manufacture consent may not be fully effective owing to the human capacity for agency: the ability for people to think purposively and deliberately and to act in a self-determining manner (see Wyn and White, 1998; Rudd and Evans, 1998). In their personal lives and through political movements, people have demonstrated this potential throughout history. However, the ability to exercise agency in the sense discussed here is sometimes a precarious matter because it is easily subverted by social pressures from peers, parents, teachers, or advertisers. More recently, corporate interests have developed extremely effective techniques for subverting this form of agency and replacing it with conformist thoughts and behaviours that only appear purposive and deliberate. The high-technology society we live in today provides the perfected tools necessary for those with power and money to undermine systematically people's potential for exercising agency by permeating the consciousness of individuals and the content of the social patterns of daily life.

In the past, these efforts to manufacture consent were less obvious because of their insidiousness; now they are so commonplace there is little attempt to disguise them. The trick is to keep people focused on immediate short-term concerns, like their appearance and how much fun they are having. This gives people a sense of personal agency, but there is little chance that they will have any impact on the political economy. Meanwhile, those who manipulate the political economy manufacture the options people have to address their immediate short-term concerns, such as their appearance and entertainment choices. From a political economy perspective, then, we can see how mass conformity is experienced by individuals as a freedom of choice. It is simply a 'multiple-choice' freedom, however, with the answers determined in advance.

As an example, consider the recent commodification of feminism and female political identity under the term 'girl power', popularized by the wildly successful British singing group, the Spice Girls. Capitalizing on the contemporary popularity of feminist politics and the increasing desire of females to assert their agency in matters of personal freedom of choice and independence of actions, the Spice Girls speak (or really sing) to a whole generation of young women and girls. However, they do so in a superficial and politically irresponsible way, seeking to convince them that they control their own lives and destinies when most of them do not. The control portrayed is often over their appearance and sexuality, which in turn are directed at potential boyfriends who are the objects of competition among these supposedly empowered girls.

What we believe is happening here is the manipulation of the notion of free choice and its redefinition to mean 'freedom of consumer choice'. In essence, however, the choice these young girls are given is really quite empty. It is either to buy or not buy a set of glitzy, prepackaged images of the Spice Girls, who were themselves recruited, trained, and marketed, along with expensive dolls, clothes, posters, and compact discs that represent a multimillion-dollar industry to the creators and owners of the Spice Girls—yes, the creators and owners. The Spice Girls are a product of a long-term marketing strategy, backed by capital, in which a large number of young women auditioned and a few were selected for their looks and trained how to sing and perform on stage in a bold and sexual manner. Clearly, the Spice Girls are a marketing vehicle, and their 'girl power' is not a means to achieve social and political justice for women.

Ideologically, then, what is at work here is the manufacture of consent and consumer compliance, as the young people who assert 'girl power' are simply asserting their right to make their own decisions around purchasing and consuming 'identity commodities' and to fight with each other over who has the coolest or hottest boyfriend. This new-found assertiveness, which is not accompanied by an appropriate impulse control, results in spending behaviour that greatly *complements* the interests of those who own and manage the associated industries. Thus, whether or not the creators of the Spice Girls deliberately set out to change the mass consciousness of teenage girls and young women is not important. At the same time, no one can disagree that they set out to make money by influencing the behaviour of this gender and age group. What is important, however, from the perspective of the earlier discussion of complementarity, is that the Spice Girls have influenced the economic behaviour, spending habits, and sense of identity among a large proportion of a whole generation of young females.

One particularly disturbing trend that may be associated with 'girl power' is the apparent rise in violence among young females as they fight with each other over their (unstable) images, possessions, and even boyfriends (Cox, 1998; Artz, 1998). These fights are no longer simply verbal, but have escalated to the types of fist fights and brawls that used to be found mainly among young males who were fighting over girlfriends. In the recent past, media and anecdotal reports of such incidents became more frequent, but the problem of violence among teenage girls is getting more social scientific attention. For example, Artz (1998: 14–15) reports that 'while the population of adolescents in British Columbia increased at a rate of 6 per cent [between 1986 and 1993], the number of male youths charged with assault increased 118 per cent . . . and the number of female youth charged increased by 250 per cent.' Artz notes that by 1993, females accounted for 42 per cent of all assault charges laid against youths, compared with 26 per cent in 1986. Similar statistics apply for the rest of Canada (a 190 per cent increase for females versus 117 per cent for males) and the US. In her own survey of students, 20.9 per cent of females (and 51.9 per cent of males) admitted to beating up a peer once or twice in the last year. While ratios reported during the 1980s of male/female violence of this sort were 4:1, Artz's ratio from 1994 was under 2.5:1, reflecting the increasing arrest trends.

Obviously, we are not blaming the Spice Girls for increases in female violence, but, wittingly or unwittingly, they definitely play a part in the new climate of sex and violence that is fast engulfing young females today. According to Cox (1998), teenage girls are under pressure to look sexy in whatever they do, and they look to the various media for images and role models as examples. Since sex and looking sexy are the primary messages from sources like the Spice Girls, those who are unsuccessful at achieving the level of attractiveness and power portrayed by these sources experience anger and frustration. This frustration brews and finds outlets mainly with peers who are seen as competitors or who are used as scapegoats. Sometimes the violence is one-to-one and sometimes it involves a group of girls ganging up on one targeted girl. In schools, many young women now find themselves literally and figuratively 'running the gauntlet' among their in-group and out-group peers.

In sum, what we are witnessing here is not the nurturing of solid feminist concerns over responsible self-determination and impulse control coupled with empathetic social responsibility, but a side-effect distortion of these into pathological social and behavioural patterns where self-restraint and empathy are mocked. The Spice Girls are but one part of a larger picture in which teenage girls have been influenced by consumer-corporate interests: consent has been manufactured among many girls as they buy corporate products, but dissent has also been manufactured as many of the same girls strike out at each other in frustration when they cannot experience the ideals of popularity and pleasure promised by these products.

Intergenerational Disparities

A major negative consequence of the attempts to manufacture consent around youth as marginal worker/mindless consumer is the lack of recognition of increasing intergenerational disparities. As we have argued, the decreasing marginal utility of the young worker has been exacerbated by changes in the technologies affecting the industrial production of goods and services. Even in the service sector, which now provides most new jobs, computer technologies continue to reduce both the number of workers required and the skill levels needed to perform service jobs. Consequently, these technological trends have tended to carve the middle out of the labour force so that workers have been in greatest demand at either pole.

Whatever the future might hold, it appears that for now the bargaining power of the young worker has been seriously reduced. In spite of being the most educated generation in Canadian history (Fournier et al., 1994; Saunders, 1996), many young workers find themselves unable even to get a foothold in the workforce, let alone pursue the types of careers that their educators and parents told them constitute the basis of happiness and success. Let us examine recent trends in more detail.

The Workplace: Youth Proletarianization

The troubled fortunes of the young can be most readily illustrated with respect to their diminishing opportunities and roles in the workplace. We note that they have recently experienced declining wages, reduced participation, and job ghettoization.

Declining Wages

Over the past 25 years there has been a steady and significant redistribution of wealth by age. For example, in the late 1960s, males aged 16–24 earned incomes that were about on par with those over 24 years of age, depending on the job (see Howe and Strauss, 1993, for US figures). Picot and Myles (1996: 17) show how the various age groups in Canada began at more or less the same wage levels in 1969, but since then there has been a steady and linear differentiation among them. By 1993, the 17–24 age group was only making about 5 per cent more than it did in 1969, while the oldest age groups were making about 30 per cent more. Adjusting for inflation, the annual earnings of those in the 17–24 age group declined by about 19 per cent, while earnings for those in the 25–34 age group fell by 10 per cent. A comparable age-based wage redistribution has been taking place for women (Logan and Belliveau, 1995: 26; Betcherman and Morissette, 1994). There is now little question about whether this is a 'real' trend, for as Morissette et al. (1993: 9) note, 'the declining earnings of younger workers is the most robust finding in the literature.'

These trends are illustrated in Table 9.1, which shows the age-based redistribution of wealth in Canada during the 1980s. These figures suggest that, contrary to media claims, what is taking place is more than a simple competition for resources between the so-called baby boomers and Generation Xers. Rather, the redistribution of wealth is continuous along age lines. Economic benefits accrued to those in the 45 and over cohorts, but in 1991 the early baby boomers were just reaching that age threshold. Contrary to public perception, the early baby-boom cohort (aged 35–44 in 1991) actually suffered losses in the 1980s. Moreover, the later baby-boom cohort (aged 25–34 in 1991) suffered even more losses. However, both cohorts were not hit as hard as the so-called Gen-X cohort (aged 25 and younger). Finally, it is telling that the groups making the bulk of the decisions about wages, benefits, etc. (those 45 and over—the cohorts before baby boomers) were the only ones who made gains during this period. On this issue, Morissette et al. (ibid., 12–13) offered the following account, based on internal labour markets theory:

in the face of downward wage pressures from globalization, older workers are better able to immunize themselves from growing wage competition as a result of seniority rules, firm-specific training and other 'institutional' barriers that favour job incumbents over new labour market entrants.

Most studies from the mid-nineties show that these trends have held (Morissette, 1997). The downward trend in wages and employment prospects has continued for young men (with high school and university educations) and women (but only those with high school educations), especially those 24 and under.[7] In addition, according to Betcherman and Morissette (1994: 8) there is little evidence that this is part of a cycle. Their analysis shows that youth wages (male and female) dropped 'within all educational levels . . . within all major industrial groups . . . and all occupational categories'. Accordingly, they conclude that the drop in earnings cannot be attributed simply to the increase in service work taken up by young workers or to fluctuations in business cycles.

Table 9.1   Change in Average Income by Age Group, 1981–1991

	Age Cohort						
	<25	25–34	35–44	45–54	55–64	>64	All ages
Families	-20.7%	-4.9%	0%	6.1%	4.3%	14.9%	3.5%
Unattached individuals	-21.7%	-13.2%	-8.4%	3.8%	4.8%	12.4%	-0.8%

Note: Percentages are adjusted to account for inflation.
Source: Adapted from Ross and Shillington (1994).

Reduced Participation

Not only are the youngest being hardest hit in earnings, but they are being marginalized in terms of opportunities for all jobs, making them even more of a reserve army of cheap labour with little bargaining power. Between 1989 and 1994 the participation rate of the young dropped dramatically (from 71 to 62 per cent), while new jobs increasingly went to the over-25 groups—and this gap seems to be widening (Little, 1995). Interestingly, this decrease in participation accounted for a drop in the overall unemployment rate at the time—to 9.7 per cent.[8] But what happened was that many would-be workers went 'missing' from official statistics, otherwise the overall unemployment rate would have been 13 per cent. In fact, between 1989 and 1994 some 300,000 young Canadians simply gave up trying to find work—became discouraged workers—so were no longer counted as unemployed.[9] Interestingly, Betcherman and Morissette (1994) argue that the drop might have been greater if it were not for the lower wages young people now make. In other words, as noted above, their low wages have enhanced their employability in some sectors.

Job Ghettoization

Studies show that young workers are not only paid less and participate in the workforce less, but they are becoming less well represented in all job categories except consumer services. Indeed, it is in the subordinate service occupations that their (cheap) labour is most in demand. Between 1981 and 1989 the proportion of jobs held by young workers (16–24) that were in the service sector rose from 69.7 to 75.8 per cent, while in the goods sector it dropped from 30.3 to 24.2 per cent (ibid.). The two most common service-sector jobs held in 1989 were retail trade (22.7 per cent) and accommodation and food (13.7 per cent). Betcherman and Morissette note 'the substantial absolute decline of youth employment in the goods sector and in public administration, health, social services, and education' and emphasize that for 'earlier generations of young people, these industries typically offered good entry-level opportunities' (ibid., 3). When broken down by gender, over 84 per cent of females aged 15–19 worked in the service sector, compared with about 60 per cent of their male counterparts (Statistics Canada, 1994: 21).

A clear picture emerges here: the jobs available to the young are increasingly deskilled, poorly paid, and of a subordinate and terminal nature, with little chance for advancement. Indeed, more than two-thirds of the new jobs created in the Canadian labour force are in the sales and service sectors (Geigen-Miller, 1994), suggesting a long-term trend that today's young people will be confronted with throughout their working lives.

Intergenerational Relations

Many young people identify with the label 'Generation X'. Certainly, the media like to play on this easy label, sometimes portraying young people as a 'lost generation'.[10] However, in spite of all the media hype, Generation X does not exist. That statement may seem strange coming from the co-authors of *Generation on Hold*. However, a more thorough academic analysis of the notions surrounding Generation X shows why it is a media artifact. Douglas Copeland, the Canadian author who coined the term, was merely in the right place at the right time to get the media attention that made him famous, for while he wrote about his age-mates, he never really defined what he meant by the term. Still, it was picked up by journalists who were hungry for a convenient label with which to characterize those who were younger than the so-called baby boomers—another media favourite.

Thomas Jefferson is noted for saying that once a theory is formed, scientists have great difficulty seeing the world in ways that do not conform to that theory. To the extent that the concept 'Generation X' constitutes the basis of a theory, social commentary on the young seems to be tainted by this descriptive, popular, journalistic term, which very few social scientists use. We emphasize this because the type of thinking that tries neatly to label people can create conceptual errors. One negative consequence is the provocation of tensions among people in different age groups. We believe this is important to recognize because the impoverishment of youth has affected not just the youngest cohorts—those in their teens and twenties—but every cohort born since World War II. In fact, there is much misunderstanding and confusion about what has happened to each cohort over this time period. Just as 'race' and gender divisions and rivalries have bedevilled the society, so, too, inter-cohort animosities have developed around the questions of who has benefited and suffered most from developments since World War II. The irony is that these misunderstandings and conflicts have also directed attention away from the sources of the difficulties that these younger cohorts have experienced.

Much has been said and written in the media about the various age groups born in the postwar period: so-called baby boomers have been accused of being greedy and self-absorbed; and so-called Generation Xers have been called whiners and slackers. Such characterizations often amount to little more than stereotypes, negative labelling, and overgeneralizations. They also tend to personalize age groups, as if some sort of original sin is associated with being born in a year that coincides with one of the labels. Thus, we find another example of victim-blaming, where the larger order is ignored in favour of individualistic, psychological explanations.

As sociologists, we are not interested in stereotypes associated with personality characteristics, as if the year one was born can predict how lazy or greedy one is. We prefer to leave that sort of stuff to astrologers. Instead, we deal with these issues at the macro, aggregate level and use concepts that help us understand long-term and widespread societal trends. Hence, we adopt here a 'cohort analysis', a heuristic device that helps us to examine what age cohorts have in common and how they differ at the aggregate level.[11]

Table 9.2 provides a categorization of the postwar cohorts that is more differentiated than the simple Generation X-baby boomer dichotomy. We have taken

Table 9.2   The Post-World War II Cohorts

	I	II	III	IV
Years born	1945–54	1955–64	1965–74	1975–84
Label	Early Boomers	Late Boomers	Busters	McBoomers
Ages in 1999	46–54	36–45	26–35	16–25
Parents' birth cohort	1915–24	1925–34	1935–44	1945–54

Source: Adapted from Allahar and Côté (1998: 155).

the liberty of using labels that are easily recognized. From this table we can see that a cycle has been completed in generational terms. That is, the first cohort has reproduced itself with the fourth cohort—the early Boomers are the parents of the McBoomers (we mean this literally in terms of 'children of the Boomers'). Moreover, the early Boomers are increasingly the guardians of the society the McBoomers are entering and will enter for another half-decade. Hence, the early Boomers have reason to be concerned about the plight of the McBoomers, as both parents and teachers. We take this as a good sign from the point of view of inter-generational justice and sharing.

The postwar cohorts have shared certain significant coming-of-age experiences: a convergence of gender roles (the experience of 'being' male or 'being' female is becoming more similar as more roles are shared); liberal gender relations (males and females as peers and casual lovers versus earlier forms of segregation and sexual puritanism); greater permissiveness accorded them by their parents and society (especially regarding sexual behaviours, drug use, and use of leisure time); the rise of mass culture and the truly mass media (especially rock music and the television industries); mass segregation in age-graded schools; and expanded opportunities for higher mass education.

While these inter-cohort experiences have varied by social class and racial/ethnic group, there are sufficient similarities to warrant the proposition that the forces shaping cohorts are also affecting the structure of inequality in Canada, thereby creating greater similarities within each successive cohort of Canadians regardless of 'race', class, or gender.[12] This seems to be due mainly to the tremendous capacity of capital to use technologies to reach and influence the masses. These technologies have been improved at an astounding pace, permitting the forces of capitalism to be further entrenched, most recently on a global scale. Consequently, we live in a 'mass-capitalist' society and, increasingly, in a world where advanced technologies intrude on virtually all aspects of people's day-to-day lives and affect almost every facet of consumption and production.

Cohort analyses can be employed to illustrate these homogenizing influences in a number of domains. For example, the term 'teenager' was first coined in the late 1930s, but because of World War II the first cohorts to be targeted as teenagers by advertisers and merchandisers were the postwar cohorts. We have traced the effects of this, noting the paradoxical rise of youth consumerism in spite of a loss of productive earning power. The consequences include a prolonged period of youth and dependence on parents (Côté and Allahar, 1996: 33–100; Allahar and Côté, 1998: 121–48). The homogenizing influences to which we refer can be illustrated with respect to the higher education and work experiences of each cohort.

Early Boomers. A significant segment of this cohort entered universities between 1963 and 1972 during the first enrolment expansion. They were the first cohort to face the prospect of a mass prolongation of youth as 'student', although most went only as far as completing high school. They rode the crest of the wave of expanding middle-class opportunities (but note that these opportunities were enjoyed more so by the cohort before them, those born in the 1935–44 period). There were good economic opportunities for university graduates, yet many have experienced a decline in earning power since the early 1980s. Although some became well positioned in the expanded middle class, as this middle class has shrunk large numbers of them have either been squeezed out or live with job insecurity and heavy debt loads (in personal loans for high-ticket purchases such as cars, mortgages, and financing their children's higher educations), and would face great difficulty in retraining.

Late Boomers. This cohort enrolled in universities in increasing numbers between 1973 and 1982, but they saw the beginning of the underemployment trend. They made the transition to the workplace as the once-expanding middle class began to contract, and there was a growing concern that economic opportunities were diminished for some graduates. Thus, underemployment has been a persistent problem for these people and significant numbers must now accustom themselves to regular job or career changes as institutional downsizing has truncated many careers. For members of this cohort, available work is increasingly contract and deskilled or in competition with younger cohorts, and the accompanying economic shortfalls and insecurities make it difficult for many to buy a home or save for retirement.

Busters. They entered university during the 1984–93 period and were part of the second enrolment expansion as a majority of the cohort went on to higher education. They increasingly found themselves caught up in a scramble for devalued credentials, with growing numbers pursuing post-graduate degrees to gain some relative advantage. A mounting disillusionment with higher education was felt by them and others, and owing to declining job opportunities, a significant portion have experienced an increased prolongation of youth as 'adults on hold', finding themselves still living with their parents in their late twenties. Many encountered increased competition for jobs with older cohorts, and having amassed student loans in the range of $20,000–$30,000 there was a growing pessimism regarding even short-term economic opportunities.

McBoomers. They began enrolling in universities in 1993 (and will continue to do so until 2003). They are among the largest cohort that has gone directly from high school to post-secondary institutions and as such are the inheritors of the 'credentialing paradox',[13] even while their educational funding is under attack by various levels of government. The bulk of this cohort find themselves locked into youth, out of 'adulthood', and still living with their parents. The 'perfunctory student' becomes a model for many—any degree will do. They witness the collapse of middle-class opportunities for their parents and the other two cohorts as governments retreat to fight deficits and corporations downsize in spite of record profits. The 'good' jobs that might have been theirs are taken by older cohorts who are themselves under pressure, and because only 'McJobs' are available for most, the short- and long-term economic prospects appear dismal for many in this cohort.

Thus, we have four cohorts with shared educational and work experiences (to varying degrees) that have reason to find common cause for complaint independent of 'race' and gender issues, although these are still very real for many and serve to complicate the matter in no small way. Certainly, the 1980s and 1990s have been hard on members from all four cohorts, but to varying degrees. Yet, we find certain tensions and resentments among them, especially between the two Boomer cohorts, on the one hand, and the two latter ones, on the other. The questions are, then, how can members of these cohorts develop the political awareness necessary if they are to arrive at a critical, structural understanding of their situation? Do they in fact have a common predicament that can override their potential age, ethnic, and gender differences and unite them on a basis that recognizes their common material interests?

Intergenerational Justice

In the foregoing we have been underlining intergenerational relations and the responsibilities generations have for each other's welfare and the sharing of collective resources. Lee (1996) argues that there is a serious generation gap, not in the simple sense of parents and their children not understanding each other but in terms of inter-cohort hostilities based on perceived self-interest. Indeed, in-group cohort identifications in the form of 'us-them' antagonisms seem to be growing, and age-based blame and recrimination are now widespread. Thus, we have a new area of inter-group relations emerging where many people—not just teens—are politically asserting identities with their age-mates. This form of identity politics, almost akin to a 'tribalization', gives people a sense of 'rightness' in terms of their privilege or oppression as against the privilege or oppression of people from other age groups.

Such intergenerational tensions are familiar media favourites, especially on the evening news. Two in particular are (a) the elderly, who fear and loathe teens, and (b) Generation Xers, who dismiss baby boomers as greedy and self-indulgent. In this context, from his study of intergenerational justice in the US, Lee (1996: 243–4) identifies the following tensions:

- The tendency to find fault with other generations is common to all generations.
- Any members of all generations falsely assume that their experiences either have been or can be duplicated by members of other generations.
- Many members of younger generations have high anger levels related to the taxes they pay to finance benefits for older generations.
- Members of older generations who came of age when good jobs with decent wages were readily available have little understanding of the job anxiety and economic insecurity experienced by many who are younger.

However widespread these tensions are, it is clear that from a justice point of view they must be set aside so that a more equitable society might be created. This may sound idealistic in a society with a history of 'tribal self-interest' and that has glorified individualism, but justice must be based on ideals. Given their economic underpinnings, Lee believes these generation gaps are more serious than any we have seen in the past, and the issues they raise cannot be casually dismissed:

> We will be strained to the breaking point if we cannot articulate a shared sense of justice based on inclusiveness and the affirmation of the dignity and significance of those of all ages. We will be torn apart if we are not responsive to the concerns and well-being of young and old alike. The years to come will be disastrous if we plunge headlong into the chasm of a war between the generations. (Ibid., xii)

Thus, we see a situation in which various age groups fight with each other over their share of the pie. Yet, in blaming each other, people miss the real cause of their financial troubles: a social and economic system in which 20 per cent of the population controls 70 per cent of the wealth (Davies, 1993: 108). For reasons of social control and political order, it is very useful for that 20 per cent of the population to have the other 80 per cent distracted and fighting over their 30 per cent share of the wealth.

Intergenerational Inequality

Some critics might read the above and argue that there have been periods when it was tough to be young in many societies, just as it has been tough to be any age, depending on the historical circumstances. For example, during the Great Depression, poverty and despair were widespread and forced many young people to move about the country looking for work, and during the two world wars, thousands of young males lost their lives in international conflicts. Indeed, young people have faced war and famine throughout history, and the physical consequences were far greater than what most young people face today. Critics might also add that the affluence of Canadian society makes the comparisons relative: is it not much better to be non-affluent in contemporary Canada than in the Canada of 200 years ago, or in a developing country somewhere else in the world today? The answer to this last question is probably yes. Yet such a pre-emptive answer ignores how things got this way and why things did not work out more equally over the past century.

As for the future, it certainly holds promise for some; indeed, change can bring great benefits, as old interest groups lose their power and conventions change. However, a key issue for the future is whether the inequalities identified here constitute part of a cycle or part of a long-term trend. The bad news for the optimists is that a consensus is emerging that workplace changes are part of long-term structural changes (Morissette et al, 1993; Davies et al., 1994). Elsewhere we consider long-term trends in the transition between the workplace and the educational system (Allahar and Côté, 1998).

What lies beyond these trends is difficult to say. Just how much more technological displacement will take place, and how much educational credentials will continue to be inflated, is also difficult to say. Certainly, there will be peaks and plateaus to these trends. For example, in the mid-1990s a plateau was reached in credentialism with a levelling in university attendance; but in the early 2000s, enrolments continue to rise. However, the danger with trends like technological displacement is that one company's employee is another company's consumer. As Rifkin argues, when a company lays off one of its employees, it is also laying off another company's consumer. In spite of the ability of capitalism to survive such crises in the past, it may only be a matter of time before companies collapse due to overproduction and the associated economic ill of under-consumption. If this becomes widespread, the largely unseen cleavages and fractures in Canadian society may well become more apparent, and inter-cohort conflict could become more overt and disruptive (Lee, 1996). It stands to reason that where a majority of young people in successive cohorts find themselves locked into structured, lifelong poverty, or into an economic situation of 'just getting by', what will appear to them as a denial of social justice could well produce political instability and violence. Recognizing the reasons for intergenerational inequalities is therefore the first step to bringing about a more just society and lessening the likelihood of misdirected social conflict.

One idea that may be useful in helping us develop a sense of intergenerational justice is the notion of a quid pro quo, or in this case an intergenerational quid pro quo. A 'quid pro quo' literally means 'something for something'. It exists intergenerationally when one generation does something for another and receives something from that other generation in return. This is a key feature of many well-functioning non-industrial societies in the sense that they are able to sustain an age-based division of labour that receives widespread intergenerational endorsement and support. Some non-industrial societies have been known to exist for centuries on the basis of an intergenerational quid pro quo that linked age cohorts across the division of labour (see Côté, 1994, for a discussion of this aspect of Samoan society).

As an advanced, industrial society, however, a somewhat different situation faces contemporary Canada, so different solutions to the problem of an insufficient intergenerational quid pro quo need to be considered. The key problem in these societies is that the youngest segments of the population have been increasingly disinherited from their share of the collective wealth. This has meant that the diminished right to be a productive member of the community has not only lowered the status of the young in general, but it has reduced their sense of obligation to other members of society. In a cycle of decline, instead of being valued for their productive contributions to the community, the youth segment has increasingly been thrust into a life of more-or-less enforced idleness or leisure in relation to older age groups. The stark fact is that we know of no societies throughout history that have enforced idleness on their hitherto most productive members (namely, young adults). When the intergenerational quid pro quo is lost in a society, the young see less reason to co-operate with their elders. This has happened in many parts of the world, particularly in developing countries, where its consequences can be quite severe for the welfare of the citizenry (ibid.). However, in countries such as Canada there is a pressing need to grant young adults greater productive social and economic roles. When this happens, not only will their social status rise, but so, too, will their willingness to co-operate in forging a new and better society. The world of the future will require new identities and roles if we are to steer the course back to one where social justice is taken to be the responsibility of each citizen, including business and political leaders.

The loss of an intergenerational quid pro quo does not apply so starkly to all young people, because some do find places in the workforce that accord with their expectations. However, it is also the case that an increasing number of the young have not been called upon to make productive contributions to their communities or societies. As a consequence, many do not feel they have a stake in the society in which they are ostensibly full citizens—instead, they feel disinherited. This paradoxical situation has had some curious consequences, as in the manufacture of dissent referred to above. Without a sense of connection to a society, people—whether young or not—do not feel it is in their interest to care about, or work for, a common good. To the extent that Canadian society as a whole is becoming a mass of disconnected people without a sense of obligation to and reward from others, we are all increasingly impoverished. No amount of corporate activity can fix that, nor will corporations try because it is not in their bottom-line interests. Certainly, intergenerational justice is not part of the agenda of the New World Order of global capitalism.

Questions for Critical Thought

1. Define the concept 'complementarity' and show its relation to social control. Provide one example each of (a) the creation of complementary conditions, and (b) the manipulation of pre-existing complementary conditions.

2. To what extent is Canada's corporate sector keenly interested in the disenfranchisement of youth? Provide and discuss an example.

3. Compared to the working-class poor and others whose poverty results from the exclusionary practices of racism and sexism, how does age discrimination constitute a special case of disenfranchisement?

4. What is the 'credentialling paradox', and how is it related to the use of schools as warehouses of the young?

5. How can intergenerational justice contribute to more amicable relations between youth and adult cohorts? How is this relevant to the notion of an intergenerational quid pro quo?

Glossary Terms

Complementarity: A system of rule aimed at securing social order. In essence it has two aspects. Those in command will examine the behaviours of a subordinate population and if they observe behaviour consistent (complementary) with their plans, they will encourage its continuation, e.g., apathy among workers. If the exhibited behaviour is not complementary to their interests, they will seek to eliminate it, e.g., trade union activism among workers.

Credentialling paradox: The idea that more education is better. This leads to a situation in which most young people who are exhorted to stay in school longer now find themselves overqualified for the jobs available. There is a blind pursuit of credentials, but collecting diplomas and degrees often has little direct relationship to the wider employment situation.

Globalization: The recent economic move that sees the entire globe as the private preserve of multinational capital. This has witnessed the homogenization of consciousness via the media and the Internet, as well as the free movement of labour, capital, and commodities across national boundaries.

Identity commodities/packages: As part of the consumer culture of contemporary society, young people are convinced that their identities are wrapped up in their material possessions. To this end, marketers and media experts are able to serve the interests of big capital by selling identity packages (designer clothing, music, fashion looks, etc.) to youth, to the tune of billions of dollars annually.

Ideology: A system of beliefs and ideas that we all carry around in our heads and use to make sense of our worlds. Ideologies are like filters through which we view social reality. There are political, economic, and religious ideologies.

Intergenerational justice: The idea that there ought to be a reciprocal relationship between generations and if we are to have a productive and harmonious society, the members of all generations or cohorts must be made to see a real or meaningful sense of equal justice and fairness across all generations. This relates to education, jobs, housing, and all other aspects of the social economy that at present seem to favour older cohorts at the expense of younger ones. As a consequence the youth are alienated, cynical, angry, and pessimistic about the future.

Social engineering: The ability of the major socialization agencies (media, schools, family) to create a specific type of citizen with a specific type of mindset. It deals with the reproduction of certain ideas, values, attitudes, and behaviours deemed non-threatening to those in positions of dominance, who benefit from a continuation of the status quo.

Youth proletariat: The notion that young people today are the cheapest, most pliable source of labour around. Like the proletariat of Marxist writing, today's youth are alienated, exploited, made to be politically apathetic, while their labour inputs are integral to the continued functioning of the capitalist machine.

Suggested Reading

Artz, S. 1998. *Sex, Power, and the Violent School Girl.* Toronto: Trifolium Books. A look at the rising rates and causes of violence among Canada's young women.

Côté, J.E., and A.L. Allahar. 1996. *Generation on Hold: Coming of Age in the Late Twentieth Century.* New York: New York University Press. An examination of theories that help explain why youth has become prolonged and hazardous, with an emphasis on political economy theory.

Currie, D. 1999. *Girl Talk: Adolescent Magazines and Their Readers.* Toronto: University of Toronto Press. A deconstruction of teenzines in terms of their role in the reproduction of gender relations of dominance and subordination.

Danesi, M. 1994. *Cool: The Signs and Meanings of Adolescence.* Toronto: University of Toronto Press. A semiotic analysis of youth culture.

Frank, T. 1997. *The Conquest of Cool: Business Culture, Counterculture, and the Rise of Hip Consumerism.* Chicago: University of Chicago Press. A serious wake-up call for those who think that consumerism among young people 'just happened'.

Kostash, M. 1987. *No Kidding: Inside the World of Teenage Girls.* Toronto: McClelland & Stewart. A sympathetic look by a journalist at the secret lives of 50 teenaged girls.

Males, M.A. 1996. *The Scapegoat Generation: America's War on Adolescents.* Monroe, Maine: Common Courage Press. A scathing attack on American society in its unfair use of stereotypes in constructing youth policies.

Tanner, J. 1996. *Teenage Troubles: Youth and Deviance in Canada.* Toronto: Nelson Canada. Image versus reality concerning youth crime, dealing with street youth and gender differences.

Notes

1. Isolated attempts to unionize have been made recently by young workers in the fast food industry, often with little success and in the face of bitter and underhanded opposition from management.

2. However, it should be noted that the state also has to mediate conflicts among different fractions of the capitalist class, and when it does so it can make false claims to independence from capital.

3. Synge (1979) indicates that men earned about twice that of women, and women would typically begin paid work in their early teens but continue working only until married (age 25 on average).

4. We should stress that the state pays most of the cost of the education for those hired by corporations, and since public revenues are raised through public taxation, average citizens do in fact subsidize the costs of educating such corporate employees.

5. Experiments using lotteries and other extrinsic reward systems to entice students to attend classes are being undertaken in both Canada and the US.

6. It is important to point out that this is not what some call a 'conspiracy theory'. Rather, the notion of complementarity speaks to the fact that the distraction may have been created by quite other circumstances and for entirely different reasons. Finding it in existence, however, any other group in the society may seek to use it to further its own aims.

7. Crompton (1996) found that men and women aged 25–9 with high school diplomas lost ground in their wages between 1979 and 1993 (as much as 17 per cent for men). Moreover, by 1993, university-educated men in this age group earned about the same in real terms as did men of the same age with high school diplomas in the late 1970s. University-educated women made gains over the same period and by 1990 were actually making more 'than their male counterparts after controlling for experience, job tenure, education and hours of work' (Wannell and Caron, 1994: ii). Note, however, that the gap closed in part because of declining earnings among males.

8. Of the G-7 countries, in 1993 Canada had the third highest youth unemployment rate (about 17 per cent), lower than France (about 25 per cent) and Italy (about 30 per cent) (*The Economist*, 19 Mar. 1994, 27).

9. Recently women over age 25 have made the most gains in employment—presumably in response to employment equity initiatives. Although they constitute 38 per cent of the workforce, they got 52 per cent of the jobs since 1990 (men over 25 got jobs in proportion to their population representation) (Little, 1995; Sunter, 1994).

10. The term 'Lost Generation' was actually coined for the youth who came of age during or after World War I and who were believed to be disillusioned and cynical.

11. Although useful, we should add some qualifications about the applicability of cohort analysis and how to recognize its limitations. First, in a cohort analysis not all individuals will be described by a pattern, but rather the experiences of the average member will be taken as the marker for the entire cohort. Assuming that the experiences examined have a 'normal distribution' around this average, there is some confidence that the majority of experiences of persons in a cohort will be 'properly' characterized. Second,

this type of analysis is further limited because of the arbitrary dividing lines defining cohorts. These lines often are based on a combination of significant events and the beginning or midpoint of a decade. Third, individuals born close to these dividing lines may share the experiences of two cohorts, so conceptual exceptions may need to be made for them. And fourth, even when differences are identified at the aggregate level, these are differences of degree, not kind. In the cohorts we examine here, certain commonalities are reflected in shared significant experiences (like underemployment) but they differ by degree. Too often cohorts are set apart from each other by the media and general public as if they are different species bent on annihilating one other. Such characterizations simply fuel misdirected inter-cohort tensions.

12. While the process is by no means complete, this can be seen in second-generation immigrant families whose cultures differ markedly from Canada's dominant norm. Take, for example, teenaged children who appear to have more in common with their fellow Canadian-born peers than with their parents, and who demand the same freedoms as those peers, such as staying out late in mixed-sex groups, drinking, choosing their own dates, and so on.

13. The credentialism paradox refers to the situation where educationally credentialled skills have little to do with the work that is eventually performed; but without the credentials, one's employability and earning power are seriously jeopardized (Allahar and Côté, 1998). See Kelly et al. (1997) for recent statistics on the problem of job overqualification.

References

Allahar, A.L., and J.E. Côté. 1998. *Richer and Poorer: The Structure of Inequality in Canada.* Toronto: James Lorimer.

Artz, S. 1998. *Sex, Power, and the Violent School Girl.* Toronto: Trifolium Books.

Baldus, B. 1975. 'The Study of Power: Suggestions for an Alternative', *Canadian Journal of Sociology* 1: 179–201.

———. 1977. 'Social Control in Capitalist Societies: An Examination of the Problem of Order in Liberal Democracies', *Canadian Journal of Sociology* 2: 37–52.

Betcherman G., and R. Morissette. 1994. *Recent Youth Labour Market Experiences in Canada.* Analytic Studies Branch Research Paper Series #63. Ottawa: Statistics Canada.

Côté, J.E. 1994. *Adolescent Storm and Stress: An Evaluation of the Mead/Freeman Controversy.* Hillsdale, NJ: Lawrence Erlbaum.

——— and A.L. Allahar. 1996. *Generation on Hold: Coming of Age in the Late Twentieth Century.* New York: New York University Press.

Cox, W. 1997. 'Girls hit with violent message', Canadian Press, 27 Nov. 1997.

Crompton, S. 1996. 'Employment Prospects for High School Graduates', *Education Quarterly Review* 3: 8–19.

Davies, J. 1993. 'The Distribution of Wealth and Economic Inequality', in J. Curtis, E. Grabb, and N. Guppy, eds, *Social Inequality in Canada: Patterns, Problems, Policies*, 2nd edn. Toronto: Prentice-Hall.

Davies, S., C. Mosher, and B. O'Grady. 1994. 'Trends in Labour Market Outcomes of Canadian Post-Secondary Graduates, 1978–1988', in L. Erwin and D. MacLennan, eds, *Sociology of Education in Canada*. Toronto: Copp Clark Longman, 352–69.

de Broucker, P., and L. Lavallée. 1998. 'Does your parents' education count?', *Canadian Social Trends*. Ottawa: Statistics Canada, 11–15.

Ewen, S. 1976. *Captains of Consciousness: Advertising and the Social Roots of the Consumer Culture*. New York: McGraw-Hill.

Fournier, E., G. Butlin, and P. Giles. 1994. 'Intergenerational Change in the Education of Canadians', in *Dynamics of Labour and Income*. Ottawa: Statistics Canada, 24–30.

Frank, J. 1992. 'Violent youth crime', *Canadian Social Trends* No. 42. Ottawa: Statistics Canada, 2–9.

Frank, T. 1997a. *The Conquest of Cool: Business Culture, Counterculture, and the Rise of Hip Consumerism*. Chicago: University of Chicago Press.

———. 1997b. 'Let them eat lifestyle: From hip to hype—the ultimate corporate takeover', *Utne Reader* (Nov.-Dec.): 43–7.

Geigen-Miller, P. 1994. 'Education no guarantee anymore', *London Free Press*, 30 Apr., A8.

Green, K.C., and A. Astin. 1985. 'The Mood on Campus: More Conservative or Just More Materialistic?', *Educational Record* (Winter): 45–8.

Hargreaves, A., and I. Goodson. 1992. *Schools of the Future: Towards a Canadian Vision*. Ottawa: Innovations Program, Employment and Immigration Canada.

Herman, E., and N. Chomsky. 1988. *Manufacturing Consent: The Political Economy of the Mass Media*. New York: Pantheon.

Howe, N., and B. Strauss. 1993. *13th GEN: Abort, Retry, Ignore, Fail?* New York: Vintage Books.

Huxley, A. 1932. *Brave New World*. London: Triad Grafton.

Kelly, K., L. Howatson-Leo, and W. Clark. 1997. 'I feel overqualified for my job . . .', *Canadian Social Trends* No. 47 (Winter): 11–16.

Keniston, K. 1975. 'Prologue: Youth as a Stage of Life', in R. Havighurst and P.H. Dreyer, eds, *Youth*. Chicago: University of Chicago Press.

Klein, H. 1990. 'Adolescence, Youth, and Young Adulthood: Re-thinking Current Conceptualizations of the Life Stage', *Youth and Society* 21 (1990): 446–71.

Lee, D.E. 1996. *Generations and the Challenge of Justice*. Lanham, Md: University Press of America.

Little, B. 1995. 'Why it's not so wonderful to be young', *Globe and Mail*, 9 Jan., A9.

Logan, R., and J. Belliveau. 1995. 'Working Mothers', *Canadian Social Trends* No. 36 (Spring): 24–8.

Mead, M. 1928. *Coming of Age in Samoa: A Psychological Study of Primitive Youth for Western Civilization*. New York: Morrow Quill.

Melton, G. 1991. 'Rights of Adolescence', in R.M. Lerner, A.C. Petersen, and J. Brooks-Gunn, eds, *Encyclopaedia of Adolescence*. New York: Garland, 930–3.

Modell, J., F.F. Furstenberg, and T. Hershberg. 1976. 'Social Change and Transitions to Adulthood in Historical Perspective', *Journal of Family History* 1: 7–31.

Morissette, R. 1997. 'Declining earnings of young men', *Canadian Social Trends* No. 46 (Autumn): 8–12.

————, J. Myles, and G. Picot. 1993. *What Is Happening to Earnings Inequality in Canada?* Analytic Studies Branch Research Papers Series #60. Ottawa: Statistics Canada.

Myles, J., G. Picot, and T. Wannell. 1988. *Wages and Jobs in the 1980s: Changing Youth Wages and the Declining Middle.* Analytic Studies Branch Research Papers Series #17. Ottawa: Statistics Canada.

Nobert, L.R., and R. McDowell. 1994. *Profile of Post-Secondary Education in Canada: 1993 Edition.* Ottawa: Ministry of Supply and Services.

Palladino. N. 1996. *Teenagers: An American History.* New York: Basic Books.

Petersen, A. 1993. 'Creating Adolescence: The Role of Context and Process in Developmental Trajectories', *Journal of Research on Adolescence* 3: 1–18.

Picot, G., and J. Myles. 1996. 'Children in Low Income Families', *Canadian Social Trends* No. 42 (Autumn): 15–19.

Proefrock, D.W. 1981. 'Adolescence: Social Fact and Psychological Concept', *Adolescence* 26, 64: 851–8.

Rifkin, J. 1995. *The End of Work.* New York: G.P. Putnam's.

Ross, D.P., E.R. Shillington, and C. Lochhead. 1994. *The Canadian Fact Book on Poverty, 1994.* Ottawa: Canadian Council on Social Development.

Rudd, P., and K. Evans. 1998. 'Structure and Agency in Youth Transitions: Student Experiences of Vocational Further Education', *Journal of Youth Studies* 1, 1: 39–62.

Saunders, D. 1996. 'Graduates Facing Postponed Beginnings', *Globe and Mail*, 22 Apr., A1, A8.

Schultze, Q.J., et al. 1991. *Dancing in the Dark: Youth, Popular Culture and the Electronic Media.* Grand Rapids, Mich.: W.B. Eerdmans.

Sheridan, C. 1996. 'Rioters without a cause', *London Free Press*, 6 July, E5.

Statistics Canada. 1994. 'Working Teens', *Canadian Social Trends* (Winter): 18–22.

Steinberg, L. 1990. 'Pubertal Maturation and Parent-Adolescent Distance: An Evolutionary Perspective', in G.R. Adams, R. Montemayor, and T.P. Gullotta, eds, *Biology of Adolescent Behaviour and Development.* Beverly Hills, Calif.: Sage.

Strasburger, V.C., and E. Donnerstein. 1999. 'Children, Adolescents, and the Media: Issues and Solutions', *Pediatrics* 103: 129–39.

Sunter, D. 1994a. 'Youths—waiting it out', *Perspectives on Labour and Income* 6, 1 (Spring): 31–6.

————. 1994b. 'The Labour Market Mid-Year Review', *Perspectives on Labour and Income* 6, 3 (Autumn): 2–10.

Synge, J. 1979. 'The Transition from School to Work: Growing up in Early 20th century Hamilton, Ontario', in K. Ishwaran, ed., *Childhood and Adolescence in Canada.* Toronto: McGraw-Hill Ryerson, 246–69.

Wannell, T., and N. Caron. 1994. *The Gender Earnings Gap Among Recent Post-secondary Graduates 1984–1992.* Analytic Studies Branch Research Papers Series #68. Ottawa: Statistics Canada.

White, L. 1994. 'Co-residence and Leaving Home: Young Adults and their Parents', *Annual Review of Sociology* 20 (1994): 81–102.

Wyn, J., and R. White. 1998. 'Young People, Social Problems and Australian Youth Studies', *Journal of Youth Studies* 1, 1: 23–38.

part four

Sociological Frontiers into the Twenty-first Century

For some, it may be difficult to envision Quebec nationalism and the environment as sociological frontiers. Our physical geography and the over 450-year evolution of North America's oldest society of European origin are hardly new phenomena. And yet, they are frontiers in the sense that there is little sociological understanding of Quebec society in English-speaking Canada, and the sociology of the environment is barely acknowledged in the panoply of programs and fields of study that are packaged in Departments of Sociology across Canada.

A widely recognized maverick of the sociology of Quebec society, Hubert Guindon, in Chapter 10, brings his insights to those in English Canada who have yet to hear 'the other voice' in the public debates about the role of Quebec in Canadian society. Too often in our deliberations about Quebec, Canadians have had to rely on a small number of hand-picked messengers to tell them what their French-speaking compatriots are talking about. Often, the message is wrong or, on occasion, is misunderstood by the messengers who were entrusted to do their job. Guindon's contribution to this volume is a narrative, that is, one person's analysis of the evolution of Quebec society. It is the story of a society's development and the role of an activist sociologist in that evolution. It is personal while it is political, as well as being supremely sociological. It is a view that may be new to many, but as Guindon tells us, readers 'may be even more surprised to learn that the analysis presented here is quite conventional in the intellectual, artistic, and academic community and among the educated youth of Quebec society.'

While pressing social, political, and economic issues face Canada, the ultimate quality of Canadian lives hinges on the future viability of our environment. As environmental sociologist Kathleen Reil explains, Canadians in recent years have begun to express increased concern about their physical surrounding and their own well-being. Increasing consciousness of the interconnections between human and societal health and the health of the biosphere have prompted the emergence of a variety of environmental groups and demands for improved governmental controls. As a result, the environment has become the focus for considerable social conflict, as governments, industries, community and environmental groups, and individual citizens struggle to assert their interests. This is all taking place within a context of economic restructuring, racial conflict, constitutional struggles, and other pressing issues. New in the struggle to achieve environmental protection and pollution control is a shift in the focus of the environmental movement from lobbying politicians to seeking an enforceable rule of law—an Environmental Bill of Rights.

chapter ten

Quebec's Social and Political Evolution Since 1945: A View from Within

Hubert Guindon

The Essay's Pitfalls

This essay is a narrative description that chronicles the social and political changes of Quebec society during the second half of the twentieth century. Such an enterprise faces two major pitfalls.

This essay is based on a text written for the XXth World Congress of the International Sociological Association held in Montreal, 16 July–1 August 1998. It was published in French in *Cahiers de recherche sociologique* no. 30 (1998): 34–78, While this is not a literal translation, its contents are essentially based on the article. A special effort was made to make it accessible to an undergraduate readership not too familiar with Quebec society. Students will quickly realize that it differs greatly from the conventional wisdom conveyed by the media and the academic literature published in English. They may be even more surprised to learn that the analysis presented here is quite conventional in the intellectual, artistic, and academic community and among the educated youth of Quebec society.

The first has to do with the ever-present concern of *looking good*. All individuals are concerned with how they are looked upon by the groups that are meaningful to them and to which they belong. It is also a characteristic of the groups themselves, whether family, village, nation, or country. This trait probably exists in all cultures, perhaps since the dawn of humanity. Since persons and groups not only see but are also seen by other persons and groups, the human condition involves a world of appearance in which every individual is a participant. Seeing and being seen become constant features of human interaction and ever-present concerns of groups as well as individuals. In the same manner and for the same reasons, one generation is concerned by the way it is looked upon by another. Everett C. Hughes[1] would explain to students that the recent past was generally the object of ambivalence and criticism by the generation reaching adulthood. He noted that in the French language, the recent past is called, in linguistics, *le passé imparfait* (the imperfect past). He would then make the point that this is true not only *linguistically speaking* but often *sociologically speaking.*

The second pitfall is linked to the first but concerns not the chronicle but the chronicler. It is always possible for the outside observer not to understand or to misunderstand the reality he claims to analyse, precisely because as an outsider and a stranger he does not grasp the meaning ascribed both to the behaviour of individuals and to the customs of the group.

It is equally true that, in complex societies, the observer *from within* may be trapped by his memberships in the social worlds of his society: the profession, the social class, the specific age group in the life cycle, the ethnic group, the religious faith he embraces or rejects, the social movements he commits to and their political agenda, sexual identity, personal ambitions, spontaneous and professionally required solidarities, sexual orientation, biography, and so many more personal circumstances that shape one's identity. Add to this the knowledge we have that all these elements of personal identity are social constructions subject to change over time and it becomes prudent to behave as the citizen described by Hannah Arendt (1959: 57), who, when speaking to peers in the public realm, begins by saying: from my vantage point, it seems to me. . . . One then is evidently speaking of opinion, not science. What is often an unspoken truth is that today's science, especially in the social sciences, often becomes tomorrow's discarded opinion.

Having said this, one need not avoid saying what may irritate many. It is the marginal observer from within who is the most susceptible to stating his mind frankly and fully because his very marginality protects him from both the fury and the blandishments of the powerful or of his own social environment in which he is never fully integrated. Hannah Arendt expected some intellectuals to be 'conscious pariahs' (those who want to be marginal) rather than 'parvenus' (those who are self-made men/women). The former she trusted more than the latter because they remained genuine or authentic human beings, whereas the self-made person was almost always looking for an angle or a 'contact' to advance her/his career.

This essay, therefore, is a personal reading of Quebec's recent past by a lone sociologist uninterested in reviewing everything written on Quebec society in sociology. The methodological approach is simple and is based principally on the frail memory of an old man remembering events he witnessed and writing a descriptive narration, which is why it is called a 'chronicle'. It is *not* a narration of events but of a succession of issues that beset Quebec society after World War II.

The postwar period (1945–60), a period I label 'Tradition under Fire', saw all the structuring institutions of Quebec's social context questioned in a climate of acrimonious debate without, however, the institutions being modified during that time. What was at stake was their legitimacy. The social edifice, labelled by sociol-ogists 'the traditional society', was described by some as the period of the great darkness (*la grande noirceur*), by others as a clerico-nationalist regime (*un régime clérico-nationaliste*), and in the other official language of the country as a *priest-ridden society*. While hatred of the Church of Rome was centuries-old for Anglo-Protes-tants, it had not spread among the Québécois people. But an antipathy emerged in this period against part of the Catholic hierarchy, not from the outside but from within—indeed, from within the Church itself. It spread in the name of 'new common values', common to the whole of North America and Western Europe, busy during the same period with its economic and social reconstruction.

Paradoxically, the Catholic Church was not opposed to these 'new common values' and the debate divided the clergy as well as the laity. These values were carried by a rising new middle class (Guindon, 1988), convinced that progress and the common good required the rapid development of institutions to house their professional careers. But their rapid implementation was resisted by the political regime of Premier Maurice Duplessis. Max Weber was the first sociologist to note that when a rising social class assimilates progress and the common good with its class interests, it gets the wind in its sails and becomes transformed into a social movement with a mission. 'Between past and future',[2] this period of Quebec soci-ety can indeed be perceived as a 'past that will no longer be and a future that has yet to become'.

These new common values, once crystallized in the postwar political culture, definitively unsettled the traditional social organization of Quebec society. They legitimated the demands for four basic changes: (1) *democracy in education* by enlarg-ing to all social classes access to secondary, college, and university training; (2) *the right of every citizen to free health care*: free hospitalization soon to be followed by free medical care; (3) *the transformation of private charity into social welfare*: private charity, locally organized and financed, and managed by community or religious organiza-tions that defined both the beneficiaries and the operative norms, was to be trans-formed into a publicly financed state system managed by state bureaucrats and professional social workers; (4) *the redistribution of wealth* by labour legislation that facilitated the emergence of working-class trade unions, soon to be extended to include state employees and state-financed social institutions.

These new common values swept through the Western world at roughly the same period. Even though it may not have had the same scope everywhere, clearly the 'Quiet Revolution' did not occur in Quebec only; in fact, all of America was involved in a process of change. The unique character of the Quiet Revolution in Quebec does not derive from its causes but in its consequences.

The narrative description that follows in more detail covers this transition period. But, before this, I must make you aware that Quebec does not have one but two versions of its history, two very different visions of historical reality distorted by fantastic legends that, though secularized, still underscore the political cultures in Canada.

A Historical Overview: The Two Histories of Quebec

A happier calamity never befell a people than the conquest of Canada by the British arms. (Parkman, 1851–92, vol. 2: 401)

According to Hannah Arendt (1961b: 23):

> In contrast to the economic structure, the political structure cannot be expanded indefinitely, because it is not based upon the productivity of man, which is indeed unlimited. Of all forms of government and organization of people, the nation-state is least suited for unlimited growth because the genuine consent at its base cannot be stretched indefinitely, and is only rarely, and with difficulty, won from conquered peoples. . . . Wherever the nation-state appeared as conqueror, it aroused national consciousness and desire for sovereignty among the conquered people, thereby defeating all genuine attempts at empire-building.

Before chronicling this historical overview, one must bring to the reader's attention and try to explain the enormous chasm separating what is written in English from what is written in French. This chasm is ever-present in newspaper articles, in letters to the editor, in history books, in introductory sociology texts, and in the writings of political scientists.

Already in the mid-sixties, the Royal Commission on Bilingualism and Biculturalism (1969) was deploring the gap in the teaching of the history of Canada in English and French. It was urging historians to narrow the gap to achieve a common history. But, quite the contrary, the gap continued to deepen all along, from the constitutional conference in Victoria in 1971 up to the Charlottetown Accord of 1992, rejected as massively by English Canadians as by Quebec Francophones.[3] The chasm has indeed become an abyss.

This historical chasm can be explained if one subscribes to Hannah Arendt's views on the role of legends in the construction of history.

> Legends have always played a powerful role in the making of history. Man, who has not been granted the power of undoing, who is always an unconsulted heir to other men's deeds, and who is always burdened with a responsibility that appears to be the consequence of an unending chain of events rather than conscious acts, demands an explanation and interpretation of the past in which the mysterious key to the future destiny seems to be concealed. Legends were the spiritual foundations of every ancient city, empire, people, promising safe guidance through the limitless spaces of the future. . . .
>
>   . . . Only in the frankly invented tale about events did man consent to assume his responsibility for them, and to consider past events *his* past. Legends made him master of what he had not done, and capable of dealing with what he could not undo. (Arendt, 1961b: 123)

The Roots of the Anglophone Legend

Francis Parkman, an American historian, was the first to provide English Canada with the fundamental legend for its history. Author of a 10-volume series entitled *France and England in North America*, he formulated it in the celebrated phrase, 'A happier calamity never befell a people than the conquest of Canada by the British arms.' The question becomes: from what calamity and for whom was the conquest a salvation? In a passage taken from his book *Pioneers of France in the New World*, Parkman reveals through what ideological glasses he views the history of New France:

> Root, stem and branch [New France] was the nursling of authority. Deadly absolutism blighted her early and later growth. Friar and Jesuit shaped her destinies. All that conflicted against advancing liberty—the centralized power of the Crown and the tiara, the ultramontane in religion, the despotic in policy—found their fullest expression and most fateful exercise. Her records shine with glorious deeds, the self-devotion of heroes and martyrs; and the result of all is disorder, imbecility and ruin. (Hamilton, 1988: 22)

Parkman's legend of British salvation found fertile soil in English-Canadian historiography and it became the prism through which English Canada viewed—and still views—Francophone society. The Parkman legend has forever become embedded in the political landscape of English Canada. In a nutshell, then, the British Conquest of New France 'rescued' the French colonists from political despotism, economic stagnation based on anti-capitalist feudal elements, and subservience to the Roman Catholic Church.

Saved from feudal France in 1763, New France was saved from itself in 1837–8 when the *patriotes* were demanding ministerial responsibility in the name of parliamentary democracy. After the military repression of the revolt, Lord Durham in his report to the British Parliament made two basic recommendations. The first one was to unite in a single state all the colonies still remaining in British possession after its defeat by the American Revolution. This recommendation became the basis of the Dominion of Canada some 25 years later, in 1867, by an act of the British Parliament: the British North America Act.

His second essential recommendation, the one that concerns us here, was pursuant to his observation that there were 'two nations warring within the bosom of the same state'. His straightforward remedy to this deplorable situation was to eliminate the French nation. This people, in the eyes of Durham, had no culture and no history. A good dose of 'stiff British rule', he notes, should achieve this objective. This enterprise has yet to be totally completed but it is still in process.

Parkman's thesis on the saving grace of the British military conquest of New France was, in fact, published during the interim between the Union Act (1840) uniting Lower and Upper Canada and the establishment of the Dominion of Canada in 1867. It arrived at the right time to unleash the passions and inflame the movement to eliminate the French nation. The spleen of the English newspapers of the period, the surprisingly bloodthirsty declarations of the Doric Club, the burning of the Canadian Parliament (then located in Montreal), as well as the nearly successful attempt by an English mob to assassinate the British governor, are a set of historical facts that show how serious, how intent, and in what manner the English Montrealers wanted to implement speedily Lord Durham's recommendation.

Anglo-Saxon historiography, on the basis of the Parkman legend, is replete with a portrait not only of New France but of Lower Canada as well,[4] and later of the province of Quebec, as a poor society, with a small population, archaic and feudal in character, with a stagnant economy, a tyrannical Church, and a corrupt and reactionary state. Meanwhile, during the same period, just south of the border, in New England, was a society in full demographic growth, a fully expanding economy, not to mention a military force able to force the British Empire to grant it its political sovereignty. How can this flagrant contrast between New France and New England be explained?

In her critique and reinterpretation of the historiography of New France, Roberta Hamilton (1988) brilliantly debunks what she considers to be a senseless question. She shows how the historians trying to locate the causes of this great demographic and economic disparity in the two colonies *themselves* are barking up the wrong tree, since the causes are to be found not in the colonies themselves, but in their respective metropoles, in the socio-economic nature of England and France.

In fact, the revolution took place in England 150 years before the French Revolution. Oliver Cromwell, a Puritan, not an Anglican, was the architect of the triumph of the bourgeoisie over the aristocracy and the feudal system. He had the king beheaded. He forced the aristocracy to choose: those who joined in the growth of bourgeois capitalism and participated in its enterprises were enriched; those who refused this alliance because of their loyalty to the past were impoverished amid their souvenirs. The peasants were *liberated* from their plots of land in spite of themselves to become an industrial proletariat. It was the first industrial revolution, fanned by the Puritan movement. It set the House of Commons under the leadership of Cromwell against the monarchy and the Church of England, which in their view retained too many features of detested Roman Catholicism.

This industrial revolution did not only change the nature of English society; it also facilitated the development of a much more prosperous colony because of its increased capital and massive emigration of the 'surplus population' of its newly emancipated peasantry to New England, joined also by members of dissident Protestant denominations in search of a more hospitable land. As a consequence, the economic and demographic growth of New England was speeded up.

The colonization of New France equally reflected the nature of its metropolis, where the transition to capitalism took place a century and a half later. The Anglophone legend, whose source is to be found in British anti-Popism and its contempt for continental feudalism and its absolute monarchy in France, led

Bishop Strachan, Anglican Bishop of Toronto and a central figure in the 'Family Compact' (at this time in our history, the ruling élite in Upper Canada, now Ontario), to claim that God, who had initially chosen the Jews as his people, had now bestowed his choice on the British Empire (Wise, 1965, 1967). When the British Empire shrank in the twentieth century, this legend disappeared in England but stayed alive in Canada.

In the second half of the nineteenth century, this Anglophone sentiment of superiority took on a racist overtone in English counter-revolutionary thought with the *Reflections on the Revolution in France* by Edmund Burke (1729-97), a reputed British political thinker in his time.[5] Confronted with the Declaration of the Rights of Man by the French Revolution, Burke retorted by declaring that the 'Rights of Englishmen' were not in need of a 'prior right' such as the 'Rights of Man'. Hannah Arendt (1961b: 176) explains his position:

> Burke's main argument against the 'abstract principles' of the French Revolution is contained in the following sentence: 'It has been the uniform policy of our constitution to claim and assert our liberties, as an *entailed inheritance* [Arendt's italics] derived to us from our forefathers, and to be transmitted to our posterity; as an estate specially belonging to the people of this kingdom, without any reference whatever to any other more general or prior right'.

Arendt continues:

> The concept of inheritance, applied to the very nature of liberty, has been the ideological basis from which English nationalism received its curious touch of race-feeling ever since the French Revolution. Formulated by a middle-class writer, it signified the direct acceptance of [a] feudal concept of liberty as the sum total of privileges inherited together with title and land. Without encroaching upon the rights of the privileged class within the English Nation, Burke enlarged the principle of these privileges to include the whole English people, establishing them as a kind of nobility among nations. Hence he drew his contempt for those who claimed their franchise as the rights of men, rights he saw fit to claim only as 'the rights of Englishmen'.

Closer to home, Ramsay Cook, the historian, and Pierre Elliott Trudeau, the politician, both claim Lord Acton as their mentor in terms of minority rights because of his declaration that 'the greatness of a State is measured by its treatment of minorities'; they neglect to tell us, however, that the states Lord Acton had in mind when he made the statement were the Austro-Hungarian Empire, for which he had particular affection, and the British Empire. The minorities he had in mind, therefore, were national minorities, not the sum of individuals that might comprise a social group. But the historian and the Prime Minister do not have the candour of Lord Durham.

Lord Acton defines more specifically what he means:

> The combination of different nations in one state is as necessary a condition for civilized life as the combination of men in society. Inferior races are raised by living in political union with races intellectually superior. Exhausted and decaying nations are revived by the contact of a younger vitality. Nations in which the elements of organization and the capacity for government have been lost, either through the demoralizing influence of despotism, or the *disintegrating action of democracy*, are restored and educated anew *under the discipline of a stronger and less corrupted race*. (Acton, 1956: 160-1; italics added)

One recognizes here echoes of Lord Durham's Report and of Francis Parkman.

Another celebrated phrase of Lord Acton concerns the corrupting effect of power: 'Power corrupts and absolute power corrupts absolutely.' Lord Acton's reference here is to the absolute monarchy in France before the revolution of 1789.

If Ramsay Cook and Pierre Trudeau had wanted fully to explain Lord Acton's thought, they would have shown that, for him, the aristocracy guaranteed *local government* in front of the absolute monarch. Louis XIV, the absolute monarch par excellence, was the king who completed the elimination of this role of the aristocracy in the political life of the realm. Lord Acton is not referring to a *local democracy* as clearly demonstrated in the previous quotations. Local democracy illustrated by the celebrated town hall meeting was initiated in the United States after their successful revolution.

They would also have perceived that the minorities Lord Acton refers to are *national minorities* recognized as such. It is clearly the case when he refers to the Austro-Hungarian Empire,[6] which he gives as an example. However, he becomes conscious that to include the British Empire in the model, he must appeal to another principle:

> The great importance of nationality in the State consists in the fact that it is the basis of political capacity. The character of a nation determines in great measure the form and vitality of a state. Certain political habits and ideas belong to particular nations, and they vary with the course of the national history. A people just emerging from barbarism, a people effete from the excesses of a luxurious civilization, cannot possess the means of governing itself; a people devoted to equality, or to absolute monarchy, is incapable of producing an aristocracy; a people averse to the institution of private property is without the first element of freedom. *Each of these can be converted into efficient members of a free community only by the contact of a superior race, in whose power will lie the future prospects of the State.* (Ibid., 167)[7]

Here Lord Acton gives a more detailed and specific picture of his definition of empire as 'a combination of different nations in one state'. Acton reveals in this passage what the nature of the combination must be. Arendt, without referring to Acton, explains why England was incapable of building an empire defined as a 'combination of different nations in a single state'. She tells us that the British 'Empire Builders putting their trust in conquest as a permanent method of rule were never able to incorporate their nearest neighbours, the Irish, into the far-flung structure either of the British Empire or the British Commonwealth of Nations.' Instead of awakening the 'slumbering genius of imperialism' (Arendt's reference to Lord Salisbury's expression) in the Irish, it had awakened the spirit of national resistance.

> The national structure of the United Kingdom had made quick assimilation and incorporation of the conquered peoples impossible: the British Commonwealth was never a 'Commonwealth of Nations', but the heir of the United Kingdom, *one* nation dispersed throughout the world. Dispersion and colonization did not expand, but transplanted, the political structure, with the result that the members of the new federated body remained closely tied to their common mother country for sound reasons of common past and common law. The Irish example proves how ill-fitted the United Kingdom was to build an imperial structure in which many different peoples could live contentedly together. (Arendt, 1991b: 126–7)

Let's return to what happens in the Canadian Confederation after its establishment in 1867. The British North America Act created provinces with legislatures that held exclusive jurisdiction on *local matters*, which included education, health, and charity. After the American Revolution, the English still loyal to the Crown took refuge in Canada and settled mainly in southern Ontario and in the Eastern Townships of Quebec. Confederation coincided with the period when secret societies flourished everywhere in the Western world (ibid., 97). At its very birth, a secret society, fiercely anti-Catholic and anti-French with the tacit approval of the Anglo-Protestant community, put pressure on the new provinces to outlaw French-language schools. It was successful in the early 1870s in Manitoba, then in the Maritime provinces, and finally in Ontario in 1912 with the public support of the Irish Catholic bishop of London, Ontario.

Clearly, all these intimidations were inspired by Lord Durham's recommendation to eliminate the French nation. The political misunderstanding in Canada, which has been constant but never openly or clearly stated, is that *national unity* in English Canada contains an underlying idea, ever since Lord Durham, of a unilingual nation. This idea is not expressed in the public political discourse of Anglophones. The Anglophones in Quebec no longer claim their 'entailed inheritance' in the name of 'the rights of Englishmen', as was their practice in imperial times, but in the name of the prior 'rights of man', an abomination for Edmund Burke and Lord Acton.

At the end of the twentieth century, the elimination of the French nation had not been completed. The dream of national unity, as conceived by Lord Durham and shared overwhelmingly in English Canada and by most of its recently landed citizens, is stalemated by the other dream: the dream of political emancipation and political independence steadily expanding in the Francophone population of Quebec: the Québécois.

The Francophones outside Quebec, who thought of themselves as part of the founding peoples of the Canadian state, are increasingly adjusting to the assimilationist policies of the governments and citizens in whose midst they live. Fearing their backlash, they duly profess their loyalty to national unity 'English-style' and dutifully condemn Quebec 'separatism'. Treated as immigrants for more than a century, they are finally behaving as immigrants as well.

The Roots of Francophone Counter-Legends

If, as Arendt contends, the function of legends is to enable human beings to appropriate a past that cannot be undone, two legends fulfil this need in the Québécois' historiography: one religious, the other political.

O Felix Culpa

In 1774, the British Parliament voted the Act of Quebec in the hope of ensuring the loyalty of its newly conquered people in the eventuality of an American Revolution. Put into effect in 1775, the Act of Quebec granted the Catholic Church the right to keep its property, a right the Catholic Church in England was still denied.

Fifteen years later, in 1789, the French Revolution took place. One of its consequences was that the Catholic Church lost its property rights (which covered one-quarter of the national territory). The Catholic Church of Quebec got a lucky break. Indeed, without the British Conquest it can be assumed that the Quebec Church would not have been spared. This event became perceived by the Church and the faithful as a providential blessing and thus the legend—O Felix Culpa[8]— was born and took on its full meaning. With this legend, French Catholic Quebec could appropriate a past that they could not undo. And the monarchist bias in the teaching of the French Revolution became an understandable corollary.

On the one hand, this legend made it possible to appropriate the painful reality of the British Conquest, a part of its recent past, and it allowed the Catholic Church to pursue its mission in North America, to keep its flock in the faith and to ensure its survival. After the Durham Report, the clergy could not be unaware that political equality was out of the question, since its avowed intention was the deconstruction of the French nation by a dose of 'stiff British rule'. And, if the Church hierarchy did not encourage the *patriotes* in 1837–8, it most probably was because it could perceive both the impossibility of a military victory and the definitive refusal to implement political reform.[9]

In any event, the Church was really concerned with the '*survivance de la race canadienne-française*' ('survival of the French-Canadian nation') and wanted to keep its flock faithful, as indicated in the well-known expression '*la langue gardienne de la foi*' ('language as guardian of the faith'). From that principle, and because of its warranted distrust of civil authority, the Church stayed concerned with keeping access to its institutions[10] for its own flock exclusively.

When, in 1867, the Dominion of Canada was created, it was without enthusiasm as well as with a warranted distrust and a noted silence that it was generally received by the Quebec hierarchy and by Monseigneur Bourget,[11] the Archbishop of Montreal, in particular. He, in fact, eventually defeated the attempt by the ruling élite in Lower Canada, the Château Clique, to establish a network of English primary schools all over Lower Canada. This was achieved by the Church taking charge of the creation of French primary parochial schools in Montreal.

The second aspect of the *Felix Culpa* legend does not concern the past but the future. It defined Quebec's mission in North America. The 'Messianic Myth' debunked by the historian Michel Brunet in the late 1950s was an outcome of that mission. Protected by providence, the Quebec people and their Church inherited the mission of keeping alive the Catholic faith in North America. The myth of agriculturalism and its distrust of industrialization equally originated from the same source. 'Anti-statism', a position the Church would drop only after the start of the Quiet Revolution, can also be understood in terms of the future. The Catholic Church in Quebec felt it was forced to distrust the (colonial and later the provincial) state after Lord Durham, the visionary conceiver of the Dominion of Canada, made the clear and unequivocal recommendation to *assimilate* the French nation in Canada.

THE TWO FOUNDING PEOPLES

The legend of the two founding peoples cannot be attributed to the Catholic Church. The Canadian confederation was created by an Act of the imperial Parliament. Its first intention was to appropriate all the territory north of the 49th parallel, from sea to sea (*a mari usque ad mare*), in order to establish a British North America. It was indeed urgent to establish it and to lay claim to the unpeopled territories of what was to become the provinces of western Canada because of the swift westward movement of the Americans towards the Pacific. Territorial integrity was to be ensured by the construction of two national railway systems spanning the whole continent from East to West. The political project included setting up an infrastructure to facilitate exporting to Great Britain, and elsewhere, western wheat and the output of emerging industrial production in Ontario.

The instigators of this project certainly did not have the intention of proclaiming that the basis of the Dominion of Canada was a pact between its two founding peoples. It is, however, precisely this popular belief that formed the basis of the consent of Francophones all across the country. It is equally the legend that gave legitimation for the Francophone élite's participation in the political life and institutions of Confederation. This legend of 'the Founding Peoples' was renamed by John Porter (1965) as the 'Two Charter Groups'. Ramsay Cook (1966, 1971) refuted its historical credibility and Pierre Elliott Trudeau trampled it politically to secure for himself a place as a *Great Canadian* in the history books of English Canada.

The night of 4 November 1981 (since then labelled by Francophone Québé-cois as the 'Night of the Long Knives') made the repatriation of the constitution possible. Until that night Quebec had a veto over changes in the constitution. That evening Trudeau obtained from Lévesque the withdrawal of Quebec's constitu-tional veto. In the preceding months, all the Anglophone premiers of the Canadian provinces had ostentatiously agreed to settle the issue of Francophone minority rights in their provinces by instituting interprovincial agreements with Quebec. With Quebec's right to veto constitutional changes out of the way, they unashamedly and triumphantly proclaimed unilaterally the very next morning the patriation of the constitution. Political trickery was required to repatriate the constitution: a great way to achieve national unity.

Quebec has refused ever since to become a signatory to the Canadian consti-tution and every attempt to meet conditions acceptable to Quebec so that it could re-enter the constitutional fold has since been thwarted: the Meech Lake Accord sabotaged by Elijah Harper with the co-operation of the Manitoba Premier and Clyde Wells. Behold the hypocrisy of Clyde Wells, who had signed it as Premier of Newfoundland and subsequently urged the provincial legislature of Newfound-land to turn it down. That political instability in Canada is as much the product of the duplicity of Trudeau and the provincial premiers is never acknowledged in English Canada. It's always the separatists. The Charlottetown Accord negotiated by Robert Bourrasa fell far short of Meech Lake. It was rejected in a Canada-wide referendum by both English Canada and Quebec Francophones.

Since then the constitutional dead end has become permanent. The federal government is imposing on Quebec a constitution it did not consent to. More than 150 years since Lord Durham's Report, about half of the Francophone Québécois still don't realize that the liquidation of the French nation in Canada remains the unstated but ever-pursued objective of the government of Canada and of its increasingly polarized citizenry.

From Tradition to Modernity, 1945–1960

The transformation of Quebec from a traditional into a modern society has been called its Quiet Revolution. This change was noted and welcomed—at the begin-ning—by the political élites of English Canada. They viewed it as Quebec's defi-nite embrace of modernity. They believed that by becoming a society more closely resembling their own, goodwill ('la bonne entente') would increase between English and French Canadians. That illusion was soon to disappear.

Laval University's Faculty of Social Sciences, headed by Reverend George-Henri Lévesque, OP, is most often credited with initiating the movement for change in Quebec. With professors trained in the immediate postwar period at Harvard University in economics and at the University of Chicago in sociology, Laval University became the centre of new thinking in Quebec.[12] Originating in postwar modern American thought, the ideas nurtured by Reverend Lévesque and the Faculty of Social Sciences at Laval spelled out the needed transformations in the postwar period. The blossoming of this new thinking in Quebec spans the period from 1945 to 1960, the transition between past and future, the past that would no longer be and the future that had not yet become.

The traditional social organization of Quebec society was soon challenged at the end of World War II. Social unrest spread progressively in all its fundamental institutions: the Church, organized labour, the class structure, the political regime, the family, as well as the health and educational systems and the caring of the poor.

The Telling Signs of Impending Modernization

The first signs of change took place within the Church itself. A conflict of perspectives arose between the Catholic Action movement and a plurality of bishops. The most active and dynamic was the Jeunesse étudiante catholique (JEC), which influenced a whole generation of youth as well as the intelligentsia. Initially, the unrest focused on the place of the laity or the congregation within the Church and its rather passive and insignificant role in Church life. At the parish level, the laity had a restricted, routinized, and customary role. The territorial base of the parish, which in the countryside encompassed a homogeneous population, had no impact on the urban workplace in full expansion where 'the meeting of two worlds'[13] was taking place. The Catholic Action movement organized outside the parish structure—in the workplace, and in social environments that were in a process of rapid social change. They were not under the control of parish priests or the bishops. They were guided by chaplain-priests who, most often, shared the unrest and the aspirations of the movement's leaders. Keenly interested in the changes taking place here and abroad, they were skilful practitioners of Emmanuel Mounier's *'philosophie personaliste'*, avid readers of the Catholic periodical *Esprit*, which he edited.[14]

Anxious to ensure a Christian presence in the rapidly growing industrial world, they were equally fascinated by this new world, its social sciences, its cinema, and so on. The JEC, for instance, was passionately interested in cinema. They encouraged the establishment of film clubs, and periodicals on the cinema saw the light of day. Meanwhile, the hierarchy still viewed the JEC with great reservations. Drive-in theatres were still forbidden by provincial fiat more than a decade after they had mushroomed elsewhere. This was perceived as a political gesture by Premier Maurice Duplessis to please the Church hierarchy. Moreover, modern dances were considered sinful and the Quebec bishops issued a collective letter condemning them. Monsignor Charbonneau, the Archbishop of Montreal, refused to sign it and the legend has it that he told his Catholic peers: 'You will not be able to keep Montreal in short pants.'

The Issue of Confessionality

The end of an era was predictable when a great debate took place within the Catholic Church on the issue of whether membership in the trade unions and in the *caisses populaires* (Church-based credit unions) should be reserved exclusively to Catholics or whether they should be open to everyone.

The Catholic trade unions as well as the Caisses Populaires Desjardins were initiated at the very beginning of the twentieth century, a time when the masses of common folk in the cities were suffering from dire poverty. Initiated by the Church, under the impulse of Pope Leo XIII's encyclical letter *Rerum Novarum,* the Confédération des Travailleurs Catholiques du Canada (CTCC) was established. The Caisses Populaires Movement, initiated by Alphonse Desjardins to provide access to financial loans for the French-Canadian population, was greatly facilitated by the close co-operation of the Catholic Church. They were welcomed all over the province and granted premises for their operation by parish churches.

The CTCC trade unions became established in Quebec City and in some other cities of the province but had little foothold in Montreal itself. The bishop of each diocese assigned to the local trade unions a chaplain who understandably remained sensitive to the bishop's directives. In Montreal, from the beginning of the twentieth century, the situation became quite different. When American capital forged ahead of British capital, the American trade union movement, which was non-denominational, followed suit. These trade unions recruited Catholic as well as non-Catholic workers. Thus arose the issue whether the Catholic trade unions should be denominational or not.

For the *caisses populaires*, which were spreading more and more throughout Montreal, the religious issue became the following: should non-Catholics be accepted as regular members? Reality eventually brought closure to the debate. Rooted in the province, but not in Montreal, the CTCC did not carry the day with large industry. The non-denominational Fédération des Travailleurs du Québec (FTQ), affiliated with the American trade union movement, became the dominant force within organized labour in Quebec. At the beginning of the Quiet Revolution, under a new name and a modified perspective, now known as the Confédération des Syndicats Nationaux (CSN), it would eventually make substantial inroads in the 1960s, not among the working class but in the new middle classes, the salaried employees of the provincial and municipal governments, and in the parapublic sectors of health and education. The CSN trade unions dropped their chaplains, became more radical, and were inspired more by Marxism than by the social doctrine of the Church.

The *caisses populaires* eventually decided to open membership to non-Catholics, though this led nonetheless to a schism between some *caisses*, which started a rival organization known as the Fédération des Caisses Populaires de Montréal. The Caisses d'économie started during this period. They set up shop in the workplace instead of the parishes (that is, in large factories, universities, police associations, hospitals, and so on), but other than this difference they operated like the *caisses populaires*. The then president of the *caisses populaires* refused to integrate them in the federation for the following reason: 'All of these persons have access to a caisse in their own parish.'[15]

One can see how both the Caisses d'économie and the Catholic Action move-ment made the same choice of operating in the workplace rather than in the parish setting. The *caisses populaires* opted to stay tied to the parish setting even though the workplace of the parishioners is overwhelmingly outside of its narrow limits. In Montreal, undergoing rapid population growth, the link between place of residence and the workplace was broken and the urban parish took on the role of a dormi-tory or one of several compartmentalized aspects of urban life, as do, from their very inception, the suburban towns, otherwise known as 'bedroom' communities.

Trade Unionism

In action terms, the trial of tradition starts in 1949 with the Asbestos Strike. This strike challenged the political regime of the Duplessis government when two bish-ops openly expressed their solidarity with the striking workers by allowing funds to be collected in every parish of their diocese.[16] It should be noted that the Catholic hierarchy had previously avoided taking sides in labour disputes, content with private rather than public interventions. Students from the Social Science Faculty of Laval, headed by the Rev. Georges-Henri Lévesque and under the lead-ership of student leaders of the JEC movement, organized collections in Catholic parishes to support the striking workers.[17] Premier Duplessis, meanwhile, declared the strike illegal and sent the provincial police to brutally suppress the demonstra-tions taking place. The intelligentsia, then, massively sided with the striking work-ers. The opening crack between the political regime and important elements of civil society would keep on widening.

The consequences of this strike (which, by the way, the workers lost) led to deep divisions within Quebec society. The conflict between the Duplessis govern-ment and the Faculty of Social Sciences at Laval deepened. Their graduates were effectively barred from employment in Quebec's public service. They were welcomed with open arms in the federal government. Father Lévesque was submitted to an ecclesiastic trial in Rome, where, due to the support he received from the religious order of the Dominicans, he was found innocent. The Duplessis government, with the collaboration of some bishops friendly to his regime, pres-sured Rome to act. Archbishop Charbonneau is said to have been shunned by his peers, not well liked by his clergy but very popular with the faithful. Badly advised, Pius XII demanded his resignation as Archbishop of Montreal, a rare gesture in Church history.[18] This forced resignation produced a spontaneous and unprece-dented movement of popular indignation. Respect for religious authority took a serious blow. The now Mgr Charbonneau exiled himself to British Columbia in a nunnery, a broken and destroyed man, where he died in 1959. His remains were brought back to Montreal and, in spite of his last wishes, he was given a grandiose funeral on television, with all the hierarchy and all the political class present. But the harm had been done. The chasm these events created between the society and the Church would only increase.

On the other hand, after the Asbestos Strike, the Catholic trade union move-ment had the wind in its sails. Important strikes in Louiseville and Murdochville received wide and popular support, as well as the support of the intelligentsia and a good part of the clergy. In fact, at that time, the great majority of the working class was not unionized and the large corporations that had been dealing with trade unions in Ontario were, in the 1950s, fiercely resisting their implementation in Quebec, where workers' wages were lower.

Trade unionism attracted attention beyond the working class and the private sector. The first to be attracted were the primary school teachers. M. Léo Guindon had attempted to establish a teachers' association to negotiate working conditions through collective bargaining. In 1948 they obtained their accreditation as a trade union from the Quebec Labour Relations Board. In 1949, after a short strike, their trade union accreditation was withdrawn under orders from Premier Duplessis. L'Alliance (the group's official name) appealed this decision in the courts and in 1952 they regained their accreditation (Gagnon, 1971: 219ff.). Meanwhile, Cardi-nal Léger,[19] who had become the new Archbishop of Montreal, set up a compet-ing professional association. This attempt eventually proved fruitless when, later, the Alliance des Professeurs Catholiques de Montréal was born.

A sign of the times, in 1966 the Alliance dropped the Catholic adjective to become simply the Alliance des Professeurs de Montréal (ibid., 275). After the reform of the Labour Code in 1964, which allowed state employees to unionize, the right to strike was also granted a year later to the teachers. And, as it often happens, at the first opportunity the Alliance went on strike, on 13 January 1967. This strike lasted a month. The teachers initially garnered widespread popular support but it fizzled away gradually as the strike dragged on. Parents, who had taken care of their children at home during the Christmas holidays, were forced to keep them at home in the thick of winter and, for many, it involved leaving their employment to do so. As a result, their support evaporated. The government real-ized that it could now call a special session of the National Assembly and enact a bill forcing the teachers back to work, which was done on 17 February. The school boards also lost their managerial independence. This pattern would be frequently used by the governments of both political parties to counterbalance strikes by unionized public and parapublic employees.[20] With such a practice, the govern-ment, a direct party to the conflict, becomes both judge and jury. This remains an unresolved problem.

At the University of Chicago, where I was a student in the early 1950s, Everett Hughes asked us one day: 'To whom do the poor in society belong?' Using the Socratic method, he made us discover that we could find the answer in ourselves. The poor used to belong to their kin. Later, they became the responsibility of reli-gious institutions. Protestants and Jews have non-profit corporations, voluntary organizations, and women's auxiliaries. In the case of Montreal, the Catholic Church had numerous religious orders that took care of the poor. Among them were (and are) the Société Saint Vincent de Paul and Le Conseil des Oeuvres, which operated for the archdiocese. Hughes then made us realize that more and more the poor become the responsibility of the state and of an assortment of professional social workers.

In Montreal, until the mid-1960s, public charity was organized on an ethnic and religious basis. There were four different charity federations: one for the French-Canadian Catholics, one for the Irish and Anglophone Catholics, one for the Jews, and one for the Anglo-Protestants. Each had its annual public subscription campaign. The reform of these four independent federations into one Centraide or United Way took place in the late 1960s or early 1970s.

In regard to financing public education, in those days large private corporations in Quebec had the privilege of choosing to which school board they would pay their taxes—Catholic or Protestant. Montreal's large corporate sector, much more Protestant than Catholic, opted for the Protestant school boards.[21] Meanwhile, the gap between the salaries paid to the teaching personnel of the two school boards was widening. The teachers of the Commission des Écoles Catholiques de Montréal (CECM) were claiming equal salary for equal qualifications. The response of the Protestant School Board of Greater Montreal (PSBGM), which was nonetheless relevant, was that they had to compete with Ontario salaries. It was inexcusable, however, to justify as public policy that the gap between the tax revenue of the PSBGM per student should amount to some $140 more than the CECM's revenue per student (ibid.).

From 1950 to 1960, Catholic parishes multiplied rapidly in Montreal due to the massive migration of population from every rural region of the province. It was also the beginning of rapidly increasing immigration from Europe. Housing developments mushroomed to fill the vacant lands within the city limits; Catholic churches and their dependencies were established, as well. Primary schools sprang up along with the all-too-familiar Steinberg supermarkets. A *caisse populaire* bearing the name of the parish[22] soon followed. When a citizen was asked where he lived in Montreal, he was more likely than not to state the name of the parish church he belonged to.

In the countryside at that time, as in the case of St Denis de Kamouraska, a small village of 700 people, the schools included all age groups: there were three schools and three different school boards, one in the village and two in the rural concessions. The teachers in the rural concessions were never nuns but young women from the parish or from neighbouring parishes. The teacher was usually well known by the schoolchildren's parents because they either had seen her grow up or knew the humble social status of her parents. It was not a rare event for parents to take issue when the teacher disciplined their children. This explanation was given to me by the parish priest to explain the tone of his sermon on a Sunday in late August before the opening of the new school year. In it he had sternly admonished the parents to uphold the teacher and not their children in such events. Parents often perceived the teacher as trying 'to pull rank' over *their* children. In a fully developed parish, nuns from outside the community would teach in the village school. Being strangers and the status of their religious calling in the community eliminated these problems.

Horace Miner, an American anthropologist, published his Ph.D. dissertation, *St. Denis: A French-Canadian Parish*, a highly readable monograph of this rural parish, describing the most traditional part of Quebec rural society. He used the four seasons and the life cycle as the parameters within which he analysed the customs and the basic institutions of kinship and religion and outlined the direction of impending social change. I revisited St Denis in 1959–60 and the data referred to here come from that field research.

The professional training of teachers took place in 'normal schools' located within a range of 50 kilometres or so from their native parishes. The training was given by nuns. The candidate would have a one-year stay after completing her primary school and would be granted a *Brevet C*, which would qualify her to teach. In the mid-1950s, when the qualification requirements were increased, nuns were the first to invade the Université de Montréal campus for summer courses and the campus took on the look of an immense convent. In the fall, the campus became peopled by a great majority of male students, dressed in the ever-present blue blazer and grey flannel trousers. This attire identified them as university students to the public and virtually every student wore this attire with pride.

When older people of St Denis were asked, in an interview, how long they had gone to school, they all would answer with a tinge of shame, 'Three years', then would hurry to add: 'I didn't drop out of school; three years is all there was; the school dropped us.'

During the forties, high schools were rare in Montreal, and the students attending them were not numerous. While enrolment grew quickly during the fifties, official statistics show that the drop-out rate in secondary schools was quite a bit higher in Quebec than in Ontario (ibid., 224).[23] In 1951, only 50 per cent of students who finished their ninth year in school registered for the tenth year. Among Anglophones, 71.5 per cent of those who finished their second year of high school were registered in the third year. (By the end of the decade, however, the drop-out rates had become similar among both Anglophone and Francophones.)

Faced with this difference, the educated Anglophones saw in this fact a difference in values, not a difference in resources. The French-Canadian culture was seen as the cause of this phenomenon rather than the political economy of the country and the poverty of the families.

Ten years later, referring to the Quebec Francophones of Montreal, Marcel Rioux and Yves Martin (see Rioux and Martin, 1964), both good sociologists and good socialists, wondered if it was not appropriate to think of the Francophone Montrealers as an *ethnic class*. The leftist intellectuals saw it as a major ideological error and sociologists became embroiled in a controversy on the concepts of nation and class. Just as the postwar Catholic Church, caught between its right wing that was refusing modernity and its left wing (the Catholic Action movement) that acclaimed it, the political left remained divided on the national question until the

The expression that Quebec was a 'priest-ridden society' was commonly used and the economic underdevelopment of Francophone Quebec was and still is explained by the 'value system' of the Catholic Church. Most of these analysts were quick to refer to Max	Weber's thesis on *The Protestant Ethic and the Spirit of Capitalism* (1958 [1930]). Needless to say, the economic underdevelopment of the Maritime provinces and Newfoundland, essentially Anglophone provinces, was not explained in the same manner.

virtual collapse of the left in Quebec in the early 1980s. However, the extreme left, like the Catholic Action movement earlier, continued to oppose the national against the social question when and if they were ever asked.

When the public high schools were not numerous, there was no shortage of 'classical colleges' to ensure the education of the future élites and the recruitment of future priests. High school diplomas did not automatically lead to university admissions reserved for candidates with the BA degree. In Montreal, the first to become preoccupied by this problem was the Faculty of Science of the Université de Montréal and the École des Hautes Études Commerciales. They initiated the establishment of *preparatory* courses in what became known as 'classical sections' in certain secondary schools. They gradually introduced at the university level an undergraduate program.

Law, medicine, and the social sciences admitted only students with a BA until well into the late 1950s. These lags in development can partly be attributed to the fact the Université de Montréal's institutional development was accelerated only in the 1930s and only after bitter struggles between Quebec and Montreal within the clergy as well as within Quebec society.

The political opposition to the Duplessis regime increased during the fifties and crystallized throughout the decade. The conflict between the Faculty of Social Sciences and Duplessis, well known by the public at large, snowballed in the university environment of Montreal. *Cité Libre*, a periodical begun by Pierre Trudeau and collaborators mainly recruited from the Catholic Action movement, became the most widely read periodical in the province. It engaged in polemics with *Relations,* a Jesuit periodical that was still defending the political regime of Maurice Duplessis. These intellectual debates were passionately followed by the intelligentsia both inside and outside Quebec. In the name of the 'social', the *Cité Librists* attacked the traditional nationalism of a good part of the Church hierarchy, claiming that it led to national socialism.[24] The Church and the values it communicated were, for those at *Cité Libre*, obstacles both to democracy and to the economic development of Quebec society (Trudeau, 1968: 103–23).

In spite of the growing unrest and alienation of the new middle classes, the regime would only end with the sudden death of Maurice Duplessis in September 1959. Two young priests,[25] in a political manifesto published in a periodical destined only to priests, *Ad Usum Sacerdotum,* raised the issue of the political immorality of Maurice Duplessis's Union Nationale because his political machine was based on patronage. Their article circulated beyond the clergy and quickly reached the larger public, Anglophone as well as Francophone, and was widely acclaimed.

In the meantime, the '*mouvement pour L'École laïque*' made modest inroads among Montreal's intelligentsia. At the end of the decade, the Association des Professeurs de l'Université de Montréal published a pamphlet whose title needs no explanation: *L'Université dit Non aux Jésuites* and, effectively, the latter were unable to obtain a university charter to change their Sainte-Marie College into a second Francophone university. L'Université du Québec à Montréal (UQAM) was to be founded some years later.[26] In it, Marxist thought supplanted Christian thinking.

The Health System and Family Life

The traditional health system and the traditional family were also put on trial. Hospitals in the late 1950s, due to higher costs brought about by increased specialization in the medical profession as well as new medical technologies, were forced to increase the costs to patients. The great majority of citizens, who could not afford the hikes, became increasingly irritated and began to question the role of religious orders in the health system. Criticism became virulent: the population was scandalized that a patient had to prove his capacity to pay before his admission to the hospital. Religious orders, one frequently overheard, were doing business, not charity. The resentment was highest among the working classes, who lacked the resources to pay these price increases.

In this context Premier Paul Sauvé, Duplessis's successor, made his famous threefold declaration: *Désormais* ('From now on'). The first concerned establishing a Royal Commission to study the feasibility of setting up a free hospitalization program. The second involved setting up *statutory grants* to universities rather than *discretionary grants*, as was customary until then. The third expressed his intention to revise the pay scale of civil servants, now called public service employees. In brief, he announced that the interests of the new middle classes would, from now on, be the Quebec state's priorities. His premature death plunged Quebec into a mood of national mourning.

What was striking in this postwar period was the speed with which unapparent but profound changes occurred in the behaviour of Quebec's population. The first surprise was the sudden and drastic drop in the birth rate. The demographers,[27] who were exhorting the population to practise family planning through birth control to ensure a better standard of living, were the first to be surprised to discover in the Canadian census of 1961 that Quebec's birth rate was suddenly below the Canadian birth rate. Clearly, in a context of rapid and massive urbanization, the small size and number of rooms in the housing stock had won against the preaching of the clergy.[28]

The other important change concerned divorce. Towards the end of the 1950s, the Speaker of the House of Commons, a prominent Quebecer, went incognito to

Las Vegas, established residence there for a month, and obtained a divorce. This information was leaked and made headlines across Canada. Greatly compromised by this scandal, the eminent parliamentarian and author of a highly noted treatise on parliamentary procedures was forced to resign as Speaker and subsequently was dropped as a candidate by the Liberal Party. He disappeared from public life, earned his living by doing translation, and died a totally forgotten person.

Divorce, at that time, was generally spurned.[29] In Quebec and Newfoundland, divorce was only granted on the grounds of adultery, by an Act of Parliament and granted by the Canadian Senate. This situation gave rise to an industry of 'simulated adultery'. The party requesting the divorce would hire a lawyer, a private detective, a photographer, and a young woman. The husband would pay the rental of a motel room and when the detective and photographer 'interrupted', as prearranged, and photographed the 'adulterous' couple lounging in loose attire on the same bed, a *legal fact* had just been created.[30]

Another Telling Strike

The period under discussion that started with the Asbestos Strike also ended with a strike: the Radio-Canada strike. In fact, it involved television, not radio. The issue was this: the TV producers of Radio-Canada wanted to form a trade union. Management claimed producers were not workers but part of management and therefore could not be unionized. The strike lasted several weeks. The TV screens in Quebec, however, were not blank. Instead, films were broadcast from morning till night. The TV viewing audience warmed to this new programing and remained rather indifferent to the strike. After some time, the artists who were hired by the producers of the Crown corporation pledged their support to the strike, and this was followed by the support of university students and, with due lag, their professors.

The only institution of the Canadian government split in two divisions on the basis of language is the CBC and Radio-Canada. Subsidized by the Canadian government, this Crown corporation is accountable to the House of Commons for its administration. Only at the top are the two divisions unified. Since the situation did not budge, the conflict became transformed from a trade union battle to a political issue. The unionized workers of Radio-Canada requested the support and solidarity of their counterparts from the Canadian Broadcasting Corporation employees' association but were turned down. The strikers brought pressure on the Canadian government to intervene, but the government failed to budge, leaving the Radio-Canada strikers to conclude that had the CBC rather than Radio-Canada been on strike, the Canadian Parliament would have intervened.

It is of interest to compare the Asbestos Strike with the Radio-Canada strike. In the first case, the company was the Johns Manville Corporation, an American multinational corporation with Anglophone managers and Francophone miners— many of whom eventually fell victim to asbestosis, a fatal lung disease. Who was blamed in the final analysis? Maurice Duplessis and the provincial police. In the case of the Radio-Canada strike, which initially involved the managers of the

French network and the Francophone producers, who was eventually criticized? The Canadian government.

This apparent contradiction can be easily explained. Michel Brunet, a history professor at the Université de Montréal, stated that there are two sets of citizens: Canadians and *Canadiens*. The latter constituted a subordinated *national minority*, and, in such a case, although democracy is defined as the government of the people, by the people, and for the people, it becomes, in such a case, the government of the majority, by the majority, and for the majority. Since Quebec is a subordinated national minority, the Canadian Parliament would not intervene. Such is the case in Canada. This perception was real to those touched by the Radio-Canada strike.

W.I. Thomas, professor at the University of Chicago in the early twentieth century, emphasized the importance of the 'definition of the situation' for what becomes socially real. With the Radio-Canada strike, the definition of the political situation was changing and would never again be the same. Once the Canadian government was blamed for the strike at Radio-Canada, the consequences became far-reaching for all of us.

In fact, the first important consequence was René Lévesque's decision to enter the field of politics. He had been a popular international correspondent for Radio-Canada. As Minister of Natural Resources, he nationalized the private electricity companies in Quebec. Another 'outcome' of the strike, the Quebec Liberal Party slogan of the 1962 election, '*Maîtres chez nous*', gave a new resurgence to the nationalist movement in Quebec. All this and more were the social consequences of the Radio-Canada strike.

The Quiet Revolution and Mores

The modernization process that all societies of the Western world underwent was based, as I stated in the introduction, on 'new common values'. In Quebec, this process was called the Quiet Revolution. The expression fits, not because of different causes, but because of its very different consequences: the *speed*, the *scope*, and the *depth* of these transformations deeply altered the social structure of Quebec society.

We can illustrate the *speed* by referring once more to the unhappy ending of Louis Beaudoin's public career. A decade or so later, with the October Crisis of 1970, after the application of the War Measures Act, it was rumoured that, because of the broad powers it contained, the police would use the legislation to dismantle organized crime in Quebec. (Ottawa, in any event, immediately denied any such intention.) In order to discredit Jérôme Choquette, the Minister of Justice in the provincial cabinet at the time, the leaders of organized crime supposedly let it be known that Choquette was not only divorced but had remarried. The leaders of organized crime, more conservative than the people, had expected public rebuke and embarrassment for the government. Not a ripple did this news create in the public. The 'Mafia' seemed unaware that a large number of the Francophone public had followed Choquette's example and that no one in the future would have to hide his or her divorced situation.[31]

A simple enumeration of the institutions affected makes evident the *scope* of the changes. For instance, in the field of labour relations, the right to strike is extended to middle-class employees of the state, city administrations, and all areas of the public service, as well as in the parapublic institutions of health and education. The social institutions are secularized and become financed by the provincial state. Public charity becomes social welfare and is bureaucratically managed; the state finances the accelerated construction of teaching and health institutions and increases substantially its share of their budgets. And free hospitalization is soon followed by free medical services.[32]

The *depth* of the changes can be measured by the massive drop in religious practice and the visible indifference, when not outright hostility, to the Christian tradition.

To finance the increased participation of the state in the rapid establishment and expanding scale of these social institutions, a new pattern was introduced, which was a carbon copy of what was practised throughout Canada and the US. It required increased taxation but also very much increased borrowing from the local and foreign financial markets by issuing provincial bonds, provincially guaranteed school board bonds, municipal bonds, and Crown corporation bonds.[33]

The growth of state expenditures to finance these new social structures was not only exponential but also continuous. To ensure free access to all citizens to these new services in health and education, the state induced these institutions to increase quickly the number of admissions and the size of the institutions. In the case of colleges and universities, the statutory grants were determined on a per capita basis and the amount increased as the level of studies increased: CEGEPs (Collèges d'Enseignement Général et d'Enseignement Professionnel, Quebec's equivalence to community colleges), undergraduate, and graduate programs. For hospitals, the grants were determined on a per diem basis per bed. To increase their budgets so they could hire more specialized professionals in all disciplines and acquire new technologies, these institutions increased the number of patients and their physical plants. Later, they could always negotiate with the state, if it proved necessary, for the required increases in government grants.

This new public, state-financed system of institutions reflected the 'new common values' that spelled the end of the traditional system. The Quiet Revolution is still celebrated by the groups that directly benefited from its implementation simply because they were able to establish lifelong careers within its institutions. And, without a doubt, today's Quebec has become a modern society, very similar to others in the Western world. Only the elderly are witnesses to the conflicts that took place before this Quiet Revolution unfolded. Since then, Quebec society has undergone all the social and political movements that took shape in the Western world: the national movements in former imperial colonies, the student movements of the 1960s, the feminist movement in the 1970s, as well as the rise and then the collapse of Marxist ideology in the early 1980s, with the current American neo-liberal legend that only a capitalist world economy can be the basis of a political democracy now holding sway.

The Quiet Revolution also had some unforeseen and unintended consequences. The two most important ones are the secularization of Quebec society and the rebirth of the national movement. They become the topics of the remainder of this essay.

The Secularization of Quebec Society

The Catholic Action movement aimed at ensuring the presence of the Church and Christian thought in the world by the concerted action of lay Catholics in society. To achieve this, the narrow limits of the Catholic parish had to be transcended, and youth had to become educated and commit themselves to change the world rather than submit to it, to challenge it instead of withdrawing from it. Some bishops and parts of the clergy perceived this as a questioning of the very teachings of the Catholic Church, which had not long ago outrightly condemned modernism.[34] This conflict led to what I have called 'the tradition on trial'.

The end product of this conflict was the secularization of the institutions founded, managed, and financed by the Church. This was followed by a massive exodus of younger priests from the ranks of the clergy, and, later, a spectacular decrease in religious practice of the laity, to such a point that it is often said that Quebec is now in need of missionaries. Those who regret as well as those who rejoice at this state of affairs share this observation. The first major social change of the 1960s was clearly the secularization of Quebec society.

The secularization of teaching institutions and the social institutions in health and public charity took place for reasons that were unrelated to the loss of faith and religious practice. For instance, concerning primary school education, what precipitated the change was a provincial government policy designed to increase the qualifications of teachers.

The secretary of the school board of Ville-Marie, a small town in the Temiscamingue region of northern Quebec, explained to me what really happened. His explanation was roughly the following:

> Not so long ago, the school boards had to be satisfied with the local school tax revenues to set up their budgets. Under these conditions, their interest was better served by recruiting nuns or teaching brothers. Since they cost less because they lived frugally and as a group, we could hire more of them with our budget. As long as the school board had to cover all their costs, they tried to recruit their teachers from the Superior General of all the religious teaching orders. With the Quiet Revolution things have now changed. The government, to induce school boards to increase the formal qualifications of teachers, makes available to the school boards special funding for this purpose. It becomes instantly more advantageous to hire lay people, men and women, than the nuns: the lay people spend nearly all their salary in the community: the car, the house or apartment, the groceries, the

insurance, the barber or the hairdresser, clothes' boutiques, and finally they equally pay taxes to the municipality from which religious orders are exempted. They contribute much more to the local economy than the nuns. Take me, for instance, I sell insurance: it brings me customers.

One must add that it was predominantly businessmen and professional people who got elected to school boards.[35] The replacement of nuns by laypersons did not need an ideological basis since the new set-up of professionally qualified and publicly paid employees made a clear contribution to the local economy without affecting religious practices or beliefs. Clearly, in the countryside, religious practice and the Catholic faith were not shattered by the onset of the Quiet Revolution.[36]

The blueprint for revamping the educational system was contained in the 1960s Report of the Parent Commission: reducing drastically the number of school boards at the primary school level, creating regional school boards to administer secondary schools, replacing the classical colleges with CEGEPs, replacing the small normal schools with faculties of education at the universities, and developing undergraduate programs in all disciplines at the university level. The Report was essentially well received and both political parties agreed with most of its recommendations.

The growth of these state-financed institutions in education and health spelled automatically the shrinking role of the Church in society and its permanent withdrawal from the institutions it had founded, funded, and managed. Only the state could muster the resources necessary to universalize access to these institutions for all social classes. It could and did raise taxes, but it also borrowed massively on financial markets and, with deficit financing prevalent until the nineties, created a debt whose interest used up nearly half of the annual budgets.

Until the Quiet Revolution, a priest who 'lost his vocation' was socially ostracized; many would leave for large American cities.[37] In the 1960s that situation rapidly changed. In the 1950s, many priests, brothers, and nuns earned university degrees and accumulated years of professional experience in teaching institutions and in hospitals and charitable organizations. Many among them had the required qualifications to enter and pass entrance exams to enter the expanding public service. The demand for qualified people far exceeded the supply, which enabled the priests and nuns who had returned to lay status to have access to these openings. During the papacy of John XXIII (1958–63), it became much easier for them to be relieved of their religious vows. In Quebec and French Canada, a massive number of young clergy, as well older priests, brothers, and nuns in religious orders, availed themselves of the new possibilities. Social ostracism had disappeared and their integration into secular society could be immediate and complete. They entered the state bureaucracies, federal and provincial, and the parapublic institutions of health, education, and social welfare. Their identities changed but their careers were not interrupted.

Their new situation, in addition, left open to them all options: to continue religious practice as lay Catholics, to join the increasing number of non-practising

Catholics, even the ranks of non-believers. All of these are personal and private choices. Since then, it has become bad taste or problematic to proclaim oneself a practising Catholic. In the recent past, it was very imprudent to proclaim oneself atheist or agnostic.

The decimated ranks of the clergy withdrew within what were formerly called parishes and are referred to today as *communautés chrétiennes*. The Church congregation is mainly composed of grey-haired elderly persons. If young people and children are to be seen, they are mostly children of immigrant Catholics from developing countries. To quite an extent the viability of many parishes is due to these new members.

The Québécois in the past indicated his/her location in the city by the name of the parish church (s)he attended. Today, if a person still knows the name of the parish, it is probably because (s)he does his/her banking at the 'Caisse Pop', which generally shares the same name. Catholic schools no longer produce a 'Catholic' youth. When they do momentarily get interested in religion, it will most frequently be a cocktail of 'outer-space cosmology', a mixture of eclectic, esoteric beliefs: believing in previous lives, in future reincarnation, with a good dose of astrology, makes sense within an environment filled with non-conventional smoke. It makes one feel good and provides a momentary liberation from a meaningless present. Meanwhile, the elderly who shun the Church rush to the casinos, lottery tickets, and video-poker machines. And when they die, we discover, in the death column of daily newspapers, that the husbands and wives of yesteryear had, in the meantime, become *conjoints et conjointes*.

If this desolate description is somewhat of a caricature of reality (and I admit it is), we are familiar with it. It reflects the complete evacuation of the Christian tradition that society so emphatically claimed to cherish not so long ago. The Québécois intellectual discovers, two centuries later, the philosophy of the Enlightenment: the people are satisfied with secular superstitions.

The complete secularization of society in so short a period requires an explanation that sociology does not bother with since it, by and large, sees this change, even today, as a liberation rather than as a desolation, an enlightenment rather than a new darkness. Even for theologians who deplore it, *secularization* is a sort of irresistible tidal wave that has unfurled onto our shores from Europe. This undefined concept is used as a substitute for a precise analysis of the complex relations between the Church and Quebec society: a substitute for the analysis of the cracks and the increasing gaps between the traditional social doctrine and the behaviour, aspirations, and dissent of well-intentioned faithful.

Let us consider, for example, the role of women in the society of that era. Traditional Church doctrine consecrated the husband as the head of the family to whom wives owed obedience. It claimed that the place of woman was in the home where she was queen, and forbade spouses to engage in any form of birth control, except continence, since by natural law sexual intercourse leads to reproduction.

In the summer of 1959, in St Denis de Kamouraska, I was a witness to a passionate discussion that a mother of 12 children was having with her four single daughters, all schoolteachers spending their summer vacation with their parents. The setting was the family kitchen with a half-dozen rocking chairs lined up along the walls, a typical pattern then in Quebec farmhouses. The daughters were ganging up on their mother, saying repeatedly, and in no uncertain terms: 'Mother, how could you, how could you accept to live like this?' The mother, not disagreeing with her daughters, could only answer: 'In those days, it was like . . . *to have to live such a life* was made abundantly clear without any deference whatsoever to the preaching of the Church.' This doctrine, however, was encouraged by the Church for many more years and, by and large, it was the daughters of such good Christian mothers who refused to honour such teachings and quit the Church for good and with an enduring resentment.

On the other hand, divorce, becoming more readily available, became a privileged solution for many, creating a phenomenon that was previously totally unknown: the single-parent family. Their number increased with the increasing divorce rate. The proportion of people excluded from the sacraments increased. Those who remarried (in a civil marriage) became guilty of the only unforgivable sin.

The breakaway of the faithful from the Catholic Church can be explained by the Church's delay in adapting to the new reality and its constraints. One reason was that positions of authority and management in all the social institutions of that traditional social structure were filled by bachelors, that is, the priests. Not only were they all bachelors, but bachelors who had all made solemn vows of chastity. Those in male or female religious orders had also made solemn vows of poverty and obedience. The secular or diocesan priests, or those not directly tied to an order or a parish, who were not committed to the vow of poverty and obedience, were held to the vow of chastity and a 'promise' of obedience. The great majority took the religious habit in early or late adolescence. No wonder that they were not as sensitive to the new realities lived by the lay people in the new 'modern society' where consumerism, increased disposable income, and increased leisure time contrasted so deeply with the rural and frugal life of yesteryear.

To claim that today's clergy in Quebec is insensitive to the difficulties faced by the population in a modern society is a falsehood. Today's clergy listen to and are willing to accompany persons who approach them since many of their own personal friends and many within their own kinship group may have left the Church and religious tradition; as well, an increasing portion of the youth have never known it. And, not unlike the mother who did not reject her daughters because of their views on the role of women in modern Quebec society, the Church cannot reject her lapsed faithful.

What Quebec society lost in this massive breakup is a common space, exclusively its own, where discussions, disputes, and, when necessary, mobilization could be achieved. The Québécois people no longer have a public space that is exclusively theirs. It is this space that enabled the establishment of the Caisses Populaires Desjardins, which allowed the organized resistance to the conscription decreed by the Canadian state in World War I. It is within this enclosure that the resistance to the suppression of French schools across the Dominion of Canada took shape.

It is within their churches that American blacks can mobilize. Synagogues constitute a private network of communication for Jews to arrive at collective decisions. It is in the Church and by the Church that the Solidarity movement was anchored to overthrow the Moscow-controlled political regime in Poland. In Quebec of the past, the Catholic parish did and could serve the same function. This is no longer the case.

It was the Catholic Action movement and not the Church that pitted the 'social' against the 'national'. The careers of those involved took place by and large in Ottawa, not in Quebec. Their spleen against the national movement of Quebec ensured their careers in the establishment of the Canadian state. What an irony that the former proponents of Catholic action became the allies, when not the emotional advocates, of a state that never repudiated Lord Durham's recommendation to suppress the French nation.

The Renewal of the National Movement

If modernity brought about the secularization of Quebec society, it also rejuvenated politically the national movement. It undermined for many Québécois their 'consent' to the Canadian state, a consent the state failed to solicit before its foundation. Having broken away from a sacred symbolic universe that was centuries old and an integral part of the foundation of New France, it should not surprise anyone that, for the Québécois, the Canadian state would also be stripped of its 'sacred' character. In opposition to the *dream of national unity,* rose *the dream of national independence.* In the beginning, the 'separatists' (as they are called in English Canada) were described by editorial writers of the English newspapers as 'the lunatic fringe'. When it became clear that the dream of national independence was taking root with an increasing number of Québécois, their slogan became: 'You'll be sorry', convinced as they still are that a sovereign Quebec would be an economic disaster. Before the referendum on the Charlottetown Accord, the Anglophone rhetoric heated up: if the disaster does not spontaneously occur, they'd make it happen. And although the 'No' vote won in the 1995 referendum, albeit but barely, the Canadian government and the Canadian corporate élite set what was called Plan B into motion.

Some day the little messiah from the Eastern Townships, Jean Charest, who was initially drafted by Toronto's Bay Street to quit the leadership of the federal Conservative Party to take over the vacant leadership of the provincial Liberal Party, will discover that he may be thrown away after being used (*'jetable après usage'*).[38]

What is ironic and worrisome is that Canadian Anglophones, as well as Quebec sovereignists, fix consent at 50 per cent plus one. To measure consent to a constitutional regime by a simple electoral majority is ridiculous. A constitution is framed to ensure the political stability of a state and to generate social stability on consent. It requires substantial and not merely formal consent. Without this consent on the basic political framework called a constitution, a state that encompasses a national minority will always remain challenged internally and its permanence will never be secure. Politically, consent to the Canadian state is consistently eroding among the Francophones of Quebec. The same principle applies to a nation aspiring to statehood. Unless it can achieve a substantial internal consent within its geographical area for its creation, it will be in peril from the very beginning of its existence. That is the present political situation in Canada.

The Parti Québécois is able to increase aspirations for statehood only among the Francophones of Quebec. This has been a constant political fact since the 1980 referendum. Although it is acutely conscious of this, the party nonetheless becomes a *political movement* for only six weeks every four years. Then, it subsequently takes its distance from its political base and does administration and reassures its intractable political enemies. It is developing at a snail's pace. The 'conscious pariahs' within the party, not the career-seekers, are keeping its purpose alive.

Quebec's National Movement in Review

The rebirth of the national movement in Quebec took place in 1963. After a series of editorials in *Le Devoir*[39] by André Laurendeau, Lester B. Pearson, then the Prime Minister of Canada, struck the Royal Commission on Bilingualism and Biculturalism. He named two co-chairmen: André Laurendeau and Davidson Dunton, the former head of the CBC and at that time the president of Carleton University.

In his first editorial, André Laurendeau clearly illustrated the urgency of setting up a Royal Commission. He quoted a memo written by a Francophone federal civil servant at the Port of Montreal to his Francophone subordinates to the effect that: 'Since everyone here is bilingual, from now on reports shall be written in English' (*Le Devoir*, 26 Aug. 1961).

My Anglophone students, the majority of whom are new Canadians, usually found this memo quite normal and functional. They did not realize that it meant that Francophones must be bilingual in Quebec but that Anglophone Quebecers can remain unilingual with no problem. The Francophone students immediately perceived the double standard: 'the rights of Englishmen' make them distinct from everyone else. The French Canadians consider themselves a national minority in Canada. The English Canadians consider French Canadians, both inside and outside Quebec, as an ethnic group and treat them as such, that is, like any other ethnic group that ought to assimilate in one or two generations.

Meanwhile, at the time of Laurendeau's editorial, the Francophones became conscious of their statistical under-representation in the managerial and higher levels of the federal bureaucracies and Crown corporations, the national railways, Air Canada, and so on. To explain this circumstance, the president of the CNR, Donald Gordon, answered to the effect that there were no qualified French Canadians. The students of the Université de Montréal rebutted that the majority of the members of the board of the CNR were of Scottish descent and that most of them only had a high school degree. Burned in effigy at Place Ville-Marie, Donald Gordon eventually understood that there was a problem. This took place in 1962.

It therefore became increasingly clear that as the Québécois received a modern education in all disciplines, they came into competition with English Canadians for new-middle-class jobs in governmental and corporate bureaucracies but faced the additional requirement of being bilingual while Quebec Anglophones did not have any such requirement.

Meanwhile, the political organizer for Paul-Gérin Lajoie, the provincial Minister of Education, a lawyer who took the train every working day from the suburban town of Vaudreuil to Montreal, decided to confront the train conductor:

> *Tickets please.*
> En français s'il vous plaît.
> *Tickets please.*
> En français s'il vous plaît.
> *Tickets please.*
> En français s'il vous plaît.

Indignant, the conductor stopped the train, called the police, and had the passenger expelled from the train. It made the headlines.

The official explanation this time: the seniority principle in the railroad companies gave first choice of routes and schedules to employees with the most seniority. (The workers refer to it as the 'bumping' principle.) Approaching retirement, all the CNR conductors in the Montreal region came from the Smiths Falls region and were therefore unilingual English. A not insurmountable solution could have been, one could argue, a three-day intensive course to learn to say: 'Bonjour monsieur, bonjour madame, billets s'il vous plaît.'

The last incident I shall note along the language frontier involved the Francophone air traffic controllers and Francophone small-craft air pilots. The traffic controllers in small and medium-size Quebec airfields such as the one in St Hubert were forced to use only English in their jobs. Significant numbers of small aircraft were piloted by Francophones who did not understand English. The Francophone controllers refused to abide by the English-only rule in these circumstances. The Canadian Air Traffic Controllers' Association (CATCA), indignant over the use of French, organized a nationally orchestrated petition in the name of 'safety in the air' to counteract the practice of the Gens de l'Air (a rival association in the making). The Canadian Airline Pilots Association (CALPA) gave their support to CATCA. Sensing the mounting displeasure of Quebec Francophones caused by the Canada-wide mobilization of English Canadians on this issue, Prime Minister

Trudeau pre-empted national television broadcasting to declare that Canada was facing the gravest crisis of its history. Then he packed his bags and went to a G-7 meeting in the Caribbean, leaving the issue to be settled by Otto Lang, the Minister of Transport. Lang gave in to the CATCA and made it a conscience issue rather than a policy question. He therefore allowed for a free vote in the House of Commons rather than a party vote. Jean Marchand was the only minister to resign from the cabinet on this issue. We had just witnessed the 'spectacular crash' of the federal policy of bilingualism and biculturalism. Pierre Trudeau, who proclaimed Canada a bilingual and multicultural country, stood in stark contrast to Lester B. Pearson, who had proclaimed Canada to be a bilingual and bicultural country. A few months later, on 15 November 1976, the Parti Québécois, led by René Lévesque, won the provincial election for the first time.

With the crash of the federal policy on bilingualism and biculturalism and the substitution of multiculturalism for biculturalism, the Canadian state assured the extinction of French culture outside Quebec. It is no longer part of a 'national culture' but an ethnic culture with no difference in terms of Canadian state support than the culture of the dozens of ethnic groups that settled here through immigration. It does not take a genius to realize that the ethnic culture of immigrants cannot survive more than two generations: memories fade and memories alone cannot feed a living culture; nor, after the first two generations, can the culture be sustained by the history of a foreign country one has never seen or heard about.

The succeeding ethnic generations are educated in the institutions of the dominant culture and, as Everett Hughes (1952) would remark, they are taught and internalize the dominant culture's attitudes towards all the other ethnic groups other than their own in the schoolyard and in the classroom. As concerns their own ethnic group, they frequently feel they are discriminated against and misunderstood.

As for Trudeau, who internalized the Anglophone legends about Quebec society after having entered the national political scene, he was, in fact, wittingly or unwittingly, aligning himself with Lord Durham's recommendation, knowing full well that this would be politically fruitful for him in Canada.

While the cultural policy at the federal level has assimilation as its long-term goal, in regard to the language conflict described above, Everett Hughes remarked to me shortly after these events that the hidden issue was one of jobs. When jobs require bilingualism, he noted, it is to the advantage of French Canadians; if they remain unilingual the jobs of Anglophones are preserved.

Finally, the greatest consequence of the Quiet Revolution in the other provinces for Francophones was the disappearance of their autonomous institutions. Previously, Francophone institutions were autonomous and did not depend on provincial financing for their continued existence. They were distinctly French institutions with full administrative autonomy. Ironically, the Quiet Revolution elsewhere in Canada forced the autonomous French institutions to become integrated into the Anglophone system of higher education and health care. The Francophones became a minority in the very institutions that their Church had historically founded, funded, and managed. It is a striking fact at the University of Ottawa. It is equally true of l'Hôpital Générale d'Ottawa, which was located next to the Catholic cathedral. The recent suppression of Montfort hospital—the only hospital left that operated in French—and its transformation into a retirement home for those awaiting the Grim Reaper, illustrates how the Quiet Revolution in Ontario and its policy of public financing suppressed the autonomy of pre-existing French institutions. Once these institutions received public funding, the Franco-Ontarians became a dominated minority within them. And they were treated as such, to be as quickly assimilated as possible into the dominant Anglophone culture of the province.

By contrast, in Quebec, the Quiet Revolution had no such effect on pre-existing English institutions in health and education. They get their full share of public funding with no legal obligation to open access to their services and employment to all citizens of Quebec—the majority of whom are unilingual French speakers. They, the English of Quebec, have kept their total institutional autonomy and receive their full share of public financing.

The Equality Party in Quebec is uninterested in this type of unequal status when it echoes Trudeau's claim that Quebec is a province like the others. For that to be true in legal and real terms, it would require that Quebec adopt the Ontario model of public financing. That is, for McGill and Concordia universities to receive public financing, for example, they would be required to implement unilingual Francophone sections in all their professional faculties and be administratively integrated into the Francophone universities. The fact of the matter is that the Anglophone cultural and social institutions have kept their autonomy, while everywhere else in Canada, state financing produced the total collapse of Francophone autonomous cultural and social institutions. Should Quebec apply the same principles as Ontario, the outcry of the Anglophone population and their media would be deafening, and would be spoken in the name of the *Rights of Man* that their ancestors loathed as a pernicious doctrine emanating from the French Revolution.

The End of a Dream?

The Quiet Revolution in Quebec is still described as *la belle époque*. People of my generation and the subsequent one perceived it as a liberation, as entering definitively into the modern world, an exhilarating and exciting period of welcomed transformation: broadened access to education, free access to the health system and medical care, the welfare state, access for the many to the bourgeois lifestyle. Education pays off (*Qui s'instruit s'enrichit*) was the popular slogan, and it was a fact for a little while. In the mid-1980s, however, after the referendum defeat, the collapse of the socialist dream, the cultural depression of the intellectuals, and the economic recession, the *vagabonds du rêve* (the dreaming vagabonds) painfully discovered the uncertainty of jobs, the precarious nature of love relationships, and gave up the hope of realizing their cherished dreams. Facing the spiritual desert that surrounds them, they are even deprived of the dream that their great-grand-parents held on to, in spite of their poverty, a dream that was handed down by their traditional religion to every generation: the hope of eternal happiness.

The Present Political Situation of Quebec

The remainder of this chronicle in a very personal reading of the political situation, not in Quebec but of Quebec. The distinction is important. The political situation *in Quebec* makes reference exclusively to its internal situation, while the political situation *of Quebec* refers to the external geopolitical context within which Quebec is located and with which it must transact.

English Canada is the immediate external geopolitical environment of Quebec and my remarks here will be limited to it. Let's note that the image of Quebec communicated to the English-speaking countries, including the United States, originates from the Canadian English-language media, since unilingualism is a common characteristic of all the English-speaking world. I intend to sketch the progressive transformation of English Canada's attitudes towards Quebec since World War II.

The image of Quebec that is current in the postwar period, as I have already outlined at the beginning of this essay, is embedded in the English–Canadian historiography on Quebec. The theoretical framework of North American social sciences since the 1950s, used to explain the differences between pre-industrial and the industrially developed societies, emphasizes that pre-industrial cultures are unadaptable to the requirements of an industrial economy. This state of affairs was imputed to the culture of the underdeveloped peoples but never to the exploitation of the overdeveloped. Feudalism under an absolute king in France accounts for the economic stagnation and the absence of political liberties in New France. The anti-modernism of a powerful and dominating Catholic Church subsequently explains the economic stagnation that persisted. These views generated in the well-meaning portion of the political class of English Canada an attitude of conde-scending compassion, albeit with a slight touch of contempt. They still expect and celebrate the co-operation of the élites of both societies, what the French Canadi-ans call 'la bonne entente'. Among the less educated, heeding the preachings of Protestant preachers ever since the French Revolution, contempt quickly overtakes condescension, since they are, to a great extent, of the same social rank as the French-Canadian rural folk.

The increasing and more vocal denunciation of the Duplessis regime by Fathers Dion and O'Neill (in spite of the reprimand by Monsignor Bernier, the Bishop of Gaspé) signalled the coming on board of the Catholic Church. A new era of mutual understanding was foreseen by the enlightened political class in English Canada whose interest in and sympathy for the new bureaucratic morality in a modernizing Quebec made headlines across the country. It kindled the hope of both a modernizing and increasingly prosperous Quebec and an enduring era of mutual understanding.

The dark side of this rosy picture surfaced on the political scene not much later. As previously detailed, the under-representation of Francophones in the federal bureaucratic establishments and in Montreal's corporate élite became a live political issue in Quebec. Federalism, and Confederation as an 'unequal union', became a political issue in Quebec, and the optimism at the outset of the Quiet Revolution became a state of perplexity illustrated by the frequently repeated question: *What does Quebec want?*

The Royal Commission on Bilingualism and Biculturalism agreed on increasing bilingualism in the workplace of federal institutions but did not reach agreement on biculturalism as the basis of constitutional reform. Trudeau settled the issue: he rejected Pearson's biculturalism for multiculturalism. The 'Two Founding Peoples' disappeared from the political vocabulary and, in fact, multiculturalism would clearly take precedence in English. With Trudeau, Canada hardened its Quebec policy, which was summarized in his political slogan, endlessly repeated in English Canada: 'Quebec is a province like all the others.' A legal fact, yes, but in terms of social reality, a legal-political fiction used to prevent the political emancipation of a politically subordinated people. For Trudeau, the Québécois were not a people, nor were they a nation. The emotional endorsement of such a view by English Canadians illustrates how committed they have remained to Lord Durham's vision of the future.

Since the failure of the Meech Lake Accord, the political climate in both French Quebec and English Canada can only be described as one of increasing exasperation and indignation. How disconnected from popular sentiment the political leaders of this country are was dramatically illustrated when 70 per cent of both English Canadians and Francophone Québécois rejected the Charlottetown Accord, the approval of which these leaders sought in a Canada-wide referendum. While the referendum restored Robert Bourassa to the status of a *good Canadian,* the premiers, to save face, concluded that the public was wary of constitutional negotiations and that they should shelve such issues.

What it did mean, however, is that English Canadians are as convinced as they have ever been that 'A happier calamity never befell a people than the conquest of Canada by the British arms.' It also illustrates Hannah Arendt's analysis that, as heirs to the tradition of 'permanent conquest' typical of the British Empire, the Québécois will never achieve political emancipation short of an organized movement of 'permanent resistance'. The Parti Québécois, an organization that does political marketing but avoids political mobilization, will never be able to deliver. Unless it becomes a political movement and remains a political movement, in or out of office, the party, and the people of Quebec, will draw no closer to political independence.

Questions for Critical Thought

1. What are the Anglophone legends of Canadian history?

2. What are the Francophone counter-legends of Canadian history?

3. Explain how modernity not only brought about the secularization of Quebec society but rejuvenated politically the national movement in Quebec?

Glossary

Two Founding Peoples: The popular belief of Francophones that the founding of Canada was a pact between its two founding peoples: the British and the French.

Asbestos Strike: A strike of asbestos miners in Asbestos, Quebec, in 1949 that was important not because the workers won (in fact, they lost) but because the consequences of the strike led to deep divisions within Quebec society—such as the deepening divisions between the Duplessis government and the Faculty of Social Sciences at Laval University and the rebirth of the Catholic trade union movement.

Quiet Revolution: The new public, state-financed system of institutions such as health, education, and welfare begun by Paul Sauvé in 1959 and continued by Jean Lesage's Liberal government after 1960.

Secularization of Quebec society: Brought about, ironically, by the Catholic Action movement because of their concern for ensuring the presence of the Catholic Church in the world. In order to achieve this, Quebec's youth had to become educated and commit themselves to change the world rather than withdrawing from it.

Radio–Canada strike of 1959: Politicized a significant number of Quebec's cultural actors since their struggle with senior management (Radio-Canada is the only national Crown corporation that has separate Francophone and Anglophone sectors) did not lead to intervention by the federal Parliament. Ottawa's seeming lack of concern politicized many of Quebec's cultural actors. For example, René Lévesque moved from being a popular international correspondent to Minister of Natural Resources in the Lesage Liberal government.

Suggested Reading

Glenday, Dan, Hubert Guindon, and Allan Turowetz, eds. 1978. *Modernization and the Canadian State*. Toronto: Macmillan. A forgotten classic in Canadian sociology that includes contributions by 23 scholars.

Guindon, Hubert. 1988. *Québec Society: Tradition, Modernity, and Nationhood*. Introduction by Roberta Hamilton and John L. McMullan. Toronto: University of Toronto Press. A collection of essays by the author that covers his life work to the mid-1980s.

Rioux, Marcel, and Yves Martin, eds. 1964. *French-Canadian Society*, vol. 1. Toronto: McClelland & Stewart. This volume of essays remains an important contribution to the sociological understanding of rural Quebec society.

Notes

1. Everett C. Hughes was Professor of Sociology at McGill University in the mid-thirties, then at the University of Chicago, finally at Brandeis University. He published a small book on Quebec society, entitled *French Canada in Transition,* a classic, that is highly readable and still pertinent. He maintained throughout his career a continuing interest in French- and English-Canadian students, as well as in the Canadian Sociology and Anthropology Association, whose annual meetings he attended until his death. He taught a year at Laval University, returned as a visiting professor at McGill in the early sixties, and in 1965 taught along with his wife, Helen McGill Hughes (an able sociologist in her own right), at Concordia University's Special Summer Institute in Sociology. To a student who dared to suggest he was getting old and a bit *passé,* my colleague Kurt Jonassohn, a former student of his, snapped back: 'He has forgotten more sociology than you'll ever learn, young man.' He was right.
2. The title of a book of remarkable essays by Hannah Arendt.
3. The Charlottetown Accord, which all the provincial premiers had approved, was submitted for approval by Canadian citizens in a referendum held on 26 October 1992. It was rejected by 70 per cent of the Anglophones outside Quebec and by over 70 per cent of the Francophones in Quebec. That is where things still stand in terms of constitutional change. Since 1982, Quebec has refused to endorse the patriated Canadian constitution.
4. The Constitutional Act of 1791 divided the colony in two: Lower Canada (Bas-Canada), with a great French majority, and Upper Canada, essentially Anglophone, which later became the province of Ontario.
5. Edmund Burke's book on the French Revolution became very popular in England as well as in monarchist circles on the Continent. His vitriolic attack on the French Revolution is, oddly enough, and one wonders why, replete with reeking anti-Semitism.
6. It survived until the Treaty of Versailles in 1918 when it decomposed into the individual nation-states over which it had ruled.
7. Hannah Arendt does not mention Lord Acton when discussing British imperialism. Her analysis, however, remains clearly a refutation of Acton's point of view. Lord Acton's views, quoted above, would have constituted for her both a description and a justification of the imperialist character of the British Empire. It is interesting to note that her analysis of imperialism is largely ignored in Anglo-Saxon historiography and political philosophy, in general, and in English Canada, in particular. See Arendt (1961b: 125–31).
8. The Latin expression could be translated as: 'Oh Blessed Mistake'.
9. This reading contradicts the argument made by Léandre Bergeron in his widely read *Petit Manuel de l'Histoire du Québec* (1970), in which he argued that the hierarchy was siding with the political rulers because of their class interests.

10. There is historical support for the continuous effort to maintain distinct institutions reserved exclusively for Francophones, which Hugh MacLennan *deplored* in his well-meaning and celebrated novel, *Two Solitudes* (1945).

11. Historians are unclear as to how the Catholic bishops responded to the BNA Act setting up the Dominion of Canada. It certainly was not acclaimed with any degree of enthusiasm. The attitude of Mgr Bourget, Archbishop of Montreal, was certainly lukewarm, if not hostile.

12. For example: Maurice Lamontagne, trained in economics at Harvard, who became one of the leading advisers to Lester B. Pearson before Pierre Elliott Trudeau appeared on the political scene; and Jean-Charles Falardeau, a sociologist who had attended the University of Chicago and, among other things, translated into French Everett C. Hughes's classic monograph, *French Canada in Transition*, under the title *La rencontre de deux mondes*. Lamontagne gained attention after he published *Le Fédéralisme canadien*, a Keynesian-inspired eulogy of Canadian federalism emphasizing the critical role of the central government in ensuring equalization of living standards across the country and stimulating the economy by public spending in times of recession. It gave rise eventually to the welfare state, which, with the recent spread of neo-liberal economics, is now frequently criticized. Both Lamontagne and Falardeau were staunch federalists.

13. This expression became the title of J.C. Falardeau's translation of Hughes's *French Canada in Transition*: *La rencontre de deux mondes*.

14. Jean Gould, a young sociologist recently trained at Laval University, brought to my attention the strong impact of Emmanuel Mounier, a French philosopher, on the postwar Catholic Action movement. The influence of his political philosophy, *personnalisme*, on Quebec society is being carried out presently by Gilles Gagné, Professor and Chairman of the Department of Sociology, and a group of graduate students at Laval University.

15. The creation of similar institutions at the workplace, one can understand, would be perceived by the parochial *caisse populaire* as unwelcome competition. In the seventies, both the credit unions and the dissident Fédération de Montréal were integrated into the Desjardins movement because of financial difficulties.

16. The strikers were recently unionized into a CTCC union but they had no strike funds.

17. This is probably what most irritated Premier Duplessis.

18. One important exception happened in postwar France when some two dozen French bishops were asked by Rome to resign under pressure of the then French ambassador to the Vatican, the internationally known and highly respected French Catholic philosopher Jacques Maritain. Their open support to the Vichy regime of Maréchal Pétain was the reason for this initiative.

19. Cardinal Léger, who had been Superior of the Canadian College in Rome and reputed to be a friend of Pius XII, took this initiative early in his tenure as bishop. It was poorly received by a good part of the intelligentsia and even more so by a majority of the teachers. Later, much more in tune with the mood of the times and the people, he was venerated by the majority of the population and praised as a 'progressive' at the Council of Vatican II.

20. The right to strike was extended to public and parapublic employees by the Jean Lesage government in 1964. It gradually spread later to all parts of Canada.

21. One must remember that, in this period, school taxes were individually fixed and raised by each and every school board in the numerous municipalities that shower the Montreal region. The Catholic school boards fixed the tax rate to Catholic property holders and Protestant school boards for Protestant property holders. The tax rate could vary considerably from one municipality to another.

22. Local sport results in the *Montréal Matin* made European tourists giggle when they read, for instance, that St Mary clobbered Saint-Joseph in a softball game.

23. Between 1949 and 1958, however, 91 primary schools were built, 8 were bought, 18 were renovated or enlarged. As for secondary schools, about a dozen benefited from programs of construction, purchase, or renovation (Gagnon, 1971: 196–7).

24. This accusation 10 years after the war refers to the fact that a good number of bishops had sympathy for the pro-Nazi Pétain regime instead of for De Gaulle, the leader of the Resistance. This was also true of the great majority of Francophones in Quebec, not excluding the readers of *Cité Libre*. The accusers knew very well that the reason for this was much more related to the fact of an imminent conscription to be authorized by the federal government in a Canada–wide referendum. On the conscription issue in World War II, Everett Hughes wrote an article in the *Dalhousie Law Review* in which he underlined that in that referendum, people seldom refer to the statistical fact that some 30 per cent of English Canadians voted against conscription. Many were farmers who needed their sons as farm workers.

25. Father Gérard Dion and Father Louis O'Neill. The former founded the Department of Industrial Relations at Laval University, the other was Professor of Philosophy, also at Laval.

26. The Anglophone community, much less numerous, already had two universities. McGill University, very old, mainly admitted students from the élites; Sir George Williams, very recent, recruited its students from the working classes, the adult population, and the postwar immigrant population by initiating an undergraduate evening as well as a day program in all disciplines.

27. The most outspoken, the better known, and the best of them was Jacques Henripin, who founded the Demography Department at the Université de Montréal.

28. The Francophone Montrealers were essentially tenants and the typical apartment consisted of four and a half small rooms. Single-family flats with six or seven rooms existed, but in much smaller numbers. Detached single-family houses of recent construction were essentially located in the growing suburbs, or in Westmount and the Anglophone West End of Montreal. During the fifties the suburbs expanded and the new middle classes were the ones able to afford housing in them.

29. Not that long before, Edward VIII, the King of England, was forced to resign his throne in order to marry an American divorced woman.

30. I used this example throughout all my teaching career to have students not confuse *legal and empirical facts*. Legal facts do not have to be real; corroborated lies make legal facts. Beware!

31. Divorce became easily accessible, and became commonplace from the start, so much so that, in order to avoid an embarrassing situation, one would no longer require incriminating news about one's spouse.

32. The free medical insurance system was rather welcomed by the general practitioners because the unpaid honoraria automatically disappeared and there was no further need to have recourse to collection agencies. The medical specialists had to resign themselves to engage in hard bargaining with the provinces.

33. A small revealing fact: Quebec bonds that find takers on the international markets always have less success in English Canada, and are equally shunned by Anglo-Quebecers. Canadian banks operating in Quebec invest in Quebec only a small fraction of the earnings made there. Speculating why can raise interesting questions. That this was always so and not only since the rise of the national movement also raises interesting questions that are seldom asked and never answered.

34. Pope Pius IX published in 1869 a *Syllabus* that gave a detailed description of the errors of modernism. It was the basis of what was called the 'anti-modernist oath'. As late as the mid-fifties this oath was taken by Université de Montréal professors, at the Mass of the Holy Ghost in the Catholic Cathedral of Montreal. I remember remarking to a priest colleague: 'But I believe everything that this oath condemns.' Most professors, I suspected, felt the same.

35. The rationale is that they are better administrators; but as the quotation above clearly reveals, they can also well perceive their individual interest.

36. Concerning secondary education, the project initially thought of establishing a school board for every high school. Such a pattern provoked local conflicts between competing towns. If the choice of the site and the town was to be made by the provincial government, the losers would be alienated from the party in power. These conflicts involved the parish priests as well as the mayors involved, and the various religious teaching orders as well as political pressures on the government. By creating, with Operation 55, one large regional school board to administer many secondary schools, the decision on their location became a regional decision and the conflicts remained an internal regional conflict.

37. Many reputedly became taxi drivers in New York and Detroit.

38. The expression comes from Michel C. Auger, one of the better political columnists in Quebec today.

39. Founded in 1910 by Henri Bourassa, this newspaper was read by a portion of the political class in both Quebec and English Canada. Its influential former editors included Gérard Filion, André Laurendeau, and Claude Ryan. Until recently, the editor was Lise Bissonnette.

References

Acton, John E.E., Lord. 1956. *Essays on Freedom and Power*. London: Thames and Hudson.

Arendt, Hannah. 1959. *The Human Condition*. Chicago: University of Chicago Press.

———. 1961a. *Between Past and Future: Six Exercises in Political Thought*. New York: Viking.

———. 1961b. *Origins of Totalitarianism*, new edn. New York: Harcourt Brace.

Bergeron, Léandre. 1970. *Petit Manuel de l'Histoire du Québec*. Montréal: Editions Québécoises.

Cook, Ramsay. 1966. *Canada and the French-Canadian Question*. Toronto: Macmillan.

————. 1971. *The Maple Leaf Forever*. Toronto: Macmillan.

Gagnon, Robert. 1971. *Histoire de la Commission des Écoles Catholiques de Montréal*. Montréal: Boréal.

Guindon, Hubert. 1988. *Québec Society: Tradition, Modernity, and Nationhood*. Toronto: University of Toronto Press.

Hamilton, Roberta. 1988. 'Feudal Society and Colonization: A Critique and Reinterpretation of the Historiography of New France', in D.H. Akenson, ed., *Canadian Papers in Rural History*. Gananoque, Ont: Langdale Press.

Hughes, Everett. 1952. *Where Peoples Meet: Racial and Ethnic Frontiers*. Glencoe, Ill.: Free Press.

————. 1963. *French Canada in Transition*. Chicago: University of Chicago Press.

Lamontagne, Maurice. 1954. *Le fédéralisme canadien: évolution et problèmes*. Québec: Presses universitaire laval.

MacLennan, Hugh. 1945. *Two Solitudes*. Toronto: Macmillan.

Parkman, Francis. 1851–92. *France and England in North America*, 10 vols. Boston: Little, Brown.

Porter, John. 1965. *The Vertical Mosaic: An Analysis of Social Class and Power in Canada*. Toronto: University of Toronto Press.

Rioux, Marcel, and Yves Martin, eds. 1964. *French-Canadian Society*. Toronto: McClelland & Stewart.

Royal Commission on Bilingualism and Biculturalism. 1969. *Report*. Ottawa: Queen's Printer.

Trudeau, Pierre E. 1968. *Federalism and the French Canadians*. Toronto: Macmillan.

Weber, Max. 1958 [1930]. *The Protestant Ethic and the Spirit of Capitalism*. New York: Charles Scribner's Sons.

Wise, S.F. 1965. 'Sermon Literature and Canadian Intellectual History', *Bulletin of the Committee on Archives*, United Church of Canada: 3–18.

————. 1967. 'Colonial Attitudes from the Era of the War of 1812 to the Rebellions of 1837', in Wise and R.C. Brown, *Canada Views the United States*. Seattle: University of Washington Press.

chapter eleven

A Poisoned Environment: Challenges for the Next Millennium

Kathleen Reil

Only when the last tree has died and the last river been poisoned and the last fish been caught will we realize that we cannot eat money.
— nineteenth-century Cree

During the last part of the 1980s and the first part of the 1990s the environment was a 'top of the mind' issue among pollsters, politicians, and the public. In the second part of the 1990s the focus shifted somewhat. Now, environmental quality is increasingly being paired with health concerns. The early and mid-1990s were also a period characterized by economic recession, corporate and government 'smart-sizing', downsizing, and out-sourcing. The scale of these structural changes was unprecedented in Canada and has affected all aspects of the environment.

This chapter will examine the recent literature in the field of environmental sociology, focus on the continuing emergence of the environment as a health-related issue, review the role of the state in environmental protection, discuss whether a paradigm shift has occurred, highlight changes in provincial environmental legislation, explore the roles of various stakeholder groups, and describe policy developments. Canadian case studies and examples are cited throughout the chapter.

Contextualizing the Environment

Environmental concerns have been recognized as important social issues throughout Canada since the early 1970s, when environmental protection and assessment legislation, regulations, and bureaucracies first emerged. Moreover, the origins of the modern Canadian environmental movement go back to the 1960s, when people began to question the effects that industrial development was having on the environment and especially on human health. It may be argued, therefore, that governments responded to the public's concern about deteriorating environmental quality in the 1960s by creating new bureaucracies and passing legislation to protect the environment. Canadian environmentalists realized the important role that the law, as a policy instrument, could play in advancing environmental interests, since environmentalists did not have the numbers or resources to scrutinize all polluting activities and needed to marshal public concern to persuade governments to pass environmental protection legislation.

In Canada and the United States environmental protection legislation has been twinned with environmental assessment legislation. Environmental assessment legislation and its administration serve to shape the public debates over the distribution and use of resources through the 'technically rational' process known as environmental impact assessment. Ideally, environmental assessments are an essential component of environmental planning and decision-making and are designed to identify and describe the full range of predicted environmental consequences of a particular project or undertaking.

However, environmental decision-making is not just dependent on the quality of the technical information available to decision-makers; rather, it is fundamentally a question of how we define the issue and how we construct our political and bureaucratic or administrative institutions to address environmental concerns. For example, although 'rational planning' may be the overt goal of an environmental assessment, no decision is purely objective or value-free. The values of the bureaucracy, political regime, proponents of a project or undertaking, professional consultants, and public stakeholders all affect and ultimately shape a decision.

Recently, a literature has emerged that focuses on what has been perceived to be a failure of public institutions to fulfil their obligations to the broader society with the degree of vigour that would be desired. This 'failure' causes the public to lose confidence and trust in the institution. The recent Red Cross 'blood scandal' in Canada is a profound example of such a failure—public officials failed to safeguard the blood supply and allowed blood contaminated with hepatitis C and AIDS to be used for blood transfusions and in the manufacture of blood products for the treatment of hemophilia. The continuing controversy over compensation for the victims of this bureaucratic failure only serves to erode further the credibility of government officials and elected politicians.

More recent examples of institutional failure among environmental officials occurred when E. coli bacteria contaminated the municipal water supply in Walkerton, Ontario in May 2000 and when a plastics recycling facility, located near a residential neighbourhood in Hamilton, Ontario, caught fire and polluted the neighbourhood with toxic chemicals, including dioxin (the fire at the Plastimet recycling factory, which occurred in 1997, will be examined in more detail later in this chapter). In this case, further attention to the threat of toxic contamination was brought by Greenpeace (a non-governmental organization dedicated to environmental protection and promoting public awareness of environmental issues). Greenpeace had its own scientific experts conduct tests of the soil for the presence of dioxins and other contaminants after residents in the area expressed concern over the inaction of the Ontario Ministry of the Environment and a lack of trust in statements made by government officials.

These examples draw our attention to the difference between 'policy statements' and 'policy implementation'. The public perceives a chasm between what an agency says it will do (through its policies, goals, missions) and the direct action that is taken (its decisions, programs, and enforcement). The impact of bureaucratic subculture and socialization may blind governmental agency officials to biases that favour the interests of industry or business. The result of this is that decisions are perceived to be based on politics and not science and that all reasonable steps to protect the environment are not taken.

Distinct governmental agency subcultures may influence loyal employees to 'forget' that the views and priorities within an agency or department may not actually reflect the views of the broader public or coincide with what the law states the agency's goals are supposed to be. The reward structure within the agency tends to reinforce the views of the bureaucratic substructure and when employees are socialized into this subculture there is an overwhelming likelihood that the agency's perspective will be accepted as the appropriate or 'real' view. The effects of bureaucratic subculture are most powerful when they are taken for granted and are unquestioned even to the extent of exerting an important influence on scientific studies. Moreover, different subcultures can exist in a single bureaucracy—for example, the scientific and technical experts may operate in a different subculture from the enforcement or legal personnel, and all employees may be affected by the overriding priorities of the bureaucracy as determined by the government in power. As a result, there is increasing difficulty for the public to gain access to and participate in the environmental decision-making process. The downsizing of bureaucracies has also served to concentrate the decision-making process in the hands of fewer people. Time demands on these fewer people and concerns about 'efficiency' have increasingly resulted in the rationalization of decision-making and of quick but not necessarily thorough decisions.

In addition, industry groups have also used international trade agreements, such as GATT and NAFTA, to challenge the environmental laws of countries that have not harmonized their environmental protection legislation with similar legislation in other countries. Particularly contentious has been the legal uncertainty over the exportation of 'bulk water' from Canada to other countries. If Canada restricts the use or entry of chemical substances (whose toxicity has not been determined) that are widely used in, for example, the United States, the industry group importing or using these substances can launch legal action against the federal or provincial government for loss of revenue (the controversy surrounding the gasoline additive MTBE is one such example).

As we have seen, the environment continues to be the focus of increasing conflict, as government, industry, community, and environmental groups and individual citizens struggle to assert their interests in the midst of economic restructuring, downloading of environmental assessment responsibilities to underfunded local or municipal governments, increasing levels of unemployment, and a slowing in the growth of the economy. Recently, the Canadian economy has shown signs of improvement and renewed growth in the new millennium and it will be interesting to see if environmental concerns once again move to a prominent position on the public agenda.

The Continuing Emergence of the Environment as a Social Issue

In recent public opinion polls the environment is increasingly linked to health concerns—particularly with respect to issues of air and water quality. In 1996, Health Canada commissioned a study by the Harvard School of Public Health, which confirmed that air pollution was causing death—particularly among individuals suffering from heart disease and respiratory illnesses. In the spring of 1998, the Ontario Medical Association also publicly acknowledged the link between air pollution and respiratory illnesses by stating that air pollution was responsible for a health crisis in Ontario, causing 1,800 premature deaths a year.

Concerns about drinking water quality also have received media attention in the last few years—particularly when the drinking water supplies of a number of urban communities experienced contamination with the E. coli bacteria[1] and the cryptosporidium parasite. For example, cryptosporidium contamination of the Milwaukee, Wisconsin, water supply in 1993 killed 100 people. Recently, Collingwood, Ontario, and Sydney, Australia, also experienced cryptosporidium contamination of their drinking water supplies. In the case of the cryptosporidium contamination of the Sydney drinking water supply, authorities at Sydney Water admitted failing consumers by not issuing early warnings to all residents and the ensuing crisis and loss of public confidence led to the government stepping in and taking over the management of the issue. A 1998 United Nations conference on managing the world's limited fresh water supplies indicated that a water shortage crisis was looming that threatened world peace, since water consumption is doubling every 20 years and one-quarter of the world's population has no access to clean drinking water.

In addition, the environment is linked to economic success, since the physical environment provides the raw materials for many production processes. In Canada, a large portion of our national economy continues to be natural resource-based: lumber, minerals, metals, oil, and natural gas. A dilemma emerges. Human societies necessarily exploit surrounding ecosystems to survive, but societies that flourish to the extent of overexploiting the environment may destroy the basis of their own survival. The management of the environment to ensure the sustainability of the physical environment and the protection of health becomes a priority of government at all levels because the physical environment is so closely interconnected with the social environment.

In addition, we are discovering that many of our products and by-products are harmful to our health and well-being and those of future generations. To increase agricultural yields, we turned to synthetic chemical fertilizers and herbicides that leached into the groundwater and contaminated aquifers. New concerns are being voiced about genetic manipulation of the food supply ('Frankenstein foods') to increase further production yields. Natural resources are becoming depleted. At the same time, populations are increasingly concentrated in urban areas that, by definition, must rely on the extra-urban environment to meet their needs. Food is often imported from foreign countries. Energy is produced at locations farther afield from urban areas and delivered to the urban population via a complex set of transmission corridors and transformer stations. As a society, we have come to expect that technology can solve our problems and maintain an ever-expanding population. In addition, people in developed countries use approximately 10 times more resources per capita than do people in developing countries. Yet, some members of society are realizing that the growth patterns, use of resources, and reliance on science and technology in accordance with the characteristics of the industrial paradigm are detrimental to their health. A 'quality of life' cannot be guaranteed for the present generations, let alone for future generations.

In the past, public concerns about environmental quality have often spurred the enactment of environmental protection legislation. For example, the enactment of the National Environmental Policy Act (NEPA) in the United States has been partially credited to a well-publicized oil spill into the Santa Barbara Channel in California in 1969. NEPA, in turn, influenced Canadian environmental laws and policy.

In fact, policy-making in the environmental arena relies heavily on the law as a policy instrument to effect social change. As such, the prevailing ideology of law as a neutral arbiter of disputes and as a positive instrument of social change makes it very difficult for persons to become aware of how the law structures social relations, mediating, advancing, or resisting certain interests. We will see, however, that as bureaucratic structures supporting the law as a policy instrument are reduced, other processes can be instituted. This situation presents both barriers and opportunities for individual members of the public, public advocacy groups, and others to become involved in environmental decision-making at a local or national level.

International law (the signing and ratifying of treaties, covenants, and protocols) continues to be the policy instrument of choice when addressing environmental protection issues on a global scale. Nevertheless, despite being a signatory to many international agreements that address the issue of air pollution, the Canadian federal government has failed to ratify these agreements and has not lived up to its promised commitments to reduce environmental pollution. Part of the problem is due to the federal-provincial division of constitutional powers in Canada—the environment is primarily a provincial responsibility. For example, the 1997 Kyoto agreement calls on governments to reduce greenhouse gases that are a major contributor to global warming; however, Canada's then federal Environment Minister, Christine Stewart, said that the federal government would not ratify this agreement until it has a consensus among all provinces and territories—the oil-producing provinces are opposed to the ratification of the agreement and the federal government does not want to do anything that would jeopardize our current economy.

Environmental sociologists recognize that different societal groups often do not perceive and respond to environmental concerns in the same ways. This observation also applies to the different levels of government bureaucracy and the various agencies within each level. However, social institutions, such as governmental agencies, tend to be characterized by decision-making processes that offer only limited opportunities for public consultation and participation, thereby favouring individuals or groups who have greater access to political, financial, educational, and legal resources—such as industry groups. Environmental concerns are addressed on a project-to-project basis and more often than not the cumulative impact of projects on the ecosystem is not assessed. More importantly, in the last few years, economic and fiscal priorities at all levels of government have overridden environmental concerns. The Ontario provincial government no longer provides intervenor funding to groups that want to participate in the environmental assessment process. Even such 'people-empowering' legislation as the Ontario Environmental Bill of Rights has been overridden by the fiscal priorities of the current Conservative provincial government. The first Environmental Commissioner (responsible for monitoring the implementation of the Environmental Bill of Rights), who had been critical of the Ontario government's efforts to protect the environment, was recently replaced by a more government-friendly appointee when her employment contract expired.

The financial and economic priorities of governments and the recent focus on deficit reduction and debt repayment have often conflicted with environmental goals. The federal Minister of Finance reduced the budget of Environment Canada by one-third between 1994 and 1998. The budget of the Ontario Ministry of the Environment has been similarly decimated, with cuts coming in such key areas as enforcement, monitoring and testing, and project assessment and approvals. The Ontario Minister of Energy, Science, and Technology has said that, as a result of the decommissioning and overhaul of certain nuclear reactors at Ontario Hydro, there would be a 70 per cent increase in coal-burning air pollutants between 1996 and 1998.

Despite the recent lack of government action on environmental issues, there are signs that the broader public and the media are starting to recognize the potential for an environmental crisis and starting to demand that governments take action to address environmental concerns.

Environmental Protection, Bureaucracy, and the State

Peace, order, and good government are the hallmarks of Canadian government. It is widely accepted that governments are supposed to act in the 'public interest'. The United Nations World Commission on the Environment (known as the Brundtland Commission) called for governments to achieve a 'sustainable' balance between environmental protection and economic growth and development.

The role of governmental agencies (ministries, departments, etc.), particularly as it relates to the management of environmental or natural resources, has been explored in an application of a seminal work by Bernstein (1955) to environmental regulatory agencies. Bernstein analyses 'institutional cycles' and concludes that regulatory agencies tend to adopt the perspective of the regulated industry, as opposed to supporting the overall 'public good', for the following reasons: the organizational structure of an industry group facilitates the exercise of political pressure, compared to the broader public; and, there is more contact between the government regulators and the industry, which promotes the shaping of a common perspective and sharing of values. As a result, the government agencies often become insulated and isolated from the broader public, allowing certain groups access to the decision-making process by excluding members of the general public who do not belong to well-organized interest groups.

Recent analyses have proffered various theories to explain the close ties between government and industry. At one end of the continuum is the 'revolving door' theory that states that bureaucrats at the top levels in government agencies do not stay in their positions for long periods of time and there is a regular exchange of personnel between the regulatory agency and the regulated industry. Although this two-way exchange does happen, it does not happen with great frequency. Moreover, with recent government and industry downsizing, governments have moved towards contract positions and out-sourcing of work to consultants, who are often former government employees. As a result, there is an increasing interaction between the regulatory agencies and the private sector—although not necessarily with regulated industries in the private sector. This phenomenon is more complex and is not really described adequately by the revolving door theory, because the exchange is more unidirectional—with personnel moving away from government to the private sector.

As a result, other theories have been posited that focus on the state and the bureaucracy as independent actors in their own right. Stone (1980) contends that the influence of business or industry in a particular environmental controversy is not as effective as the revolving door theory suggests. Stone suggests that the predisposition of public officials results partly from the fact that government bureaucrats have economic constraints and rarely have the budget allotments to do everything they wish to do, and partly from the recognition of the importance of 'associational considerations'—the fact that various groups in society have the power to support or block a bureaucrat's goals. In other words, Stone's theory recognizes that bureaucrats have goals and interests of their own and, more often than not, the most powerful groups in society tend to be the same groups that have the greatest power to facilitate or interfere with the achievement of the goals of bureaucrats.

Still other theorists have focused on the bureaucracy in the context of the political and economic system in general. Such theorists as Offe (1984) and Block (1987) have questioned the ability in a capitalistic system of any government agency to impose regulations that would interfere with the economic profitability of an industry group. In a capitalist society, government agencies are expected to met the demands of two, often conflicting, roles—they are expected to protect the broader public, while at the same time they are under intense pressure not to impose significant costs on regulated industries.

One way to meet these potentially conflicting demands is for the government agency or bureaucracy to seek a co-operative relationship with regulated industries, particularly when the industry has more resources to expend in challenging government regulations in the political and legal arenas and the ruling government does not express the political will to ensure that industry regulations are enforced.

Another way to accommodate these conflicting demands is for the government agency to direct its efforts towards actions that are highly symbolic in value, but low in the actual costs they impose on industry. The enactment of laws and regulations that are broad, ill-defined, or not enforced serves a symbolic purpose: politicians and government officials realize that it is more important that they demonstrate their concern to the broader public in some way, even if the 'solution' is legislation that has little instrumental value and is merely symbolic (Gusfield,1975). For example, although environmental assessment legislation was designed to facilitate the identification of the full range of predicted environmental consequences of a particular project or undertaking, the actual environmental assessment process occurs within a political and bureaucratic structure that is characterized by conflict: the bureaucracy is attempting to maintain itself and make appropriate decisions (as it defines them); politicians are vying for individual power and recognition within their respective parties; scientific or technical experts are operating within political environments and within an environment characterized by uncertain and rapidly changing knowledge; and, members of the broader public are lobbying for 'something to be done' and for increased involvement in decision-making. This conflict is highly structured since bureaucratic and political interests have influenced the interpretation of this legislation in a manner that both serves their interests and maintains the 'appearance' of protecting the environment.

This 'contained conflict' does not threaten the underlying structure and interest of the government or economy. Schnaiberg and Gould (1994) argue that bureaucracies or government agencies are structured in such a manner that the dual role of government (protecting the environment and ensuring economic growth, stability, and the well-being of the citizenry) is maintained because economic interests have paramountcy. While environmental assessments are designed ostensibly to gather and assess empirical research and data on aspects of the environment (defined in the Ontario Environmental Assessment Act as land, air, water, plant, and animal life and the social, economic, and cultural conditions that influence man or a community), they have been used to assist decision-makers to delay decisions, to select among alternatives, to ensure the 'wise use of public funds', to justify a proposed action, as vehicles for public consultation, or some combination thereof.

It should be noted that environmental assessment legislation has no legislative standards that must be met, nor is the scope of the assessment or the criteria defined legally. Rather, the interpretation and definition of 'environment' and the criteria for assessing impacts are determined, in large part, by the proponent of the project or undertaking. Ultimately, then, an environmental assessment is a 'balancing act' or a 'strategically crafted argument' (Stone, 1988), where the problem is subject to different interpretations and definitions.

Historically, the environment has been managed or regulated under all three levels of government: federal, provincial, and municipal. This is notable because the environment itself is not confined neatly into geopolitical boundaries. The federal government has been involved in environmental protection and enhancement as secondary issues associated with its jurisdiction over oceans, fisheries, and national health and welfare. The federal mandate is to control and regulate environmental contaminants on the ecosystem and to reduce the level of associated negative health implications. Ottawa has jurisdiction to protect and enhance federal lands (including some Native reserves), waters, federal works, national parks, and federal undertakings. It can also establish specific interjurisdictional relationships by separate agreement. The International Joint Commission (IJC) is an intergovernmental body with representatives from the federal, provincial, and state governments in the US and Canada that explores issues related to the Great Lakes.

The primary regulatory instrument of the federal government is the Canadian Environmental Protection Act (CEPA), which provides environmental guidelines for use by federal agencies in the exercise of their authority and in the operation of their duties. CEPA also establishes the requirements for monitoring and assessing environmental emissions. The federal government has recently enacted the Canadian Environmental Assessment Act (CEAA), which is designed to assess proactively the impacts of proposed projects. There is much controversy over the application of CEAA, since projects are scoped initially to determine what level of analysis, if any at all, is required. Further, criticism has been voiced over the applicability of CEAA for Canadian projects in non-Canadian settings, for example, the installation of CANDU nuclear reactors in Southeast Asia. The current situation is that CEAA has not yet been applied in non-Canadian settings, even though the proponents of the project are Canadian federal agencies.

It has been argued that the institutional arrangements reflecting the tenets of the industrial paradigm have led to wide variations in environmental protection and enforcement of legislation throughout Canada and have prevented a holistic environmental perspective from emerging.

Theoretical Paradigms: Society, Technology, and Ecology

Thomas Kuhn proposed the concept of a paradigm to explain the development of scientific knowledge. A paradigm or world view can be applied to a particular realm of social life that leads to ideologies, beliefs, and assumptions about the world. Because any given social paradigm is limited to a specific realm, numerous paradigms can exist simultaneously.

Olsen, Lodwick, and Dunlap (1992: 175) assert that 'sociologists must formulate theoretical principles linking social paradigms with the overall process of social organization.' They posit seven principles regarding paradigms.

Social paradigms arise from, and hence reflect, currently existing technological, social, economic, political, and other conditions.

Social paradigms are created and held by communicative communities, or sets of people who share common interests and communicate with one another who share common interests to some extent.

Social paradigms are viewed by their holders as expressions of social reality, and consequently have a semi-autonomous existence apart from the conditions that give rise to them or the people who create them.

Social paradigms act as 'mental lenses' to shape—but not fully determine—the manner in which their holders perceive and interpret their social world.

Social paradigms therefore influence—but do not fully determine—many of the actions and activities of their holders.

Social paradigms change through time as a consequence of emerging new technological, social, economic, political, and other conditions.

Social paradigms that exist at any given time tend to incorporate ideas from previous paradigms, and to affect future paradigms. (Olsen et al., 1992: 175–6)

Much of the conflict evident in the environmental field is a reflection of the different world views held by different stakeholders. To understand more fully the emergence of the environment as an issue one should look to our beliefs about the relationships between nature and humans. Environmental sociology, or sociology of the environment, has been concerned with the difficulties conceptualizing the human society-physical environment interrelationship or the 'society and nature' interrelationship. At the extremes of the debate are the positions that (a) the social and the physical are truly different and that the physical environment is irrelevant to sociological analysis and (b) that the social and the physical environments are intertwined and interdependent—that society influences the physical environment and the physical environment influences society (see Buttel,1986; Humphrey and Buttel, 1982; Dunlap and Catton, 1979; Catton, 1980; Schnaiberg, 1980; Schnaiberg and Gould, 1994). Environmental sociologists depart from traditional sociologists in that they do not believe that social facts are explained by other social factors. Environmental sociologists or social ecologists add the physical environment as another dimension that both effects and is affected by social behaviour.

While environmental sociologists acknowledge the integral importance of the physical environment, other stakeholders in the environmental arena adhere to a different paradigm also known by various names including the industrial paradigm, the dominant social paradigm, the human exemptionalist paradigm, the technological social paradigm, or one that assumes man is apart from and dominates nature. The defining characteristics of the technological social paradigm or dominant social paradigm are:

- People are fundamentally different from all other creatures on earth over which they have dominion.
- People are masters of their own destiny; they choose their goals and learn to do whatever is necessary to achieve them.
- The world is vast, and thus provides unlimited opportunities for humans.
- The history of humanity is one of progress; for every problem there is a solution, and thus progress need never cease.

As we will see, these different world views affect the structure of legislation and bureaucratic institutions, and shape the patterns of human/environment interaction. Also, when adherents of the different paradigms come together to 'solve' problems, as we will see in the case studies illustrated later in this chapter, each stakeholder has a different definition of the problem and a different conception of the appropriate solution. Further, it may be argued that the biophysical environment shapes socio-political structure and conflict. Social institutions and social structures can have a profound impact on public awareness of environmental issues.

At present, the jurisdictional boundaries among municipal, provincial, and federal governments are unclear with respect to many environmental issues. Individuals, environmental groups, and industry groups often face complex, ponderous, and conflicting bureaucratic structures. Downsizing within government bureaucracies has resulted in 'brain drain' in that more knowledgeable and experienced staff have left the public service. This further exacerbates the interaction with bureaucrats since many less experienced bureaucrats themselves are unaware of the structure and are learning at the same time as are their clients (individuals, industry groups, and environmental groups). Further, because decisions are made on a project-by-project basis, one facility may operate without environmental conditions attached to its permit (known as an approvals certificate) and an identical facility, operating in another area, may have onerous environmental conditions attached to its permit.

The postwar expansionist period (industrial paradigm) was characterized by almost unbridled consumption: the growth of subdivisions, super-highways, increased use of plastics and synthetics, high-technology farming, high-rise housing, big government, and big business. People were attempting to gain and exert control over their environment—to harness it for their own benefit without the realization that they were a component in a closed system and that their activities would have repercussions. Virtually all growth was considered good since growth meant economic prosperity and a higher standard of living. The industrial paradigm valued growth as a measure of prosperity.

This is not to suggest that pollution and environmental degradation were ignored; rather, pollution was dealt with on a piecemeal basis. If a plant was discharging too much particulate pollution, a filter was added. The solution was a technological addition—not a re-examination of the production and consumption patterns associated with a particular product or industrial process.

The industrial paradigm holds the belief that humans are superior to every other species on earth and perpetuates the notion that humans can dominate other species and have the ability to alter ecosystem equilibrium: to use it to further human goals. Humans, through science and technology, have been able to dominate nature and to exploit natural resources for the accumulation of wealth. Nature, or the resource itself, is not valued unless it can be transformed by humans into a product that can be consumed.

A stand of old-growth forest, according to this industrial paradigm, would be valued for the wood products it could produce. This same stand of forest is seen to have no value for the other components of the ecosystem (plants, animals, atmosphere, the terrestrial and aquatic environments) because humans are regarded as dominant and their needs and wants must be satisfied first. The natural resource is consumed in the most efficient and cost-effective way. Science and technology operate as integral tools used to dominate nature and to devise processes and methods to increase efficiency and reduce the costs of using natural resources.

This industrial paradigm also contains a time dimension. The well-being and wealth of the present generation is of primary concern. The conservation and preservation of a resource or natural feature is not a primary goal because the paradigm assumes that science and technology can 'fix' any shortcomings. Science and technology can be called on as well to correct an ecosystem disequilibrium. According to the industrial paradigm, a genetically engineered fish that grows rapidly could be introduced to ensure the supply of fish stock: a relative quick fix.

People are led to believe that they must accept the increased risk associated with technology or the mechanical domination of nature because not accepting these risks would impede progress as defined by the industrial paradigm. This is not to suggest that risks are ignored; rather, risks are minimized through the use of additional technology. Often, however, the technology is so new that the range of risks is not known. This is a particular concern in the widespread use of biotechnology and gene transplantation from one species to another or from animal to vegetable. Knowledge about the environmental impacts from biotechnology is still in its infancy, yet more bioengineered, genetically altered products enter the marketplace on a daily basis.

Perhaps equally disquieting is the industrial paradigm's assumption that natural resources are unlimited. It therefore follows that the most efficient and cost-effective practices should be used to maximize resource use. Humans are assumed to be apart from the ecosystem, not a part of it. This assumption has had profound ramifications for the way we have structured our society, how we define success and growth, and how we frame our policy objectives.

The industrial paradigm has been challenged by the ecological social paradigm. This paradigm is almost diametrically opposed to the industrial paradigm in its basic assumptions. Perhaps the most blatant distinction is the ecological social paradigm's view of science and technology and of humans' relationship with nature.

Technological and scientific advances enabled humans to extract natural resources and to dominate nature in ways that were previously incomprehensible. Humans can alter the course of rivers (e.g., Chicago), traverse the globe with rapid speed (e.g., the Concorde), visit space, communicate with others via the Internet and e-mail. We have come to expect change—rapid change—and are accustomed to being able to control the direction of that change.

Yet, increasingly, we are discovering that many of our products and by-products are harmful to our health and well-being and to those of future generations. The El Niño weather patterns, including the ice storm of 1998 that caused massive power outages in Quebec and Ontario, and the flooding of the Red River and Saguenay regions are but stark reminders that technology is still subsumed by nature. A reliance on technology proved devastating for many people and livestock farms in Ontario and Quebec during the ice storms. Livestock froze in barns that were unheated; dairy cattle suffered because they could not be milked due the lack of electricity to operate the milking machines; and still other animals suffocated due to the failure of ventilation systems. Water supplies were unreliable, since electric pumps were required to draw the water from the ground. In urban areas, the city came to a virtual stop due to lack of electrical power. Due to various government policies, electrical power is the preferred method of heating in Quebec. Further, government decisions to construct above-ground transmission lines exacerbated the problems associated with the ice storm. As we can see, the concentrated reliance on electrical technology in the organization of farming, heating, and ventilation practices, coupled with an ice storm of a magnitude previously unseen, had severe social and economic consequences.

According to the ecological social paradigm, fundamental problems of society cannot be solved by technology: fundamental social change is also required. The paradigm does not renounce all growth, technology, or scientific advances, but calls for proactive participatory consultation and planning of projects and policies. It also assumes that there will be an assessment of potential impacts of proposed projects, technologies, and policies before their implementation. Table 11.1 summarizes the differences between the two paradigms.

Different segments in society favour one paradigm over the other and conflict results since both sets of actors are trying to make the world a 'better place' according to their beliefs. In fact, most people in the developed world believe in aspects of both paradigms: they strongly believe in environmental values but are also striving for material wealth and financial security.

There is also a further elaboration of some of the social-physical environment interrelationship approaches contained within the ecological social paradigm. The intent here is to present the view that, even within a paradigm, different theoretical positions are possible. There are primarily three different approaches that focus on the society-physical environment interrelationship within the ecological social paradigm. They are the environment and materialism approach, the environment and society approach, and the social ecology approach. All of these approaches can be grouped under the paradigm known by various names: the new environmental

Table 11.1   Components of the Existing Industrial Paradigm and the Ecological Social Paradigm

Existing Industrial Paradigm	Ecological Social Paradigm
Environmental Components	
Humans can control nature and use it to their advantage to improve life.	Humans are part of the earth's ecosystem and must live within nature.
The natural environment is valuable because it provides necessary resources.	The natural environment is valuable in itself and must be protected at all costs.
Natural resources are ample for all human needs.	Natural resources are limited and must be preserved.
The earth could support a considerably larger human population.	World population has reached the earth's carrying capacity and must be controlled.
Technological Components	
Technology can eventually solve most human problems.	Technology creates at least as many problems as it solves.
Technology should be continually improved, expanded, and utilized.	The advantages and disadvantages of all technology should be continually assessed.
Hard and/or high technology is usually most desirable.	Soft and/or low technology is often most desirable.
The most advanced technology should always be used.	The most appropriate technology should always be used.
Economic Components	
A market economy based on private property and operated to maximize profits is desirable.	A planned economy based on both public and private ownership of property and operated to serve human needs is most desirable.
Unlimited economic growth and material progress are possible.	Economic growth and material progress are limited by ecological conditions.
The primary economic goal should be increased production to create greater wealth.	The primary economic goal should be sustainable sufficiency to meet human needs.
Emphasis on market control.	Emphasis on foresight and planning.
Our economic future will be characterized by abundance.	Our economic future will be characterized by scarcity.

Table 11.1   cont'd

Political Components

Extensive centralized government is necessary in modern society.	Limited, decentralized government is necessary in modern societies.
Authority should be hierarchically structured.	Authority should be non-hierarchical and participatory.
Political decisions should be made by experts on the basis of factual knowledge.	Political decisions should be made by citizens on the basis of valuative concerns: consultative and participatory.
The primary function of government is to preserve law and order in society.	The primary function of government is to promote individual and collective well-being.

Organizational Components

Organizations are most effective when they are large-scale and complexly structured.	Organizations are most effective when they are small-scale and simply structured.
Organizations are most effective when they are centralized and use formal operating procedures.	Organizations are most effective when they are decentralized and use informal operating procedures.
The most fundamental concerns of organizations should be order and stability.	The most fundamental concerns of organizations should be innovation and change.

Source: From Olsen, Lodwick, and Dunlap (1992: 3–7).

paradigm, the ecocentric paradigm, the emerging industrial paradigm, the transindustrial paradigm, the metaindustrial paradigm, the alternative social paradigm, or the post–industrial paradigm.

Environment and Materialism

Marx developed a 'historical materialism' that focused on the differences between the conceptual and the material—an analytic separation of the social from the natural world. This is not to suggest that Marx ignored nature. Marx conceived the *mode of production* of material life as 'condition[ing] the social, political and intellectual processes of life in general' (Marx and Engels, 1955: 363). O'Connor (1998) presents an ecological Marxist perspective by examining the relationship between the economy, nature, and society. O'Connor argues that Marx indeed incorporated the notion of ecology. O'Connor asserts Marx had 'a vision of society in which the appropriation of nature is not based on the logic of capitalist accumulation but rather on individual and social need . . . and "ecologically rational" production.' According to O'Connor, Marx did have a view of nature not merely as a productive force to be harnessed and used by humans for the creation of surplus value, but nature is also valued as an end, in and of itself. However, Marx acknowledges that nature can be 'dominated' through the application of science and technology to increase production and the productivity of nature. Nevertheless, he argues that environmental and social crises pose a growing threat to capitalism itself—one of its inherent contradictions.

Environment and Society: Causal Patterns

In this view of the environment-society interrelationship the debate centres around the paramountcy of either the physical or social environments—a chicken and egg debate, if you will. Within this realm are the environmental determinists at one end of the spectrum and human exemptionalist (see Dunlap and Catton, 1979) adherents at the other end. Environmental determinants believe that physical environmental features determine socio-cultural patterns. Conversely, according to Dunlap and Catton, human exemptionalists believe in socio-cultural determinism.

Social Ecology

One of the primary tenets of ecology is the notion of interconnectedness or 'web of life' conceptualizations—that every action has a reaction—where the goal is a state of equilibrium. This biological concept of ecology has been applied to social life and is known as human ecology. In human ecology, the environment is an integral component of social relations. Our behaviour, structures, and institutions are shaped by and shape our physical environment. Both the biophysical and social environments are of relatively equal prominence. Humphrey and Buttel (1982) and Buttel (1986, 1987) are most often associated with this perspective. The environment is seen as both a facilitator and a limiting factor in social activities.

Towards a New Paradigm

It has been argued that the inclusion of the 'environment' as a factor in social activities is indicative of an emerging paradigm shift. Although there has always been a relationship between society and nature, a paradigm shift may be emerging. This newer paradigm accords a greater emphasis and role to the natural or biophysical environment *for understanding a set of socio-political conflicts.* Freudenburg, Frickel, and Gramling (1995: 372), in their discussion on resource use, argue that socio-cultural factors provide necessary but not sufficient conditions for any resource use. They argue that while physical characteristics *do* matter, it is essential to understand the assumptions underlying what is characterized as 'natural' or 'strictly social'. In this regard, it is important to understand the social meanings ascribed to natural phenomena and to understand the interaction between what is deemed to be 'natural' and what is deemed to be 'social'.

Freudenburg et al. (1995: 387) further assert that 'there may actually be no such thing as a "natural" resource—only a complex mix of social, technological, and biophysical conditions through which a given element of the natural environment, at a particular time, comes to be socially defined as valuable.'

On the other hand, some theorists, such as Schnaiberg and Gould (1994), concur with the work of Offe (1984), and contend that the inclusion of environmental concerns is not necessarily indicative of a paradigm shift, but rather is part of an 'enduring conflict' in modern capitalist system, with the 'environment' providing the 'economic treadmill' with the supply it demands. According to these theorists, ecological sustainability and economic development are interdependent, that is, without a sustained resource base, economic development is ultimately self-limiting and this underlies the contradictions inherent in capitalism with its emphasis on continuous capital growth. Consequently, in order to maintain this 'treadmill', the state has enacted many pieces of environmental protection legislation over the last 20 years.

According to Schnaiberg and Gould (1994) this treadmill and its associated class structure are reproduced by a shared commitment of members of advanced industrial societies (or post-industrial societies) to some form of economic expansion in order to meet their needs. The treadmill of production is neither a global nor a local institution—it is a network of regional, national, and increasingly, multi-national economic organizations. These organizations are linked to regional and national government agencies, providing them with economic resources and cultural approval. The modern 'treadmill' has emerged from co-ordinated social, political, and economic decisions.

Schnaiberg and Gould focus on the conflict between the role of the treadmill that requires more and more to produce the goods and services it creates a demand for, and our desire to avoid the damage that this system creates. Environmental problems are rooted in conflicts about the scarcity of these environmental resources, as experienced by groups and social classes. These environmental conflicts focus on resource allocation decisions and the values members of society place on environmental resources—such as clean air, pure water, and old-growth forests. However, since the major institutions of modern society are structured by and linked to economic growth and treadmill expansion, concepts such as 'sustainability' are filtered through this 'economic growth perspective' and every effort is made to ensure that the treadmill is maintained.

Conversely, other theorists (see Freudenburg et al., 1995) have challenged the work of Schnaiberg and Gould. The analysis conducted by Schnaiberg and Gould is hampered by their acknowledged choice not to discuss legal institutions.

However, it is precisely the legislative and bureaucratic framework that is shaped by environmental assessment legislation, which sets the boundaries (however broadly defined) of the range of environmental factors to be considered in decision-making. In this regard, Finsterbusch (1994) contends that the inclusion of an assessment of the social environment in an overall environmental assessment serves several purposes that may conflict with the economic treadmill model posited by Schnaiberg and Gould. Finsterbusch asserts that the policy-making process should be characterized by cycles of information-gathering and decision-making and that through the inclusion of the 'social environment' in an overall environmental assessment, different stakeholders can gain access to the information-gathering and decision-making process. It is through these mechanisms that problem definition and the environmental impact assessment itself can affect the direction and pace of the 'treadmill'.

The first and perhaps best-known example of a full-scale inclusion of social factors in an environmental assessment of a project is the Mackenzie Valley Pipeline Inquiry (the Berger Inquiry). Justice Thomas Berger recommended that the Arctic Gas project be deferred largely because of the potential social and cultural effects such a project would have on the Aboriginal population. Prior to the Mackenzie Valley Pipeline Inquiry, it was commonplace for environmental assessments to focus only on the physical environment or natural resource concerns. Social factors are usually incorporated in the form of a social impact assessment. Even though social impact assessments have been conducted in Canada for over 20 years, there are still many concerns regarding the content and methods of analysis of social data and the incorporation of such information into an environmental impact assessment.

Further, in the Ontario context, it is through the environmental assessment and approvals processes that projects are assessed on the basis of broader criteria. To cite recent examples, the Ontario Waste Management Corporation's search for a hazardous waste landfill site and the Ontario Hydro Demand and Supply Plan are illustrations of what can occur when other perspectives are brought to bear on projects. In the first example, the application for a proposed hazardous landfill site was denied, and in the second, Ontario Hydro withdrew its proposal due to public concern about the lack of attention paid to managing the social demand for electrical power and absence of any assessment of the effect of the implementation of energy conservation measures to meet this demand, as opposed to just simply increasing supply.

Environmental decision-making occurs within a context characterized by a plurality of stakeholders and interests. Environmental legislation and the administration of this legislation serve to shape the debates over the distribution and use of resources. However, the framework within which the decision-making process operates can shape the direction of the gathering of information and ultimately affect the decision itself. It may be argued, therefore, that the 'treadmill model' is too economically deterministic and it cannot adequately address the de facto policy changes that result from individual project decisions.

Risk Assessment, Risk Management, Standard Setting, and Health Effects

Environmental standards are developed to protect society against harm from the release of toxic and/or polluting substances. Standard-setting is very much a social process of determining 'how safe is safe enough'. Social definitions of safety are linked to perceptions and assessments of risk and technology. As technology advances, our ability to identify and measure smaller and smaller amounts of substances is enhanced. Further, as scientific epidemiological research is amassed, substances previously defined as safe or 'harmless' are now defined as harmful. 'Harm' or hazard has traditionally been defined in terms of the concept of risk.

The term 'risk' has two distinct meanings. It can mean a hazard, that is, an event or act that has adverse consequences such as a fire, plane crash, or nuclear accident. In addition, risk can be interpreted more broadly to connote the probability or chance of experiencing an adverse consequence within a specific set of conditions—such as varying concentrations or amounts of a substance during a period of time. 'Risk perception' is a social psychological process during which risk is defined. This perception process can occur at both the individual and social group levels. Many factors influence the risk perception and risk assessment (a determination of whether there is a risk and the level of that risk) process. In addition, a number of other factors are involved in risk perception. These include familiarity or experience with the event or substance, whether there is voluntary or involuntary exposure and/or involvement, previous experience with an event or substance, gender, language, education, and whether the event is technological or natural. An element in the risk perception process that is often overlooked is the 'language' used in describing the event or substance. For example, there are certain 'trigger phrases' that have connotations attached that may not be evident initially. The word 'reactor' is frequently used among scientists and technical experts to describe the vessel in which a process occurs. The same word repeated to members of the general public is almost always assumed to be associated with nuclear energy. Therefore, even though 'reactor' is used by petrochemical engineers to describe a heater used in the production of petrochemical by-products, such as lubricants used in cosmetics, members of the general public assume all 'reactors' are 'nuclear reactors' (since these are the only type of 'reactors' that they are aware of) and may perceive an unwarranted level of risk (the risk associated with nuclear reactors) simply due to the different socially constructed meanings attached to the word.

Whether one is familiar with or has had experience with a substance and/or event affects the perception of the risk and the assessment of it. An annual flooding is perceived to be a relative non-event provided that flooding control devices and strategies have been developed and successfully implemented in the past. The Red River flooding in Manitoba in 1997 represented an event of greater magnitude than previously experienced; however, the city of Winnipeg had knowledge of the more severe (than anticipated) flooding impacts from US communities that had already experienced the cresting of the river. Winnipeg was able to prepare and hence reduce the perception and assessment of the risk of the flood that they were soon going to experience. In addition, Winnipeg had previously constructed a spillway for the annual cresting of the Red River. Although significant additional resources and reinforcements were required to manage the flood, the city of Winnipeg, unlike Grand Forks, North Dakota, was largely spared flood damage.

In another example, a fire occurred in Hamilton, Ontario, within a plastics recycling warehouse. The community and fire departments were concerned about the conditions at the recycling facility before the fire. Fire officials cited the company for Ontario Fire Code violations. In addition, members of the neighbouring community had written letters to local politicians about both the previous and existing owners of the property, voicing their concerns about site management. Complicating the situation even further was the fact that there appeared to be a gap in jurisdictional control over the site: the province did not issue approvals for recycling facilities and the municipal permitting process did not address environmental concerns.

A problem was identified by various individuals and agencies yet the 'tools' were not developed to adequately address the problem. Some residents believed that 'there were a lot of safety precautions could have been taken, but they weren't and the city and the Ministry of the Environment have to share the blame' (*Toronto Star*, 1998: E1). In addition, questions were raised regarding the business practices and criminal records of the previous and/or existing owners of the Plastimet site. Hamilton is characterized as an industrial city, being the home to two major steel producers. Residents and local politicians alike are familiar with the practices of industry.

The Plastimet fire burned for four days. Initially, residents were advised to stay indoors. As the fire continued to burn, nearby homes were evacuated while toxic smoke enveloped the community. Media accounts indicated the smoke was laden with dioxins and other toxic chemicals. It was reported that fire officials were not entirely aware of what materials were stored in the warehouse. Public health officials instructed local residents not to eat vegetables from their gardens until contaminant testing could be completed. A number of weeks later, the ban was lifted when contaminant testing indicated that the levels of contaminants were within acceptable levels. Residents were advised by officials to return to their homes once the fire was extinguished and that the ensuing clean-up efforts would achieve 'acceptable levels' of pollutants. Residents were wary. Was this safe? Would children be harmed from inhaling the smoke, eating home-grown vegetables, or playing in neighbouring playgrounds? Why were responses littered with phrases such as 'acceptable levels' as opposed to 'safe' and 'health'? There were no definite answers because not enough scientific knowledge has been amassed about the exposure of residents to the chemicals released through an industrial fire. Residents had no benchmarks with which to compare their situation and evaluate their perceptions of risk. The scientific experts from the Ministries of Environment and Health could present information on 'acceptable levels'. These levels, however, were established during an era of domination by scientific and technical experts in the environment standard-setting process, with very little or no involvement of the public. In addition, standards are developed on a single contaminant level, not on the combination of substances involved in the creation of plastics or the combination of substances that may have been created during the fire.

Greenpeace stepped in to conduct its own testing after the affected residents expressed great dissatisfaction with the actions and responses of Ministry of the Environment personnel. Greenpeace helped to publicize this 'environmental crisis' and put pressure on the Ministry of the Environment to act to clean up the Plastimet site.

There is abundant literature to confirm that scientific experts tend to view the public's perceptions of risk as unscientific and irrational. The literature also confirms that scientific experts and members of the public perceive, assess, and respond to risk differently and use different criteria in the processes. Even though government scientific experts have assured the residents surrounding the Plastimet fire site that contaminants are within acceptable levels, residents *felt* they had been negatively affected or harmed. In addition, residents were angered by the inaction of government officials who did not act when concerns about the site were previously brought to their attention.

Feelings of helplessness and hopelessness lead to demoralization in people trapped by a situation that exposes them to toxic substances. One of the most important predictors of demoralization is a perceived threat to physical health, and the inability to do anything about it, that is, a *lack of control* and a sense of not being taken seriously. As a result, the impact of an event is influenced by its perceived controllability—if one believes he or she has control there is less stress. Since governmental agency support is often ineffective, affected populations frequently experience disillusionment (with 'experts') and government officials experience a loss of credibility and trust. It is not surprising then that residents were less than relieved by the assurances of government officials and technical experts.

Technological disasters differ from natural disasters. In the two examples cited above people in the man-made facility fire experienced additional stress because there is an expectation that society had instituted a series of checks and balances—in the form of permits, licences, inspections, and monitoring. Technological accidents are assessed as having greater risk precisely because of the failure of the systems that were designed to prevent them. Technological accidents are perceived as having greater risk, since they do not occur in a predictable fashion (hence the term accidental) and, as such, the effects are less known. Natural disasters, such as floods, may be perceived as having less risk, since the effects, albeit large-scale and devastating, are known and people have experienced them in the past.

Critics of risk assessments that rely on quantitative statistical techniques for the determination of 'acceptable limits' note that the indirect consequences of hazards, the qualitative differences associated with the consequences of different types of hazards, the decision-making context in which the hazard occurs, and the decision-making context of the decision about the limit itself are *not* considered. Members of the public tend to have broader definitions of risk when compared with scientific experts. The public incorporates values, beliefs, ideas of social equity, history, economics, culture, and politics in their perceptions and assessments of risk. For example, historical relationships with proponents of projects are incorporated in the public assessment of risk. Factors such as a reluctance to be forthcoming with information, actively misleading/deceiving the public in the past, previous incidents/accidents, not responding to public concerns or a history of acrimonious labour relations all become incorporated into a public assessment of risk. Such factors usually result both in an intensification of perception of risk and in an assessment of greater severity of risk. Further, when technological projects such as water purification facilities, waste landfills, or major highway projects are planned for predominately rural areas, the concern about the impact on the social fabric and culture are issues generally initially raised by members of the public who are concerned about a change in their 'way of life'. It should also be noted that even scientific determination of 'acceptable limits' requires subjective judgements.

Alberta has instituted a definition of standards in its Environmental Protection and Enhancement Act as being something more than a numerical limit. Standards are applied through approvals, guidelines, or codes of practice. They 'can be numerical limits, narrative statements, or best management practices'. The province of Alberta differentiates between technology-based and ambient-based standards. This is an attempt to incorporate social information in a traditionally technical process. Technology-based standards ensure a minimum level of treatment and pollution prevention and a level playing field among industrial and municipal sectors. Ambient-based standards are applied where protection of the environment requires more stringent levels of treatment and pollution prevention. Alberta's legislation is a relatively recent statement on environmental standards and acknowledges that numerical limits are only part of the picture. It is through the 'narrative' statement that social values and subjective beliefs can be integrated.

The Multi-Stakeholder Advisory Group Process

In this section, two examples of multi-stakeholder group process will be examined. As the name implies, a multi-stakeholder group represents multiple interests as expressed by different stakeholders. There are a number of different processes, each characterized by different levels of stakeholder participation and decision-making ability. The philosophy behind the formation of a multi-stakeholder group is that decisions made through consensus are more likely to ensure success and diminish the expression of conflict. Since it is logistically impossible to incorporate the interests of everyone, an important sociological question is 'Who becomes involved in the process?' A number of questions follow logically. On what basis are stakeholders selected? What interests do they represent? Do stakeholders accurately represent their constituencies? This was a particular concern a few years ago in a British Columbia logging practice protest when Greenpeace indicated that they represented the interests of Aboriginal groups. Various Aboriginal groups objected, indicating that Greenpeace was imposing *its* values and did not represent the Aboriginal groups' values.

Additional considerations involved in multi-stakeholder group processes include: Are there any structural barriers that prevent participation in a multi-stakeholder group? Are all 'voices' equal within the group or are some 'voices' given greater authority or power than others? A multi-stakeholder group process involving representatives of the public is an attempt by government to facilitate public participation in decision-making. The amount of influence multi-stakeholder groups have on decisions, however, depends on the issue. Our society is governed through a representative, democratically elected Parliament. Stakeholders represent a constituency but are rarely duly elected. Since stakeholders are rarely elected, what is the nature of their responsibility to consult directly with their constituencies? How are individual interests represented in multi-stakeholder group settings? Are group members given adequate time to inform and consult with their constituencies and thus ensure that they have a mandate to speak on behalf of their constituencies? The answers to these questions depend on the interests and structure of the group involved in the process and on the structure of the multi-stakeholder group itself.

Although there are many different forms of multi-stakeholder group consultative processes there are two general approaches. In one approach the multi-stakeholder group has problem-defining and decision-making capability. Problems are defined in a group context and the resolution of the problem may also be within the purview of the multi-stakeholder group. In the other approach, the multi-stakeholder group is advisory only, providing comment to and minor modification to a 'draft' decision. The problem has been scoped and defined by another party— usually the result of a political or bureaucratic decision.

Environmental Contaminant Standard Setting

In the following example of air quality standard-setting, the multi-stakeholder process in Ontario is currently in development. Although the Ministry of Energy, Science, and Technology wishes to pursue a multi-stakeholder approach, it is not certain at this point whether the multi-stakeholder group will be able to determine a list of air pollutants for which standards will be developed or use a list of priority pollutants already identified by the Ministry of Energy, Science, and Technology.

Multi-stakeholder group processes can pose a threat to traditional decision-making approaches formulated under the existing industrial paradigm. If stakeholders are involved in problem definition and problem resolution, there is a distinct possibility that the interests of those adhering to other paradigms will be able to influence the 'problem' definition and hence the solution to the problem.

The National Pollutants Release Inventory

The federal government, in an effort to determine the magnitude of environmental pollution, introduced the National Pollutants Release Inventory (NPRI) in 1993 in response to the 1990 federal Green Plan. The Green Plan committed to the creation of a publicly accessible national database on environmental emissions as the first in a series of steps designed to evaluate the nature and extent of various environmental pollutants. The NPRI is a voluntary reporting of environmental pollutants. The conditions required for reporting were size of the facility, amount of substance released, and the type of substance released. It is an important non-regulatory mechanism for encouraging pollution control.

The NPRI was developed as a result of consultation with a multi-stakeholder advisory group consisting of representatives from different levels of government, industry, and non-governmental organizations. Representatives of nine industry associations, including the mining, pulp and paper, and petrochemical sectors, contributed. Labour, health, and environmental groups and provincial and territorial governments were also involved. The result of this consultation process identified 178 substances and criteria for reporting. The multi-stakeholder process resulted in an approach that was acceptable to those involved and represented a significant change in environmental decision-making—one more closely associated with the ecological paradigm.

The use of a multi-stakeholder group in the development of criteria for reporting and measurement represents a notable change in the operation of government in the development of pollution control programs and policies. Prior to the formation of a multi-stakeholder group process, consultation on various government initiatives would occur with a select group (determined on the basis of the issue or by the ministry/agency involved) of influentials, primarily scientific experts. A multi-stakeholder group process permits the formal involvement of public interest groups who may or may not have recognized scientific expertise.

The results of the NPRI are published in major national and local newspapers, although there are no sanctions attached. It is hoped that industries would reduce their pollutant releases, where possible, through moral suasion. Further, making the database accessible to the public ensures a certain level of public scrutiny and potential public pressure to reduce releases. The multi-stakeholder group also played a key role in defining the problem and its resolution. This is not to imply that there are no detractors of the multi-stakeholder group process. The NPRI, however, represents one of the first federal examples where groups of stakeholders are brought together to jointly design a program and therefore it represents an example of decision-making that is more in keeping with the principles of the ecological social model.

In 1995, the first NPRI data were widely publicized throughout the print and electronic media with headlines as such: 'Canada's worst polluter' or ' Highest on the list for pollutants'. Although the guidelines of the NPRI clearly state that the physical tonnage of a particular substance does not necessarily relate to the toxicity levels of the substances involved and that toxic micro-pollutants such as dioxin and furans were not included, the effect of the public release of data provided an impetus for various reporting facilities and industries to examine their operations.

Recent Changes in Environmental Legislation

The focus in this section will be on Ontario as the case study. Ontario is selected because it has the largest population in Canada, it has been acknowledged as having some of the most comprehensive environmental legislation, and because in October 1998 Ontario was identified as the 'third worse polluter in North America'— despite its amendments to environmental assessment and protection legislation and the enactment of environmental rights legislation.

Environmental Bills of Rights

While the public's right to a healthy environment is enshrined under various pieces of provincial and federal legislation (for example, under the Canadian Environmental Protection Act [CEPA], the Fisheries Act, the National Parks Act, the Migratory Bird Convention Act), few provinces in Canada have specific comprehensive environmental bills of rights. Environmental rights in Canada are tools to assist members of the public in the protection of the environment. The enactment of Environmental Bill of Rights (EBR) legislation in Canada is a significant step in the advancement of a paradigm shift. A rights-based approach to environmental quality entrenches the involvement of members of the 'public'. EBR legislation establishes each citizen's right to a healthy environment and a provision acknowledging that the government has a public trust obligation to protect the environment for future generations. It is a significant departure from previous pieces of legislation because of its emphasis on *individual* rights. Individual people now have access to information, the right to ask for an environmental investigation, and the right to comment on policies, permits, and processes. In addition, EBR legislation usually involves provisions and/or processes for:

- access to information;
- right to notice and comment;
- requests for investigation;
- private prosecution/right to make a complaint;
- grounds for actions;
- informant/employee 'whistle-blowing' protection;
- petitions to the Minister of Environment to review the issue;
- annual reports.

The Northwest Territories was the first Canadian jurisdiction to enact a comprehensive environmental rights law, the Northwest Territories Environmental Rights Act, 1990. This was followed by the Yukon Environmental Act, 1991. The Yukon's protection of environmental rights is arguably the most comprehensive in Canada. In 1992, Saskatchewan proposed its own environmental bill of rights. Yet, in 1993 a Standing Committee on the Environment reviewed the bill and recommended that the minister should use the bill as a foundation for further consultation on rights and responsibilities legislation. British Columbia has environmental rights outlined in its recently enacted Environmental Protection Act.[2] Another piece of relatively new environmental legislation, An Act respecting environmental rights in Ontario, more commonly known as the Ontario Environmental Bill of Rights (EBR), came into effect in February 1994.

It was the then NDP government's hope that Ontario's Environmental Bill of Rights would become a landmark for the environment and for democracy in Ontario. More importantly, its objective was to reinforce Ontario's commitment to the goal of sustainable development championed in the 1987 Brundtland Report, which recognized the global nature of environmental problems.

The Ontario Environmental Bill of Rights has been praised as giving individuals new rights and remedies in dealing with environmental issues. Its proponents say it represents a new era in environmental decision-making, one characterized by *enhanced public participation, citizen empowerment, and greater accountability of decision-makers.* The EBR was enacted by Ontario's NDP government in response to the perceived public demand to open up the government's environmental decision-making process to much greater public scrutiny and also in response to requests by the business community that the environmental approvals process for projects be streamlined and made more uniform and predictable—in other words, more efficient. Are these two goals contradictory? Does increased public participation in decision-making create more efficient and uniform decision-making? Specifically, the EBR has been described as 'a win-win' situation for everyone. Ontario's long-term health and prosperity, after all, depend on our success in restoring and protecting the environment. The Ontario EBR was paired with encouraging a healthy economy in one of the clearest statements on sustainability issued by government: '*A clean environment creates incentives for jobs in Ontario, bringing with it real economic growth and opportunities for job creation.*' This is interesting because, by enacting the EBR, the NDP legally entrenched certain *values* in the Environmental Bill of Rights Act. For example, section 2 of the Act states that:

> the purposes of this Act are to protect, conserve, and where reasonable, restore the integrity of the environment; to provide *sustainability* of the environment; and, to protect the health of the environment . . . including the following: the prevention, reduction and elimination of the use, generation and release of pollutants that are an unreasonable threat to the integrity of the environment; the *protection and conservation* of biological, ecological and genetic diversity; and, the protection and conservation of natural resources, including plant life, animal life and ecological systems.

Which parts of the environment are sustained? Which parts are protected? Which, conserved? Who chooses? And how is sustainability defined? What unit of analysis is used to measure and define the concept of sustainability? Is sustainability a measurable concept?

In addition, it is important to understand the 'ecosystem' approach employed by the EBR. The EBR applies not only to the Ministry of Environment but to almost all the ministries; however, the Ministry of Finance has been specifically exempted. The ministries will draft Statements of Environmental Values (SEVs) stating how each ministry will take the environment into account in its decision-making and that the public can comment on acts, policies, and instruments that can effect the environment. To date, the majority of public activity concerning the EBR has been related to the Ministry of Environment.

The Environmental Bill of Rights also represents a joining of science and the law within the context of policy-making. An argument can be made for the fact that science is a major social institution that constructs environmental risks, knowledge, crises, and solutions. The law is also a major social institution and when one looks at the purpose of the Environmental Bill of Rights and its emphasis on biology and science where the current state of knowledge is far from certain, one cannot help but wonder about the appropriateness of subjecting uncertain scientific knowledge to the rules of evidence/standards of proof etc. in a courtroom. Is the law (EBR) supposed to determine what is acceptable science?

The appropriate means of participating is through *written comment*, which limits those without a facility in written English and French, a particular concern in a multi-ethnic area such as greater Toronto. Furthermore, the process is for comment only; there is no provision for individual feedback or response to those who provide comment. Although comments from the public must be considered in decisions, there are no guidelines or frameworks for how these comments will be considered. The practice has been to enumerate the comments and provide a précis of the concerns indicated, followed in some cases by an action that may/may not address the comments. Participation through the EBR is highly structured and time lines are rigidly specified. On one hand, this provides a measure of certainty; it also limits the debate and assumes that the public has a sufficient knowledge base to provide meaningful comment.

However, an even more important question is whether a legal rights perspective is the best way to increase public access to environmental decision-making for all people in Ontario. In particular, Aboriginal legal commentators have contended that the traditional legal rights paradigm is the artifact of a specific cultural and historical orientation (Turpel, 1993).

The political will to implement the EBR will clearly be a factor in its success. The question remains as to what the EBR will be able to do to promote environmental protection. The 1998 environmental report card for Ontario was not promising. It is still unclear whether the EBR is an indication of the beginning of a paradigmatic shift in environmental policy-making.

What we are seeing is that environmental protection or pollution control is a new subject of law. A very large and very complex environmental bureaucracy has been built over the last thirty years, its separate parts built independently and sometimes without much awareness of the whole structure. Most environmental laws have brought increasing responsibilities to governments. Increasingly, the duty to implement these laws is falling to provincial or municipal governments. Environmental responsibility has shifted downward without the needed funds to implement the programs the laws mandate. Nevertheless, there has been an exponential growth in environmental laws. Moreover, if one looks at the membership of the Bill of Rights Task Force—struck to facilitate the implementation of the Ontario Environmental Bill of Rights—the members were predominantly lawyers. Arguably, this group can be defined as an 'epistemic community' (to borrow Haas's term), which was first used in the context of international environmental treaty-making referring to a group of like-minded officials with shared beliefs about ecological principles and similar ideas about the policies needed to address environmental concerns.

The Environmental Bill of Rights Task Force can be regarded as an 'epistemic community' because they are shaping the issues to fit the 'law' as the policy instrument of choice. They all share a view about the appropriateness or legitimacy of law as a policy tool and the use of the courts or quasi-judicial boards to resolve disputes. The use of these 'experts' and the emphasis on law, the courts, and the resolution of disputes in an adversarial setting fits in more with the industrial social paradigm than with the ecological social paradigm.

Recent amendments to the EBR by the Conservative government make it unlikely that the EBR will be a spur to paradigmatic change with respect to environmental policy-making. For example, the Ontario Conservative government has been criticized as impeding progress towards a healthy and sustainable environment by suspending parts of the EBR in 1995. According to a report to the legislature prepared by the Environmental Commissioner this suspension was 'snuck' through the legislature in late November 1995 without notice and profoundly affects the EBR (Poole, 1996: 334). The Environmental Commissioner alleged that the Minister of Environment and Energy had violated both the spirit and intent of the EBR. In particular, the Environmental Commissioner's most pointed criticisms were aimed at Ontario Regulation 482/95, which was passed on 29 November 1995 (ibid.). This regulation temporarily revoked the parts of the EBR that require the 14 ministries to publicize, through an electronic environmental registry, laws or regulations that might affect the province's environment. The Conservative government had suspended that requirement for any policy or other decision related to *cost-cutting* measures, making all ministries exempt until 30 September 1996 (ibid.). The Finance Ministry is now exempted permanently. The Environmental Commissioner was particularly critical of the government for compounding the problem by failing to post a regulation on the registry (where it would be accessible to every individual) and she was concerned that unless there is a procedure for tracking what the ministries do, vis-à-vis the environment, there would be no incentive for government to be accountable for their activities (ibid.).

Most importantly, by exempting the Ministry of Finance from the requirements of the Bill of Rights, decision-makers in that ministry will tend to focus on priorities that seem more important than the environment. In fact, all ministries will view financial issues as separate from and more important than environmental issues, thereby destroying the possibility of making 'sustainable development' a reality. The view that there is an interconnectedness and interdependence between the economy and the environment clearly is not shared by the Conservative government.

The regulation not posted on the EBR bulletin board also suspends for 10 months the public notice requirements for environmentally significant proposals linked to government cost-cutting. In other words, public comment opportunities were weakened at precisely the time when numerous changes were occurring in Ontario's environmental policy and regulatory framework through the implementation of the Environmental Bill of Rights. For example, significant changes to environmental legislation introduced through Bill 26—the government's so-called omnibus bill—were not open to public comment through the Environmental Bill of Rights.

In failing to post the regulation on the environmental registry, the Minister of Environment did not comply with the public notice requirements of the Environmental Bill of Rights, effectively denying the public a chance to evaluate the importance of removal of the Ministry of Finance from the requirements of the Environmental Bill of Rights. The passage of this regulation (again, using the law as a policy tool) has effectively removed the opportunity for public participation and has suppressed any public expression of disapproval, while at the same time ensuring that the purposes of the Environmental Bill of Rights are never achieved. The Environmental Bill of Rights has been gutted. Only its symbolic shell remains—making it appear as if the Conservative government is responsive to environmental concerns.

The Ministry of Finance has responded to the Environmental Commissioner's concerns by saying that its inclusion in the list of ministries subject to the Environmental Bill of Rights was inappropriate. The Ministry of Finance is arguing that the EBR, in practice, had little application to the Ministry of Finance since the EBR already exempts proposals for policies and Acts that are predominantly financial or administrative in nature from notice requirements. The government argued that the regulation was not placed on the electronic registry for the same reason—it was predominantly financial and administrative in nature. It argued that the suspension of the electronic registry until September 1996 was an administrative regulation only that in no way weakens any environmental protection in this province. It is further stated that the time spent in public consultations would undermine the administration's ability to curb spending and reduce the deficit.

These initiatives represent a change in approach to environmental issues in Ontario that is consistent with other policies promulgated by the Conservative government to encourage growth and reduce spending. The government also proposes to conduct a cost-benefit analysis (going back to rational decision-making and a belief in the supremacy of the market as a regulator of human activities) of any new environmental regulation or legislation that is introduced. The Conservative government appeared to be taking steps to ensure that the Ministry of Environment and Energy (MOEE), now known again as the Ministry of Environment (MOE), did not interfere with its plans for development in the province—the announcement of the layoff of 272 MOEE employees is one example of this. The downsizing at MOE was proportionally larger than the downsizing at any other ministry. The message to investors is clear: Ontario is open for business at all costs—there is no mention of 'sustainable development'.

Although many efforts of the Conservative government have truncated the scope of the EBR, some important features remain. In an era of downsizing, the electronic bulletin board has increasingly become an important information resource used by both organized groups and individuals. Organized groups include: environmental activists, consultants, lawyers, advocacy organizations, and business. The annual reports published by the Environmental Commissioner's Office have been seen as 'report cards' on the state of the environment in Ontario. Instead of being lost in a bureaucratic quagmire, these reports and the EBR provide individuals or groups with concise sources of information on a wide range of environmental issues and provide a valuable entry point for delving into environmental issues in more detail. This is not to suggest that the EBR has been operating without problems. Every law and every process has difficulties. Some potential problems with the EBR include: information access in a multicultural society; the potential to create a situation of public interest where one does not exist, or exist to the degree presented; the equity issues associated with individuals and groups commenting on projects/policies that do not directly affect them; and having non-local interest overwhelm the interests of local populations. In this regard, the EBR has facilitated the access to information, however, it has also created a decision-making environment wherein decision-makers may have to incorporate a multiplicity of interests never before imagined.

Needless to say, the amendments to the EBR underscore a very important question: What are the values and the goals that are reflected in environmental legislation? Are these values and goals ultimately irreconcilable, at least in the short-term?

Conclusions

There is growing recognition that the major obstacles to solving environmental problems are no longer technical—they are in large part sociological. Concurrently, there is also a realization on the part of government that the social or human dimensions of environmental problems are more difficult to incorporate into government policies. The recent government focus on deficit and debt reduction has conflicted with environmental protection, further evidence of the persistence of the industrial paradigm in our society. Responsibility for environmental assessment of projects has been downloaded to municipal governments, which are not adequately funded to undertake an adequate assessment of environmental impacts.

It appears that the goals of sustainable development and ecosystem management seem harder to achieve than ever before. Too often, assumptions are made that more often than not reflect the 'professional' orientation of the bureaucratic staff rather than the views of the public.

Policy-making in the environmental arena relies heavily on the 'law' as a policy instrument to effect social change and promote sustainable development. Arguably, however, sustainability is as much a political-economic dimension as an ecological one; what can be sustained is only what political and social forces in a particular historical context define as 'in need of protection'.

It may be argued that the environment is an arena of intersecting and competing social and cultural definitions and interests. Different stakeholders are contesting the nature and gravity of environmental threats, the dynamics underlying them, the priority accorded one issue over another, and the optimal means for mitigating or ameliorating conditions that have come to be defined as problematic.

If one were to view society as a 'political economy' instead of a 'market' (in the economic sense) it is possible to consider the struggle over ideas and to analyse the shared meanings that motivate people to action and transform individual actions into collective action. Ideas are at the centre of all political conflict. Policy-making, in turn, is a constant struggle over the definition of the problem, the criteria for classification, the boundaries of categories, and the definition of values and ideals that guide the way people behave. There are multiple understandings of what appears to be a single concept; different views on how these understandings are created and manipulated as part of a political strategy. So, it may be argued that what we are seeing in the recent environmental legislation is the legal construction of objectives and boundaries that structure both participation and conflict in environmental decision-making. It is important to recognize the role of law, as a social institution, in fixing the boundaries of politics—particularly in defining legitimate political expression. It is equally important to analyse the multi-stakeholder processes that result in programs such as the NPRI and standard-setting. It is through these processes that a multiplicity of social values *can* be incorporated.

The concept of 'need' is often socially and culturally defined. Yet, most environmental assessments concentrate on the acceptability of the undertaking and the provisions for mitigation. By not examining the need for an undertaking, sound planning cannot occur since the benefits and costs of the undertaking are assessed without a context. Unless all reasonably foreseen biophysical, socio-economic, and cultural effects, as well as their interconnections to the project, plan, or policy, are taken into account, effective ecosystem management cannot take place since cumulative effects cannot be assessed adequately. Furthermore, a more complete understanding of the impact of a project could be obtained if 'socio-economic' impacts were disaggregated into 'social' and 'economic' cumulative impacts. Processes such as the EBR and environmental assessment present an opportunity for the emergence of the ecological paradigm. However, as we saw above, competing interests are operating to limit the scope of policies, plans, projects, and permits included under EBR.

Complicating these issues even further is the fact that many of society's institutions, such as the law, adhere to classical economic beliefs, i.e., viewing the ecosystem as a collection of resources for human growth and development. There is the additional difficulty of integrating scientific information into the 'adversarial' court process, specifically with respect to the rules of evidence and the presentation of expert testimony.

Nevertheless, recent court decisions indicate that even legal institutions are moving towards the ecological paradigm. For example, in a recent decision of a three-judge panel of the Ontario Divisional Court, it was found that the Ontario Natural Resources Ministry is violating the Crown Forests Sustainability Act by not having a comprehensive plan in place to regulate logging in six major areas of Ontario. In effect, this decision means more accountability and much more public involvement in determining logging practices on Crown lands. The panel of judges found that ministry regulators had failed in duties spelled out in the new legislation—which emphasizes 'sustainability'—defined as the long-term health of the Crown forest. The objective of the Crown Forests Sustainability Act is to accommodate a variety of stakeholder interests, including wildlife, conservation, recreation, logging, wilderness preservation, and jobs, and to sustain the forest for multiple uses for future generations. The panel of judges further noted that the difficulty in compliance with the law was not a reflection of the professional foresters or local ministry employees, rather, it was due to the 'institutional failure' of the Ministry of Natural Resources to appreciate and fulfil its legal obligations. This decision helps to ensure that the public is not deprived of access to the procedures for direct public involvement in the forestry management planning process.

The courts are playing a role in environmental protection as a 'public watchdog' and interpreter of environmental laws to ensure that governments fulfil their obligations to the public as mandated in the recent environmental legislation. Further, in the future, environmental advocacy groups, such as Greenpeace (through its association with the Sierra Legal Defence Fund), will have an increasing role to play in ensuring that the public is aware of environmental issues and that government does not abdicate or ignore its environmental 'safeguarding' responsibilities. The public's perception of the ineffectiveness of governments to solve environmental problems will likely lead to a rise in environmental social activism and an increase in the membership of environmental watchdog organizations—that can marshal more resources to challenge both industry and government in what is increasingly a legal battle.

However, each individual Canadian must recognize that he or she also is part of the environmental problem—it is not just an 'us against them' problem. In fact, a recent study, commissioned by the Earth Council (an international organization), found that Canadians are among the worst abusers of the environment in the world. This study of 52 large nations (which account for 80 per cent of the world's population and 95 per cent of its economic output) focused on 'ecological impact' and found that only four other countries caused more environmental degradation per capita than Canada. The report concluded that Canadians consume four times above the level that is environmentally sustainable; the world now has 1.7 hectares of biologically productive space available for each human being and the economic and consumption patterns of Canadian society use seven hectares per person. Canada's consumption pattern is part of a larger trend seen in the last five years; humans now use one-third more of the earth's carrying capacity than nature can regenerate over the long term. In 1992, humans used one-quarter more of the earth's carrying capacity than nature can regenerate over the long term. There is clearly an alarming trend towards a decrease in the long-term sustainability of nations around the globe.

The looming worldwide environmental crisis raises profound ethical issues concerning equity and fairness and the question of the compatibility of the capitalist industrial paradigm with its emphasis on increasing consumption and growth with environmental protection and sustainability. The question that we must all address is: 'Do developed nations have the right to appropriate this much of the earth's resources at the expense of the developing nations and future generations?'

Questions for Critical Thought

1. What effect does political ideology have on the structuring of our institutions and (a) the creation or definition of problems; (b) the resolution of problems?

2. What steps can be taken to prevent 'institutional failures' from occurring or recurring?

3. In this era of shrinking government, what opportunities and challenges face watchdog groups and the general citizen? Can you think of ways to minimize these challenges?

4. What is the effect of corporate globalization and free trade on Canada's natural resources? For example, if bulk freshwater exports are permitted, what societal changes do you foresee for both Canada and the receiving country, in terms of corporate interests and national sovereignty?

Glossary

Environmental impact assessment: The systematic examination of social (including economic, cultural, archaeological dimensions), physical, and biological factors that may be affected by a proposed project, program, or policy as a part of the process of environmental decision-making.

Institutional failure: When the expectations and primary roles of institutions are not met. The problem is often compounded by denials, delays, and attempts by government officials and politicians to 'control' the problem in the media and avoid accepting responsibility.

Multi-stakeholder group: A collectivity of people with different perspectives on an issue, brought together to aid in, and ultimately influence, decision-making. In environmental impact assessments stakeholders include: federal, provincial, and municipal governments (both the elected officials and the bureaucrats at all three levels of government), the proponent of the project or program, grassroots opposition groups, environmental groups, regional pressure groups, local chambers of commerce and industry associations, and the general public.

Paradigm: A 'world view' or fundamental image of the subject matter within a science (or social science). It subsumes the assumptions, beliefs, and values of the discipline. It determines what should be studied, what questions should be asked, and what 'rules' should be followed in interpreting the research. A paradigm is the broadest unit of consensus and serves to differentiate one discipline (or subdiscipline) from another.

Sustainable development: A new perspective to development and environmental impact, according to the Brundtland Commission (1987), which perceived sustainable development broadly as meeting the economic and social needs of present generations without compromising the needs of future generations. It is a process of change in which the management of resources, economic investment, technological development, and institutional change reflect future as well as present needs.

Suggested Reading

Betchel, Robert, Robert Maran, and William Micheson, eds. 1987. *Methods in Environmental and Behavioral Research*. New York: Van Nostrand. This volume provides a comprehensive overview to the differences associated with conducting environmental-social research compared with traditional social research. It provides the reader with important methodological insights and strategies for conducting research in this area, including geospatial analysis and time series analysis.

Hannigan, John A. 1995. *Environmental Sociology: A Social Constructionist Perspective*. New York: Routledge. This work provides a constructionist perspective to environmental issues, risks, and problems. Canadian case studies are cited. This is an important contribution to the field of Canadian environmental sociology, and contains a perspective on the nature of 'risk' and its social construction.

Meinesz, Alexandre. 1999. *Killer Algae: The True Tale of a Biological Invasion*. Chicago: University of Chicago Press. A detailed account of the efforts of a French marine biologist to alert the political and scientific establishment about the spread of a 'bio-invader' algae off the coast of Monaco. This work contextualizes the human dimension of the phenomenon of 'institutional failure', as it details the lack of action, denials, and attempts to control the media spin on the issue by key political and scientific authorities.

Muldoon, Paul, and Richard Lindgren, in conjunction with Pollution Probe. 1995. *The Environmental Bill of Rights: A Practical Guide*. Toronto: Edmond Montgomery. This book provides an overview and background to environmental bills of rights across Canada. It illustrates the differences between the provinces and highlights the benefits associated with legal instruments such as environmental bills. It is easy to follow and written in a comprehensive manner for both non-legal and legal audiences.

Perrow, Charles. 1984. *Normal Accidents: Living with High Risk Technologies.* New York: Basic Books. This classic work provides an enlightening perspective on the structure of modern technology, bureaucracy, and industrial processes. The work highlights the thesis that accidents are a normal result of 'tightly coupled' organizations—organizations that are structured to fail.

Note

1. An outbreak of deadly *E. coli* (0157:H7) bacteria was found in the municipal water supply of Walkerton, Ontario in May 2000. The outbreak appears to have been caused by a combination of factors including: the breakdown of a chlorination unit, an overflow of storm run-off, problems with wells, and factory farming practices in the area. An investigation into the precise cause or causes is ongoing. At least six people died as a direct result of the outbreak and over 2000 people became ill, in a town with a population of approximately 4500 people. The local medical officer of health took the responsibility for informing the public and media of the situation.

   The crisis has been attributed to a variety of circumstances: lack of timely notification of contamination, severity of the strain of bacterial contamination, poorly trained municipal water technicians, ill-informed municipal officials, province wide re-structuring of water testing, downsizing, privatization, and reallocation of responsibilities.

   The tragic result was clearly an institutional failure on many levels. This outbreak gained international recognition and serves as a world-wide public reminder of the importance of government's role in ensuring the health and safety of its citizens.

2. For additional information on environmental rights legislation, the reader is advised to consult the specific provincial legislation and appropriate Ministry of Environment for the administrative and policy details.

References

Bernstein, Marver. 1955. *Regulating Business by Independent Commission.* Princeton, NJ: Princeton University Press.

Block, Fred. 1987. *Revisiting State Theory: Essays in Politics and Postindustrialism.* Philadelphia: Temple University Press.

Buttel, Frederick. 1986. 'Sociology and the environment: The winding road toward human ecology', *International Social Science Journal* 38: 337–56.

———. 1987. 'New directions in environmental sociology', *Annual Review of Sociology:* 488.

Catton, William. 1980. *Overshoot: The Ecological Basis of Revolutionary Change.* Urbana: University of Illinois Press.

Dunlap, Riley, and William Catton. 1979. 'Environmental Sociology', *Annual Review of Sociology* 5: 243–73.

Finsterbusch, Kurt. 1994. 'In Praise of SIA—A Personal Review of the Field of Social Impact Assessment: Evaluation, Role, History, Practice, Methods, Issues, and Future', paper presented at the annual meeting of the International Association of Impact Assessment, Quebec City, 14–18 June.

Freudenburg, William, Scott Frickel, and Robert Gramling. 1995. 'Beyond the Nature/Society Divide: Learning to Think About a Mountain', *Sociological Forum* 10, 3: 361–92.

Gusfield, J. 1975. 'Moral Passage: The Symbolic Process in Public Designation of Deviance', in F. Davis and R. Stivers, eds, *The Collective Definition of Deviance*. New York: Free Press.

Humphrey, Craig, and Frederick Buttel. 1982. *Environment, Energy and Society*. Belmont, Calif.: Wadsworth Press.

Marx, Karl, and Frederick Engels. 1955. *Karl Marx and Frederick Engels: Selected Works in Two Volumes, vol. 1*. Moscow: Foreign Languages Publishing House.

O'Connor, James. 1998. *Natural Causes: Essays in Ecological Marxism*. New York: Guilford Press.

Offe, Claus. 1984. *Contradictions of the Welfare State*. London: Hutchins.

Olsen, Marvin, Dora Lodwick, and Riley Dunlap. 1992. *Viewing the World Ecologically*. Boulder, Colo.: Westview Press.

Ontario Bill of Environmental Rights Act, 1993.

Poole, K. 1996. 'Bill of Rights Gutted', *Environmental Policy and Law*: 334.

Schnaiberg, Allan. 1980. *The Environment: From Surplus to Scarcity*. New York: Oxford University Press.

———— and Kenneth Gould. 1994. *Environment and Society: The Enduring Conflict*. New York: St Martin's Press.

Stone, Clarence. 1980. 'Systematic Power in Community Decision-Making: A Restructuring of Stratification Theory', *American Political Science Review* 74: 978–90.

Stone, Deborah. 1988. *Policy Paradox and Political Reason*. New York: HarperCollins.

Toronto Star. 1998. Insight, Section 'E', 11 Apr., E1–E4.

Turpel, M. 1993. 'Patriarchy and Paternalism: The Legacy of the Canadian State for the First Nations Women', *Journal of Women and the Law* 6: 174.

World Commission on Environment and Development. 1987. *Our Common Future*. Oxford: Oxford University Press.

Some Final Thoughts

In the six years that have passed since the first edition of this book was published, Canadian society has undergone some significant structural changes and has seen the rise of a number of social movements. The criticisms of society these social movements express have grown stronger. Those concerned with the environment, for example, have taken new directions, pursuing struggles on the legal front instead of concentrating their energies on the agendas of party politics in Canada. The publication of this new edition affords an opportunity to look at these recent developments, especially the women's movement, gays and lesbians, Canadian youth, and Quebec nationalism, and to add some reflections on the hard choices that remain and the new challenges that await Canadians in the coming years.

At the start of the 1990s, the depressed economic climate exacerbated the demoralization of many Canadians. The numerous pressing social issues confronting Canadians seemed to defy optimistic analysis. Among these issues were the following: the undermining of organized labour's opposition to the socio-economic status quo; the failure of government policy to address adequately global economic restructuring; increasing social class polarization; the growing popularity of openly racist, sexist, and homophobic organizations; the failure of so many English Canadians to examine and understand Quebec's history and struggle; the overwhelming presence of the American cultural and economic empire; and Canadians' documented sense of powerlessness in addressing environmental concerns.

Times have changed. For some, Canada has changed for the better. For many others, some things have changed for the better but much remains to be done. And then there is Quebec.

The present economic climate in Canada provides opportunities that were absent at the beginning of the last decade. Unemployment is down, the federal government can boast of a budget surplus, and Canada seems poised to take advantage of the Information Age. And yet, the more things change, the more they seem to stay the same. While unemployment is down, Canadians see more and more homeless, more and more children living in poverty, and young working families struggling harder to make ends meet. The federal government's surplus is spent on tax breaks while health care, education, and social programs are given crumbs. Canadians continue to fret about our social fabric and what makes us distinct from our neighbours to the south. As the provinces continue to gain in power at the expense of the federal authority, it seems that the federal government has become the resource of last resort. That is, instead of taking a leadership role in the politics of the nation, the federal government appears content to take the path of least resistance, except in regard to Quebec.

What can we in the social sciences offer Canadians as we face the hard choices ahead of us? The role of the 'soft' sciences (that is, the social sciences of sociology, political science, economics, and history), for example, and their concern for social justice can provide much in the way of understanding. We are not proposing that the social sciences are capable of providing some panacea for Canadians and their problems. However, the analyses advanced in the essays contained here are clearly central to a full understanding of the complexities of Canadian social issues.

Perhaps one of the greatest challenges to Canada's future is an unwillingness on the part of many (the 'haves' of society) to pay attention to the issues raised in this text, or a refusal to listen at all to the plights, grievances, and views of other Canadians, or a highly selective attention only to a few fashionable issues and a few 'official' spokespersons. Clearly, one text won't change the attitudes of those who inhabit the world of the 'haves'. Nor can we hope to convince everyone that the arguments presented here exhaust the critical analyses of Canadian society. What we do suggest is the pivotal role sociology can and must play in this debate. We urge students of Canadian society to learn more, both by reading some of the many excellent sources cited in each chapter but also by becoming involved, if they are not already, in that issue which is most central to their concerns. Only by involvement (as we have found ourselves) can one really understand the meaning and power of the issues.

As the women's movement emphasized in the 1960s, the personal is political, and vice versa. Every personal act, even the simple act of buying a cup of coffee at the local Tim Horton's franchise, has social and even global ramifications ranging from support for part-time work to destruction of tropical rain forests. Making these connections between the personal and the political is part of being conscious of both the roots and consequences of our acts. However, we shouldn't become paralysed or obsessed by these connections. We are not asking for 'true believers'. We endeavour to inform. We are seeking what American sociologist C. Wright Mills termed 'the sociological imagination'. Being knowledgeable about the principal patterns of power and influence, conflict and contradiction, along with recognizing the key players and pivotal institutional, group, and interpersonal linkages in Canadian society, is fundamental not only to social action but to personal liberation. This consciousness is, in turn, fundamental to any real possibility of democracy and freedom. As we have presented in this volume, visible minorities, women, union activists, environmentalists, gays and lesbians, and others have worked out this public/private connection and have found it to be the key to both personal liberation and public empowerment.

List of Contributors

ANTON L. ALLAHAR is Professor of Sociology at the University of Western Ontario.

JAMES E. CÔTÉ is Professor of Sociology at the University of Western Ontario and editor of *Identity*.

HUGUETTE DAGENAIS is Professor of Anthropology at Laval University and co-founder and past director of *Recherches féministes*.

ANN DUFFY is Professor of Sociology at Brock University.

DAN GLENDAY is Professor of Sociology and Director of the Centre for Labour Studies at Brock University.

HUBERT GUINDON is Professor Emeritus at Concordia University.

KELLY HANNAH-MOFFAT is Assistant Professor in the Department of Sociology at the University of Toronto.

GARY KINSMAN is Associate Professor of Sociology at Laurentian University. He is the author of *The Regulation of Desire* and a gay liberation and social activist.

DAVID W. LIVINGSTONE is Professor of Sociology at the Ontario Institute for studies in Education (OISE) at the University of Toronto.

NANCY MANDELL is Associate Professor of Sociology at York University.

RICK PONTING is Professor of Sociology at the University of Calgary.

NORENE PUPO is Associate Professor and Chair of the Department of Sociology at York University.

KATHLEEN RIEL is a doctoral candidate at the University of Toronto, Sociology Department, and the President of Holistic Impax Group Inc.

PETA TANCRED is Professor of Sociology and past Director of the Centre for Research and Teaching on Women, McGill University.

Index